iMovie '08 & *iDVD*

THE MISSING MANUAL

*The book that
should have been
in the box*

iMovie '08 *& iDVD*

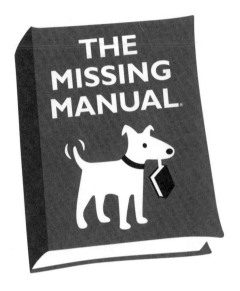

David Pogue

POGUE PRESS™
O'REILLY®

Beijing · Cambridge · Farnham · Köln · Paris · Sebastopol · Taipei · Tokyo

iMovie '08 & iDVD: The Missing Manual
by David Pogue

Published by O'Reilly Media, Inc., 1005 Gravenstein Highway North,
Sebastopol, CA 95472.

O'Reilly Media books may be purchased for educational, business, or sales
promotional use. Online editions are also available for most titles: *safari.oreilly.
com*. For more information, contact our corporate/institutional sales department:
(800) 998-9938 or *corporate@oreilly.com*.

October 2007:   First Edition.
December 2007:   Second Printing.

This book uses a durable and flexible lay-flat binding.

ISBN-10: 0-596-51619-3
ISBN-13: 978-0-596-51619-2

Table of Contents

Part Two: Editing in iMovie

Part Three: Finding Your Audience

Part Four: iDVD '08

The Missing Credits

About the Author

 David Pogue (author, indexer) is the weekly tech columnist for the *New York Times*, an Emmy-winning correspondent for *CBS News Sunday Morning*, 2006 winner of an Online News Association award, and the creator of the Missing Manual series. He's the author or co-author of 43 books, including 17 in this series and six in the *"for Dummies"* line (including *Macs, Magic, Opera,* and *Classical Music*). In his other life, David is a former Broadway show conductor, a magician, and a pianist.

News, photos, links to his columns and weekly videos await at *www.davidpogue.com*. He welcomes feedback about his books by email at *david@pogueman.com*.

About the Creative Team

Tim Geaney (still photos) has shot editorial photos for *Self, GQ, Mademoiselle,* and *Glamour* magazines, among others. His commercial photography clients include Victoria's Secret, Nautica, J. Crew, Spiegel, Nordstrom, Neiman Marcus, and Saks Fifth Avenue. Web: *www.timgeaney.com*.

Aaron Miller (technical editor, author of many useful bits) lives in Orem, Utah with his wife and three boys. He is a part-time lawyer, Mac consultant, and professor, and runs a software company serving nonprofit organizations. In all of his spare time, he authors the blog "Unlocking iMovie '08" (*http://imovie08.blogspot.com*), his own little way of trying to make the Mac world a better place. If he's not at his computer, he's probably playing Ultimate Frisbee or "tickle monster." Email: *ilifer08@gmail.com*.

Teresa Noelle Roberts (copy editor) is a freelance copy editor and proofreader, as well as a published fiction writer and poet. When she can tear herself away from the computer, she may be found gardening, belly dancing, or enjoying the beautiful beaches of New England. Email: *safirasilv@comcast.net*.

Phil Simpson (design and layout) works out of his office in Southbury, Connecticut, where he has had his graphic design business since 1982. He is experienced in many facets of graphic design, including corporate identity/branding, publication design, and corporate and medical communications. Email: *pmsimpson@earthlink.net*.

Lesa Snider (screenshot supervisor and graphics gooddess) assists David Pogue on many projects. As Chief Evangelist for iStockphoto.com and a veteran writer for international graphics publications, Lesa is on a mission to teach the world how to create beautiful graphics. You can see more of her work at *TheGraphicReporter.com*, and catch her live at many conferences.

Erica Sadun (iDVD chapters, previous editions) holds a PhD in Computer Science from the Georgia Institute of Technology. She has written, co-written and contributed to almost two dozen books about technology, particularly in the areas of programming, digital video, and digital photography. An unrepentant geek, Erica has never met a gadget she didn't need. Her checkered past includes run-ins with NeXT, Newton, and a vast myriad of both successful and unsuccessful technologies. When not writing, she and her geek husband parent three adorable geeks-in-training, who regard their parents with unrestrained bemusement. Email: *erica@mindspring.com.*

Acknowledgments

The Missing Manual series is a joint venture between Pogue Press (the dream team introduced on these pages) and O'Reilly Media (a dream publishing partner).

A special group did great favors for this project: Helpful writings by Jim Kanter, Irene Lusztig, Karl Petersen, and Tim Franklin, prepared for earlier editions, live on in this one; those guys were my video gurus and technical advisers. Sohaila Abdulal, Kate Briggs, Stephanie English, Sada Preisch, and Ellen Keyne Seebacher shared proofreading duties on this edition. Shawn King was indispensable, fast, and funny during the creation of the index.

For this edition, iMovie product manager Dion Scoppettuolo and his team shared their expert advice, answers, and—most importantly—their enthusiasm for the project. I'm also grateful to David Rogelberg, my agent.

Finally, thanks to Kelly, Tia, and Jeffrey, my favorite iMovie stars, and my wife, Jennifer, who made this book—and everything else—possible.

The Missing Manual Series

Missing Manual books are superbly written guides to computer products that don't come with printed manuals (which is just about all of them). Each book features a handcrafted index; cross-references to specific page numbers (not just "See Chapter 14"); and RepKover, a detached-spine binding that lets the book lie perfectly flat without the assistance of weights or cinder blocks. Recent and upcoming titles include:

- *Mac OS X: The Missing Manual,* Leopard Edition by David Pogue
- *iPhone: The Missing Manual* by David Pogue
- *iPhoto '08: The Missing Manual* by David Pogue
- *Switching to the Mac: The Missing Manual,* Tiger Edition by David Pogue
- *AppleScript: The Missing Manual* by Adam Goldstein
- *AppleWorks 6: The Missing Manual* by Jim Elferdink and David Reynolds
- *iWork '05: The Missing Manual* by Jim Elferdink
- *Office 2004 for Macintosh: The Missing Manual* by Mark H. Walker, Franklin Tessler, and Paul Berkowitz

- *Windows Vista: The Missing Manual* by David Pogue
- *Windows XP Home Edition: The Missing Manual,* by David Pogue
- *Windows XP Pro: The Missing Manual,* by David Pogue, Craig Zacker, and L.J. Zacker
- *Access 2007: The Missing Manual* by Matthew MacDonald
- *CSS: The Missing Manual* by David Sawyer McFarland
- *Creating Web Sites: The Missing Manual* by Matthew MacDonald
- *Digital Photography: The Missing Manual* by Chris Grover and Barbara Brundage
- *Dreamweaver CS3: The Missing Manual* by David Sawyer McFarland
- *Flash CS3: The Missing Manual* by E. A. Vander Veer and Chris Grover
- *eBay: The Missing Manual* by Nancy Conner
- *Excel 2007: The Missing Manual* by Matthew MacDonald
- *FileMaker Pro 8: The Missing Manual* by Geoff Coffey and Susan Prosser
- *FrontPage 2003: The Missing Manual* by Jessica Mantaro
- *Google: The Missing Manual,* 2nd Edition by Sarah Milstein and Rael Dornfest
- *Home Networking: The Missing Manual* by Scott Lowe
- *The Internet: The Missing Manual* by David Pogue and J.D. Biersdorfer
- *iPod: The Missing Manual,* 6th Edition by J.D. Biersdorfer
- *PCs: The Missing Manual* by Andy Rathbone
- *Photoshop Elements 5: The Missing Manual* by Barbara Brundage
- *PowerPoint 2007: The Missing Manual* by Emily A. Vander Veer
- *QuickBooks 2006: The Missing Manual* by Bonnie Biafore
- *Word 2007: The Missing Manual* by Chris Grover

For Starters

The "For Starters" books contain just the most essential information from their larger counterparts—in larger type, with a more spacious layout, and none of those advanced sidebars. Recent titles include:

- *Windows Vista for Starters: The Missing Manual* by David Pogue
- *Windows XP for Starters: The Missing Manual* by David Pogue
- *Access 2007 for Starters: The Missing Manual* by Matthew MacDonald
- *Excel 2007 for Starters: The Missing Manual* by Matthew MacDonald

- *Quicken 2006 for Starters: The Missing Manual* by Bonnie Biafore
- *Word 2007 for Starters: The Missing Manual* by Chris Grover
- *PowerPoint 2007 for Starters: The Missing Manual* by Emily A. Vander Veer

Introduction

iMovie is video editing software. It grabs a copy of the raw footage from your digital camcorder or still camera. Then it lets you edit this video easily, quickly, and creatively.

That's a big deal, because over the years, home movies have developed a bad name. *You* know what it's like watching other people's camcorder footage. You're captive on some neighbor's couch after dessert to witness 60 excruciating, unedited minutes of a trip to Mexico, or 25 too many minutes of the baby wearing the spaghetti bowl.

Deep down, most people realize that the viewing experience could be improved if the video were edited down to just the good parts. But until iMovie came along, editing camcorder footage on the computer required several thousand dollars' worth of digitizing cards, extremely complicated editing software, and the highest-horsepower computer equipment available. Unless there was a paycheck involved, editing footage under those circumstances just wasn't worth it.

Then along came iMovie, the world's least expensive version of what the Hollywood pros call nonlinear editing software. The "nonlinear" part is that no tape is involved while you're editing. There's no rewinding or fast-forwarding; you jump instantly to any piece of footage as you put your movie together.

The world of video is exploding. People are giving each other DVDs instead of greeting cards. People are watching each other via video on their Web sites. People are quitting their daily-grind jobs to become videographers for hire, making money filming weddings and creating living video scrapbooks. Video, in other words, is fast becoming a new standard document format for the new century.

If you have iMovie and a camcorder, you'll be ready.

The Difficult Birth of iMovie '08

Within six months of its release in October 1999, iMovie had become, in words of beaming iMovie papa (and Apple CEO) Steve Jobs, "the most popular video editing software in the world."

Apple only fanned the flames when it released iMovie 2 in July 2000 (for $50), iMovie 3 in January 2003 (for free), and then—as part of the iLife software suite—iMovie 4, iMovie HD, and iMovie 6 in successive Januaries.

Then, in August 2007, Apple dropped a bombshell. Or, rather, it dropped iMovie.

The company's new consumer video editing program, called iMovie '08, was, in fact, not iMovie at all. It was a totally different program, using all-new code and a different design, and built by different people. It was conceived, according to Steve Jobs, by an Apple programmer who wanted to edit down his vacation footage—but found the old iMovie too slow and complicated. So the guy sat down and wrote his own little program, focused primarily on editing speed above all. Steve loved it, and decided that it would replace the old iMovie.

Many people were stunned by Apple's move—and I, your humble author, was among them. In my *New York Times* email column, I wrote about just how different iMovie '08 was from its predecessors:

> "iMovie '08 has been totally misnamed. It's not iMovie at all. It's designed for an utterly different task.
>
> "The new iMovie, for example, is probably the only video editing program on the market with no timeline—no horizontal, scrolling strip that displays your clips laid end to end, with their lengths representing their durations. You have no indication of how many minutes into your movie you are.
>
> "The new iMovie also gets a D for audio editing. You can't manually adjust audio levels during a scene (for example, to make the music quieter when someone is speaking). All the old audio effects are gone, too. No pitch changing, high-pass and low-pass filters, or reverb.
>
> "The new iMovie doesn't accept plug-ins, either. You can't add chapter markers for use in iDVD, which is supposed to be integrated with iMovie. Bookmarks are gone. 'Themes' are gone. You can no longer export only part of a movie. And you can't export a movie back to tape—only to the Internet or to a file.
>
> "All visual effects are gone—even basic options like slow motion, reverse motion, and fast motion. Incredibly, the new iMovie can't even convert older iMovie projects. All you can import is the clips themselves. None of your transitions, titles, credits, music, or special effects are preserved.
>
> "On top of all that, this more limited iMovie has steep horsepower requirements that rule out most computers older than about two years old."

Pretty harsh, I know. But listen, I was an absolute whiz at iMovie 6. I knew it like the back of my mouse. And it looked to me like Apple was junking that mature, powerful program for what amounted to a video slideshow program.

Now, all of those "doesn't haves" are still there. iMovie 6 still is more powerful than iMovie '08 in many ways—which may be why Apple makes iMovie 6 available as a free download to anyone with iMovie '08. You can even take a single movie back and forth between the two programs, capitalizing on the strength of each. (See Chapter 13.)

But according to Apple, iMovie '08 was an inevitable development, because *people don't edit video anymore.* People don't have three hours to spend whittling down a vacation video. Apple's internal studies showed that iMovie use, among the iLife applications, had dropped to a distant second behind iPhoto. People just weren't using it.

So iMovie '08 is designed for them: the people who had given up on video editing. It's just as good a program—but designed for a different crowd.

Once you accept its new mission, it's much easier to make peace with the new iMovie. It's far more modern than the old iMovie, for example. It's equally adept at importing video from the new tapeless camcorders (DVD, hard drive, or memory-card models)— and from digital still cameras—as it is at importing from tape. And it's all hooked up to the Web, so that a single command can post your masterpiece on YouTube.

Then there are the cool features that the old iMovie could only dream about. The color-correction and frame-cropping tools are unprecedented in a consumer program. You can really, truly delete unwanted pieces of your clips, thus reclaiming hard drive space. (iMovie, on the other hand, preserves an entire 20-minute clip on your hard drive even if you've used only 3 seconds of it.)

iMovie '08 creates titles, crossfades and color adjustments instantly. There's no "rendering" time, as there was in the old iMovie. So you gain an exhilarating freedom to play, to fiddle with the timing and placement of things.

So, no, iMovie '08 is not a descendant of the old iMovies. It's a different program, with a different focus and a different audience. But it's here to stay, and it has charms of its own.

iDVD

As you may have noticed, this iMovie book comes with a free bonus book: *iDVD '08: The Missing Manual,* which constitutes Chapters 18 through 21. iDVD can preserve your movies on home-recorded DVDs that look and behave amazingly close to the commercial DVDs you rent from Netflix or Blockbuster.

iDVD '08 wasn't a huge update from the previous version, but there are a few useful changes. It's faster, for one thing. It accepts more video formats, and comes with more predesigned menu-screen themes.

New alignment guides appear when you're dragging objects around on your menu screens, to help you keep your buttons in a row; a new Buttons palette makes it easy to make your buttons "light up" in creative ways when operated with the remote control;

and a refined Drop Zone editor makes it much easier than before to customize your DVD menus' design schemes.

There's also a new encoding scheme for burning your finished DVDs, which Apple calls Professional. What it should have called it was "Twice the video quality—in twice the time." You wait a long time for one of these DVDs to pop out of your little Mac toaster, but the visual quality will make you glad you did.

About This Book

Don't let the rumors fool you. iMovie and iDVD may be simple, but they're not simplistic. Unfortunately, many of the best techniques aren't covered in the only "manual" you get with iLife—its electronic help screens.

This book was born to address two needs. First, it's designed to give you a grounding in professional filming and editing techniques. The camcorder and iMovie produce video of stunning visual and audio quality, giving you the *technical* tools to produce amazing videos. But most people don't have much experience with the *artistic* side of shooting—lighting, sound, and composition—or even how to use the dozens of buttons packed onto the modern camcorder. This book will tell you all you need to know.

Second, this book is designed to serve as the iMovie/iDVD manual, as the book that should have been in the box. It explores each iMovie feature in depth, offers illustrated catalogs of the various title and transition effects, offers shortcuts and workarounds, and unearths features that the online help doesn't even mention.

About the Outline

iMovie '08 & iDVD: The Missing Manual is divided into five parts, each containing several chapters:

- Part 1, **Shooting Great Video,** covers what happens before you get to iMovie. It explains the various modern camcorder formats, helps you learn to use the one you bought, and offers a crash course in professional film technique.

- Part 2, **Editing in iMovie,** is the heart of the book. It leads you through transferring your footage into iMovie, editing your clips, placing them into a timeline, adding crossfades and titles, working with your soundtracks, and more.

- Part 3, **Finding Your Audience,** helps you take the cinematic masterpiece on your screen to the world. iMovie excels at exporting your work to the Web, to YouTube, to an iPod or iPhone, to an Apple TV, to a QuickTime file on the hard drive, or to iDVD for burning (your best bet for maintaining the visual quality of the original). This part of the book offers step-by-step instructions for each of these methods, and also shows you how you can use QuickTime Player Pro to supplement the editing tools in iMovie.

- Part 4, **iDVD '08,** is just what you'd expect: a bonus volume dedicated to the world's easiest-to-use DVD design and burning software. It goes way, way beyond the basics, as you'll see.

At the end of the book, four appendixes await:

- **Appendix A** provides a menu-by-menu explanation of iMovie menu commands.

- **Appendix B** is a comprehensive troubleshooting handbook.

- **Appendix C** is a master cheat sheet of iMovie's keyboard shortcuts.

- **Appendix D** is a visual reference to all of the little symbols, stripes, badges, and color-coded doodads that, sooner or later, will clutter up your iMovie window and leave you bewildered. Turn to this two-page cheat sheet in times of panic.

About→These→Arrows

Throughout this book, and throughout the Missing Manual series, you'll find sentences like this one: "Open your Home→Library→Preferences folder." That's shorthand for a much longer instruction that directs you to open three nested folders in sequence, like this: "In the Finder, choose Go→Home. In your Home folder, you'll find a folder called Library. Open that. Inside the Library window is a folder called Preferences. Double-click to open it, too."

Similarly, this kind of arrow shorthand helps to simplify the business of choosing commands in menus, as shown in Figure I-1.

Figure I-1:
In this book, arrow notations help to simplify folder and menu instructions. For example, "Choose ⬤→Dock→Position on Left" is a more compact way of saying, "From the ⬤ menu, choose Dock; from the submenu that then appears, choose Position on Left," as shown here.

Technical Notes for PAL People

If you live in the Americas, Japan, or any of 30 other countries, your camcorder, VCR, and TV record and play back a video signal in a format that's known as *NTSC*. Even if you've never heard the term, every camcorder, VCR, TV, and TV station in your country uses this same signal. (The following discussion doesn't apply to high-definition video, which is the same across continents.)

What it stands for is National Television Standards Committee, the gang who designed this format. What it *means* is incompatibility with the second most popular format, which is called PAL (Phase Alternating Line, for the curious). In Europe, Africa, the Middle East, Australia, and China (among other places), everyone's equipment uses the PAL format. You can't play an American tape on a standard VCR in Sweden—unless you're happy with black-and-white, sometimes jittery playback.

Tip: France, the former Soviet Union countries, and a few others use a third format, known as SECAM. iMovie doesn't work with SECAM gear. To find out what kind of gear your country uses, visit a Web site like *www.vidpro.org/standards.htm*.

Fortunately, iMovie converses fluently with both NTSC and PAL camcorders. When you launch the program, it automatically studies the camcorder you've attached and determines its format.

However, most of the discussions in this book use NTSC terminology. If you're a friend of PAL, use the following information to translate this book's discussions.

The Tech Specs of NTSC

Whether you're aware of it or not, using the NTSC standard-definition format means that the picture you see is characterized like this:

- **30 frames per second.** A *frame* is one individual picture. Flashed before your eyes at this speed, the still images blend into what you perceive as smooth motion.

- **575 scan lines.** The electron gun in a TV tube paints the screen with this number of fine horizontal lines.

- **The DV picture measures 720 x 480 pixels.** This figure refers to the number of screen dots, or *pixels,* that compose one frame of image in the *DV* (digital video) version of the NTSC format.

The Tech Specs of PAL

When iMovie detects a PAL camcorder (or when you inform it that you're using one), it makes the necessary adjustments automatically, including:

- **25 frames per second.** Video fans claim that the lower frame rate creates more flicker than the NTSC standard. On the other hand, this frame rate is very close to the frame rate of Hollywood films (24 frames per second). As a result, many independent filmmakers find PAL a better choice when shooting movies they intend to convert to film.

- **625 scan lines.** That's 20 percent sharper and more detailed than NTSC. The difference is especially visible on large-screen TVs.

- **The DV picture measures 720 x 576 pixels.** This information may affect you as you read Chapter 12 and prepare still images for use with iMovie.

About MissingManuals.com

At *www.missingmanuals.com,* you'll find news, articles, and updates to the books in this series.

But if you click the name of this book and then the Errata link, you'll find a unique resource: a list of corrections and updates that have been made in successive printings of this book. You can mark important corrections right into your own copy of the book, if you like.

In fact, the same page offers an invitation for you to submit such corrections and updates yourself. In an effort to keep the book as up to date and accurate as possible, each time we print more copies of this book, we'll make any confirmed corrections you've suggested. Thanks in advance for reporting any glitches you find!

In the meantime, we'd love to hear your suggestions for new books in the Missing Manual line. There's a place for that on the Web site, too, as well as a place to sign up for free email notification of new titles in the series.

The Very Basics

You'll find very little jargon or nerd terminology in this book. You will, however, encounter a few terms and concepts that you'll see frequently in your Macintosh life. They include:

- **Menus.** The *menus* are the words in the lightly striped bar at the top of your screen. You can either click one of these words to open a pull-down menu of commands (and then click again on a command), or click and *hold* the button as you drag down the menu to the desired command (and release the button to activate the command). Either method works fine.

Note: Apple has officially changed what it calls the little menu that pops up when you Control-click (or right-click) something on the screen. It's still a *contextual* menu, in that the menu choices depend on the context of what you click—but it's now called a *shortcut* menu. That term not only matches what it's called in Windows, but it's slightly more descriptive of its function. Shortcut menu is the term you'll find in this book.

- **Clicking.** This book offers three kinds of instructions that require you to use the mouse or trackpad attached to your Mac. To *click* means to point the arrow cursor at something onscreen and then—without moving the cursor at all—press and release the clicker button on the mouse (or laptop trackpad). To *double-click,* of course, means to click twice in rapid succession, again without moving the cursor at all. And to *drag* means to move the cursor while keeping the button continuously pressed.

  When you're told to ⌘-*click* something, you click while pressing the ⌘ key (next to the Space bar). Such related procedures as *Shift-clicking, Option-clicking,* and *Control-clicking* work the same way—just click while pressing the corresponding key on the bottom row of your keyboard.

Note: On Windows PCs, the mouse has two buttons. The left one is for clicking normally; the right one produces a tiny shortcut menu of useful commands. (See the previous Note.) But new Macs come with Apple's Mighty Mouse, a mouse that looks like it has only one button but can actually detect which side of its rounded front you're pressing. If you've turned on the feature in System Preferences, you, too, can right-click things on the screen.

That's why, all through this book, you'll see the phrase, "Control-click the photo (or right-click it)." That's telling you that Control-clicking will do the job—but if you've got a two-button mouse or you've turned on the two-button feature of the Mighty Mouse, right-clicking might be more efficient.

- **Keyboard shortcuts.** Every time you take your hand off the keyboard to move the mouse, you lose time and potentially disrupt your creative flow. That's why many experienced Mac fans use keystroke combinations instead of menu commands wherever possible. ⌘-P opens the Print dialog box, for example, and ⌘-M minimizes the current window to the Dock.

  When you see a shortcut like ⌘-Q (which closes the current program), it's telling you to hold down the ⌘ key, and, while it's down, type the letter Q, and then release both keys.

If you've mastered this much information, you have all the technical background you need to enjoy *iMovie '08 & iDVD: The Missing Manual.*

Part One: Shooting Great Video

1

A Field Guide to Camcorders

To edit video using iMovie, you must first *shoot* some video, which is why the first three chapters of this book have nothing to do with your iMovie software. Instead, this book begins with advice on buying and using a camcorder, getting to know the equipment, and adopting professional filming techniques. After all, teaching you to edit video without making sure you know how to shoot it is like giving a map to a 16-year-old without first teaching him how to drive.

In previous editions of this book, "digital camcorder" meant only one thing: digital *tape* camcorders—MiniDV cassette camcorders. But since 2005 or so, the camcorder industry has radically changed. Sales of tape camcorders have plummeted. People are using their digital *still* cameras to record video, and leaving their bigger, heavier, less spontaneous camcorders at home.

The camcorder industry has responded by trying to make their new models smaller, lighter, cheaper—and unshackled by the limitations of tape (like waiting to rewind). Nowadays, camcorders can record onto built-in hard drives (just like the ones in iPods); onto removable memory cards (just like the ones in digital cameras); or onto miniature, burnable blank DVDs.

Fortunately, iMovie '08 can import and edit the video from almost all of these new camcorder types. Unfortunately, embracing one of these new camcorder formats means sacrificing some features and picture quality along the way.

This chapter guides you through the ever-more-complicated jungle of camcorder types, their pros, and their cons.

Meet Digital Video

Technically speaking, you don't need a camcorder to use iMovie. You can work with QuickTime movies you find on the Web, or use it to turn still photos into slide-shows.

But to shoot your own video—and that's the real fun of iMovie—you need a camcorder.

Note: If your video is on tapes in one of the *really* old analog formats, like VHS, S-VHS, VHS-C, or 8mm, see Chapter 4. But from this day forward, shoot all of your new footage with a *digital* camcorder like one described in this chapter. You'll gain a whole new world of convenience, picture quality, and footage longevity.

One thing all current camcorders have in common: They all record video and audio *digitally*, recording it on that tape/hard drive/memory card/DVD as a series of computer files. A digital camcorder therefore offers enormous advantages over previous formats.

It's Smaller

The size of the camcorder is primarily determined by the size of whatever it records onto. A MiniDV cassette (tape cartridge) is much smaller than the old VHS camcorders, as shown in Figure 1-1, for example, and memory-card camcorders can be smaller still.

Figure 1-1:
How's this for a tech museum? The standard-size VHS cassette (back) is nearly extinct. 8mm and Hi-8 cassettes (right) are fading fast. MiniDV tapes (left), like the ones required by most digital camcorders, are the highest quality, least expensive format, but even their popularity is fading.

Small size has lots of advantages. You can film surreptitiously when necessary. Small camcorders don't make kids or interview subjects nervous like bulkier equipment. The batteries last a long time, because they've got less equipment to power. And, of course, smaller means the camera is easier to take with you.

Astounding Quality

Video quality is measured in *lines of resolution,* the number of tiny horizontal stripes of color the playback uses to fill your TV screen. As you can see by this table, digital camcorders blow every previous tape format out of the water. (All camcorders, TVs, and VCRs have the same vertical resolution; this table measures *horizontal* resolution.)

Tape Format	Maximum Lines of Resolution
VHS, VHS-C	240
8mm	280
Live TV broadcast	300
S-VHS, Hi-8	400
Digital satellite broadcast	400
MiniDV	500
High definition	720 or 1080

The sound quality of digital is dramatically better than previous formats, too. In fact, it's better than CD-quality sound, since most digital camcorders record sound at 48 kHz instead of 44.1 kHz. (Higher means better.)

Tip: Most DV tape camcorders offer you a choice of sound-quality modes: 12-bit or 16-bit. The lower quality setting is designed to leave "room" on the tape for adding music after you've recorded your video. But avoid it like the plague! If you shoot your video in 12-bit audio, your picture will gradually drift out of sync with your audio track—if you plan to save your movie to a DVD. Consult your manual to find out how to switch the camcorder into 16-bit audio mode. Do it *before* you shoot anything important.

No Generation Loss

This is a big one. You probably know that every time you make a copy of VHS footage (or other non-DV material), you lose quality. The copy loses sharpness, color fidelity, and smoothness of color tone. Once you've made a copy *of* a copy, the quality is terrible. Skin appears to have a combination of bad acne and radiation burns, the edges of the picture wobble as though leaking off the glass, and *video noise* (jiggling static dots) fills the screen. If you've ever seen, on the news or *America's Funniest Home Videos,* a tape submitted by an amateur camcorder fan, you've seen this problem in action.

Digital video is stored on the tape as computer codes, not as pulses of magnetic energy. You can copy this video from digital camcorder to digital camcorder, or from camcorder to Mac, dozens of times, making copies of copies of copies. The last generation of digital video will be utterly indistinguishable from the original footage—which is to say, both will look fantastic.

Note: Technically speaking, you can't keep making copies of copies of a digital tape infinitely. After, say, 20 or 30 generations, you may start to see a few video *dropouts* (digital-looking specks), depending on the quality of your tapes and duplicating equipment. Still, few people have any reason to make that many copies of copies. (Furthermore, making infinite copies of a *single* original poses no such problem.)

Longevity of the Recordings

Depending on how much you read newspapers, you may remember the depressing story the *New York Times* broke in the late 1980s: Because home video was such a recent phenomenon at the time, nobody had ever bothered to check out how long videotapes last.

The answer, as it turns out, was: not very long. Depending on storage conditions, the signal on traditional videotapes may begin to fade in as little as 10 years! The precious footage of that birth, wedding, or tornado, which you had hoped to preserve forever, could in fact be more fleeting than the memory itself.

Your first instinct might be to rescue a fading video by copying it onto a fresh tape, but making a copy only further damages the footage. The bottom line, said the scientists: There is *no way* to preserve original video footage forever!

Fortunately, there is now. Because the quality of digital recordings never degrades when you make copies, you'll glow with the knowledge that your grandchildren and *their* grandchildren will be able to see your movies with every speck of clarity you see today—even if they have to dig up one of those antique "Macintosh" computers or gigantic, soap-sized "camcorders" in order to play it.

Note: This handy feature refers to the digital *recordings*—not necessarily to the discs or tapes they're recorded *on.* That, in fact, remains a serious concern; see page 31.

Editability

The best advantage of digital video may be iMovie itself. Once you've connected your camcorder up to your Mac (as described in Chapter 4), you can pour the footage from camcorder to computer—and then chop it up, rearrange scenes, add special effects, cut out bad shots, and so on. For the first time in history, it's simple for anyone, even non-rich people, to edit home movies with professional results. (Doing so in 1990 required a $200,000 Avid editing suite; doing so in 1995 required a $4,000 computer with $4,000 worth of digitizing cards and editing software—and the quality wasn't great because it wasn't digital.)

Furthermore, for the first time in history, you won't have to press the fast-forward button when showing your footage to family, friends, co-workers, and clients. There won't *be* any dull footage worth skipping, because you'll have deleted it on the Mac.

Tip: Before you get nervous about the hours you'll have to spend editing your stuff in iMovie, remember that there's no law that every video must have crossfades, scrolling credits, and a throbbing music soundtrack. Yes, of course, you *can* make movies on iMovie that are as slickly produced as commercial films; much of this book is dedicated to helping you achieve that standard. But many people dump an hour's worth of footage onto the Mac, chop out the boring bits, and dump it right back onto the camcorder—only about 15 minutes' worth of work after the transfer to the Mac.

What's It Good For?

If you're reading this book, you probably already have some ideas about what you could do if you could make professional-looking video. Here are a few possibilities that may not have occurred to you. All are natural projects for iMovie:

- **Home movies.** Plain old home movies—casual documentaries of your life, your kids' lives, your school life, your trips—are the single most popular creation of camcorder owners. Using the suggestions in the following chapters, you can improve the quality of your footage. And using iMovie, you can delete all but the best scenes (and edit out those humiliating parts where you walked for 20 minutes with the camcorder accidentally filming the ground bouncing beneath it).

  This, too, is where iMovie '08's Internet smarts come into play. Instead of burning and shipping a DVD of your home movies, you can shoot the finished product up to a Web page or YouTube, where your lucky, lucky family and friends can enjoy them.

- **Web movies.** But why limit your aspirations to people you know? This is the YouTube Era, dude. If you've got something funny or interesting on "film," why not share it with the Internet population at large? In iMovie '08, YouTube is only one menu command away—and that's just the beginning. New film festivals, Web sites, and magazines are springing up everywhere, all dedicated to independent makers of *short* movies.

- **Business videos.** It's very easy to post video on the Internet or burn it onto a cheap, recordable CD or DVD, as described in Part 3. As a result, you should consider video a useful tool in whatever you do. If you're a real estate agent, blow away your rivals (and save your clients time) by showing movies, not still photos, of the properties you represent. If you're an executive, quit boring your comrades with stupefying PowerPoint slides and make your point with video instead.

- **Video photo albums.** A video photo album can be much more exciting, accessible, and engaging than a paper one. Start by filming or scanning your photos. Assemble them into a sequence, add some crossfades, titles, and music. The result is a much more interesting display than a book of motionless images, thanks in part to iMovie's Ken Burns effect (page 247). This emerging video form is becoming very popular—videographers are charging a lot of money to create such "living photo albums" for their clients.

- **Just-for-fun projects.** Never again can anyone over the age of eight complain that there's "nothing to do." Set them loose with a camcorder and the instruction to make a fake rock video, commercial, or documentary.

- **Training films.** If there's a better use for video than providing how-to instruction, you'd be hard-pressed to name it. Make a video for new employees to show them the ropes. Make a video that accompanies your product to give a humanizing touch to your company and help the customer make the most of her purchase.

Make a DVD that teaches newcomers how to play the banjo, grow a garden, kick a football, use a computer program—and then market it.

- **Interviews.** You're lucky enough to live in an age where you can manipulate video just as easily as you do words in a word processor. Capitalize on this fact. Create family histories. Film relatives who still remember the War, the Birth, the Immigration. Or create a time-capsule, time-lapse film: Ask your kid or your parent the same four questions every year on his birthday (such as, "What's your greatest worry right now?" or "If you had one wish…?" or "Where do you want to be in five years?"). Then, after five or 10 or 20 years, splice together the answers for an enlightening fast-forward through a human life.

- **Broadcast segments.** Want a taste of the real world? Call your cable TV company about its public-access channels. (As required by law, every cable company offers a channel or two for ordinary citizens to use for their own programming.) Find out the time and format restraints, and then make a documentary, short film, or other piece for actual broadcast. Advertise the airing to everyone you know. It's a small-time start, but it's real broadcasting.

- **Analyze performances.** There's no better way to improve your golf swing, tennis form, musical performance, or public speaking style than to study footage of yourself. If you're a teacher, camp counselor, or coach, film your students, campers, or players so that they can benefit from self-analysis, too.

- **Turn photos into video.** Technically, you don't need a camcorder at all to use iMovie; it's equally adept at importing and presenting still photos from a scanner or digital camera. In fact, iMovie's Ken Burns effect brings still photos to life, gently zooming into them, fading from shot to shot, panning across them, and so on, making this software the world's best slideshow creator.

Tape vs. Tapeless

If you already own a camcorder, you can safely skip to the next chapter. If you're in the market for a new one, though, you can consider the rest of this chapter a handy buying guide.

For years, when you said "camcorder," it was understood that you meant "*tape* camcorder." And, to be sure, the least expensive and most popular camcorder type today (by a hair) records onto tape: MiniDV cassettes.

The popularity of digital tape camcorders is crashing, however. Their sales have been declining 10 to 15 percent a year.

As you can imagine, these numbers are causing some consternation at the headquarters of Sony, Canon, and other camcorder makers. What's going on? Don't people want to preserve memories of their lives anymore?

As best they can tell, the problem is the cassettes themselves. They're too hard to find in the drawer when the neighbors want to see the highlights of your latest vacation, and it takes too long to rewind and fast-forward.

What the world wants, the camcorder manufacturers have decided, is *random access:* the ability to jump directly to any scene without having to wait. In theory, a tapeless camcorder also saves you time when transferring the video to your computer for editing, because you don't have to play the video from the camcorder in real time. The video files are stored on memory card, hard drive, or DVD as regular computer files, which you should be able to simply drag and drop onto your Mac's hard drive. (In practice, it doesn't quite work out that way—see page 91—but you get the idea.)

That's why the industry has been flooding the stores with *tapeless* camcorders: cameras that record onto memory cards, onto hard drives, or onto little DVDs—anything but tape.

The Downsides of Tapeless

Unfortunately, at least at this writing, few tapeless camcorders offer the incredible video quality of MiniDV camcorders. In order to store a reasonable amount of video onto that tiny memory card, hard drive, or DVD, the camera must *compress* it to an alarming degree, using less information to describe each frame of video. Video recorded onto MiniDV tapes, on the other hand, is essentially uncompressed. What you see on playback is what the camera recorded.

Remember, too, that each kind of tapeless camcorder has its own kinds of storage limitations:

- **DVD camcorders.** The miniature blank DVDs used by DVD camcorders generally hold only 20 minutes of video apiece—only 15 minutes in high definition. (Some models can record onto the newer double-sided discs, which roughly doubles the recording time.) And you can't play the resulting disc in a regular DVD player unless you first "finalize" it, a sort of software shrink-wrapping process that can take 10 or 15 minutes inside the camcorder.

  In fact, you can't play the resulting DVDs in a *Mac* at all. Macs expect full-size DVDs; these miniature, 8-centimeter discs can literally trash your drive.

FREQUENTLY ASKED QUESTION

What's Digital About DV

I was a little surprised to find, when I bought my MiniDV camcorder, that it requires tapes, just like my old nondigital one. If it still needs tapes, how can they call it digital?

Your confusion is understandable. After all, digital cameras don't require film, and digital TV recorders (such as the tapeless TiVo and ReplayTV "VCRs") don't use videotape.

Today's MiniDV camcorders are really only half digital. They

store their signal in digital form as a bunch of computer codes, but still record it on videotape just like the old camcorders. You still have to rewind and fast-forward to find a particular spot in the footage. (Until you transfer the footage to iMovie, that is.)

In other words, MiniDV is old-fashioned tape that stores a modern digital signal.

- **Hard-drive camcorders** can record several hours of video (say, five hours at best quality) before running out of space—but at that point, you're dead in the water. Your camcorder is useless until it has a date with your computer, so you can dump the video off the camcorder to empty its hard drive.

- **Memory-card camcorders** might be able to store, for example, one hour of video on a four-gigabyte memory card. And you can carry a couple of extras around in case of emergency. But memory cards are far too expensive for long-term storage. In other words, nobody but Donald Trump can afford to buy a new memory card for every vacation, holiday, and wedding. Everybody else empties out the camcorder onto the computer every time the memory card gets full.

Note: The new world of tapeless camcorders is filled with exceptions, footnotes, and caveats. Apple has noted a few of the quirks here–*http://docs.info.apple.com/article.html?artnum=306171*–but the best advice is to use Google before you buy any camcorder to ensure its compatibility with iMovie. (Search for *Sony SR7 imovie 08,* for example.)

High Definition

A growing number of camcorders film in gorgeous, widescreen, ultrasharp *high definition.* The video looks absolutely incredible when viewed on an HDTV set. Your own life looks like it was filmed by a Hollywood movie crew.

If you're shopping for a camcorder now, you should seriously consider going to high-def right now. High-definition camcorders are available in both tape and tapeless models. The really cool thing about the tape models, in fact, is that they record onto ordinary MiniDV cassettes, exactly the same ones used by regular tape camcorders. The signal recorded on these tapes is different, of course—it's in a format called

Figure 1-2:
High-def camcorders like the Canon HV20 record onto ordinary MiniDV tapes. The image quality, however, is anything but ordinary.

HDV—but you still gain the convenience and economy of those ordinary drugstore tapes (Figure 1-2).

High-def camcorders cost more than standard-definition models. But it's worth paying the premium, because high definition is the video format of the future; sooner or later, the transition to HD will be complete. You may as well start filming your life in high definition now, because in a few years, standard definition will look as quaint as daguerreotype photographs.

AVCHD, MPEG-2, and Other Such Jargon

The new generation of tapeless camcorder stores video as ordinary computer files—on DVD, hard drive, or memory card—that you can copy to your Mac and edit in iMovie. But what *are* those files? Every computer document is *some* format, whether JPEG (the usual format for photos) or TXT (text files). What format are these video files?

Some digital camcorders, especially old ones, record in formats called MPEG-1, MPEG-2, and MPEG-4. (The abbreviation stands for Motion Picture Experts Group, the association of geeks who dream up these standards.) iMovie '08 recognizes and imports MPEG-2—usually. Unfortunately, there are multiple *flavors* of MPEG-2, and iMovie doesn't recognize all of them.

iMovie can also work with the movies created by most digital *still* cameras, like .MOV, .AVI, and MPEG-4 files. Here again, though, your mileage may vary.

Tip: It's worth repeating: If you're tempted to buy a certain camcorder, but you're not sure if iMovie works with it, Google it.

The good news is that iMovie '08 also recognizes *AVCHD*, which is already the most popular file format for high-definition tapeless camcorders. (It stands for Advanced Video Coding/High Definition, and yes, it's an annoying acronym. Do they really think they're going to make video editing *more* attractive by dreaming up names like this?)

Anyway, AVCHD is a high-def format concocted by Sony and Panasonic in 2006, and is now available on camcorders from Sony, Panasonic, Canon, and Samsung. This format offers roughly the same video quality as MPEG-2 or MPEG-4, but takes up even less space on your camcorder's memory card, miniDVD, or hard drive.

As it turns out, AVCHD is the same as H.264, which is the video format as Blu-ray high-definition DVD discs (and also the format of videos from the iTunes Store). That's a handy feature for people who own both an AVCHD camcorder that records onto miniature DVDs and a Blu-ray DVD player (or Playstation 3), because you can pop the DVD right out of the camcorder and into the Blu-ray player to play on your TV.

That's the good news. The bad news is that AVCHD still takes up a lot of space; a DVD camcorder of this type holds only 15 minutes of best-quality video per disc. (On the newer double-sided discs and camcorders that accept them, you get 27 minutes.)

The bigger bummer is that AVCHD does not take kindly to being edited. When you import AVCHD video to iMovie, for example, your Mac first converts it to another format that *can* be edited (page 100), which takes a very long time. In fact, one hour's worth of video takes over *two* hours to convert, which neatly erases the importing-time advantage that your tapeless camcorder would have had over a MiniDV tape camcorder.

Camcorder Features: Which Are Worthwhile?

Like any hot new technology, digital camcorders started out expensive ($2,500 in 1996) and continue to plummet in price. At this writing, basic models start at $300; prosumer models hover around $1,500; many TV crews are adopting $2,800 models like the Canon XL2 or Sony's high-definition FX7; and the fanciest, professional, commercial-filmmaking models go for $7,000 or more. All of these camcorders are *teeming* with features and require a thick brochure to list them all.

Useful Features

So how do you know which to buy? Here's a rundown of the most frequently advertised camcorder features, along with a frank assessment of their value to the quality-obsessed iMovie fan.

Note: As you read, you'll encounter one slightly depressing trend: Some of the handiest little features that were once standard are missing from the latest camcorder models. That's because, in an effort to prop up sagging camcorder sales, camcorder companies have been stripping away features to cut costs and lower prices. Among the features they're deleting: FireWire jacks; microphone inputs; headphone jacks; analog inputs; and a Backlight button.

FireWire connector

FireWire is Apple's term for the tiny, compact connector on the side of most MiniDV tape camcorders. When you attach a FireWire cable, this jack connects the camera to your Mac. Other companies have different names for this connector—you may see it called IEEE-1394, i.Link, DV In/Out, or DV Terminal.

On tapeless camcorders, FireWire jacks are usually missing altogether. That's OK; you have other ways to get your video off the camcorder and onto the Mac, as described in Chapter 4.

Analog inputs

This single feature may be important enough to determine your camcorder choice by itself. *Analog inputs* are connectors on the camcorder (Figure 1-3) into which you can connect older, pre-DV equipment, such as your VCR, your old 8mm camcorder, and so on.

Unfortunately, this is one of those features that the camcorder makers have been quietly eliminating in an effort to shave costs. That's too bad, because there's no easier, less expensive method of transferring older footage into your digital camcorder—or directly into iMovie.

This technique is described in more detail in Chapter 4. For now, note only that the only *other* method of transferring pre-DV footage into digital format is to buy a $200 converter box.

RCA connectors   S-video connector

Figure 1-3:
Look for a camcorder with RCA connectors as inputs for older, analog video. (Actually, what you'll probably get is a special cable with RCA connectors on one end and a miniplug on the camcorder end, like the one shown here. Don't lose this cable! You also need it to play your camcorder footage on TV.) A few older models offer an S-video connector too, for much higher quality.

GEM IN THE ROUGH

Digital8 format

Here's another plan for getting your older footage into iMovie: Buy what Sony calls a *Digital8* camcorder. This fascinating hybrid doesn't use the MiniDV videotapes used by all other DV camcorders. Instead, it accepts the less expensive 8mm or, as Sony recommends, Hi-8 tapes.

Onto these cassettes, Digital8 camcorders record the identical DV signal found on MiniDV camcorders. But they can play back *either* digital video or traditional, analog video. (When recording digital video, however, the camera runs twice as fast—you still get only one hour of recording per tape, just as on MiniDV tapes.)

This kind of camcorder, in other words, may be a good solution if you have a library of old 8mm tapes that you'd like to edit in iMovie. Your Mac can't tell which kind of tape the Digital8 camcorder is playing.

On the other hand, full-blown MiniDV camcorders and tapes are only slightly more expensive than their 8mm predecessors, and Sony's Digital8 camcorder family has begun to wind down. In fact, at this writing, there's only one model left.

Three chips (CCDs)

Professional camcorders offer three individual image sensors, one for each color component of a video picture: red, green, and blue. These camcorders are advertised as having three chips or *CCDs (charge-coupled devices*—electronic plates, covered with thousands of individual light sensors, that convert light rays into a digital signal). The result is even more spectacular picture quality, resolution, and color rendition than the less-expensive, one-CCD cameras.

Unfortunately, three-chip camcorders tend to be more expensive than one-chip cams—but they deliver much better color.

Not all three-chip models are big and pricey. Panasonic, in particular, has developed a line of three-chip camcorders that aren't much larger or more expensive than one-chip models. Note, however, that they usually contain three very *small* CCDs, so the quality improvement is visible primarily in bright, outdoor scenes.

LCD viewfinder

In the olden days, you'd set up your shots and monitor your filming by looking through a tiny glass eyepiece. Today, virtually all camcorders offer a small swing-out LCD screen (Figure 1-4). (LCD stands for *liquid crystal display,* the technology used to produce the image. As you may have noticed, it's the same technology used in laptop screens.)

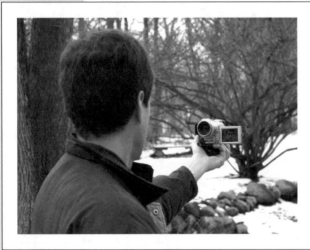

Figure 1-4:
Your camcorder's LCD screen can rotate 180 degrees to face front; that's useful when you want to film yourself. Without an LCD screen, you'd have no idea whether or not you were centered in the frame. You can usually flip the LCD so far around, in fact, that you can press it flat against the camcorder, screen side out. That's a nice way to play back your footage for a couple of onlookers.

The LCD means that when you're shooting, you can see what the camcorder sees without having to mash your face against the eyepiece. Better yet, after shooting, you can play back your footage. And thanks to the small, built-in speaker found on every sub-$1,500 camcorder, you can watch and hear your work played back on the LCD screen while still "on location." (Professional camcorders don't have any speakers.)

Now, what you see isn't *exactly* what you get. For one thing, the LCD panel usually has its own brightness control, which, if not adjusted perfectly, may trick you into thinking a scene is lit better (or worse) than it actually is. The color and exposure revealed by the LCD screen may not exactly match what's going onto the tape, either.

When picture perfection counts, therefore, use your camcorder's eyepiece viewfinder instead of the LCD panel. You may also want to use the eyepiece when it's very bright and sunny out (the LCD display tends to wash out in bright light), when you don't want people around you to see what you're filming, and when you're trying to save battery juice. The LCD display depletes your battery about 50 percent faster than when the LCD is turned off.

Tip: The size of the LCD viewfinder is relative to two things: the size of the camcorder and its price. A camcorder with a 2.5-inch screen may cost hundreds of dollars less than one with a 4-inch screen.

Image stabilizer

Certain film techniques scream "Amateur!" to audiences. One of them is the instability of handheld filming. In a nutshell, professional video is shot using a camera on a tripod (Woody Allen's "handheld" period notwithstanding). Most home camcorder footage, in contrast, is shot from the palm of your hand.

A stabilizing feature (which may have a marketing name, such as Sony's SteadyShot) takes a half step toward solving that problem. As shown in Figure 1-5, this feature neatly eliminates the tiny, jittery moves present in handheld video. (It can't do anything about bigger jerks and bumps, which are especially difficult to avoid when you're zoomed in.) It also uses up your battery faster.

This kind of anti-shake feature comes in two forms:

- Electronic or digital stabilization is what you get on cheaper camcorders. Its workings are described in Figure 1-5.

Figure 1-5:
Digital stabilization features work by "taking in" more image than you actually see in the viewfinder. Because the camcorder has some buffer, its computer can compensate for small bumps and jitters by keeping an "eye" on prominent features of the image. On less expensive camcorders, unfortunately, this buffer zone means that your camcorder is absorbing less video information, to the detriment of picture quality.

• Optical stabilization is much preferable. This mechanism involves two transparent plates separated by a special optical fluid. As the camera shakes, these plates create a prism effect that keeps handheld shots clearer and steadier than electronic (digital) stabilizers. The images are clearer because optical stabilizers don't have to crop out part of the picture as a buffer, unlike the stabilizers illustrated in Figure 1-5.

Manual controls

Better camcorders let you turn off the automatic focus, automatic exposure control, automatic white balance, and even automatic sound level. This feature can be useful in certain situations, as you'll find out in the next chapter. If you've decided to pay extra for this feature, look for a model that lets you focus manually by turning a ring around the lens, which is much easier than using sliders.

Optical zoom

When you read the specs for a camcorder—or read the logos painted on its body—you frequently encounter numbers like "12X/300X ZOOM!" The number before the slash tells you how many times the camera can magnify a distant image, much like a telescope. That number measures the *optical* zoom, which is the actual amount that the lenses themselves can zoom in. Such zooming, of course, is useful when you want to film something that's far away. (As for the number *after* the slash, see "Digital zoom," later in this chapter.)

You should know, however, that the more you've zoomed in, the shakier your footage is likely to be, since every microscopic wobble is magnified by, say, 12 times. You also have to be much more careful about focusing. When you're zoomed out all the way, everything is in focus—things near you, and things far away. But when you're zoomed in, very near and very far objects go out of focus. Put into photographic terms, the more you zoom in, the shorter the *depth of field* (the range of distance from the camera that can be kept in focus simultaneously).

Finally, remember that magnifying the picture doesn't magnify the sound. If you're relying on the built-in microphone of your camcorder, always get as close as you can to the subject, both for the sound and for the wobble.

Tip: As you'll discover in the next chapter, professional video and film work includes very little zooming, unlike most amateur video work. The best zooming is subtle zooming, such as when you very slowly "move toward" the face of somebody you're interviewing.

For this reason, when shopping for camcorders, test the zooming if at all possible. Find out if the camcorder has *variable-speed* zooming, where the zooming speed increases as you press the Zoom button harder. Some camcorders offer only two different speeds—fast and faster—but that's still better than having no control at all. (Variable-speed zooming isn't something mentioned in the standard camcorder literature; you generally have to try the camcorder in the store to find out how it does.)

Minutes-remaining readout

Fortunately, the problems exhibited by camcorder batteries of old—such as the "memory effect"—are a thing of the past. (When you halfway depleted a pre-digital camcorder battery's charge several times in a row, the battery would adopt that half-way-empty point as its new *completely* empty point, effectively halving its capacity.) Today's lithium-ion battery technology eliminates that problem.

Some camcorders—mostly from Sony, JVC, and Canon—even display, in minutes, how much juice the battery has remaining. A glance at the viewfinder or the LCD screen tells you how many minutes of recording or playback you've got left—a worthy feature.

Tip: The number of minutes' recording time advertised for camcorder batteries is *continuous* recording time—that is, the time you'll get if you turn the camcorder on, press Record, and go out to lunch. If you stop and start the camera to capture shorter scenes, as almost everyone does, you'll get much less than the advertised amount of time out of each battery charge.

Built-in light

As you can read in the next chapter, insufficient lighting is one of the leading causes of "amateuritis," a telltale form of poor video quality that lets viewers know that the footage is homemade. In the best—and most expensive—of all possible worlds, you'd get your scene correctly lit before filming, or you'd attach a light to the "shoe" (light connector) on top of the camera. Those few cameras that have such a shoe, or even have a built-in light, give you a distinct advantage in filming accurate colors.

Preprogrammed exposure options

Most DV camcorders come with a number of canned focus/shutter speed/aperture settings for different indoor and outdoor environments: Sports Lesson, Beach and Snow, Twilight, and so on. They're a useful compromise between the all-automatic operation of less expensive models and the all-manual operation of professional cameras.

Remote control

Some camcorders come with a pocket-sized remote control. It serves two purposes. First, its Record and Stop buttons give you a means of recording *yourself,* with or without other people in the shot. Second, when you're playing back footage with the camcorder connected to your TV or VCR, the remote lets you control the playback without needing to have the camcorder on your lap. You may be surprised at how useful the remote can be.

Backlight mode

As you can read in the next chapter, modern camcorders take much of the guesswork out of shooting video. For example, they can focus automatically.

Although few consumers appreciate it, today's camcorders also set their *aperture* automatically. The aperture is the hole inside the barrel of your camcorder's snout that gets bigger or smaller to admit more or less light, preventing you from under- or overexposing your footage. (Inside the camera is an *iris*—a circle of interlocking, sliding panels that move together to reduce or enlarge the opening, much like the one in a still camera.)

The automatic aperture circuitry works by analyzing the image. If it contains a lot of light—such as when you're filming against a snowy backdrop or aiming the camera toward the sun—the iris closes automatically, reducing the opening in the camera lens and thus reducing the amount of light admitted. The result: You avoid flooding the image with blinding white light.

Unfortunately, there may be times when you have no choice but to film somebody, or something, against a bright backdrop. In those cases, as you may have discovered through painful experience, the person you're trying to film shows up extremely dark, almost in silhouette (see Figure 1-6). Now the background is correctly exposed, but the *subject* winds up underexposed.

Figure 1-6:
Without the backlight mode, your camcorder is likely to turn your subject into a silhouette (left). The Backlight button compensates by brightening everything up (right).

A Backlight button, then, is a valuable (but increasingly rare) asset on a camcorder. Its purpose is to tell the camera, "OK, look, it's a bright scene; I can appreciate that. But I'm more interested in the subject that's coming out too dark at the moment. So do me a favor and open that aperture a couple of notches, will you?"

The camera obliges. Your subject no longer winds up too dark. In fact, modern camcorders do a great job at making sure the subject turns out just right. But overriding the automatic aperture control undoes the good the automatic iris originally did you—now everything *around* your subject is several shades too bright. Alas, there's no in between. *Either* your subject or the background can be correctly exposed in very bright settings—but not both.

Tip: If your camcorder has a manual-exposure control, you can similarly compensate for backlit scenes, but with much more control. Professionals and semi-pros, in fact, turn the auto-exposure feature off *completely.* True, they must now adjust the exposure knob for every single new shot, but their footage is then free from the bizarre and violent darkening or brightening that auto-exposure electronics can create as you pan across a scene.

FlexiZone or Push Focus

All camcorders offer automatic focus. Most work by focusing on the image in the center of your frame as you line up the shot.

That's fine if the subject of your shot *is* in the center of the frame. But if it's off-center, you have no choice but to turn off the autofocus feature and use the manual-focus ring. (Using the camcorder isn't like using a still camera, where you can point the camera directly at the subject for focusing purposes, and then—before taking the shot—shift the angle so that the subject is no longer in the center. Camcorders continually refocus, so pointing the camera slightly away from your subject makes you lose the off-center focus you've established.)

Some Canon, Sony, and Sharp camcorders let you point to a specific spot in the frame that you want to serve as the focus point, even if it's not the center of the picture. (This feature is called FlexiZone on the Canon models, or Push Focus on high-end Sony models. On Sony cams with touch-screen LCD panels, it's especially easy to indicate which spot in the frame should get the focus.) If the model you're eyeing has this feature, it's worth having.

Night-vision mode

Most Sony camcorders offer a mode called NightShot that works like night-vision goggles. In this mode, you can actually film (and see, as you watch the LCD screen) in total darkness. The infrared transmitter on the front of the camcorder measures the heat given off by various objects in its path, letting you capture an eerie, greenish night scene. Rent *The Silence of the Lambs* for an idea of how creepy night-vision filming can be. Or watch any episode of *Survivor*.

The transmitter's range is only about 15 feet or so. Still, you may be surprised how often it comes in handy: on campouts, during sleepovers, on nighttime nature walks, and so on.

Still photos

All modern camcorders can take still photos. The camcorder freezes one frame of what it's seeing, and records it either on the tape (for, say, a 7-second stretch) or as a regular JPEG photo file on a memory card.

The photo quality, unfortunately, is pretty terrible. The resolution may be OK (some camcorders offer two- or even three-megapixel resolution), but the quality isn't anywhere near what you'd get using a dedicated digital still camera. It turns out that the lenses and circuitry that best serve video are all wrong for stills.

If the camcorder you're considering offers this feature, fine. But it may be redundant for the iMovie owner. iMovie can grab one-megapixel still frames from *any* captured video, as described in Chapter 12.

Progressive-scan CCD

This special kind of image sensor is primarily useful for capturing still images. It ensures that the *entire* image is grabbed, not just one set of alternating, interlaced scan lines (the usual video signal). If you plan to catch still frames from your camcorder, a progressive-scan CCD will spare you some of the jagged lines that may appear. However, if your primary goal is to make movies, this expensive feature is not worth paying for, especially since you can buy a digital *still* camera, with much greater resolution, for about the same added cost.

Useless Features

Here are some features you'll see in camcorder advertising that you should ignore completely (and definitely not pay extra for).

Title generator

Some camcorders let you superimpose *titles* (that is, lettering) on your video as you film. In your case, dear iMovie owner, a title-generating feature is useless. Your Mac can add gorgeous, smooth-edged type, with a selection of sizes, fonts, colors, and even scrolling animations, to your finished movies, with far more precision and power than the blocky text available to your camcorder. (Chapter 10 shows you how.)

Tip: A title generator on the camcorder is actually *worse* than useless, because it permanently stamps your original footage with something you may wish you could amend later.

In fact, as a general rule, you should avoid using (or paying for) *any* of the in-camera editing features described in this chapter—title generator, fader, special effects—because you can do this kind of editing much more effectively in iMovie. Not only are they redundant, but they commit you to an editing choice in advance, thus limiting how you can use your footage.

Audio dubbing

In a few fancy camcorders, you can rerecord the soundtrack on a piece of tape you've already shot. You could conceivably use this feature to add, for example, an accompanying rock song to a montage of party scenes.

But iMovie offers far more flexibility. For example, iMovie lets you add a piece of music to a scene *without* deleting the original voices, as your camcorder's audio-dub feature would.

Special effects

Most DV camcorders offer a selection of six or seven cheesy-looking special effects. They can make your footage look solarized, or digitized, or otherwise processed (see Figure 1-7).

Avoid using these effects. iMovie '08 doesn't have any of these special effects, but iMovie 6 (which you still have—see page 3) has a huge collection of them. And it gives you far greater control over when they start, when they end, and how intensely they affect the video. Even then, unless you're shooting a documentary about nuclear explosions or bad drug episodes, consider avoiding these effects altogether.

Date/time stamp

Every camcorder offers the ability to stamp the date and time directly onto the footage. As you've no doubt seen (on *America's Funniest Home Videos* or *America's Scariest Cop Chases*), the result is a blocky, typographically hideous stamp that permanently mars the footage. Few things take the romance out of a wedding video, or are more distracting in spectacular weather footage, than a huge **20 SEP 06 12:34 PM** stamped in the corner.

Figure 1-7:
Using the stock collection of special effects built into your camcorder, you can create special, hallucinogenic visuals. The question is: why?

Nor do you have to worry that you'll one day forget when you filmed some event. As it turns out, digital camcorders automatically and invisibly date- and time-stamp *all* footage. You'll be able to see this information when you connect the camcorder to your Mac; *then* you can choose whether or not to add it to the finished footage (and with much more control over the timing, location, and typography of the stamp).

Control-L or Lanc

You'll find this feature on some Canon and all Sony camcorders. It's a connector that hooks up to special editing consoles.

You, however, have a far superior editing console—iMovie. Control-L and Lanc are worthless to you.

Digital zoom

Much as camera owners mistakenly jockey for superiority by comparing the megapixel rating of their cameras (more megapixels don't necessarily make sharper pictures), camcorder makers seem to think that what consumers want most in a camcorder is a powerful digital zoom. Your camcorder's packaging may "boast" zoom ratings of "50X," "100X," or "500X!"

When a camcorder uses its *digital* zoom—the number after the slash on the camcorder box—it simply enlarges the individual dots that compose its image. Yes, the image gets bigger, but it doesn't get any *sharper*. As the dots get larger, the image gets chunkier, coarser, and less recognizable, until it ends up looking like the blocky areas you see superimposed over criminals' faces to conceal their identity on *Cops*. After your digital zoom feature has blown up the picture by 3X, the image falls to pieces. Greater digital zoom is not something worth paying extra for.

Where and How to Buy

Most of the usual electronics suspects make camcorders these days, including Sony, Panasonic, JVC, Samsung, Sanyo, Hitachi, and Canon. Each company releases a new line of models once or twice a year; the feature list always gets longer, the price always gets lower, and the model numbers always change.

Cameras come in all sizes, shapes, and price ranges (see Figure 1-8). In magazine reviews and Internet discussion groups, Sony and Canon get consistently high marks for high quality. Still, each manufacturer offers different exclusive goodies, and each camcorder generation improves on the previous one.

Figure 1-8:
The model lineup changes constantly, and new formats come and go. Here, for example, are three 2007-era digital camcorders.

Top left: This Panasonic high-def camcorder records onto memory cards in AVCHD format.

Top right: JVC pioneered the hard-drive camcorder in its Everio series.

Bottom: Pros and semi-pros, however, are still using tape. In the right camcorder, like this semi-pro model from Sony, the results are stunning.

To look over a company's latest camcorders, start by reading about them at the relevant Web site:

- Sony. Visit *www.sonystyle.com*, and then navigate your way to the Handycam Camcorders page.

- Canon. Go to *www.canondv.com* to view the various models.

- Panasonic. Start at Panasonic.com and burrow your way in through Consumer Electronics, or just use this shortcut: *http://tinyurl.com/ywm42h*.

• JVC. These camcorders' headquarters are at *http://camcorder.jvc.com*.

Camcorders, as it turns out, are famous for having hopelessly unrealistic list prices. The high-definition Sony FX7, for example, has an official price tag of $3,500, but you can find it online for less than $2,500.

Once you've narrowed down your interest, then, go straight to a Web site like *www. shopper.com* to see what the real-world price is. Such Web sites specialize in collecting the prices from mail-order companies all over the world. When you specify the camcorder model you're looking for, you're shown a list of online stores that carry it, complete with prices. (All of the prices in this chapter came from listings on those Web sites.)

As you'll quickly discover, prices for the same camcorder cover an *extremely* large range. Use the price-comparison Web sites if saving money is your priority.

Of course, you can also find DV camcorders at electronics and appliance superstores (Circuit City, Best Buy, and so on), mail-order catalogs, and even photo stores.

The Long-Term Storage Problem

No matter which kind of camcorder you choose, you have more to consider than just features and prices; you have the future to consider. Every kind of camcorder types presents serious challenges if you hope to preserve your video for future generations.

• **DVD camcorders.** Nobody has yet figured out how long those home-burned DVDs actually last. They don't last essentially forever, as Hollywood DVDs do. In Hollywood, they *stamp* DVDs, pressing a pattern into the plastic. Home DVD burners, though, record a pattern in a layer of organic dye on the bottom of the disc—a dye that can take between several *weeks* and several *decades* to break down.

• **Memory-card and hard-drive camcorders.** Once the card or drive is full, you're finished shooting for the day. The camcorder is worthless until you offload the video to a computer, thereby freeing up space to continue shooting.

But what then? Are you going to burn hour after hour of captured video onto DVDs? Not only is that practically a full-time job, but then you're stuck with those homemade DVDs and their questionable lifespan.

You could, of course, just keep the video on hard drives, even though that's a very expensive and bulky solution. Here again, though, you have to wonder: Will the hard drive you buy today still be functioning 50 years from now?

• **Tape camcorders.** Digital tapes may deteriorate over a decade or two, just as traditional tapes do.

The solution to all of these problems, of course, is simple vigilance. Every 10 or so years, you'll have to copy your masterworks onto newer tapes, discs, hard drives, or whatever the latest storage format happens to be.

Turning Home Video into Pro Video

W hen you turn on the TV, how long does it take you to distinguish between an actual broadcast and somebody's home video? Probably about 10 seconds.

The next question is: *How* can you tell? What are the visual differences between professionally produced shows and your own? Apple's advertising claims that a digital camcorder and iMovie let you create professional-quality video work. So why do even iMovie productions often have a homemade look to them?

WORD TO THE WISE

Maybe Homemade Is What You Want

If you want to learn how to upgrade your filming techniques to make your finished videos look more professional, then this chapter is your ticket.

That's not to say, however, that "professional" *always* means "better." Not every video has to be, or should be, a finished-looking production. There are plenty of circumstances in which homemade-looking video is just fine. In fact, it's exactly what an audience of family members is probably expecting. When watching your footage of a one-of-a-kind scene for which preparation was obviously impossible, such as a baby's first steps or the eruption of a local volcano, rest assured that nobody will be critiquing your camera work.

Furthermore, sometimes amateur-looking video *is* the look your professional project calls for. In some movies, filmmakers go to enormous lengths to simulate the effect of amateur camcorder footage. (The color segment of *Raging Bull,* for example, is designed to look as though it's composed footage shot by a home movie camera.)

In other words, polished-looking video isn't necessarily superior video for every situation. Nonetheless, you should know how to get professional results when you want them; even Picasso mastered traditional, representational drawing before going abstract.

As it turns out, there are a number of discernible ways that home movies differ from professional ones. This chapter is dedicated to helping you accept the camcorder deficiencies you cannot change, overcome the limitations you can, and have the wisdom to know the difference.

Film vs. Videotape

There's only one crucial aspect of Hollywood movies that you can't duplicate with your DV camcorder and iMovie: Real movies are shot on *film,* not video. Film, of course, is a long strip of celluloid with sprocket holes on the edges. It comes on an enormous reel, loaded into an enormous camera. After you've shot it, a lab must develop it before you can see what you've got.

Videotape is a different ball game. As you know, it comes on a cartridge and doesn't have to be developed. Many TV shows, including sitcoms and all news shows, are shot on video.

Visually, the differences are dramatic. Film and videotape just look different, for several reasons:

- Film goes through many transfer processes (from original, to positive master, to negative master, to individual "prints," to movie screen), so it has a softer, warmer appearance. It also has microscopic specks, flecks, and scratches that tell you you're watching something filmed on film.

- Film has much greater resolution than video—*billions* of silver halide crystals coat each frame of the film. As a result, you see much more detail than video can offer. It has a subtle grain or texture that you can spot immediately. Furthermore, these specks of color are irregularly shaped, and different on every frame. A camcorder's sensors (CCDs), on the other hand, are all the same size and perfectly aligned, which also affects the look of the resulting image.

- Film is also far more sensitive to color, light, and contrast than the sensors in camcorders, and different kinds of film stock have different characteristics. Hollywood directors choose film stock according to the ambiance they want: One type of film might yield warmer colors, another type might offer sharper contrast, and so on.

- Film is composed of 24 individual frames (images) per second, but NTSC video (page 5) contains more flashes of picture per second (30 complete frames, shown as 60 alternating sets of interlocking horizontal lines per second). All of that extra visual information contributes to video's hard, sharp look and lends visual differences in the way motion is recorded. This discrepancy becomes particularly apparent to experts when film is *transferred* to video for broadcast on TV, for example. Doing so requires the transfer equipment to *duplicate* a frame of the original film here and there.

Of course, the *content* of the film or video is also a telltale sign of what you're watching. If it has a laugh track and a brightly lit set, it's usually videotape; if it's more carefully and dramatically lit, with carefully synchronized background music, it's usually film.

Film-Technique Crash Course

The bottom line is that two different issues separate film from video: the *technology* and the *technique*. What you can't change is the look of the basic medium: You're going to be recording onto tape, not film.

Tip: If the grain and softness associated with film are crucial to your project, you're not utterly out of luck. With the addition of a 320 video-processing program called Adobe After Effects and a $550 software add-on called CineLook (from DigiEffects), you can get very close to making video look like film. CineLook adds the grain, flecks, and scratches to taped footage, and plays with the color palette to make it look more like that of film. Another popular add-on called CineMotion (from the same company) adds subtle blur processing to make the *motion* of video look more like film, simulating 24-frames-per-second playback. (Needless to say, few iMovie fans go to that expensive extreme.)

What you can change with iMovie alone, however, is almost every remaining element of the picture. Some of the advice in this chapter requires additional equipment; some simply requires new awareness. Overall, however, the tips in this chapter should take you a long way into the world of professional cinematography.

The Very Basics

If you're using a camcorder for the first time, it's important to understand the difference between its two functions: as a camera and as a VCR.

The most obvious knob or switch on every camcorder lets you switch between these two modes (plus a third one known as Off). These two operating-switch positions may be labeled *Camera* and *VTR* (for Video Tape Recorder), *Camera* and *VCR,* or *Record* and *Play.*

But the point is always the same: When you're in Camera mode, you can record the world; the lens and the microphone are activated. When you're in VTR mode, the lens and the mike are shut down; now your camcorder is a VCR, complete with Play, Rewind, and Fast-Forward buttons (which often light up in VTR mode). When you want to *film* a movie, use Camera mode; to *watch* the movie you've recorded, put the camcorder into VTR mode. (You'll also have to put the camera in VTR mode when it comes time to record your finished iMovie creation, or when you want to copy video to or from another camcorder or VCR.)

Here, then, is the usual sequence for filming:

1. **Prepare the microphone, lighting, angle, and camera settings as described in this chapter.**

   This is the moment, in other words, to play director and cinematographer, to set up the shot. You can read about all these important techniques in the rest of this chapter. They're extremely important techniques, at that: If the raw footage has bad sound, bad lighting, or the wrong camera settings, no amount of iMovie manipulation can make it better.

2. **Turn the main knob or switch to Camera (or Record) mode.**

You've just turned the power on. The camera's now in standby mode—on, but not playing or recording anything. (See Figure 2-1.)

Figure 2-1:
The main button on every camcorder lets you turn the camera on by switching it into Camera or VTR mode (left). The red Record button is the trigger that makes the tape roll (right).

3. **Take off the lens cap.**

Some lens caps are built-in and automatic (hurray!). But most still dangle from a short black string that you've looped around a corresponding hole on the front of the camera (or hooks onto the handstrap).

4. **Frame your shot (aim the camera).**

Do so either by looking at the LCD screen or by looking through the eyepiece. Adjust the zoom controls until the subject nicely fills the frame. Get your performers ready (if they're even aware that they're being filmed, that is).

5. **Press the Record button.**

It's usually bright red and located next to your right thumb. (The left-handers' lobby has gotten absolutely nowhere with camcorder manufacturers.)

Some camcorders have an additional Record button on the top or side, plus another one on the remote control, for use when you're filming yourself or holding the camcorder down at belly level.

In any case, now you're rolling.

6. **Film the action as described in this chapter. When you've filmed enough of the scene—when you've *got the shot*—press the Record button to stop rolling.**

At this point, the camcorder is back in standby mode. It's using up its battery faster than when it's turned off. Therefore, if you don't expect to be filming anything else within the next few minutes, push the primary switch back to its Off position. (If you forget, no big deal; most camcorders turn off automatically 5 minutes or so after your last activity.)

Now you, like thousands before you, know the basics. The rest of this chapter is designed to elevate your art from that of camera operator to cinematographer/director.

Get the Shot

Rule No. 1: Get the shot.

If you and the camcorder aren't ready when something great happens—whether you're trying to create a Hollywood-style movie with scripted actors or just trying to catch the dog's standoff with a squirrel—then everything else in this book, and in your new hobby, are for naught.

Both human and mechanical obstacles may conspire to prevent you from capturing the perfect footage. Here are some examples:

Is the Camera Ready?

Your camcorder is only ready when its battery is charged and it's got fresh tape or free space inside. MiniDV cassettes these days cost about $4 apiece (from, for example, *www.bhphoto.com* or warehouse discount clubs like Costco); blank miniDVDs are about $7. If you bite the bullet and buy a box of 10 or 50, you'll save even more money, you won't have to buy any more for quite a while, and you'll be able to keep a couple of spares with the camera.

If you have a hard-drive or memory-card camcorder, you can't exactly buy more recording space at a drugstore. Planning ahead is part of the game with these machines.

Tip: Professional broadcast journalists never go anywhere without fully charged batteries and blank tape in the camera. Even if you're not a pro, having enough tape and power at all times can pay off, since you can make good money selling your video to news shows because you caught something good on tape.

The same goes for battery power. The battery that comes with the camcorder is adequate as a starter battery, but buying a second one—especially if it's one of the fat, heavy, longer-capacity batteries—is further insurance that some precious shooting opportunity won't be shut down or lost by equipment failure.

Remember, too, that today's lithium-ion batteries are extraordinarily sophisticated. But even though they're rechargeable, they're not immortal; most can be recharged only a few hundred times before you start to notice a decrease in capacity. In other words, use the power cord whenever it's practical.

Tip: Camcorder batteries are far more fragile than they appear. Keep them dry at all costs. If one gets damp or wet, you may as well throw it away.

Are You Ready?

There's a human element to being ready, too. For example, remember that from the moment you switch on the power, your camcorder takes about 8 seconds to warm up, load a little bit of tape, and prepare for filming. It's a good idea to flip the power on, therefore, even as you're running to the scene of the accident, earthquake, or amazing child behavior.

Is the Camera Actually Recording?

Every day, somewhere in the world, a family sits down in front of the TV, expecting to watch some exciting home movies, and instead watches 20 minutes of the ground bumping along beneath the camcorder owner's hand.

As you begin to shoot, *always* glance at the viewfinder to confirm that the Record indicator—usually a red dot, or the word REC or RECORD—has appeared. Make it a rigid and automatic habit. That's the only way you'll avoid the sickening realization later that you punched the Record button one too many times, thus turning the camera *on* when you thought it was *off*, and vice versa.

If your subject is a family member or friend, they may be able to confirm that you're getting the shot by checking the *tally light*—the small light on the lens end of the camcorder that lights up, or blinks, while you're recording. Most videographers, however, turn off the tally light (using the camcorder's built-in menu system) or put a piece of black tape over it. If you're trying to be surreptitious or to put your subject at ease, the light can be extremely distracting, especially when it starts *blinking* to indicate that you're running out of tape or power.

Similarly, make sure the indicator disappears when you punch the Record button a second time. Sometimes this button sticks and doesn't actually make the camera stop filming.

Tip: If the recording-the-ground syndrome has struck you even once, check your camcorder's feature list. Some models, including most Sony camcorders, offer a special feature that's designed to eliminate this syndrome. When you slide a switch into a mode Sony calls Anti-Ground Shooting, the camcorder records only *while* you're pressing the Record button. As soon as you remove your thumb, the camera stops recording. This scheme isn't ideal for long shots, of course, and it ties up your hands during shots when you might need to adjust the zoom or focus while filming. But it's extremely good insurance against missing important moments.

How Much to Shoot

For years, books and articles about camcorders have stressed the importance of keeping your shots *short*. In the pre-iMovie era, this was excellent advice. When you show your footage to other people, there's absolutely nothing worse than endless, monotonous, unedited scenes of babies/speeches/scenery. If you don't want your guests and family members to feel that they're being held hostage during your screenings, strive for short shots and very selective shooting. So goes the usual advice.

But the iMovie revolution turns that advice on its head. Yes, it's still agonizing and tedious to watch hours of somebody's unedited video, but thanks to iMovie, you won't be showing unedited video. By the time an audience sees it, your stuff won't be endless and boring. In fact, it will be far better than a bunch of short, selective shots on the average person's camcorder, because you'll have had a much greater selection of footage from which to choose the most interesting scenes.

In other words, it's safe to relax about how much you're shooting. It's much better, in the iMovie Age, to shoot too much footage than too little. After all, if your camcorder stops rolling too soon, you might miss a terrific moment. (Almost everyone who's used a camcorder has experienced such unfortunate timing.)

In Hollywood and professional TV production, in fact, shooting miles of footage is standard practice. When filming movies, Hollywood directors shoot every scene numerous times, even if nothing goes wrong in most of them, just so that they'll have a selection to choose from when it comes time to assemble the final film. (As an extreme example, legend has it that during the making of Stanley Kubrick's *Eyes Wide Shut,* the director asked the actors to repeat a scene 140 times, on the premise that eventually they'd no longer be acting—it would be *real.*) The more takes you get "in the can," especially if they're shot different ways (different angles, zoom levels, and so on), the more flexibility and choice you'll have when editing, and the better the finished product will be.

Don't go overboard, of course; there *is* still such a thing as shooting too much footage. You should still think in terms of capturing *shots* that you've thought about and framed in the viewfinder; don't just roll continuously, pointing the lens this way and that. And you should still remember all the extra time you'll have to spend transferring the footage into iMovie, reviewing it, and editing it. The more you shoot, the greater the editing time.

But it's certainly safe to say that in the age of iMovie, you'll improve your odds of catching memorable moments on tape if you keep the camera rolling as long as the kid/animal/tornado is performing.

Replace the Microphone

The built-in microphone on your camcorder can't be beat for convenience. It's always there, it's always on, and it's always pointing at what you're filming.

Unfortunately, camcorder microphones have several disadvantages. For example:

- **They're usually mounted right on the camera body.** In quiet scenes, they can pick up the sound of the camcorder itself—a quiet grinding of the electronic motor, or the sound of the lens zooming and focusing.

- **If your subject is farther than a few feet away, the sound is much too faint.** The powerful zoom lens on modern camcorders exaggerates this problem. If your subject is 50 feet away, the zoom may make it look as though you're right up close, but the sound still has to come from 50 feet away.

"Camcorder sound," that hollow, faraway sonic quality present on most home videos (including the ones shown on your cable station's public-access channel late at night), is one of the most obvious differences between amateur video and professional work. Even if viewers can't quite put their finger on *how* they know that something was shot with a camcorder, they'll know that it *was* shot with a camcorder just by listening.

Clip-on (Lavalier) Microphones

Few camcorder accessories, therefore, are more useful than an external microphone. And it doesn't have to cost a lot. (See Figure 2-2.)

Of course, if the problem of camcorder audio is that it gets worse when the subject is far away, an external microphone with a six-foot cord isn't of much use. Therefore, consider buying a couple of extension cords for your microphone; they come in lengths of 20 feet or more, and cost about $10. You can plug one into the next, using standard miniplug connectors (like the ones on the end of Walkman headphones).

Tip: In certain situations, plugging one cable into the next, as you do when connecting an external microphone to an extension cable, can introduce a hum on your soundtrack. To avoid ruining otherwise great footage, carry with you a pair of cheap Walkman headphones. Whenever you're using an external microphone, plug these headphones into the headphone jack on your camcorder and listen as you film. (In fact, you're wise to use headphones *anytime* you're filming.)

If a humming or buzzing does arise, try exchanging cables, eliminating extension cords, and running the camcorder on battery instead of AC power, until you've isolated the source of the problem.

FREQUENTLY ASKED QUESTION

Automatic Gain Control

Where's the recording-volume knob on my camcorder?

There isn't one. Modern consumer camcorders use something called *automatic gain control* (AGC). They set the volume level automatically as you record.

That may sound like a neat feature, but it drives professionals nutty. AGC, in essence, strives to record all sound at exactly the same level. When something is very loud, the AGC circuit quiets it down to middle volume; when something is very soft, the AGC circuit boosts it to middle volume.

Over the years, automatic-gain circuitry has dramatically improved. The electronic boosting or quieting is smoother and less noticeable than it once was. Even some modern camcorders, however, sometimes exhibit the unpleasant side effects of AGC circuitry: Try filming something that's very quiet, and then suddenly clap right next to the microphone. On lesser camcorders, when you play the footage back, you'll

hear how the sudden, loud sound made the AGC back off, cutting the volume way down in anticipation of further loud noises. It takes the camcorder several seconds to realize that the surrounding sound is still quiet (and to boost the volume level back up where it had been).

Fortunately, that sudden-adjustment syndrome is a rare and usually harmless occurrence. For most purposes, camcorders do an excellent job of setting their own volume level (although it certainly evens out the dynamic highs and lows of, say, a symphony performance).

Besides, you don't have much of an alternative. Only a few, more expensive camcorders permit you to override the AGC circuit (and adjust the sound level manually). Even if you plug in an external microphone, most camcorders take it upon themselves to adjust the sound level automatically.

Wireless Mikes

One of those inexpensive tie-clip microphones is ideal when you're filming interviews, speeches, or scripted dialog with actors. But in other situations, a cabled microphone like this is impractical, such as when you're shooting a jogger, somebody in a car, or an undercover agent.

For those circumstances, consider buying or renting a *wireless* microphone. These microphones come in two parts: the microphone held or worn by the actor or speaker, and a receiver that clips onto your camcorder and plugs into the Mic In jack. The receiver picks up the sound signal that's transmitted by radio waves. (Here again, be aware of interference. As you film, wear Walkman headphones to monitor the incoming sound. There's nothing worse than tender words of love being drowned out by a nearby trucker cursing on his overamplified CB radio that's picked up by your receiver.)

Figure 2-2:
A tie-clip microphone, known in the business as a lavalier *mike ("lava-LEER"), is a very inexpensive way to dramatically improve the audio on your footage, especially when accompanied by an extension cable or two. You plug it into the Mic In jack on the side of almost every DV camcorder. (This jack may be concealed by a protective plastic cap.)*

For $20, Radio Shack will sell you a tie-clip microphone like this one.

Other Microphones

If you're shooting documentary-style, it's impractical to attach *any* kind of microphone to the people you're filming. Depending on how serious you are about your filming, you have alternatives. A *shotgun mike* is elongated and thin; it's designed to pick up a distant sound source with pinpoint accuracy. (In Hollywood thrillers, shotgun mikes appear onscreen in the hands of the characters almost as often as they do behind the scenes.) Semi-pro camcorders like the Canon XL1 and the Sony VX2000 have shotgun mikes built right in. Clip-on shotgun mikes are available for less expensive Canon and Sony camcorders, too.

There's also the *boom mike,* which requires a helper to hold over the head of the actor on a long pole—another staple of professional film production. Unfortunately, this kind of mike, too, is likely to dampen your spontaneity.

Where to Buy Them

You won't find these fancier microphone types, which cost $100 or more, in the local Radio Shack. Online, however, they're everywhere. Video-supply companies like *www.markertek.com* and *www.bhphotovideo.com* are good starting points for your shopping quest.

Limit Zooming and Panning

In a way, camcorder manufacturers are asking for it. They put the zoom-in/zoom-out buttons right on top of the camcorder, where your fingers naturally rest. That tempting placement has led millions of camcorder owners to zoom in or out in almost every shot—and sometimes even several times *within* a shot. For the camcorder operator, zooming imparts a sense of control, power, and visual excitement. But for the viewer, zooming imparts a sense of nausea.

In other words, most home-movie makers zoom too much. In professional film and video, you almost never see zooming, unless it's to achieve a particular special effect. (Someday, rent a movie and note how many times the director zooms in or zooms out. Answer: almost never.)

Tips for Keeping Zooming Under Control

To separate yourself from the amateur-video pack, adopt these guidelines for using the zoom controls:

- The zoom button is ideal for adjusting the magnification level *between* shots, when the camcorder is paused—to *set up* a new shot. Be conscious of how many times you're using the zoom while the tape is rolling.

- Sometimes you may be tempted to zoom in order to create an *establishing shot*—to show the entire landscape, the big picture—before closing in on your main subject.

   That's a worthy instinct, but zooming isn't the best way to go from an establishing shot to a closeup. Instead, consider an effect like the extremely effective, more interesting one that opens such movies as *Citizen Kane*: a series of successive shots that dissolve, one into the next, each closer to the subject than the previous. (See Figure 2-3.) Open with a wide shot that shows the entire airport; fade into a medium shot that shows the exiting masses of people; finally, dissolve to the worried face of the passenger whose luggage has vanished. Naturally, you can't create the fades and dissolves while you're shooting, but it's a piece of cake to add them in iMovie. Your job while filming is simply to capture the two or three different shots, each at a different zoom level.

- You don't have to avoid zooming altogether. As noted above, professional movie-makers rarely zoom. One of the exceptions, however, is when the director wants to pick one face out of a crowd, often just as some horrific realization is dawning. Furthermore, when you're filming somebody who's doing a lot of talking, a very slow, almost imperceptible zoom is extremely effective, especially if you do it when the speech is getting more personal, emotional, ominous, or important.

The point is to use zooming *meaningfully*, when there's a reason to do it.

- For the lowest motion-sickness quotient, use the *hold-zoom-hold* technique. In other words, begin your shot by filming without zooming for a moment; zoom slowly and smoothly; and end the shot by holding on the resulting closeup or wide shot. Don't begin or end the shot in mid-zoom.

Tip: Documentary makers frequently film with this pattern: Hold for 5 seconds; zoom in, and then hold for 5 seconds; zoom out again, and hold for 5, then stop the shot. This technique gives the filmmaker a variety of shots, providing choice when editing the final movie.

All of this sheds light on another reason to hold at the end of a zoom, and another reason to avoid zooming in general: When editing, it's very difficult to make a smooth cut during a zoom. Cutting from one nonzooming shot to another is smoother and less noticeable than cutting in mid-zoom.

Figure 2-3:
Zooming, as represented here by several sequential frames (left), is a dead giveaway that the movie is homemade.

Try a more professional sequence to set up your shot: Hold on a wider, scene-establishing shot, cut to a medium shot, and then cut to a closeup (right).

Zooming

Cutting

- Consider how much to zoom. There's no law that says that every zoom must use the entire 500X magnification range of your camcorder.

- Did you ever see *Wayne's World*—either the movie or the *Saturday Night Live* skit on which it was based? *Wayne's World,* of course, was a spoof of a hilariously amateurish public-access cable TV show that was supposedly shot with a camcorder in somebody's basement. The show's trademark camerawork: multiple zooms in a single shot. (Such annoying shots are always accompanied by Wayne and Garth shouting, "Unnecessary zoom!")

As rare as zooming is in professional TV and film, *multiple* zooms in a single shot are virtually unheard of. To avoid creating a *Wayne's World* of your own, consider zooming only once, in only one direction, and then *stop* to focus on the target. Don't zoom in, linger, and then continue zooming; and don't zoom in, linger, and then zoom back out (unless you intend to discard half of that shot during editing). Furthermore, on camcorders equipped with a variable-speed zoom, keep the zoom speed consistent. (The slowest zoom is usually the most effective.)

Note: There's an exception to the avoid-zooming-in-and-out-while-shooting rule. That's when you're filming a one-of-a-kind event and you're desperate to keep the camera rolling for fear of missing even a second of priceless footage. In that case, zoom all you want to get the shots you want. But do so with the understanding that the good stuff won't be the zooming footage—it will be the scenes *between* zooms.

Later, you can eliminate the unnecessary zooms during iMovie editing.

Panning and Tilting

Panning is rotating the camera while recording—either horizontally, to take in a scene that's too wide to fit in one lensful, or vertically (called *tilting*), to take in a scene that's too tall.

In general, panning is justifiable more often than zooming is. Sometimes, as when you're filming a landscape, a skyscraper, or a moving object, you have no alternative. Standard camcorder lenses simply aren't wide-angle enough to capture grand panoramas in one shot, much to the frustration of anyone who's tried to film New Zealand landscapes, New York skyscrapers, or the Grand Canyon.

Even so, some of the guidelines listed above for zooming also apply to panning:

- Pan only when you have good reason to do so. One of the most common reasons to pan is to *track* a moving target as it moves through space. (Interestingly, professionals pan most of the time from left to right, the way people read, except when a shot is meant to be deliberately disturbing.)

    In fact, almost *any* pan looks better if there's something that "motivates" the camera movement. A car, train, bird flying, person walking, or anything else that draws the eye justifies the pan and gives a sense of scale to the image.

- Begin and end the pan by holding, motionless, on carefully chosen beginning and ending images.

- Make an effort to pan smoothly and *slowly*. This time, you can't rely on the camcorder's electronics to ensure smoothness of motion, as you can when zooming. Bracing your elbows against your sides helps. (If you pan too fast, you may create what's known as a *swish pan*—a blurry shot that's *intended* to be disorienting, as when the main character, being chased through a crowd, is desperately turning his head this way and that in an effort to spot his pursuers.)

- Avoid panning more than once in a shot. Make an effort not to perform such classic amateur maneuvers as the Pan/Linger/Pan or the Pan-to-the-Right, Get-Distracted, Pan-Back-to-the-Left.

- If you're especially gifted with your camcorder, remember that you can also pan and zoom simultaneously. This, too, should be considered a special effect used rarely. But when you are, in fact, filming a closeup of somebody saying, "Look! The top of the building is exploding!" nothing is more effective than a smooth zoom out/pan up to the top of the building.

- *Practice* the pan, tilt, or zoom a couple of times before rolling tape. Each time, the result will be smoother and less noticeable.

- Be careful about panning when your camcorder's image stabilizer is turned on. If you're doing a slow pan when the camcorder is on a tripod (as it should be), the shot gets jittery and jumpy as the camera tries to hold onto (or "stabilize") one scene as you rotate a new one into view. If your camcorder is on a tripod, it's safe for you to turn off the electronic stabilization anyway. (*Optical* stabilization doesn't exhibit this problem.)

Tip: If you plan to save your finished iMovie work as a QuickTime movie—a file that plays on your computer screen (Chapter 16)—panning and zooming slowly and smoothly is especially important. iMovie's compression software works by analyzing the subtle picture differences from one frame to another; if you zoom or pan too quickly, the QuickTime compressors won't understand the relationship between one frame and the next. Blotchiness or skipped frames (which cause jerky motion) may result in the finished QuickTime movie.

Keep the Camera Steady

Here's another difference between amateur and pro footage: Most camcorder movies are shot with a camera held in somebody's hand, which is extremely obvious to people who have to watch it later. Real TV shows, movies, and corporate videos are shot with a camera that's mounted on a massive rolling base, a hydraulic crane, or a *tripod.* (There are a few exceptions, such as a few annoying-to-watch Woody Allen movies. However, they were shot with handheld cameras for an artistic reason, not just because it was too much trouble to line up a tripod.)

It's impossible to overstate the positive effect a tripod can have on your footage. Nor is it a hassle to use such a tripod; if you get one that's equipped with a quick-release plate, the camcorder snaps instantly onto the corresponding tripod socket. Tripods are cheap, too. You can buy one for as little as $20, although more expensive tripods have more features, last longer, and are less likely to nip your skin when you're collapsing them for transport.

Tip: If the camcorder on the tripod isn't perfectly level, the picture will start to tilt diagonally as you pan (the car will appear to be driving up or down a hill instead of across a flat plain). To prevent this phenomenon, make sure that the camera legs are carefully adjusted—slow and tedious work on most tripods. But on tripods with *ball-leveling heads* (an expensive feature, alas), achieving levelness takes just a few seconds: Just loosen a screw, adjust the head until it is level, and tighten the screw down again.

Of course, tripods aren't always practical. When you're trying to film without being noticed, when you don't have the luggage space, or when you must start filming *immediately,* you may have to do without. In those instances, consider one of these alternatives:

- **Turn on the image stabilization feature.** As noted on page 23, every modern camcorder includes an *image stabilization* feature, which magically irons out the minor jiggles and shakes associated with handheld filming. Using electronic/digital (as opposed to optical) image stabilization drains your battery faster, so feel free to turn it off when you're using a tripod. But at all other times, the improvement in footage is well worth the power sacrifice.

- **Make the camera as steady as possible.** If you can steady it on top of a wall, on top of your car, or even your own knee, you'll get better results. If there's absolutely nothing solid on which to perch the camcorder, keep your camcorder-hand elbow pressed tightly against your side, use two hands, and breathe slowly and with con-

---

Recording Entrances and Exits

When it's possible, record the "entrances and exits" of moving subjects in to, and out of, your camcorder's field of vision. For example, if you're filming two people walking, film the space where they're *about* to appear for a moment—and then, when they enter the frame, pan the camcorder to follow their movement. Finally, stop panning and let your subjects walk clear out of the frame.

Entrances and exits like this make more interesting footage than simple follow-them-all-the-way shots. By letting the motion occur within the frame, for example, you emphasize the motion. If a car zooms *across* the screen, and then exits the frame, your viewers can *see* how fast it was going. But if you track the car by panning all the way, you diminish the sense of motion. It's hard to tell how fast a car is moving if it's always centered in a panning shot.

More important, frame entrances and exits can help make your editing job easier, thanks to their ability to disguise discontinuous action. Suppose, for example, that you've got a medium shot of a schoolgirl starting to raise her hand. But the shot ends when her hand is only as high as her stomach. Now suppose that the next shot, a closeup of her face, begins with her hand *entering the frame* from below, whereupon it heads for, and finally scratches, her nose. You can safely cut from the stomach shot to the nose shot; because of the hand's entrance into the frame, your cut looks natural and motivated. The "entrance" disguises the fact that the hand was at stomach level in one frame and at face level in the next.

Without that entrance, you'd wind up with a *jump cut*—an irritating discontinuity in time from one shot to the next.

---

trol. When you pan, turn from the waist, keeping your upper body straight. Bend your legs slightly to serve as shock absorbers.

Tip: Regardless of your camcorder model, you'll get the best and steadiest results if you use your free hand to brace the *bottom* of the camera. Holding both *sides* of the camcorder isn't nearly as steady.

• **Zoom out.** When you're zoomed in to film something distant, magnifying the image, say, 10 times, remember that a one-millimeter jiggle gets magnified many times. When you're zoomed in a lot, it's easy to produce extremely unsteady footage. Keep this in mind when deciding how much you want to zoom; the most stable picture results when you're zoomed out all the way.

• **Consider a monopod.** Despite the enormous boost in stability that a tripod gives your footage, you don't always have the time to unlatch, extend, and relatch each of the three legs. If the kind of shooting you do frequently requires such fast setup and takedown, consider a *monopod*. As much as it sounds like a creature from a sci-fi movie, a monopod is actually a closer relative to a walking stick. It's a collapsible metal post for your camcorder. When using a monopod, you still have to steady the camcorder with your hands (jiggles are still possible), but the monopod eliminates motion from one of the three dimensions (up and down), which is much better than nothing. And the monopod, of course, takes very little time to set up and take down.

• **Get a clamp.** You can also buy viselike clamps equipped with camera plates. You can clamp them to car windows, chair backs, tops of ladders, skateboards, and so

---

BUYERS' GUIDE

How to Buy a Tripod

A tripod has two parts: the legs and the *pan head.* The camera attaches to the pan head, and the legs support the head.

You can buy a tripod with any of three pan head types. *Friction heads* are the simplest, least expensive, and most popular with still photographers. Unfortunately, they provide the bumpiest pans and tilts when used for videotaping. *Fluid heads* are the most desirable kind; they smooth out panning and tilting. They're more expensive than friction heads, but are well worth the money if you're after a professional look to your footage. Finally, *geared heads* are big, heavy, expensive, and difficult to use. These are what Hollywood productions use, because they can handle heavy film cameras.

The tripod's legs may be made of metal, wood, or composite. Metal is light and less expensive but easier to damage by accident (thin metal is easily bent). Wood and composite legs are much more expensive and are designed for heavier professional broadcast and film equipment. The bottoms of the legs have rubber feet, which is great for use indoors and on solid floors. Better tripods also have spikes, which work well outdoors on grass and dirt.

Good tripods also have *spreaders* that prevent the legs from spreading apart and causing the entire apparatus to crash to the ground. If your tripod doesn't have spreaders, you can put the tripod on a piece of carpet, which prevents the legs from slipping apart.

In general, you adjust a tripod's height by extending the legs' telescoping sections. Some tripods have a riser column, too, that lets you crank the pan head higher off the legs. Remember that the higher the camera is lifted up, the more unsteady it becomes, so sturdiness is an important characteristic.

---

on, for even more stable-shooting options. (Put a piece of cloth between the clamp and the surface to prevent scratching.)

Video Lighting: A Crash Course

Today's camera optics are good, but they're not human eyeballs. Every camera, from your camcorder to professional TV and film models, captures truer color, depth, and contrast if lighting conditions are good. The need for bright light is even more critical on today's consumer camcorders than it is on film, because video picks up an even smaller range of light and shadow. A movie whose acting, sound, and dialog are exceptional can be ruined by poor lighting.

This desperate need for light explains why some camcorders have a small built-in light on the front. Unfortunately, such lights are effective only when shooting subjects just a few feet away. Better still are clip-on video lights designed precisely for use with camcorders. Not every camcorder has a *shoe*—a flat connector on the top that secures, and provides power to, a video light. But if yours does, consider buying a light to fit it. The scenes you shoot indoors, or at close range outdoors, will benefit from much better picture quality.

If your camcorder doesn't have a light attachment, or if you want to get more serious yet, consider deliberately lighting the scene, just like TV and film cinematographers the world over.

Going to this extreme isn't always necessary, of course. If it's just you filming the New Year's Eve party, you're better off not asking the revelers to sit down and be quiet while you set up the lights. But when you're conducting interviews, shooting a dramatic film, making a video for broadcast, or making a QuickTime movie for distribution on a CD, lights will make your footage look much better.

The following discussion is dedicated to illuminating those more important filming situations. When you want the very best footage, lit the way the pros would light it, the following guidelines, theory, and equipment suggestions will serve you well indeed.

(If you're just shooting kids, relatives, or animals indoors, at least turn on every light in the room.)

Lighting Basics

Cinematographers spend entire careers studying the fantastically complex science of lighting. Here's what they worry about.

Exposure

Exposure refers to light—the amount of illumination the camera picks up. When the scene is too dark, you lose a lot of detail in dark shadows. Worse, your camcorder's AGC (Automatic Gain Circuit, the video equivalent of the audio-leveling circuitry described in the previous section) tries to amplify the available light. The result, which you can see for yourself by filming in dim light, is video *noise* (colored speckles) and unrealistic colors (black becomes a noisy, milky dark gray).

If the scene is too bright, on the other hand, details can wash out, disappearing in white areas.

Contrast

The *contrast ratio* is the ratio of the brightest highlights in a scene to the darkest shadows. Professional filmmakers often set up huge arrays of extra lights to *reduce* the contrast ratio, thus evening out the illumination so that the camera can record more detail accurately. (When watching a movie being filmed, you sometimes see huge lights set up, even in daylight: They're there to fill in the shadow areas, so that the camera can "see," for example, the actors' eyes.)

Film cameras can photograph details in a scene that has a 10:1 contrast ratio (highlights are 10 times brighter than the dark shadow areas). Video, on the other hand, can't capture details outside a contrast ratio of about 3:1 or 4:1. That's another reason lighting is much more important when using a camcorder, as noted above.

Hard light vs. soft light

Hard light comes from a small light source falling directly on an object. It creates hard edges between the highlight and shadow areas. For example, when someone's standing in direct sunlight, the shadows on his face are harsh and dark. This high contrast emphasizes wrinkles, skin blemishes, baggy eyes, and other facial features. In other words, hard light is unflattering light.

Soft light, on the other hand, is less direct, offering softer, smoother gradations of light from brightest to darkest areas. You get soft light from a large light source, usually reflected or diffused, like the outdoors light on an overcast day or the light reflected from the umbrellas used by photographers. The result: soft shadows or no shadows; everything is lit fairly evenly.

Soft light is much more flattering to human subjects, because it de-emphasizes wrinkles and other facial contours. Unfortunately, soft light can also make your subjects appear flat and lifeless. Harder light can reveal contours, shapes, and textures, making objects more interesting and three-dimensional.

The best video lighting, therefore, comes from direct light sources that are mechanically softened. That's why many video lights have milky translucent covers.

Key, fill, and backlight

In professional film and TV work, the most common lighting arrangement is called the *three-point lighting setup.* It requires that you set up at least three light sources, as shown in Figure 2-4:

- The *key* light is the primary source of illumination in a scene. This can be the light on the camera, the sun, the overhead light above a table, or the light from a window, for example.

- The *fill* light comes from a second light source. It's designed to fill in the shadows caused by the key light. By doing so, fill light reduces the *contrast ratio,* allowing the camcorder to pick up more details. If your camcorder has a built-in light, that's usually a fill light, too. It softens the shadows cast by the key light (such as the room lights).

- The *backlight* comes from behind the subject. It helps to separate the subject from the background. Backlight is especially helpful in distinguishing a dark subject (such as a person's hair) and a dark background, because it casts a glow around the rim of the subject's outline.

  Be careful, of course: When the light behind the subject is *too* bright, camcorders respond by dimming the entire picture, as described on page 25.

- In professional film and video, technicians sometimes set up a fourth light: the *background* light, which is pointed at the background to make it easier to see (especially in very dark scenes).

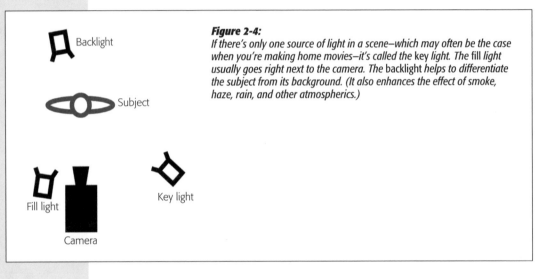

Figure 2-4:
If there's only one source of light in a scene—which may often be the case when you're making home movies—it's called the key light*. The* fill light *usually goes right next to the camera. The* backlight *helps to differentiate the subject from its background. (It also enhances the effect of smoke, haze, rain, and other atmospherics.)*

Color temperature

Believe it or not, even ordinary daylight or room light also has a *color*. In general, daylight has a bluish cast, fluorescent light is greenish, and household bulbs give off a yellowish light.

Filmmakers call these color casts the *color temperature* of the light. We don't usually notice the color casts of these common light sources because our eyes and minds have adjusted to it. DV camcorders usually do an excellent job of compensating to avoid noticeable color casts, thanks to the *automatic white balance* in the circuitry of every modern model.

If, even so, you notice that certain shots are coming out too blue, green, or yellow, you can help the camcorder along by switching on one of its *programs* (as several manufacturers call them)—presets for Daylight, Indoor Light, Snow and Ski, and so on. Each is represented in your viewfinder by an icon (such as a sun or a light bulb).

When you use these presets, the camcorder shifts its color perception accordingly.

And if even those adjustments don't fix a particular color-cast problem, your camcorder may offer *manual* white balance. White balancing means identifying to the camera some object that's supposed to look pure white, so that it can adjust its circuitry accordingly. To use the manual white-balance feature, focus on something white that's illuminated by the key light—for example, a clean T-shirt or piece of paper. Zoom in until the white area fills the screen, then press the White Balance button. The camcorder responds by compensating for the dominant color in the light.

The 45/45 rule

This lighting guideline suggests that the key light be at a 45-degree angle to the camera-subject line and at a 45-degree angle above the ground. (See Figure 2-5.)

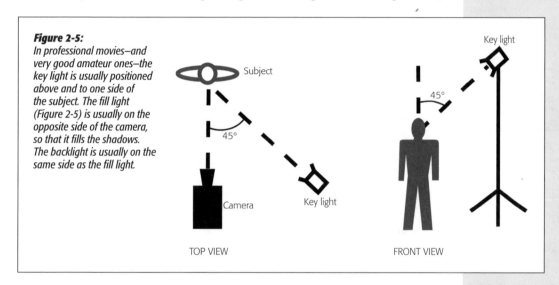

Figure 2-5:
In professional movies—and very good amateur ones—the key light is usually positioned above and to one side of the subject. The fill light (Figure 2-5) is usually on the opposite side of the camera, so that it fills the shadows. The backlight is usually on the same side as the fill light.

General Guidelines for Lighting

The preceding discussion gives you the theory of lighting design. Here's the executive summary—a distillation of that information down into just a few points to remember for the most professional-looking lighting:

- The subject should be brighter than the background. Don't shoot people with a bright window or doorway behind them, unless you want them to disappear into silhouette.

- If the background is bright, and you can't shine additional lights on the subject, use your camcorder's Backlight button or manual-exposure knob, if it has one, so the subject is correctly exposed (even if that makes the background too bright).

- Stand so that the key light—the sun, for example—is behind you. Don't shoot a subject with the sun behind her (unless you want silhouettes).

- Avoid a key light that's *directly above* your subject. That arrangement causes ugly, heavy shadows under the eyes, nose, and chin. (The cinematographers for the *Godfather* movies set up lights this way on purpose, so that the mobsters' eyes would be hidden in shadows. That's not the effect you want when filming the mothers-in-law at a wedding ceremony. Usually.)

- If you decide to add lights to your setup, you don't need expensive movie lights. At the hardware store, buy some inexpensive photoreflector lights (those cheap, silver, bowl-shaped fixtures) and equip them with photoflood or tungsten work-light bulbs.

- If you're aiming for professional quality, create soft fill lights by bouncing light off a big square of white foam-core board (which you can get at Kmart, Home Depot, and so on), or a big piece of cardboard covered by foil or newspaper. This arrangement creates a beautiful soft light—great for closeups.

  Bouncing lights off a white ceiling makes for a pleasantly soft key light, too.

- Tracing paper, tissue paper, and translucent plastic (such as shower-door material) make great diffusers for soft light, too. (Just don't put the paper in *contact* with the bulb; this kind of paper, especially tissue paper, ignites easily if it gets too hot.)

- Be alert to the presence of shiny surfaces like windows, glass, chrome, and highly polished wood in your shots. They can reflect your lights into the camera, making it look as though someone is shining a light directly into the lens.

- If the backlight spills into the lens, you get *flares*—those oddly shaped patches of light that move across the frame as the camera pans. The sun behind the subject, or car headlights, often cause flares. If you can avoid this effect, do so.

Keep It in Focus

A camcorder is a camera, just like any other. If its lenses aren't focused on the subject, you wind up with a blurry picture.

In theory, the autofocus feature of every modern camcorder takes care of this delicate task for you. You point the camera, it analyzes the image and adjusts its own lens mechanisms, and the picture comes out in sharp focus. But in practice, the autofocus mechanism isn't foolproof. Camcorders assume that the subject of your filming is the *closest* object; most of the time, that's true. But now and then, your camcorder may focus on something in the foreground that *isn't* the intended subject. As a result, what you actually wanted to capture goes out of focus, as Figure 2-6 makes clear.

Another autofocus hazard is a solid or low-contrast background (such as a polar bear against a snowy background). The autofocus method relies on contrasting colors in the image. If you're aiming the camcorder at, say, a white wall, you may witness the alarming phenomenon known as autofocus *hunting,* in which the camcorder rapidly goes nearsighted, farsighted, and back again in a futile effort to find a focus level that works.

Other situations that freak out the autofocus include shooting when it's dark, shooting through glass, filming a subject that's not centered in the frame, and high-contrast foregrounds (such as prison or cage bars, French-window frames, and so on), which compete for the autofocus's attention.

Figure 2-6:
When you're filming the school play, somebody's head or hat may confuse the autofocus. When you're filming scenery, a nearby branch may similarly fool it (top). The front bars of zoo cages are also notorious for ruining otherwise great shots of the animals inside them. The only solution is to use manual focus (bottom).

Manual Focus

Fortunately, most camcorders offer a *manual focus* option: a switch that turns off the autofocus. Now you can (and must) set the focus by hand, turning a ring around the lens (or pushing + and – buttons) until the picture is sharp.

If neither you nor your subject has any intention of moving during the shot, that's all there is to manual focus. Moving shots are trickier, because as the distance between you and your subject changes, you may not have time to fiddle with the focus ring. The best approach is to keep the camera zoomed out all the way as you pan to track the action.

Another potential problem: zooming. When you zoom, your focus changes, too. Fortunately, there's an ancient and very clever trick that circumvents this problem: the zoom-out-and-focus trick. It goes like this:

1. **Zoom all the way in to your subject.**

   You haven't yet begun to record. You're just setting up the shot.

2. **Focus the camcorder manually.**

3. Zoom back out again.

As you zoom out, notice what happens: The camcorder remains in perfect focus all the way. (Figure 2-7 shows this sequence.) Now you can begin to film, confident that even when you zoom in, the picture will remain in sharp focus.

Figure 2-7:
For freedom of zooming without worrying about going out of focus, begin by zooming in all the way (top). Then use the focus ring to focus (middle). Now you can zoom in or out to any level, before or during the shot (bottom), and your focus remains sharp all the way.

Be careful, though: Don't zoom in so far that you make the camcorder's digital zoom kick in. Most camcorders zoom in optically (true zoom) for several seconds, and then, as you continue to press the Zoom button, begin the artificial digital zoom that makes the image break up. You can detect the end of the optical zooming in two ways: First, a bar graph in the viewfinder usually identifies the ending point of the true zoom's range. Second, your camcorder may introduce a very short pause in the zooming as it switches gears into digital mode.

Either way, when using the manual focus trick described here, you want to zoom in all the way using only your true, optical zoom.

In other words, once you've focused at the maximum zoom level, you're free to set the zoom to any intermediate level without having to refocus (*if* you're zooming sparingly and with a purpose, of course).

Video Composition: A Crash Course

The tips in this chapter so far have been designed to turn you from an amateur into a more accomplished technician. Now it's time to train the artist in you.

Even when shooting casual home movie footage, consider the *composition* of the shot—the way the subject fills the frame, the way the parts of the picture relate to each other, and so on. Will the shot be clearer, better, or more interesting if you move closer? What about walking around to the other side of the action, or zooming in slightly, or letting tall grass fill the foreground? Would the shot be more interesting if it were framed by horizontal, vertical, or diagonal structures (such as branches, pillars, or a road stretching away)? All of this floats through a veteran director's head before the camera starts to roll.

As an iMovie-maker, you, unlike millions of other camcorder owners, no longer need to be concerned with the sequence or length of the shots you capture, since you can rearrange or trim your footage all you want in iMovie. Your main concern when filming is to get the raw footage you'll need: You can't touch the composition of a shot once you're in iMovie.

Kinds of Shots

You'll hear film professionals talk about three kinds of camera shots: *wide, medium,* and *close* (Figure 2-8):

- When you're zoomed out all the way, so that the camera captures as wide a picture as possible, you're using a *wide shot.* Wide shots establish context. They show the audience where we are and what's going on. Wide shots make great *establishing* shots, but they can also reveal a lot about the scale and scope of the action even after the scene has begun. (There's a famous crane shot in *Gone With the Wind* that starts on a medium shot of Scarlett O'Hara and then moves up and wide as she walks through a compound filled with hundreds of dying confederate soldiers to reveal a tattered Confederate flag. Thanks to the wide shot, you can see the people she's passing completely, from head to foot.

Figure 2-8:
A wide shot captures the camcorder's biggest possible picture (top). It gives viewers a sense of place and direction. A medium shot (middle) begins to direct the audience's attention, but still captures some of the surroundings. And a closeup (bottom) is delightful for all concerned, especially if you plan to export your finished iMovie production as a QuickTime movie.

- *Medium shots* are useful because they eliminate many distractions from the background. By zooming in part way, you let your viewers concentrate more on individuals, and you establish a relationship between objects in the frame. People in medium shots are usually visible only from the waist up. Medium shots are by far the most common ones on TV.

- When you're zoomed in a lot, so that your subject fills the screen, you're using a *close shot, tight shot,* or *closeup.* These shots reveal detail, such as a character's reactions, which have a huge impact on how the audience reacts. Close shots are the best kind of shot if you plan to show your movie on a small screen, such as in a QuickTime movie or on a small TV.

Note: You'll hear professionals talk about lots of other kinds of shots, too: the extreme closeup, the extreme long shot, the medium closeup, and so on—but they're all variations on the Big Three.

Choosing your shots

After you're finished editing your video in iMovie, will it be viewed primarily on a computer screen or a TV screen? This important question may affect your choice of zoom level for each shot.

If you plan to make QuickTime movies (for playback on computer screens), use a lot of closeups. Remember that most QuickTime movies play in a small window on the computer screen. Beware the wide shot that looks great on the TV or in the viewfinder, but when shrunk to QuickTime-movie size, reduces faces to white specks on the screen.

Tip: If you're concerned about the *file size* of the finished QuickTime movies—if you intend to email them or post them on a Web site, for example—simpler and steadier shots work best. When iMovie creates the QuickTime movie, it reduces the file size by *discarding* information about parts of the frame that don't change from one frame to the next. Frames filled with clutter, and moving shots, therefore, result in larger QuickTime movie files that take longer to email and download from the Web.

If your iMovie productions are instead destined to be sent back to your camcorder for viewing on a TV, you don't need to be quite so worried about using mostly closeups (although they're still extremely effective on TV). Medium shots are fine, and so is *variety* in your shots, as described in the next section.

Combining shots

When editing footage, professional editors often use a wide shot to show where something is happening, then cut between medium and close shots. Example:

1. **A wide shot reveals the hustle and bustle of a city market.**

   No individual details stand out.

2. **Cut to a medium shot of two people standing next to each other, back to back.**

   Their hands are by their sides.

3. Cut to a closeup showing the hand of one person passing a small envelope to the other.

4. Cut back to a medium shot.

   The exchange was barely noticeable.

5. Cut away to someone reading a newspaper.

6. Cut in to a closeup of the newspaper guy, showing that he's not actually reading, but is looking over the top of the paper.

7. Cut to a wide shot of the two people who made the hand-off, now starting to walk away from each other.

8. Cut to a medium shot of the person with the newspaper. As he stands up, someone sitting at the table behind him also gets up.

   The audience didn't even notice the second person before, because the first shot of the newspaper guy was a closeup.

Of course, you'll do all of this fancy footwork in iMovie, during the editing phase. But you can't create such a dramatic sequence unless you capture the various close, medium, and wide shots to begin with—as you're filming.

As noted earlier, footage that you'll eventually save as a QuickTime movie file should consist mostly of closeups. But regardless of the final format, the best movies feature a variety of shots—a fact that doesn't occur to every camcorder operator.

Tip: It's an excellent idea to set a new scene with an establishing shot, but *when* you film that shot is unimportant. Ever watch a TV sitcom? Almost every segment that takes place in, for example, the Cosby family's apartment begins with an exterior establishing shot of the brownstone building's exterior. Needless to say, those interior and exterior apartment shots were filmed on different days, in different cities, by different film crews. The magic of video editing made it seem like the same time and place.

Mind the Background

Most home videographers don't pay much attention to the background of the shot, and worry only about the subject. The result can be unfortunate juxtapositions of the background *with* the foreground image—tree branches growing out your boss's head, for example, or you and your camcorder accidentally reflected in a mirror or glass, or a couple of dogs in furious amorous passion 20 feet behind your uncle.

When possible, set up the shot so that the background is OK, and then place your subjects in front of it. If you have no such control—if you're shooting home-movie, reality-TV, or documentary style—move *yourself*. Find a spot where the subject looks better relative to the background, whether it's 6 inches away or 20 feet away.

Professional camera operators, in fact, train themselves to watch the *edges of the frame* while filming, rather than the actors' faces. Doing so ensures that they take in the background, spot such accidental intrusions as reflections of people standing behind the camera, and stand ready to pan or tilt if the subject should move into or out of the frame. If you pay some attention to the shapes rather than people in the frame, composing the shot well becomes much easier. (You can always watch the subject later when you play back your footage.)

> **Note:** Even with years of training, Hollywood film crews nonetheless occasionally catch unwanted reflections, equipment, and technicians on film. The Internet Movie Database (*www.imdb.com*), for example, maintains message boards where observant moviegoers can report gaffes, such as the scene in *Titanic* where both crew members and equipment are visible as a reflection in Rose's TV.

Framing the Shot

Another way to make a shot more interesting is to let something in the environment *frame* it, subtly altering the shape of the square image of the frame. You might, for example, shoot through a door or window, shoot down a hallway, and so on. Even a tree branch stretching across the top of the frame, emphasizing the horizontal component of the image, makes an interesting shot.

The Rule of Thirds

Most people assume that the center of the frame should contain the most important element of your shot. As a result, 98 percent of all video footage features the subject of the shot in dead center. For the most visually *interesting* shots, however, dead center is actually the *least* compelling location for the subject. Artists and psychologists have found, instead, that the so-called Rule of Thirds makes better footage.

Imagine that the video frame is divided into thirds, both horizontally and vertically, as shown in Figure 2-9. The Rule of Thirds says that the intersections of these lines are the strongest parts of the frame. Putting the most interesting parts of the image at these four points, in other words, makes better composition.

Figure 2-9:
The Rule of Thirds: Don't put the good stuff in the middle. When shooting someone's face, frame the shot so that the eyes fall on the upper imaginary line, a third of the way down the frame. When two people are in the frame, zoom in so that they're roughly superimposed on the two vertical "rule of thirds" lines. When shooting a panorama, put the horizon line at the bottom-third line to emphasize the sky or tall objects like mountains, trees, and buildings; put the horizon on the upper-third line to emphasize what's on the ground, such as the people in the shot.

Save the center square of the frame for tight closeups and "talking heads" (shots of people standing alone and talking to the camera, as in a newscast). Even then, try to position their eyes on the upper-third line.

Camera Angle

The camera angle—that is, where you place the camcorder relative to your subject—is your greatest compositional tool. What position in the room or setting gives you the best framing, the best lighting, the least background distraction? Which position gives the shot the best composition?

You know the old stereotype of the movie director who walks slowly in a circle, squinting, peering through a square he frames with his thumbs and index fingers? It's a cliché, for sure, but old-time directors did it for a good reason: They were trying out different camera angles before committing the shot to film.

If you want to capture the best possible footage, do exactly the same thing (although you can just check the camcorder's screen instead of looking through your fingers like a weirdo). Before recording *any* shot, whether it's for a casual home movie or an independent film you plan to submit to the Sundance Film Festival, spend at least a moment cataloging your camera placement options.

The *vertical* angle of the camera counts, too. Will you be shooting down on your subject, up at it, or straight on? In commercial movies, camera angle is a big deal. Shooting up at somebody makes him look large, important, or threatening; shooting down from above makes him look less imposing.

In home movies, you don't have as much flexibility as you might when shooting a Hollywood film. About all you can do is hold the camcorder while lying down, squatting, sitting up, standing, or standing on a chair. Still, that's a lot more flexibility than most camcorder owners ever exploit.

Tip: Choosing the angle is especially important when filming babies, toddlers, or other cuddly animals. Too many people film them exclusively from a parent's-eye view; you wind up with tapes filled with footage shot from five feet off the floor. As anyone who has ever watched a diaper commercial can tell you, baby footage is much more compelling when it's shot from baby height. Kneel or squat so that the camera puts the viewer in the baby's world, not the parent's.

Capturing Multiple Angles

When you make a movie, you're trying to represent a three-dimensional world on a two-dimensional screen. To give the audience the best possible feeling for the environment where the filming was done—and to create the most interesting possible videos—consider *varying* your shots.

When you're shooting longer scenes, such as performances, interviews, weddings, and scripted movies, consider changing the camera position during the same session. You get two benefits: First, it gives your audience a break; whenever the camera angle changes, your footage benefits from a small boost of energy and renewed interest.

In fact, whenever you're shooting something important, cover the same action from different angles and with different kinds of shots.

When shooting two people in conversation, get more than the standard "two shot" (a composition containing two people, equally prominent, in the same frame). Shoot the two people talking in a wide shot that establishes where they are and how their positions relate. Get a closeup of one person by shooting over the shoulder of the other subject. If you can, shoot the conversation again, this time from over the other person's shoulder. Keep rolling even when that person's just listening, so that you'll have some *reaction shots* to edit into your finished iMovie.

The second advantage of capturing the same scene from different angles is that it gives you the luxury of *choice* when you assemble your movie in iMovie. You'll be able to conceal a flubbed line or a bad camera shot by cutting to a continuation of the action in a different piece of footage. Because the new footage will have been shot from a different angle or zoom level, the cut won't feel forced or artificial.

Capture Footage for Cutaways and Cut-Ins

Capturing a scene from more than one angle is a great precaution for another reason, too: You'll often find it extremely useful to be able to *cut away* to a shot of a secondary subject, such as an onlooker or the interviewer's face.

For example, when you're making a scripted movie, the first 30 seconds of dialog may have been terrific in the first take, but the next few lines may have been better in take number 4. You'd want to avoid simply editing the second take onto the end of the first; doing so would introduce a *jump cut,* an obvious and awkward splice between two shots of exactly the same image. But if you conceal the snip by briefly cutting away to, for example, the reaction of an onlooker, your viewers will never suspect that the dialog came from two different takes.

Another example, one that's especially pertinent when you're making training or how-to videos: Capture some footage that you can use for *cut-ins.* Cut-ins are like cutaways, in that they're brief interpolated shots that inject some variety into the movie. But instead of splicing in a wider shot, or a shot of somebody who's observing the scene, you splice in a *closer* shot.

When you're filming somebody for a cooking show, you can cut in to a closeup of the whisk stirring the sauce in the bowl. When you're filming a dramatic scene, you can cut to a closeup of the actor's hands twitching, a trickle of sweat behind the ear, or a hand reaching slowly for a weapon.

You'll do all of this cutting in and cutting away during the editing, not while you're filming. Nonetheless, the point in all of these cases is to make sure you've captured the necessary footage to begin with, so that you'll have the flexibility to use such techniques when it comes time to edit. Shoot cutaway candidates near and around your subject—clouds in the sky, traffic, someone sitting at a café table sipping cappuccino, a bird in a tree, and so on—*something* so that you'll have some shot variety when you assemble your final footage.

Tip: Imagine the difficulty of shooting and editing a movie like *My Dinner With André* (1981)—a conversation between two men seated at the same restaurant table for the *entire* two-hour movie. If this movie had been shot with a single camcorder on a tripod, its audiences would have gone quietly insane. Only the variety of shot types, angles, shot length, and so on make the single setting tolerable. (That and the conversation itself, of course.)

Dolly Shots

One of Hollywood's most popular shot types is one that never even occurs to most camcorder owners: the *dolly shot* or *tracking shot.* That's when the camera moves while shooting.

To create a dolly shot, filmmakers mount the camera on a platform car that glides along what looks like baby train tracks. The purpose of this elaborate setup is, of course, to move the camera along with a moving subject—to follow Kevin Costner running with wolves, for example, or to circle the passionately embracing Joseph Fiennes and Gwyneth Paltrow at the end of *Shakespeare in Love.* As a film technique, this one works like gangbusters—not only is it a very exciting shot to watch, but it also puts the viewer directly into the action.

Note: A dolly shot that moves forward isn't the same as simply zooming in. As a quick experiment will show you, the visual result is completely different.

When you zoom, the camera enlarges everything in the picture equally, both foreground and background. When you move forward through space, on the other hand, the distant background remains the same size; only the subject in the foreground gets bigger, which is a much more realistic result. Your viewers are more likely to feel as though they're part of the action and actually in the scene if you dolly forward instead of just zooming.

As a camcorder owner hoping to film, for example, your daughter's field hockey championship, you may find that this business of laying down train tracks on the field isn't always well received by the other parents.

But don't let the expense and dirty looks stop you. When it counts, you can improvise. You can lean out of a car window or sunroof, holding the camcorder as steady as you can, as a relative drives slowly alongside the action. You can film while riding a bicycle. You can persuade a family member to drag you along in an actual Radio Flyer–style wagon in the name of getting more interesting, more professional footage.

The wheelchair solution

Or use a wheelchair. Wheelchairs are remarkably popular with low-budget filmmakers who want to create dolly shots inexpensively. Wheelchairs don't require tracks, are comfortable to sit in while shooting, and provide a stable moving platform.

GlideCam and Steadicam JR

You might also consider buying or renting a special camera mount called GlideCam, a padded brace that keeps the camera steady (about $170, Figure 2-10), or even a Steadicam JR (about $550), a scaled-down version of the popular Hollywood tracking device. Both devices incorporate variations of a *gimbal* (a universal ball joint) that intercepts jerks and twists before they can reach the camera; they also distribute the camcorder's center of gravity to keep it even steadier. As a result, the camera stays level and stable even while you're running in a crowd, up and down stairs, and so on.

These ideas may sound extreme, but you'd be surprised at how effective they are. Suddenly you have access to one of Hollywood filmmakers' favorite tricks. Sure you'll feel silly riding through the neighborhood in your kid's Radio Flyer wagon—but how do you think professional camera operators feel riding along on their little choo-choos?

Figure 2-10:
Both the GlideCam, shown here, and the Steadicam JR require lots of practice and a strong arm, but can create spectacular moving shots. Both Bonfire of the Vanities *and* Goodfellas *include very long shots where we follow the main character as he crosses the street, enters a building, goes downstairs, through a hallway, and so on—all in one continuous, very steady shot, thanks to the Steadicam.*

The "180 Degree" Rule

When you're filming a scene from several different angles, don't cross "the Line." That's the invisible line that connects two people who are conversing, the two goalposts of the football field, and so on. Change camera angles and positions all you like, but stay on the same *side* of the action.

That's the "180 degree" rule they'll teach you about in film school. If you were to cross this 180-degree angle between the right and left objects in your shot, you'd confuse the audience. Imagine, for example, how difficult it would be to follow a football game if one shot showed the Browns rushing to the right side of the screen, and the next shot (of the same play) showed them running left. Similarly, the audience would become confused if an interviewer and interviewee shifted sides

of the frame from one shot to another. And if you're showing two people talking, you can imagine how disconcerting it would be if you cut from a closeup of one person to a closeup of the other, each facing the *same direction.*

As you watch TV and movies in the coming days and weeks, notice how rigidly directors and cinematographers obey the 180-degree rule. Once the right-to-left layout of the room, scene, or conversation has been established, it doesn't change for the duration of the scene.

The only exception: when the audience *sees* the camera cross the line, so that they get their new bearings as the camera moves. What you should avoid is *cutting* to a different shot on the other side of the 180-degree line.

Special Event Filming

I f all you intend to do with your camcorder is to capture random events of childhood charmingness around the house, you can skip this chapter. Just keep your camcorder lying handy, its battery charged and its tape compartment occupied, and you'll be all set.

Chances are, however, that once you've got the iMovie bug, you may become more inspired. It may occur to you to take your camcorder out of the house—to shoot the school play, your kid's sports game, your cousin's wedding, and so on. Maybe you'll decide to use the camcorder for more serious work, such as transferring your old photos to preserve them forever, creating a family history by interviewing relatives, shooting a documentary, or even making a scripted movie.

Each of these situations can benefit from a little forethought, plus a few tips, tricks, and professional techniques. This chapter is designed as a handbook to help you make the most of these common camcorder-catchable events.

Interviews

What's great about an interview is that you know it's coming. You've got time to set up your tripod, arrange the lighting, and connect an external microphone, as described in Chapter 2. (Do all of this before your subject arrives, by the way, since nothing makes an interview subject more nervous than having to sit around beforehand, just growing apprehensive.) Because you've got this extra time to plan ahead, there's no reason your interview footage can't look almost identical in quality to the interviews you see on TV.

Chapter 2 describes the basics of good camcorder footage. Well, in an interview situation, the same tips apply. Lighting is important: Avoid having the brightest light behind the subject's head. Sound is critical: Fasten a tie-clip microphone to your subject's lapel or collar.

Above all, use a tripod. You'll be glad you did, not only because the picture will be stable, thus permitting the audience to get more "into" the subject's world, but also for your own sake. Even the lightest camcorder is a drag to hold absolutely motionless for more than 5 minutes.

But interviews offer some additional challenges. If you've ever studied interviews on TV, such as the *60 Minutes* interviews that have aired every Sunday night since 1968, you realize that the producers have always thought through these questions:

- **What's the purpose of the interview?** The answer affects how you shoot the scene. On *60 Minutes,* the purpose is often to demonstrate how guilty or shifty the subject is. Bright lights and a black background help to create this impression, as do the ultra-closeups favored by the *60 Minutes* crew, in which the camera is zoomed in so tight that the pores on the subject's nose look like the craters on Mars.

  In interviews that aren't designed to be especially incriminating, however, the purpose of the interview is often to get to know the subject better. The setting you choose can go a long way toward telling more of the subject's story. Set the interview somewhere that has some meaning for, or tells something about, your subject. If it's a CEO, shoot it in her office across her handsome mahogany desk; your wide establishing shot will telegraph to your viewers just how magnificent this office is. If it's your grandfather, shoot it in his study or living room, where the accumulated mementos on the end tables suggest his lifetime of experiences. (When possible, get these cutaway and establishing shots before or after the actual interview, so as not to overwhelm your interviewee or waste his time.)

- **Who's going to ask the questions?** In professional interviews, of course, the camera person doesn't ask the questions. One person operates the camera, while another conducts the interview. If you can arrange to have a buddy help with your interview, it'll go a *lot* better. She (or you) can chat with the subject while the lights and microphones are being adjusted, for example.

  If you, the camcorder operator, absolutely must double as the interviewer, take your microphone situation into account. If your subject is wearing a tie-clip microphone, then your questions will be recorded very softly, as though coming from far away. If you're not using an external microphone, you'll have the opposite problem. Since you're standing right next to the camera, the sound of your voice will be very loud on the finished tape, in unfortunate contrast to the much fainter sound of your subject's replies.

  You can usually find solutions to all of these problems. For example, you can use a single, *omnidirectional* mike (covers all directions) that sits between you and your subject. Or you could connect *two* external mikes to your camcorder by way of a portable mixer, which accepts (and lets you adjust the volume of) several inputs simultaneously. (Radio Shack and video-equipment Web sites sell these items.)

Tip: If you are both the camera operator and the interviewer, and you decide that you want to be on-camera along with your interview subject, use the remote control that comes with most camcorder models. Open the LCD screen and rotate it so that it's facing you as you sit in front of the camera—that's the only way for you to frame the shot when you're not actually standing behind the camcorder.

- **Is the interviewer part of the interview?** In other words, will the audience see the person asking the questions? If so, you've got a challenge on your hands. You've got two people sitting across from each other, facing opposite directions, but only one camera to film them with.

  If you ever saw the 1987 movie *Broadcast News,* you know how TV professionals solve this problem. Before or after the interview, they capture some establishing-shot footage of the two people sitting there face to face. They also take some footage of the interviewer alone—nodding sagely in agreement, smiling in understanding, frowning in concern, and so on. They film him asking the questions again, even after the interview subject has left the scene. Later, when editing the finished product, they splice these reaction shots into the interview footage, as you can do in iMovie. The audience never suspects that the entire interview was shot with one camera.

  On the other hand, in many interviews, you don't see the interviewer at all. You hear her voice, but you don't see her on-camera. (A disembodied voice like this is called a *voiceover.* Voiceovers are extremely common in TV ads, movies with narration, and episodes of *The Wonder Years.*)

  Sometimes you don't see *or* hear the interviewer, such as when the producer just wants a comment or sound bite from the interview subject. In those situations, invite your subject to phrase his answers as complete sentences. Otherwise, after the questions have been edited out, you'll be left with an interview subject saying, "Yes…that's right…no, I don't think so," and other unhelpful utterances.

Tip: If you, the interviewer, will ultimately be edited out of the movie, you can greatly assist your own cause by framing your questions cleverly. Avoid yes-or-no questions. Don't ask, "Were you happy with your performance?" Instead, ask, "Tell us about how you felt," for example.

That's what professionals do. Now you know why, when asked "You just won the Olympics. Where are you going to go now?" nobody in the Disney World ads ever just says, "Disney World!"

- **How long will the interview be after editing?** If the finished product will be more than a couple of minutes long, think about keeping your viewers' interest up by introducing some variety into the camera work, as described in the previous chapter.

  Capture some wide shots, for example, for use as cutaways. That way, when you edit the interview in iMovie, you'll be able to offer a refreshing change of shot now and then.

CHAPTER 3: SPECIAL EVENT FILMING

Cutaways are also ideal for masking cuts in the interview footage. It's a convenient fact of life that you can't see somebody's lips moving when filming from behind them, or when the camera is far away. In other words, you can use a cutaway even while your interview subject is still talking. Your viewers won't be able to detect that the cutaway footage was actually shot at a different time. (TV news editors use this technique all the time—they briefly cut to a shot behind the subject's head in order to conceal an edit between two parts of the same interview.)

• **How conservative is the interview?** The answer to this question affects how you frame the subject in your lens. Some interviews are designed to be hip, like the ones on MTV, the *Bunting's Window* computer show shown on airplanes, or fight sequences in the old *Batman* series. These might feature a handheld camera, off-center framing, or even a camera mounted off-kilter on its tripod for that added wackiness.

If wackiness isn't exactly what you're going for, however, the framing shown in Figure 3-1 is about right.

Figure 3-1:
As in any footage, interviews should offer some variety of composition and zoom amount. But for maximum viewer comfort, most pro video interviews capture the speaker from shoulders up, with a little bit of space left above the head. (Here, you're seeing more of the subject's torso, just so you can see the tie-clip microphone.) If the subject is supposedly looking at something off-camera—the interviewer, for example—professionals leave some talk space in the shot. That is, a little extra room in front of the person's face, as shown here.

• **How is the shot set up?** In most interviews, the interview subject doesn't look directly into the camera—except when she's recording a Last Will and Testament. Usually she's looking just off-camera, at a spot a couple of feet to one side of the camcorder, or even directly across the camcorder's line of vision. That's where the interviewer should sit, so that the subject looks at the right spot naturally.

The camcorder should be level with the subject's face, which is yet another argument for using a tripod.

Tip: If you're the interviewer, here's one tip that has nothing to do with the technicalities of your camcorder and tripod: *Listen* to the answers. Many inexperienced interviewers are so busy thinking about the next question that they miss golden opportunities for further lines of questioning. Worse, the interview subject will detect that you're not really paying attention, so the interview won't go nearly as well as it could.

Music Videos

Few camcorder endeavors are as much fun as making a music video, whether it's a serious one or a fake one just for kicks.

Of course, your interest in this kind of video technique may depend on your age and taste. But music videos are worth studying, no matter who you are, because they frequently incorporate every conceivable camera trick, editing technique, and shooting style. The day you shoot a music video is the day you can try punching every button on your camcorder, unlocking those weird special effects you've never even tried, and using all the unnecessary zooms you want. Better yet, this is the day when you don't care a whit about microphones or sound. Eventually, you'll discard the camcorder's recorded sound anyway. As you splice your footage together in iMovie, you'll replace the camcorder's soundtrack with a high-quality original recording of the song.

Figure 3-2:
Because you have iMovie, you can pull off a fascinating visual stunt that's very common in rock videos: the jumping-flea-musician effect, in which, every few seconds, everybody in the scene blips into a new position (or appears and disappears), sometimes in time to the music. (You're actually creating jump cuts, *which you should avoid except when creating special effects like this.) Creating this effect is simple—if your camcorder has a tripod. Just shoot each segment, moving your musicians around when the camera isn't moving. In iMovie, the splices will be exactly as sharp and convincing as they are on MTV (or* Bewitched*).*

Some music videos are lip-synched—that is, the performers pretend that they're singing the words on the soundtrack. Other videos are voiceover, narrative, or experimental videos. In these videos, you don't actually see anybody singing, but instead you watch a story unfolding (or a bunch of random-looking footage). If you decide to create a lip-synched video, take a boom box with you in the field. Make sure it's playing as you film the singers, so that they're lip-synching with accurate timing.

When it comes time to edit the music video in iMovie, you'll be able to add crossfades, transitions, graphics, and other common rock-video elements. (See Figure 3-2.)

Live Stage Performances

Filming a live stage performance, such as a play, musical, concert, or dance, is extremely challenging. It poses four enormous challenges: capturing the sound, getting power, capturing the picture, and getting permission in the first place.

Getting Permission

At most professional performances, the management doesn't permit camcorders. Whether union rules, copyright rules, house rules, or simple paranoia is at play, the bottom line is that using a camcorder (or any camera) is usually forbidden.

That leaves you two alternatives: Confine your footage to performances where camcorders are OK, such as the choir concert at the elementary school—or film surreptitiously. (As the size of camcorders shrinks year by year, the latter option is becoming ever more popular among people who don't mind flouting the rules.)

Capturing the Sound

When you're filming a performance from the audience, your camcorder gets hopelessly confused. It's programmed to record the closest sounds, which, in this case, are the little coughs, chuckles, and seat-creaks of the audience members around you. The people on stage, meanwhile, come through only faintly, with the hollow echo that comes from recording people who are far away from the microphone. As any camcorder buff who's filmed her kid's school play can tell you, the resulting video is often very unsatisfying.

You have alternatives, but they require some effort. One option is to equip your camcorder with an external microphone—a *unidirectional*-style one. Mount it on a pole that puts the microphone over the audience's heads.

If the show has its own sound system—that is, if it's miked and amplified—you may be able to snake an external microphone up to the speaker system, so that your camcorder is benefiting from the microphones worn by every actor. Better yet, you can sometimes persuade the management to let you hook up your camcorder to the sound system itself. Connect the cable to the *audio* input of your camcorder, if you have one. (Unfortunately, connecting it to the *microphone* input may overload your sound circuitry and produce distortion.)

Getting Power

Before worrying about the visual quality of your live-performance footage, worry about the power. Are the batteries charged? Do you have enough battery power to film the entire show? If so, have you thought about when you can swap batteries without missing something good?

If you're filming with permission, you may be able to plug your camcorder into a power outlet, which neatly solves this problem. Unfortunately, because of the extension cord tripping hazard, this solution presents itself fairly rarely. (If you do get permission to lay down extension cords, tape them to the floor using duct tape, like generations of professional film crews before you.)

Capturing the Picture

Now you've got to worry about where you're going to sit or stand. Sometimes you don't have a choice—you'll just have to sit in your seat and do the best you can. (Keep your screen closed when shooting; keeping it open both distracts the other audience members and gets you in trouble with management.)

Thanks to the powerful zoom on today's camcorders, standing at the back of the theater is frequently a more attractive alternative. There you may even be able to use a tripod, much to the benefit of your footage and the relief of your muscles. Doing so means that the camcorder will be able to shoot over the heads of the audience members—another real advantage over shooting from your seat.

Technically speaking, filming a live performance on a fairly distant, brightly lit stage requires three special considerations:

- **Use the manual focus trick.** Nowhere is this secret (see page 53) more useful than when you're filming a live stage performance. Autofocus generally fails you in these circumstances, because the camera tries to focus on the nearest object—the head of the lady in row 34. This autofocus syndrome, which arbitrarily blurs the picture as you film, is the number-one destroyer of homemade performance videos.

  Use the manual focus to get the picture sharpened up in its fully zoomed-in state before you begin rolling tape. Then you'll be able to zoom in or out during the performance without ever worrying about the focus.

- **Adjust the exposure.** Stage lights and spotlights throw camcorders for a loop. These lights pour very bright light onto the performers' faces, but throw normal light on the rest of the set. The result is a broad spectrum of brightness—too broad for a camcorder's sensors. The auto-exposure feature of your camcorder does its best to figure out its mission, but it usually makes a mess of things in medium or wide shots, turning every actor's face into a radioactive white blur with no features at all (Figure 3-3).

  Solving the problem requires you to *override* the auto-exposure feature. Consult the camcorder's manual for instructions. On Sony camcorders, for example, you press the Exposure button on the left side of the camera and then turn a thumb knob to adjust the exposure. Turn this knob downward to make the picture darker. After a moment, you'll see the features return to the actors' faces.

Be ready to turn that exposure knob the other way on short notice, however. You can expect the stage lights to be full up during the big, full-cast, song-and-dance numbers, but other scenes may be lit dimly for dramatic effect. Such scenes are equally troublesome for camcorders, since turning up the exposure knob can help a lot but may introduce graininess to the picture. There's not much you can do in this situation, because camcorders simply thrive on light.

Tip: Whenever you use your camcorder's manual exposure control, be very careful about trusting your LCD monitor for feedback. On most camcorders, this screen has its *own* brightness control, which, when set to a very bright or very dim setting, can lead you astray as you set your exposure knob. For best results, gauge the effect of your manual exposure fiddling by looking only through the eyepiece viewfinder.

Figure 3-3:
The solution to the bright-face syndrome in shows (left) is to turn down the exposure (right). Unfortunately, when the actors' faces look good, the set may wind up too dark.

- **Know the show.** The best performance videos are made by somebody who's familiar with the performance. Only they know in advance when to use a wide shot, when to use a closeup, and so on.

When you're zoomed out all the way, you can't see any faces—a distinct drawback in a dramatic performance. For this reason, you'll be tempted to use the zoom a lot when you're filming a theatrical performance. Unfortunately, actors have a habit of *moving* during the scene—from the camcorder operator's standpoint, a distinctly annoying behavior. No sooner have you found your kid and zoomed into his face when he *moves,* leaving you to film 7 seconds of empty set as you try to hunt for a human being. (Professionals learn to keep both eyes open when shooting. One eye is on the eyepiece when framing, and the other eye occasionally looks around to see what else is happening in the scene and to prepare for subjects that might enter the frame.)

If it's possible to attend a dress rehearsal or a previous performance, therefore, your footage will be vastly improved. You'll know in advance when the big, full-stage moments come, and when to zoom in for closeups.

Tip: If the show is really important, consider shooting it *twice*. At the second performance, position the camera in a different place and shoot different kinds of shots. Later, you can use iMovie to combine the footage from the two performances. By splicing in one camera's shot, then the other—thereby changing camera angles and zoom amounts without missing a beat—you simulate the effect of having two cameras at the same performance.

You also have a backup in case you missed a key entrance, joke, or pratfall during the first performance.

Speeches

What to worry about when filming talks, presentations, and speeches: the sound. Exactly as when filming live stage performances, your camcorder's built-in microphone does a lousy job of picking up a speaker more than 10 feet away. To remedy the problem, use a tie-clip microphone on extension cords, get a wireless mike, or run an external microphone to the loudspeakers (if the talk is amplified) or even directly to the sound system's mixing board.

Otherwise, the only other problem you'll encounter is the question-and-answer session, if there is one. In an auditorium situation, not only will you have a terrible time (because there isn't *enough* time) trying to train the camera on the person asking the question, but you won't pick up the sound at all. You can only pray that the guest speaker will be smart enough to repeat the question before providing the answer.

Tip: Capturing audience reaction shots for use as cutaways is a great idea when you're recording a talk. Splicing these shots into the finished iMovie film can make any speech footage more interesting, and gives you the freedom to *edit* the speech if necessary.

If your goal is to capture the entire talk, and you've got only a single camcorder, you'll have to get the reaction shots *before or after* the talk. Don't just pan around to the audience while the speaker is speaking.

Sports

Filming sporting events is, in general, a breeze. Most take place outdoors, neatly solving all lighting problems, and the only sound that's important at a sporting event is usually the crowd's reaction, which your camcorder captures exquisitely. Most of the time, you'll be zoomed out all the way, because there's too much motion to worry about closeups. (And when you *do* want closeups, you'll know exactly when to zoom out again, thanks to the structured nature of most sports. Every baseball play begins the same way, for example.)

If your aim is to film a player for training purposes, or to study a golf swing or tennis stroke as it's played back in slow motion or frame by frame, consider using your camcorder's *high-speed shutter* feature. When you use this special recording mode, the camcorder records the action in a strange, frame-flashing sort of way. When you play this footage back, you can use the slow-motion or freeze-frame controls on your camcorder with sensational, crisp, clear results.

Caution: The high-speed shutter is effective only in *very* bright, sunny, outdoor light. If you try to use it indoors, outdoors when it's overcast, or in shadow, all kinds of unpleasant side effects result. You may get flickering and stuttering motion, the autofocus feature may stop working, colors may not look right, and the picture in general will seem too dim.

Photos and Old Movies

Most people associate video with *moving* images, but video "slideshows" can be extremely satisfying to watch, especially if you add commentary or music in iMovie. With a tripod, a music stand, and good lighting, your camcorder is all set to preserve your family photos forever.

If the photos were taken with a digital camera, there's nothing to it: Just import them as described in Chapter 12.

The challenge is what to do about photos that *aren't* digital—the old kind, the paper kind, the kind you'll confront if you put together a biographical video about anyone who's more than six years old.

Old Photos

Tactic one: Get the old pictures into the Mac using a scanner. As described in Chapter 12, you can then drop them into your iMovie storyboard electronically, without having to mess with lights, focus, tripod, and so on.

Tactic two: Film the photos with the camcorder. Take each photo out of its frame, prop it on a music stand or tape it to the wall, and slip a big black piece of cardboard behind it. Set up the camcorder so that it's directly aimed at the photo; otherwise, the photo may look skewed or distorted when filmed. Use the manual focus on your camcorder, zoom in an appropriate amount, position the tripod and lights so that there's no glare, and begin shooting. If you're getting glare from the photo, use two lights, one on each side of the photo, each at a 45-degree angle to it.

Scanning produces a more professional effect. Still, filming the photos gives you some interesting creative possibilities, like surrounding each photo with meaningful memorabilia, capitalizing on late-afternoon sun slanting in through a window, and so on.

Shooting Slides

You can transfer slides to your movie in either of two ways:

- Project the slides onto a slide screen or white wall, and then film them with your camcorder. To make the slide's image sharper, put the projector as close as possible to the screen. Position the camera right next to the projector, so that it doesn't wind up filming the projected slide at an angle.

- Have a Kodak shop or a local service bureau scan your slides, transferring them to a CD. (If your scanner has a slide attachment, you may even be able to do this yourself, although it can be a finicky procedure.) Then you can import the slides electronically into iMovie, as described in Chapter 12. This method ensures the highest possible quality and saves you a lot of setup hassle.

Transferring Old Movies to Digital

Transferring old movies to the camcorder is another good idea. If these older movies are on videotape, such as VHS cassettes or 8mm videotapes from an older camcorder, you're in good shape. Transferring them onto your digital camcorder is fairly easy, if you have the right equipment. (See Chapter 4.)

Transferring old *film* to your camcorder is a more difficult proposition. Photographic catalogs sell mirror-based gadgets just for this purpose. In essence, this apparatus lets you run the film projector, which projects the old movie onto a tiny movie screen. Your camcorder simply films the film. Unfortunately, the camcorder can pick up quite a bit of grain and picture deterioration in the process.

You can also send your old reels out to a commercial transfer shop. Most local photo-developing outfits and camera shops will handle this transaction for you.

Weddings

Ah, weddings! Everybody loves weddings—especially camcorder manufacturers. Talk about once-in-a-lifetime (all right, very-*few*-times-in-a-lifetime) occasions! What bigger event could there be to drive somebody to buy a camcorder?

Where to Stand

If you're just a friend or family member in the audience, you've got no choice about where to position the camcorder. You'll have to shoot from your seat or stand in the back.

But suppose that you're a wedding videographer—or becoming one. (That's an excellent idea, by the way, if you've been thinking about going into business for yourself. You, with your *digital* camcorder and iMovie, can advertise your superior equipment, lower costs, and greater editing flexibility when compared with all the poor slobs still lugging around older, analog equipment.)

From the videographer's standpoint, weddings are tricky. If you've only got one camcorder, where do you stand during the vows? From the spectators' side, where you can't capture the faces of the bride and groom? Or from the opposite side, where you get the bride and groom, but can't see the scene the way the spectators see it? Here are a few solutions:

- **Film the rehearsal.** The idea is that later, in iMovie, you can splice in some of this footage as though it were captured with a second camera on the day of the wedding. The rehearsal isn't usually "in costume," of course, so you won't fool anyone with your footage of the bride and groom in their sweatshirts and blue jeans. But the presiding official (minister, rabbi, justice of the peace) may well be in official garb at rehearsal time. At the very least, you can grab some footage of him at the rehearsal. With his lines and reaction shots already in the can, you can spend your time during the actual ceremony standing and filming from behind him.

• **Really use a second camera.** Videographers make about $1,000 per wedding, so after one wedding, you'll have made enough money to buy a second camcorder. If you have an assistant who can operate it, you've solved your "where should I stand?" dilemma.

But if you don't have an assistant, you can set this second camcorder up in the back of the hall, in the balcony, or behind the presiding official, and just let it run unattended. Once again, iMovie will be your salvation; you'll be able to incorporate footage from the second camcorder whenever your editing instincts tell you that it's time for a refreshing new angle.

• **Shoot from behind the official.** If none of these ideas work for you, film some of the wedding from the audience's point of view. But during the vows, get yourself up onto the dais and shoot over the official's shoulder. In the end, what everybody wants from your wedding video is to see the faces of the bride and groom as they pledge their love forever—something they *didn't* get to see during the actual wedding.

Getting the Sound

This is the big one. If there was ever an event where recording the words was important, this is it. If you're just a friend shooting from the audience, the sound will probably be weak unless you use one of the tricks described on page 68.

If you're the hired videographer, however, your responsibility to get clearly audible sound is even greater. Maybe you bought one of the pro camcorders with a shotgun mike. It will do splendidly if you film from behind the presiding official, only a few feet from the bride and groom.

Otherwise, equip the groom with a wireless mike, if he'll permit it. This usually entails slipping a little transmitter into his pocket and running a tiny wire up to his lapel.

If he objects, well, it's his wedding. But remind him that his one wireless mike will also pick up the words of the bride and the official, too, thanks to their close proximity during the vows.

And for goodness' sake, wear Walkman headphones to monitor the sound when you shoot the actual ceremony. Your videography career will come to a quick and miserable end if you play back the footage and discover that the wireless mike wasn't transmitting.

Tip: Many professional videographers these days invest in a Sony MiniDisc recorder, which looks like a Walkman but contains a half-size, recordable CD. It records extremely high-quality sound, and serves as a great backup sound-recording unit at weddings. When you return to your Mac, you can transfer the audio into the computer and then import it into iMovie. The sound won't perfectly match the video for more than a few minutes at a time, but your clips are probably short enough that such "sync drift" won't be a problem.

Being Unobtrusive

Anyone who hires a wedding videographer has already swallowed hard and accepted that there's going to be somebody running around the ceremony with a bunch of

22 Shots for Your Wedding Video

Take it from a wedding-video veteran, Doug Graham of Panda Video Productions: There's a certain set of shots you've *got* to include if you're the one who's been asked to film it. Here they are:

1. Bride and bridesmaids dressing. (Keep it G-rated!)

2. Exterior of the church.

3. Wedding party arriving at church.

4. Continuous roll of the ceremony, from prior to bride's entrance to the couple's walk down the aisle at the end. Use two cameras, if you can—place one in the back third of the church. Using the handheld, position yourself on the bridesmaids' side of the aisle at the altar steps. Shoot the procession. After the bride arrives, move to a tripod placed behind the officiant and on the groom's side. This gives the best shot of the bride during the vows. (Coordinate and clear this with the officiant beforehand.)

If you can, take a moment later to film a reenactment of the ring ceremony. Get a good closeup of rings being slipped onto fingers, which you can splice into iMovie later.

5. Any special touches in the ceremony, like a solo song, unity-candle lighting, and so on.

6. Reaction shots of bride's and groom's families.

7. The photographer's formal posed shots.

8. Wedding party leaving church.

9. Wedding party arriving at reception. (This'll take some good planning and fast driving on your part!)

10. Bride and groom entering reception.

11. First dance.

12. Mom's dance with the groom.

13. Dad's dance with the bride.

14. Best man's toast.

15. Cake cutting.

16. Garter toss.

17. Guestbook signings.

18. Special dances and ceremonies at the reception.

19. Interviews with guests.

20. Interview with the bride and groom.

21. Footage for use as cutaways: cake, presents, decorations, flower arrangements, the DJ or band. Get a copy of the wedding announcement, and souvenirs (such as specially printed napkins), so that you can film them for closeups later.

22. Guests saying goodbye.

Don't shoot: People eating. Backs of heads. People backlit by windows. Drunks.

Interviews at a wedding are a real art. I just have the guests pass around the mike and ask them to "say a few words to the happy couple." Some good leading questions might be:

- What can you tell me about how Bill and Sue met?

- What did you feel when you learned they were engaged?

- What do you think Bill should do to keep Sue happy?

- Where do you think Bill and Sue will be years from now?

- What do you think Sue loves most about Bill?

When interviewing the bride and groom, I do it individually, rather than together. I ask each of them the same questions: How did you meet? Tell me how the relationship grew. When did you first know Tim was "the one"? Tell me about how he proposed? What are your plans for the future?

Then I cut the responses together when editing. The juxtaposition of the two viewpoints can be funny, touching, or poignant.

I always remind my on-camera folks to answer questions in complete sentences. For example, if I ask "What's your name?", I don't want, "Joe." I want, "My name is Joe." That way, I can edit out my questions later, and the response will be complete in itself.

electronics. Fortunately, your equipment is much smaller than non-DV equipment—a great feature at weddings.

Still, you should use as much tact and foresight as possible. Scope out the hall before the ceremony, and speak to the presiding official to discuss your plans. Use video lights if you can, but accept that your clients may object to the clutter. And use only battery power, as duct-taping extension cords to the carpeting doesn't always go over well in houses of worship.

Tip: If it's your responsibility to film a wedding or some other important event, take an extra fully charged battery and extra blank tapes. You may think that this is obvious advice, but there's absolutely nothing worse than forgetting it and missing half of the most important day of your client/friend/sister's life.

Actual Scripted Films

For a steadily growing subset of camcorder owners, this is the Big Kahuna, the *raison d'être,* the Main Event: making a real movie, complete with dialog, actors, and a plot. Ever since *The Blair Witch Project* made $150 million—a movie made by recent film-school grads with a camcorder, no funding, and no Hollywood connections—independent films have become a *very* big deal.

You can post your homemade movies online, where 200 million Internet citizens can watch them. The most popular ones get Hollywood-studio attention. There are even a growing number of film festivals dedicated to showing homemade (usually video) films. In the 1960s, Americans used to say that anyone could grow up to be president. Today, we say that anyone can make a Hollywood movie.

The world, and the library, is filled with books on making traditional movies. However, the process is much more difficult than making the kinds of movies described so far in this chapter. In addition to all of the technique and technical considerations you've read about so far, you now have to worry about plot, scripts, continuity, marketing, actors, characters, costumes, props, sets, locations—and budget. You'll go through these phases of creation:

- **Writing the screenplay.** Most movies begin with a script—or at the very least, a *treatment* (a 5- to 30-page prose synopsis of the movie's story line that's usually designed to attract interest from backers).

  If you send your screenplay to Hollywood in hopes of getting it made into a movie, your competition is 250,000 other people every year who also send unsolicited scripts. Like them, you'll get yours back soon enough, too; to avoid being accused of stealing ideas, Hollywood studios don't even open unsolicited scripts. Even if you have a connection to someone who'll look at your screenplay, it won't be taken seriously unless it's prepared using extremely specific page formatting, which you can read about in any of dozens of screenwriting books.

Fortunately, if you're going to make your own movie, it doesn't make one bit of difference how your screenplay is formatted. Format it however you like, just so your actors can read it.

- **Location.** You'll have to figure out where you're going to shoot each scene—and get permission to shoot there. Does the restaurant owner know, for example, that you'll be bringing in lights and sound equipment?

Tip: Instead of traveling to a special location for shooting, you can often save money and hassle by turning your own backyard or living room into a set. Just a few key props and set dressings may be enough to suggest, for example, an office, jungle, or police station—especially if it's preceded, in your movie, by an establishing shot showing your characters going *into* such a building.

- **Preproduction.** Before shooting, make "shopping lists." Go through the script and make lists of which actors are in which scenes, what clothes and props they'll need for those scenes, and so on. *Preproduction,* the planning phase, is where a production is set up to succeed or fail.

  You should also make a written list of the shots that you want to get, so that when everyone arrives on the set and all hell breaks loose, you won't forget any critical shots. Lists prevent memory blocks.

- **Actors.** Who's going to star in your movie? You can get friends to do it, of course. You can recruit people from acting classes, colleges, or theaters in your area. They'll probably be delighted to participate, in exchange for nothing but the experience, good treatment, and *good food.* (You'd be surprised how important the food is.)

  Or you can get professional actors, with the help of a talent agency. You choose them by holding an audition, and you pay for their participation.

- **Editing.** After you've shot the various scenes of your movie—which, of course, you don't have to do in sequence—you'll assemble the film in iMovie. This is where you decide how long each shot should take, which camera angle to use, which *take* to use (which of several versions of the scene you've shot), and so on.

  In the real film world, this editing phase, called *postproduction,* often takes longer than the actual filming. Incredible magic takes place in the cutting room; the film editor alone can make or break the feeling, mood, and impact of the movie. You can read more about editing tricks in Chapter 13.

If you've never made an actual movie before, start small. Make a *short* (a brief movie), which, in the age of independent films, is becoming an increasingly popular format. (In March 2000, Woody Allen made a *6-minute* movie to protest the construction of a skyscraper in a beloved area of Manhattan.) Starting with a short film is a great idea not just because it prevents you from biting off more than you can chew, but also because the average Mac's hard drive can't hold more than about 60 minutes of raw footage at a time.

Making a short is also excellent practice for reducing a movie down to its absolutely essential elements, trimming out the superfluous shots and scenes—a highly prized talent that will pay off when you graduate to full-length movies. As they say in the biz: "If it doesn't move the story forward, it holds it back." (More editing advice in Chapter 13.)

Part Two: Editing in iMovie

2

Importing Video

Phase 1 is over. You've captured the raw footage on your camcorder: You've assembled the ingredients you need, and you're ready to enter the kitchen. Now it's time for Phase 2, the heart of this book: editing your footage on the Mac using iMovie. This chapter introduces you to iMovie and its importing window, which is equally adept at slurping in video from tape camcorders, tapeless camcorders, and old iMovie projects. It can also record video live, in real time, from a camcorder or an iSight video camera.

iMovie: The Application

So far in this book, you've read about nothing but *hardware*—the equipment. In the end, however, the iMovie story is about *software*, both the footage as it exists on your Mac and the iMovie program itself.

iMovie on a New Mac

If you bought a new Mac since September 2007, iMovie '08 is probably already on your hard drive. Open the Macintosh HD icon→Applications folder. Inside is the star-shaped icon for iMovie itself.

Its icon is probably in your Dock, too.

iMovie for an Existing Mac

If your Mac didn't come with iMovie '08, you can buy it as part of the $80 iLife '08 software suite. That's one DVD containing the latest versions of GarageBand, iMovie, iPhoto, iWeb, and iDVD. (It's available from Apple's Web site, Apple stores, or popular Mac mail-order sites like *www.macmall.com* and *www.macwarehouse.com*.)

Apple says that iMovie requires a Mac (running Mac OS X version 10.4.9 or later) in one of these categories:

- Any Mac with an Intel processor (MacBook, MacBook Pro, Mac Pro, recent iMacs). An Intel-based Mac is required if you want to work with *AVCHD* video (page 19).

- A Power Mac G5 with dual 2.0-gigahertz chips or faster

- An iMac G5 whose chip runs at 1.9 gigahertz or faster

Apple also recommends a machine with at least 1 gigabyte of memory—and *requires* it if you want to work with high-def video.

It goes without saying, of course, that the more memory you have, the bigger your screen, and the faster your processor, the happier you and iMovie will be. This program is *seriously* hungry for horsepower.

If you've bought iLife, now run its installer and choose which programs you want.

Tip: Consider installing GarageBand even if you're not a musician. You'll need it to assist iMovie with things like adding DVD chapter markers and editing sound.

When the installer is finished, you'll find an icon called iMovie in your Applications folder and in your Dock.

Tip: If you've got the previous version of iMovie already on your Mac, the installer thoughtfully preserves it. You'll find a folder called "iMovie (previous version)" in your Applications folder, ready to run when necessary.

To find out why Apple left the old version on your hard drive, read page 2.

".0.1" Updates

Like any software company, Apple occasionally releases new versions of iMovie: version 7.1, version 7.2, and so on (or even 7.1.1, then 7.1.2, etc.). Each free upgrade adds better reliability to the program. They're well worth installing for any program, but they're especially important for iMovie; Apple realizes that the new iMovie isn't nearly as full-featured as the old one, and promises to restore some of the most beloved missing features.

You don't have to look far to find these updates. One day you'll be online, and the Mac's Software Update dialog box will appear, letting you know that a new version is available and offering to install it for you. You can also download the updates from within iMovie by choosing iMovie→Check for Updates.

When the updater finishes, your original copy of iMovie '08 has morphed into the newer version of the program. (One way to find out what version of iMovie you have is to open the program and then choose iMovie→About iMovie.)

This book assumes that you have at least iMovie 7.1.

Getting into iMovie

After you've installed iMovie, open it by double-clicking its icon in the Applications folder, or by single-clicking its star-shaped icon in the Dock.

Note: At this point in a book about any previous version of iMovie, you'd be cautioned about your screen resolution. "Anything lower than 1024 by 768 pixels," would go the warning, "and iMovie won't even be able to run."

Fortunately, no Mac capable of running the new iMovie *has* a lower resolution than that. And it wouldn't matter anyway; iMovie '08 has no problem running on tiny screens or at low resolutions, like 800 by 600 pixels.

Now, just in case it had somehow slipped your attention that iMovie is a totally new program, a special starter screen appears to let you know (Figure 4-1).

Figure 4-1:
This window welcomes you to the new concepts of iMovie. The most significant element of this billboard is the Video Tutorials button, which takes you online to see some videos that go over iMovie's basic features. Click OK to close the welcome screen and get down to work.

When you click OK, you arrive at the main iMovie screen. Figure 4-2 is a cheat sheet for iMovie's various screen elements, but spend no time memorizing their functions now; the rest of this book covers each of these tools in context and in depth.

• **Project Library.** If you're used to the old iMovie, the new iMovie's way of doing things may come as a shock.

You create new movie projects the same way as always, by choosing File→New Project (or pressing ⌘-N). But now, after you type a name for the new movie, you're not asked where you want to save it. Instead, iMovie just adds its name to this Project Library list, alongside all of your projects, past and present. More on projects in the next chapter.

• **Project storyboard.** You'll spend most of your editing time up here. Here's where you see your movie represented as *filmstrips*—short sequences of representative frames from each clip. Parallel colored strips indicate blocks of sound that play simultaneously.

• **Viewer.** You watch your footage in this window.

• **Toolbar.** Here's where you'll find most of iMovie's onscreen controls.

• **Event Library.** In the new iMovie scheme, *all* your raw footage is available to *all* your movie projects at all times. The Event Library lists all the video you've ever imported into iMovie '08, on all of your hard drives. It's organized by *event*—wedding, vacation, graduation, and so on. You can read much more about Events on page 90; for now, it's enough to know that your Events are listed here, organized into folders by year.

• **Event browser.** This area stores the raw, unedited *clips*—"filmstrips" of footage, individual shots—that you'll rearrange into a masterpiece of modern storytelling. Exactly what you see here changes; it shows the contents of whatever Event whose name you click in the Event Library.

• **Playhead.** The Playhead is like the little handle of a normal scroll bar. It shows exactly where you are in the footage.

Figure 4-2:
Here's a quick grand tour of iMovie at its most forlorn-looking. It will soon be seething with filmstrips, clips, pictures, and sound.

If you've just opened iMovie, it probably looks pretty barren at the moment. But you'll fix that.

Importing from a Tape Camcorder

If you have a MiniDV tape camcorder, high-def or not, transferring your recordings to the Mac for editing is straightforward. All you have to do is connect your two machines—the camcorder and the Mac—with a cable.

It's called a FireWire cable, and it looks like the one in Figure 4-3. The big end of the cable goes into the FireWire jack on the front, side, or back of your Mac; it's marked by a radioactive-looking ☢ symbol.

Figure 4-3:
Plug the larger end of the FireWire cable—the six-pin end, as Apple calls it—into the corresponding jack on the Mac. The tiny end may look almost square, but it fits in only one particular way, thanks to a little indentation on one side. Be gentle with it.

On the other end is a much smaller, squarish plug (the four-pin connector). Plug this tiny end into the FireWire connector on your camcorder, which, depending on the brand, may be labeled "FireWire," "i.Link," or "IEEE 1394." It's almost always hidden behind a plastic or rubber door or flap on the camcorder.

This single FireWire cable communicates both sound and video from the camcorder to the Mac. Once it's connected, proceed like this:

1. **Turn on the camcorder. Switch it into Play mode (Figure 4-4).**

   The camcorder's playback mode may be labeled Play, VCR, VTR, or just ▶.

   At this point, iMovie's big blue Import window is supposed to open automatically. If it doesn't, run through the troubleshooting checks described on page 425.

Tip: You'll probably want to open the camcorder's LCD screen, which also turns on its speaker. Otherwise, you'll have no way to hear the audio as you play back the tape.

---

2. **Specify what you want to import.**

If you want to import the whole tape, make sure the Automatic/Manual switch (lower left) is on Automatic, and then click Import. This is a convenient option, since you can walk away and do other things while iMovie works. The "Save to" dialog box appears (Figure 4-5); skip to step 3.

Figure 4-4:
Your camcorder's Play Mode should be a fairly prominent knob or menu setting. If you can't find it, check the manual.

Figure 4-5:
This dialog box wants to know: Where do you want to save the incoming clips (which hard drive)? What Event do they belong to? And how big do you really need hard drive footage to be?

If you want to import only some of what's on the tape, set the Automatic/Manual switch to Manual. At this point, the window sprouts a set of playback control buttons (Figure 4-6). You can actually use the ◄◄, ►►, ■, and ► buttons on the screen to control the camcorder.

Tip: You have to keep the mouse button down on the ◀◀ and ▶▶ buttons continuously to make them work. If you use these buttons while the video is playing, you scan through the video; if you click Stop (■) first, these buttons zoom much faster through the tape, but of course you can't see where you are until you hit ▶ again.

Figure 4-6:
*There are no
keyboard short-
cuts for these
buttons. Use
your mouse to
operate the cam-
corder by remote
control, or just
use the playback
controls on the
camcorder itself.*

What you're doing now, of course, is scanning your tape to find the sections that you want to include in your edited movie. When you find a shot that's worth bringing onto the Mac, click the Import button at the lower-right corner of the window. The "Save to" dialog box appears (Figure 4-5); read on.

3. **Indicate where you want to save the imported video clips.**

   Most people, most of the time, save incoming video onto the main Mac hard drive. But true iMovie addicts wind up buying additional hard drives to hold their movies. That's why the "Save to" pop-up menu appears here—so that you can choose a different hard drive to hold your video.

4. **Specify an Event.**

   The pair of choices shown in Figure 4-5 let you answer these questions: Were the scenes you're about to import filmed at a new Event? Or should they more properly be filed along with scenes you've already imported as part of an existing Event?

   Answering this question, of course, requires that you know what Apple means by an Event. See the box on page 90.

Note: What you see in the "Add to existing Event" pop-up menu depends on which hard drive you've selected. That's because iMovie only "knows about" the Events on the currently selected hard drive.

5. **If you have a high-definition camcorder, choose either "Large – 960x540" or "Full – 1920x1080."**

   This final option (Figure 4-7) appears only when you're importing video from a high-definition camcorder, one that captures video in the so-called 1080i format. (That term refers to the fact that it reproduces a scene using 1,080 fine horizontal lines, which is very sharp indeed. Actually, the "i" means that you see two sets of 540 lines, odds and evens, interlaced with each other, flashed alternately on the screen.)

   iMovie is offering you the chance to import a quarter-scale version of that gigantic video canvas, for the purposes of saving hard drive space. For assistance in making the Large vs. Full decision, see the box on the facing page.

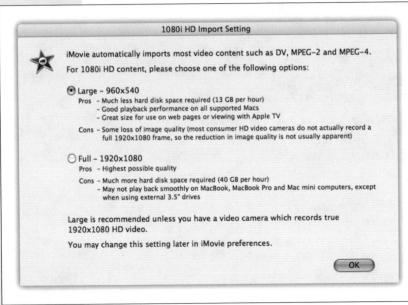

Figure 4-7:
When you're importing high-def video, iMovie offers you an opportunity to suck in a quarter-scale version of the original. You'll save an immense amount of hard drive space, but you probably won't see much difference in the picture quality.

6. **Click OK.**

   If you chose the Automatic option, iMovie now rewinds the tape to the beginning, then commands the camcorder to begin playback. As it plays, iMovie captures the video and stores it on your Mac. You can interrupt the process by clicking Stop, if necessary; at this point, iMovie displays a little congratulations message, revealing how many minutes' worth of video you imported. You can click OK and then import some more, if you like, starting from step 2.

Or you can walk away while iMovie works. You can even surf the Web, crunch some numbers, organize your pictures in iPhoto, or whatever you like. Since iMovie is a Mac OS X program, your Mac doesn't have to devote every atom of its energy to capturing video. It continues to give priority to capturing video, so your other programs may act a little drugged. But you can get meaningful work or reading done while you're dumping your footage into iMovie in the background.

If you let the Automatic importing proceed without interruption, iMovie auto-rewinds the tape when it reaches the end.

If you chose the Manual setting, you can use playback controls to operate the tape, shuttling through it to find the parts you want; use the Import button (and its alter ego, the Stop button) to capture only the good parts.

UP TO SPEED

Large vs. Full

High-def is great and all. Truly it is. It's mind-blowingly sharp, clear, and colorful. One frame of a true high-def 1080i picture is made up of 1,920 by 1,080 pixels. (Compare that with the pathetic dimensions of standard TV: 640 by 480 pixels.)

But high-def video also takes up a ridiculous amount of hard drive space: 40 *gigabytes per hour*. (Standard-resolution DV video takes up less than a third that much space.)

If your 160-gig hard drive is already half full with programs, photos, music, and other software, then you've got room for only 120 minutes of high-def video. And depending on how trigger-happy you are as a videographer (and how cute your kids are), that's not very much at all.

Apple is pointing out here, though, that 1080i video is actually overkill for most of the things people do with their home movies. It's much too big for a standard DVD, for example, whose picture is only 640 by 480 pixels. It's way too big to watch from a Web page. That size image may even be too big to fit on your monitor (an Apple 20-inch screen has a maximum resolution of 1,680 by 1,050 pixels—too small for a full 1080i movie).

So Apple is offering you the opportunity here to import your video at a *scaled-down* size: 960 by 540 pixels. If you do the math, you'll realize that that's actually only *one-quarter* the area of the original high-def picture (half in each dimension), which makes Apple's name for this—"Large"—a little suspicious.

Still, importing your high-def video at the Large (quarter-size) setting means that each hour of video takes up only 13 gigabytes per hour instead of 40. You'll also get smoother playback on slower Macs. And for most end-result showcases—like the Web, a DVD, or computer-screen playback—the resolution is still sensational. It's unlikely that you'd see any difference between the Large and the Full settings.

There *are* times when the Full setting is appropriate, however. You'd want that setting when you plan to export your edited version to Final Cut Pro (Apple's professional video editing program); when you intend to broadcast it on TV or use it in an actual, professional movie; or when you hope to burn it to a *high-definition* DVD someday (when such burners become available on the Mac).

Furthermore, as you weigh this decision, just remember one thing: You're making this choice *forever*. Hard drives will get bigger and cheaper. High-def DVDs will eventually become commonplace. Computer horsepower will someday double or quadruple. If you're working with precious, important video that you expect to be watched for decades to come, it might be worth keeping the full resolution just in case.

Note: Check your camcorder's manual. Not all camcorders advertised as "1080i high-def" do, in fact, record at the full 1,920 by 1,080 pixels. And if yours *doesn't*, there's very little downside to using the "Large" option here.

Tip: When you come to a scene you want to bring into iMovie, capture 3 to 5 seconds of footage before and after the interesting part. Later, when you're editing, that extra leading and trailing video (called *trim handles* by the pros) will give you the flexibility to choose exactly the right moment for the scene to begin and end. Furthermore, you need extra footage at the beginnings and ends of your clips if you want to use crossfades or similar transitions between them.

Unfortunately, the process isn't the speedy joyride it was in the previous version of iMovie, where you could just tap the Space bar (or click Import) every time you wanted to start or stop importing during playback.

In iMovie '08, each time you click Stop, iMovie locks you out for a minute or two while it displays the "Generating Thumbnails" message. That's iMovie's way of saying, "I'm processing this video and making some live, 'skimmable' filmstrips" (which are described on page 123).

Once that message disappears, you can use the playback controls to find the next bit of video that's worth importing—but you'll have to fill out the box shown in Figure 4-5 all over again, every time.

These frequent "Generating Thumbnails" and "Save to" interruptions are, for many people, a pretty strong argument for avoiding the Manual settings. The Automatic setting winds up saving you a lot of time—and doesn't cost you any extra disk space. (See the box on the facing page.)

7. **When you and iMovie are both finished, click Done.**

UP TO SPEED

The Definition of an Event

In iMovie terms, an Event is an organizational tool, like a label or a filing folder.

Sometimes, what constitutes an Event is obvious. A wedding, a graduation, a birthday party, and a ski trip would all be considered individual Events. You'd want all of the video scenes for somebody's wedding filed under a single heading, even if they were filmed over the course of a whole wedding weekend.

Sometimes, though, "Event" is a little nebulous. What if you film little scenes of your new baby every other day for a couple of months? Would they all be one Event called "August"? Or would you have a lot of little Events like "Overturned spaghetti bowl" and "First steps" ?

Or what if you take a 10-day cruise, featuring a stop every other day in a different port of call? Would the Event be "Mediterranean Cruise"? Or would you create individual Events for "Naples," "Monaco," and "Tunisia"?

The answer is, of course, "That's up to you." And that's why the options in Figure 4-5 appear at this point. If you want to create a new Event, type a name for it into the "Create new Event" box. But if you're importing more footage into an Event category you've already created, click "Add to existing Event," and then choose which Event from the pop-up menu.

Note: If you opt to create a new Event, you're also offered a checkbox called "Split days into new Events." If this option is turned on, then each day's worth of shooting becomes an Event all its own, even if it was all shot on the same vacation or wedding weekend. iMovie automatically adds day numbers to the Event names, like "Wedding – Day 1" and "Wedding – Day 2."

The Import window goes away. You return to the iMovie screen, where you can click the name of the Event you specified in step 4 to see the newly imported clips within it. Proceed to Chapter 5.

Automatic Scene Detection

You'll notice a handy iMovie feature when the importing is all over: It automatically creates an individual filmstrip (clip) for each scene you shot. An hour's worth of tape doesn't wind up as a single, mega-chunk of video—instead, you wind up with 30 or 40 individual clips, just the way you shot them.

What iMovie is actually doing is studying the *date and time stamp* that digital camcorders record into every frame of video. When iMovie detects a break in time, it assumes that you stopped recording, if only for a moment, and therefore that the next piece of footage should be considered a new shot. It turns each new shot into a new clip.

In general, this feature doesn't work if you haven't set your camcorder's clock. Automatic scene detection also doesn't work if you're playing from a nondigital tape using one of the techniques described on page 101.

Importing from Tapeless Camcorders

The beauty of tapeless camcorders is that, because they store video as computer files on a hard drive, DVD, or memory card, you don't have to wait for them to play into your Mac in real time. Instead, the importing process takes only as much time as iMovie needs to copy those files onto your Mac's hard drive. (At least in theory; read on.)

Note: If you have a camcorder that records onto miniature DVDs, see page 96 for some additional notes.

Once you're ready to transfer some video from your camcorder, here's how you should proceed.

1. **Connect the camcorder's USB cable to the Mac.**

FREQUENTLY ASKED QUESTION

Reclaiming Disk Space

I'm worried about using the Automatic importing option. It seems like overkill if it brings in a whole hour of video, and I wind up using only 10 minutes of it.

Yes, it's true that imported digital video eats up 13 gigabytes of disk space per hour of footage. (And that's standard-definition video. High-definition video eats up 40 gigs, at least if you choose the Full option described on page 89.)

The good news: As you work on your project, you can always delete the pieces you're not using—and reclaim the disk space they were using.

Details appear on page 153, but the point is this iMovie '08 feature is a big improvement over the previous iMovie version, where deleting part of a clip did not, in fact, reclaim any disk space. (iMovie 6 hung onto the *entire* clip, behind the scenes, just in case you ever changed your mind about which piece you were using in your movie.)

Most tapeless camcorders connect to the Mac using a USB cable, which comes right in the box. It connects to any of the Mac's skinny rectangular USB jacks, as shown in Figure 4-8.

2. **Turn on the camcorder. Switch it into PC mode.**

Figure 4-8:
Tapeless camcorders generally come with a USB cable. The little end plugs into the camcorder; you may have to open some tiny plastic doors on the camera to find the jack. The big end plugs into any of your Mac's USB jacks.

The wording might vary, but every tapeless camcorder has a mode for making PC or Mac connections (Figure 4-9).

At this point, iMovie should open automatically, if it wasn't open already. If

Figure 4-9:
Every camcorder has a switch or command that lets you connect it to a PC (or, in this case, a Mac). Most tapeless camcorders have a dedicated position on the main mode dial for this purpose, like this one.

everything is going well, a message appears at the top of the screen that says, "Generating thumbnails." Then, after a minute, you see the Importing screen depicted in Figure 4-10.

If iMovie does *not* open, or if the Importing screen does *not* appear, then run through the troubleshooting steps described on page 425.

You're about to experience one huge payoff of using a tapeless camcorder: instant access to individual scenes on the camcorder. That means, first of all, that you don't have to rewind or fast-forward to find a certain shot.

Furthermore, as you can see in Figure 4-10, iMovie lets you import only the shots you want, leaving the duds behind. That feature alone can represent a huge time savings over the old "import the whole tape" method.

Tip: If your camcorder stores its video on memory cards—SD cards, for example—then you have another option at this juncture. You could remove the card from the camcorder and insert it into a *card reader* that's attached to your Mac. (Card readers are supercheap—under $10. They're like tiny disk drives that attach to your Mac's USB jack.)

The advantage of the card-reader method is that you don't use up the camcorder's battery power while you're transferring your video.

Figure 4-10:
You can select individual scenes for importing without rewinding or fast-forwarding. You can also preview the recorded scenes before you bother importing them to the Mac. If your intention is to bring in most of the clips, just turn off the checkboxes that you don't want. If you want to import less than half of them, though, click Uncheck All, and then turn the checkboxes back on for the shots that you do want.

3. **Inspect the shots on the camcorder to see what's worth importing.**

   To play a shot, click its thumbnail and then click the ▶ button. Click the ◄ or ►
   buttons to skip to the previous or next shot on the camcorder (or just click the
   thumbnails on the screen in front of you).

4. **Specify which shots you want to import.**

   If you want to import everything on the camcorder, click Import All; then skip
   to step 5.

   If you want to import only some of the shots, move the Automatic/Manual switch
   in the lower-left corner of the Import window to Manual. Now you'll see little
   checkboxes appear on the shot thumbnails. All of them start out with checkmarks,
   meaning that iMovie intends to import all of them. See Figure 4-10 for tips on
   selecting the scenes you want. Once the correct shots have checkmarks, click
   Import Checked.

   At this point, the top of the window sprouts a little sheet of options (Figure 4-11).

Figure 4-11:
*This dialog box looks just like
the one that appears when
you import from tape. Once
again, it wants to know:
Where do you want to save
the incoming clips (which
hard drive)? What Event do
they belong to? And how big
do you really need hard drive
footage to be?*

5. **Indicate where you want to save the transferred video clips.**

   Most people save the incoming clips onto the main Mac hard drive. But if you've
   bought additional hard drives to hold your movies, you can use the "Save to" pop-
   up menu to choose a different hard drive to hold your video.

6. **Specify an Event.**

   The pair of choices shown in Figure 4-11 let you answer these questions: Were
   the scenes you're about to import filmed at a new Event? Or should they more
   properly be filed along with scenes you've already imported as part of an existing

Event? See the box on page 90 for the definition of an Event—and suggestions on what to choose here.

7. **If you have a high-def camcorder, choose either "Large – 960x540" or "Full – 1920x1080".**

You may not see the final option shown in Figure 4-11. It appears only when you're importing video from a high-definition camcorder, one that captures video in the so-called 1080i format.

See the box on page 89 for a discussion of this option and advice on what to choose.

8. **Click Import.**

Now iMovie swings into action. It begins slurping in the video from the camcorder's hard drive, DVD, or memory card. As it works, a progress counter ticks off the remaining shots left to import (Figure 4-12).

Figure 4-12:
Top: The counter here not only tells you how much longer you have to wait in "minutes: seconds" format, but also shows you how many video shots remain to be imported.

Bottom: When it's all over, the word "Imported" appears on each thumbnail. That's a handy reminder when you've only opted to import some of the clips.

Considering that fact that a tapeless camcorder is supposed to spare you the real-time importing process of a tape, you may be surprised at how much time the importing takes. AVCHD footage, in particular (page 19), takes a long time because iMovie has to convert it into an editable format; depending on the speed of your computer, you may wind up waiting 2.5 minutes for each minute of video. An hour's worth of video, in other words, can take two and a half hours to import.

You've been warned.

But never mind that; once the job is done, a message appears to congratulate you. It lets you know how many minutes and seconds of video you've imported, total, and how many clips (Figure 4-13).

Import complete

Imported 23 seconds from 1 clip.

OK

Figure 4-13:
Hey, you did it! You successfully imported some video from the camcorder to the Mac. You can now turn off the camcorder and put it away.

9. **Click OK.**

The congratulations message goes away.

10. **Click Done.**

The Import screen goes away. You arrive at the main iMovie screen, where your new video appears in the Events list at the left side of the screen. Page 84 describes this structure in more detail.

Note: Sony's HDR-SR1 and SR7 camcorders can record video in either of two formats: AVCHD and MPEG-2. iMovie can import both types, no problem (although, of course, an Intel-based Mac is required to import the AVCHD stuff.)

Here's a funny thing, though: If you've stored *both* formats on the camcorder's hard drive, iMovie can't see the AVCHD videos until you *first* import the MPEG-2 files and then erase them from the camcorder.

Importing from DVD Camcorders

In general, the routine for importing video from a DVD camcorder—at this writing, the most popular format on the market—is exactly the same as it is for other tapeless camcorders. The instructions begin on page 92.

There are, however, a few caveats:

- iMovie '08 doesn't import video from DVD camcorders that use the AVCHD video format (page 19). Unfortunately, that pretty much rules out all the *high-definition* DVD camcorders.

- Thanks to the hostility of the engineers who dreamed up the recordable DVD camcorder disc, most DVD camcorders offer multiple recording *formats*, with such cheerful names as DVD-Video and DVD-VR. Each has tradeoffs: One plays back in more DVD players, another lets you erase scenes before committing the DVD to plastic, and so on.

The thing is, you have to choose which format you want *at the time you put the blank DVD into the camcorder.* That's when the screen offers you the choice of formats.

The key here is to choose the DVD-Video format, sometimes called Standard. If you choose VR or DVD-VR instead, iMovie won't be able to import your recorded video. (When you connect the camcorder, it thinks that you've just inserted a DVD, rather than thinking that you've attached a disk full of video.)

Note: Apple cites Sony's DCR-DVD 403 and 505 models, Canon's DC20, and Panasonic's D300 as camcorders whose DVDs you have to format correctly as you put in the discs.

Recording Live from a Camcorder or iSight Camera

iMovie is also happy to capture video straight from a camera, sending whatever it "sees" directly into iMovie, live. You can perform this stunt in either of two ways:

- **Using an iSight camera.** All recent Mac laptops and iMacs have this tiny Apple video camera built right in, just above the screen (Figure 4-14). You can also buy an external iSight camera/microphone for use with other Mac models.

- **Using a camcorder.** Alternatively, you can connect a camcorder to your Mac and use it as a glorified eyeball.

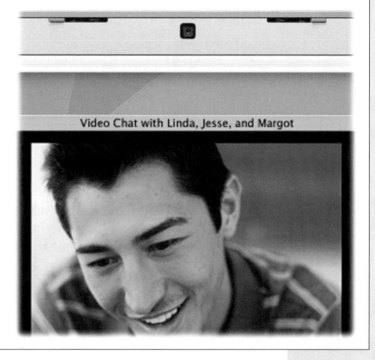

Figure 4-14:
This tiny lens, in the top of every MacBook, MacBook Pro, or iMac, records live video with surprisingly good quality.

Video Chat with Linda, Jesse, and Margot

Note: You can even use an ordinary Webcam, as long as it has a FireWire connector. Not many do.

Here are the steps:

1. **If you're using a camcorder, set its mode switch to Camera or Record (rather than VCR or Play, as you would if you were importing something you'd already recorded).**

   If you're using an iSight or FireWire Webcam, you can skip this step.

2. **Choose File→Import from Camera (⌘-I), or click the camcorder-shaped button at the left side of the screen.**

   Either way, the Import window opens. If everything's going your way, you'll see a live video image from your camera.

Note: If you have *more than one* camera connected—a camcorder connected to a Mac with an iSight, for example—choose the camera you want to use from the Import From pop-up menu (at the lower-left corner of the Import window).

3. **Click Capture.**

   Now the usual "Save to" dialog box appears, just as shown in Figure 4-5.

4. **From the "Save to" pop-up menu, choose a hard drive's name.**

   You're specifying where you want the imported video to be saved.

5. **Specify an Event.**

   The pair of choices shown in Figure 4-5 let you answer these questions: Were the scenes you're about to import filmed at a new Event? Or should they more properly be filed along with scenes you've already imported as part of an existing Event? See the box on page 90 for details on this choice.

6. **Click OK.**

   iMovie begins to import the live video image.

7. **To end the recording, click Stop.**

   iMovie enters its usual "Generating Thumbnails" state of catatonia for a few minutes.

   To record some more, repeat all this from step 2.

8. **When you're finished recording, click Done.**

   Your video recording appears in the Event you specified, ready for editing.

Importing Old iMovie Projects

Most software companies, most of the time, stick with certain time-honored traditions concerning software upgrades. One of them happens to be compatibility: If you release BeeKeeper Pro 7, it goes without saying that it can open files created by BeeKeeper Pro 6.

iMovie '08, though, is not actually an updated version of iMovie 6; it's a completely different program, written from scratch. Its ability to import older iMovie projects is extremely limited.

To bring in an older iMovie project, choose File→Import iMovie HD Project. The dialog box shown in Figure 4-15 appears. Here, you should make two decisions before choosing the old iMovie project you want to open:

- **Where you want to save the imported, converted project.** The "Save to" pop-up menu lists your hard drives and shows you how much space is available on each one.

- **How you want iMovie to handle high-definition video projects.** See page 89 for details on making a choice here.

Once you've made those choices, navigate to the iMovie project you want to import, and double-click its name or icon.

Figure 4-15:
In this dialog box, you specify what, where, and how you want to open an older iMovie project.

iMovie '08 springs into action, importing the video clips (making a new copy of them) and generating the filmstrip thumbnails that you'll work with as you edit. This process can take a good long time.

When it's all over, whatever clips you had placed into the iMovie timeline appear in the Project (storyboard) area, in the correct sequence, correctly trimmed. Leftover clips (the ones that were left unused on the Clips pane of the old project) are brought in, too. They show up in the Event that contains your project, just in case you want to add them to the project later.

On the other hand, iMovie '08 brings in only a few basic elements of the original iMovie project. To be precise:

- **You get only the clips.** iMovie '08 ignores all effects, titles, and credits.

- **You lose *all* audio work you've done.** iMovie '08 ignores everything in the old iMovie's two audio tracks, including music, narration, sound effects, or the audio "paste-over" cutaways.

- **You lose all special transitions.** If you used any transition effects in your older iMovie project, iMovie '08 replaces them all with generic crossfade dissolves.

If you really, truly want to go to all this trouble, you can now start over again, repairing and reconstructing the movie, restoring the elements that got lost during the import

---

UP TO SPEED

Apple Intermediate Codec

iMovie can *edit* lots more formats than before, including MPEG-2 SD (from memory-card camcorders), MPEG-4, iSight video (Photo JPEG), H.264, and DV.

But if you import the two high-definition camcorder formats, HDV (high-def tape camcorders) and AVCHD (high-def tapeless), it must first convert them to AIC.

A-I-what?

AIC stands for Apple Intermediate Codec. The conversion from high-def into AIC is what takes so bloomin' long when you try to import AVCHD clips.)

There's a good reason for this: HDV and AVCHD were never intended for editing. They were intended to store a lot of video quality in very little space on camcorders. So when you import them to the Mac, you're dealing with gigantic, unwieldy files that would make your processor wheeze

and gasp.

Enter AIC. The AIC format retains all the quality of the original video, but is much faster to edit, play, copy, paste, and so on.

When Apple calls this converter "intermediate," it's not kidding; the video remains in this format only while you're editing. When you finally do something with the finished movie, it's usually converted *back* into another format, like the H.264 format for YouTube or the .Mac Web Gallery (Chapter 15).

All of this explains, by the way, why you can't drag movies into the main iMovie window to import them. You have to drag them into an *Event* or use the File→Import Movies command. Both of those mechanisms convert incoming movies into the AIC format (and create filmstrip thumbnails for them) to prepare them for editing.

---

process. You might find the effort worthwhile if you want to use some of the iMovie '08 tools that aren't available in the old iMovie, like video cropping or rotation or one-click exporting to YouTube.

Otherwise, though, you might want to consider leaving your old iMovie projects just as they are. As Chapter 13 makes clear, the old iMovie version is still perfectly usable and freely available to you, so it might make more sense to leave it in its original format.

Dragging Video In from the Finder

iMovie can import movies directly from your hard drive, too—no camcorder needed. Position the iMovie window so that you can see the movie files in the Finder, and then drag their icons directly onto an Event in the Event list.

Alternatively, use the File→Import Movies command to find and select the movies you want to import. You'll be asked at that point which Event you want to contain the imported flicks.

Either way, you wind up with your digital movie files installed in an Event and ready to edit.

Importing Footage from Non-DV Tapes

We live in a transitional period. Millions of the world's existing camcorders and VCRs require VHS, VHS-C, or 8mm cassettes—that is, analog tapes instead of digital.

These days, people are buying only digital camcorders. But in the meantime, how are you supposed to import and edit the footage you shot before the digital era? Fortunately, this is fairly easy to do if you have the right equipment. You can take any of these four approaches, listed roughly in order of preference.

Note: When you use any of these approaches, iMovie won't be able to chop up the video into individual scene clips automatically, as it does for digital video. That's because old analog camcorders didn't stamp every frame of every shot with an invisible time code, so iMovie doesn't know when you stopped the camcorder.

Approach 1: Use a Recent Sony or Canon Camcorder

If you're in the market for a new digital camcorder, here's a great idea: Buy a Sony or Canon MiniDV camcorder with analog-to-digital *pass-through conversion.* In other words, the camcorder itself acts as a converter that turns the signal from your old analog tapes into a digital one that you can edit in iMovie.

The footage never hits a tape. Instead, it simply plays from your older VCR or camcorder directly into the Macintosh. (Not all camcorders have this feature, so ask before you buy. And on some models, you must use the camcorder's own menu system to enable the live pass-through.)

If you've got a drawerful of older tapes, such a camcorder is by far the most elegant and economical route, especially if you're shopping for a new camcorder anyway.

Approach 2: Record onto Your DV Camcorder

Even if your newish digital camcorder doesn't offer *real-time* analog-to-digital conversion, it may have analog inputs that let you record your older material onto a MiniDV tape in your *new* camcorder. If so, your problem is solved.

1. **Unplug the FireWire cable from the DV camcorder.**

   Most camcorders' analog inputs switch off when a FireWire cable is hooked up.

2. **Connect RCA cables from the Audio Output and Video Output jacks on the side of your older camcorder or VCR. Connect the opposite ends to the analog inputs of your DV camcorder.**

   Put a blank tape into your DV camcorder.

Tip: If both your old camcorder and your DV camcorder have *S-video* connectors (round, dime-sized jacks), use them instead. S-video connections offer higher quality than RCA connections. (Note that an S-video cable doesn't conduct sound, however. You still have to connect the red and white RCA cables to carry the left and right stereo sound channels.)

---

3. **Switch both camcorders into VTR or VCR mode.**

   You're about to make a copy of the older tape by playing it into the camcorder.

   By now, every fiber of your being may be screaming, "But analog copies make the quality deteriorate!" Relax. You're only making a single-generation copy. Actually, you're only making half an analog copy; it's being recorded digitally, so you lose only half as much quality as you would with a normal VCR-to-VCR duplicate. In other words, you probably won't be able to spot any picture deterioration. And you'll have the footage in digital format now forever, ready to make as many copies as you want with no further quality degradation.

4. **Press the Record button on the DV camcorder, and press Play on the older camcorder or VCR.**

   You can monitor your progress by watching the LCD screen of your camcorder. Remember that a DV cassette generally holds only 60 minutes of video, compared with 2 hours on many previous-format tapes. You may have to change DV cassettes halfway through the process.

When the transfer is finished, you can rewind the newly recorded DV cassette in the DV camcorder and then import it into iMovie exactly as described in this chapter.

Approach 3: Use a Media Converter

If your DV camcorder doesn't have analog inputs, you can buy an *analog-to-digital converter*—a box that sits between your Mac and your VCR or older camcorder (Figure 4-16). It's an unassuming half-pound gray box, about 3 by 5 inches. Its primary features include analog audio and video (and S-video) inputs, which accommodate your older video gear, and a FireWire jack, whose cable you can plug into your Mac.

Figure 4-16:
The Canopus ADVC-55 (http://canopus.com, about $210) requires no external power because it draws its juice from the Mac, via FireWire cable. It also offers double sets of inputs and outputs, so you can keep your TV and VCR hooked up simultaneously. And it can handle both NTSC (North American) or PAL (European) video signals.

You'll be very pleased with the video quality. And when it comes to converting older footage, the media-converter approach has a dramatic advantage over DV camcorders with analog inputs: You have to sit through the footage only once. As your old VCR or camcorder plays the tape through the converter, the Mac records it simultaneously. (Contrast with Approach 2, which requires you to play the footage *twice:* once to the DV camcorder, and then from there to the Mac.)

Unfortunately, you can't control these devices using iMovie's playback controls, as described in this chapter. Instead, you must transfer your footage manually by pressing Play on your VCR or old camcorder and then clicking Import on the iMovie screen. In that way, these converters aren't as convenient as an actual DV or Digital8 camcorder.

Approach 4: Use a Digital8 Camcorder

Sony's Digital8 family of camcorders accommodate 8mm, Hi-8, *and* Digital8 tapes, which are 8mm cassettes recorded digitally. (Low-end models may not offer this feature, however, so ask before you buy.) Just insert your old 8mm or Hi-8 cassettes into the camcorder and proceed as described in this chapter. iMovie never needs to know that the camcorder doesn't contain a DV cassette.

Actually, a Digital8 camcorder grants you even more flexibility than that. Most Digital8 camcorders also have *analog inputs,* which let you import footage from your VCR or other tape formats, just as described in Approach 2.

The Lay of the Land

I f you're coming to iMovie '08 from a previous version of iMovie, you're likely to be a bit confused; the design of this program is completely different. If you're coming to iMovie '08 from any *other* video editing program, you'll be equally baffled. And if you've never used any video editing program at all, well, you'll probably have no clue what's going on.

Before you delve into the actual experience of chopping and rearranging your video into a finished masterwork, therefore, it's worth sampling this brief chapter on what, exactly, iMovie is up to. Here's where you'll learn what's where on the screen, how to tailor the setup to your work habits, and where iMovie actually stores your video.

The Concept of Movie Projects

A *project,* in iMovie lingo, is an edited movie. The reason you're learning iMovie in the first place is to create these projects.

In previous versions of iMovie, a project was an icon on your desktop. It was really a cleverly disguised folder, and inside, you'd find all the gigantic movie clips that you'd used in your movie. This was convenient in one way—you could move the whole thing to another computer or back it up easily, for example.

But in another way, it wasn't ideal. If you wanted to use a particular piece of video in more than one project, you'd have to duplicate it (by pasting it into the second project), which ate up a lot more hard drive space.

iMovie '08 operates on a totally different system. The idea here is that your Events list (lower left of the iMovie window) shows every piece of video on your entire Mac—even video on other hard drives. All of it is available to all your projects, all the time.

When you choose a video clip to use in a project, you're not moving it anywhere.
You're just providing a *pointer* for the project, showing iMovie where to look for each
piece of video you want it to play.

This new system has a number of implications:

• You can use the same video clips in dozens of different movie projects, without
  ever eating up more disk space. (See Figure 5-1.)

Figure 5-1:
*An orange line across the
bottom edge lets you know
which chunks of a source clip
you've used in your project.
When you click a different
project, you'll see the orange
lines jump around. It's showing that you've used a different chunk of the same source
clip in the second project.*

• You can create multiple versions of the same project—a long one and a short one,
  for example—without worrying about filling up your hard drive.

Note: Yes, each project takes up disk space, but only an infinitesimal amount—about as much as a word
processor document. It contains only a text list of *pointers* to bits of video on your hard drive.

• There's no longer any easy way to back up or move a single project. Yes, there's a
  folder that contains your individual project files. (It's the Home→Movies→iMovie
  Projects folder.) But if you attempt to drag one of these project files to another
  disk, you'll have nothing, because you'll be leaving behind the raw video that it
  points to.

When you're finished editing a project, you'll probably want to *send* it somewhere: to
YouTube, to a DVD, to a QuickTime movie, or whatever. Only then does iMovie meld
together the editing information stored in the project file with the video information
stored in the clips—and produce a single, sharable movie file.

Creating a Project

To create a new project, you have three choices:

• Choose File→New Project.

• Press ⌘-N.

• Click the **+** button beneath the Projects list.

In each case, the New Project sheet appears, as shown in Figure 5-2. Here's where you give the project a name, and choose an *aspect ratio* for it. See page 109 for details on aspect ratios.

Figure 5-2:
Name your new project and specify the shape of the movie frame. The project will appear in the list at lower left.

Duplicating a Project

It's often useful to create several versions of the same project. You could have a short and a long version; an R-rated and a PG-rated version; or several differently edited cuts so you can get feedback on which one works best.

The beauty of iMovie '08 is that you can do this easily and simply, without filling up your hard drive with duplicated video files. Each version of the project calls upon the *same* underlying video files.

To duplicate a version, click its name, and then choose File→Duplicate Project. You'll see the new project appear in the Project Library, complete with a temporary name. (If the original was called "Baby Spaghetti on Head," the new one is called "Baby Spaghetti on Head – 1.") The naming rectangle appears open and highlighted, so you can simply type a new name right over what's there.

You can now get to work editing the new version independently of the original.

Renaming a Project

To give a project a new name, double-click the old name. The renaming rectangle opens so you can type a new title.

Project Folders

It's great to have every project you've ever done right at your fingertips at all times. But when your projects start to pile up, and the list gets unwieldy, you can create virtual folders to organize them.

Just click in the Project list and then choose File→New Folder. iMovie creates a new folder icon in the list, much the way iPhoto creates albums or iTunes creates playlists. Conveniently enough, you'll see these folders any time you use the Media Browser (page 282) to incorporate your iMovie work into iDVD, Keynote, and so on.

You can rename a folder by double-clicking it, or delete it (*and* everything inside it, as described next) by choosing File→Move Folder to Trash (⌘-Delete).

Deleting a Project

To get rid of a project, click its name, and then choose File→Move Project to Trash, or just press ⌘-Delete.

POWER USERS' CLINIC

Behind the Scenes at iMovie '08

In this chapter, you'll read about some sneaky ways to go behind iMovie's back. For example, if you delete a project or an Event by accident, you can rescue it by opening your Mac's Trash and manually restoring the files to their rightful place.

That's because, in the end, iMovie '08 is nothing more than a glorified front end for the files that actually sit on your hard drive. And knowing the relationship between what you see in iMovie and what you find in the Finder can be extremely useful.

It turns out that every project, Event, and camcorder clip that you see in iMovie corresponds to an icon in the Finder. Want to see them?

Then open your Home folder (in the Finder, choose Go→Home), and then double-click the Movies folder. (Alternatively, click Movies in the Sidebar at the left side of *any* Finder window.)

Here they are, the two special folders created by iMovie '08. One, called iMovie Projects, contains the icons for every project you've made in iMovie '08.

The other, called iMovie Events, contains individual *folders* for each import job you've done—one for each bunch of

video you've imported. And inside *those* folders are the actual QuickTime video clips that you imported that day.

Every time you open iMovie '08, what you see in the Project Library and the Event Library is nothing more than a mirror of what's in the Finder, in those two iMovie folders within the Movies folder. (OK, you also see the videos you keep in iPhoto, but that's another story.)

In general, you shouldn't ever need to muck around in these Finder folders—but there's no harm in doing so. If you rename, delete, or add to these files, you won't mess anything up; you'll just see those changes reflected in iMovie's lists the next time you open the program.

(In fact, you can Control-click any filmstrip in iMovie and, from the shortcut menu, choose Reveal in Finder. You'll go right to the corresponding QuickTime clip.)

Keep your knowledge of this one-to-one correspondence tucked away for the day when you delete a project or an Event by accident. You'll be grateful that you know how to restore them by putting them back manually (see Figure 5-3 on the facing page).

Behind the scenes, iMovie moves the selected project to the *Macintosh* Trash. (To prove it to yourself, click the Trash icon on your Dock and open the iMovie Temporary Items folder.)

It may have disappeared from iMovie, but it's not *completely* gone until you return to your Desktop, choose Finder→Empty Trash, and click OK.

Tip: Once you've created a project and have started working on it, you may as well *hide* the Project list; it's just eating up screen space, after all. See page 117.

Undeleting a Project

On the other hand, what if you delete a project—and then change your mind? Or you delete the wrong one by accident?

As long as you haven't yet emptied the Macintosh Trash, you can get that project back. Figure 5-3 shows the procedure.

Figure 5-3:
Behind the scenes, every iMovie project is represented by an icon in your Home→Movies→ iMovie Projects folder (front window). To rescue a project you've deleted by accident, then, open the Trash (click its Dock icon), open the iMovie Temporary Items folder, and then drag the project's icon from the Trash back into the iMovie Projects folder. The next time you open iMovie, you'll find the project right back in the Projects list, ready to go.

Aspect Ratios: The Missing Manual

Aspect ratio is an annoying geek term for *shape of the movie frame.* Having to learn about aspect ratios is an unfortunate requirement if you're going to master video editing.

A standard 1980 TV set's screen is not the same shape as a movie screen. The TV is almost square; the movie is wide and short. They have different *aspect ratios*.

Standard TV sets have a 4:3 aspect ratio. Those are the horizontal:vertical proportions. So if your screen is 4 feet high, it's 3 feet wide.

Figure 5-4:
iMovie offers you a choice of three aspect ratios: Standard (like a traditional TV), Widescreen (like a high-def TV), or iPhone (which has a nonstandard screen shape). You can always change your mind later.

High-def TV screens, on the other hand, are 16:9. If the width is 16 feet wide, then the height is 9 feet (and you have a *heck* of a big TV).

Note: Weirdly, 16:9 is *not* the standard aspect ratio for Hollywood movies! Those are usually 1.85:1 or, believe it or not, 2.35:1. (Don't ask why movie aspect ratios always have 1 in the denominator. Nobody ever accused the video industry of being consistent.)

Believe it or not, those aren't even the only common aspect ratios. Consider the iPhone, which, of course, Apple hopes that everybody also owns. *Its* screen is 3:2!

Every time you create a new project, then, iMovie asks you, "What aspect ratio would you like, O Master?"

If the result will play on a standard TV, choose "Standard (4:3)." If it will play on a high-def TV screen, choose "Widescreen (16:9)." If it will play on an iPhone, well, you can guess.

And if it will play on the Internet or as a QuickTime movie, the aspect ratio really makes no difference. Choose the one that best fits the original video shape.

Mismatched Aspect Ratios

One cool thing about iMovie '08 is that it can handle *multiple* aspect ratios in the same movie. You can mix and match source video, filmed in different aspect ratios, within a single fixed-shape project.

How is this possible? Because whenever iMovie encounters source video that doesn't fit the frame, it does one of two things:

- Adds black letterbox bars above and below the picture (or on either side).

- Blows up the video large enough to fill the frame. In the process, of course, some of the picture gets chopped off at the top and bottom of the frame, or on the right and left sides.

Figure 5-5 shows both situations.

Figure 5-5:
Top: If you choose the Standard frame for your movie, then standard video fits fine—but widescreen video, shown here, has to be either cropped or letterboxed.

Bottom: If you choose Widescreen for your movie, then standard 4:3 video, shown here, also has to be either cropped or letterboxed. (Actually, when the black bars are vertical, some people call them pillarbox bars.)

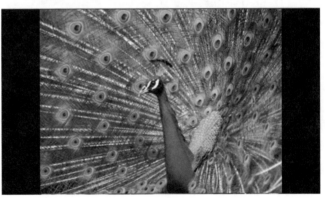

So those are iMovie's two solutions: letterbox bars or cropping. But *you* have to tell it which solution you prefer.

To do that, click the name of the project, and then choose File→Project Properties (⌘-J). In the Project Properties dialog box (Figure 5-6), use the "Initial Video Placement" pop-up menu to choose either Crop (the misfitting video gets enlarged to fill the frame, even though you'll lose some at the edges) or Fit in Frame (you get letterbox bars).

Click OK.

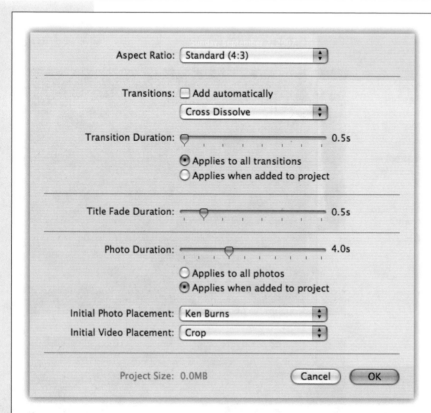

Figure 5-6:
The Project Properties dialog box lets you specify how you want misfitting video wedged into your chosen movie-frame shape: by cropping or by zooming. Here, you can also change the aspect ratio for a project—even one that's underway.

Changing Your Project's Aspect Ratio

Yes, iMovie asks you what aspect ratio you want when you first create a project. But you're not locked in. You can change your mind at any moment.

Suppose, for example, that you chose Widescreen when you created the project—but later, after editing for a while, you realize that the vast majority of your footage is standard-definition video. In that case, you'll probably want to make the whole project Standard, to minimize the amount of time your audience spends staring at letterbox bars.

To change aspect ratios for a project that's already underway, click its name, and then choose File→Project Properties (⌘-J). In the Properties dialog box (Figure 5-6), choose a new aspect ratio from the Aspect Ratio pop-up menu at the top, and then click OK.

iMovie dutifully reformats the movie, adding *different* letterbox bars as necessary, or zooming mismatched videos *differently.*

All About Events

At the lower-left corner of the iMovie window, you see the Event library. It's supposed to be a massive repository of all the video on your entire computer, from all sources (Figure 5-7).

Figure 5-7:
When you click an Event name (left), iMovie shows you all the video clips that it contains (right).

It's organized like this:

- **Last Import.** Click this heading to view, in the clips area, all the video clips that you *most recently* imported from your camcorder. Often, this is precisely what you want.

- **iPhoto Videos.** Click this icon to see all the movie clips you've shot with your digital *still* camera (not your camcorder). In the Great iLife Master Plan, of course, it's not iMovie that handles photos and videos from still cameras—it's *iPhoto.* So here, iMovie is giving you handy, one-click access to all the videos that you've imported into iPhoto from your still camera.

- **2007, 2006, 2005....** These year headings organize your camcorder video collection into annual clumps. Click the flippy triangle to expand or collapse the year heading, so that you can see all the video batches within it.

What you actually see in one of these expanded lists is all the individual import jobs you performed during that year, each with whatever name you gave it. If you click one of these Event names, the right side of the window shows you all the video clips inside it.

Fine-Tuning the Events List

iMovie offers a copious slew of options designed to help you manage big video collections. (Some of these options make it clear that Apple expects all of us to have multiple two-terabyte hard drives in the very near future.)

- **Break it down by volume.** In the View menu, you'll find a command called Events by Volume. Here, Apple doesn't mean *audio* volume; it doesn't even mean *quantity*. Apple is using the term "volume" to mean "disk."

  So if you choose View→Events by Volume, iMovie adds headings representing each of your hard drives, showing which video is stored on each.

- **Break it out by month.** You can also make iMovie break down each year's worth of Events by *month*. Just choose View→Events by Month. Now iMovie adds month subheadings within each year category: May, August, or whatever. (To save space, it adds headings only for the months when you actually shot video.)

- **Reverse the sort order.** Ordinarily, iMovie lists your events in reverse chronological order—from oldest to newest. If you choose View→Most Recent Events at Top, then the sorting order is flipped. Newest video appears at the top.

- **Adjust the font size.** Out of the box, iMovie assumes that you have a lot of video to manage. If you don't, or if you have a nice big monitor (or aging eyes), you can ask iMovie to enlarge the type size for the Events and Projects lists. Choose iMovie→ Preferences, and then turn on "Use large font for project and Event lists."

- **Add the dates.** Having your footage grouped by month is handy, but it can be even handier to see the exact *dates* of your filming. Once again, asking iMovie to display

---

POWER USERS' CLINIC

Changing the Date of an Event

It could happen. Maybe your camcorder didn't date-stamp your video properly. Or maybe you just need a serious alibi. Either way, you'll be happy to learn that you can manually change the date and time stamps on your video clips, and therefore the way that iMovie sorts them. (This works with video imported by iMovie '08—not, for example, movies that you import from the hard drive or from iMovie 6.)

To make the change, find the actual video files on your hard drive. They're in the iMovie Events folder described on page 108.

Inside the individual Event folders, the files have names like "clip-2007-11-15 19;18;11.dv." The first set of numbers represents the year, month, and date. The second set, with semicolons, represents the hour (on a 24-hour, military-style clock), minute, and seconds.

If you change these numbers to match the date you want for your footage, the next time you open iMovie, it will recreate the thumbnail clips and sort the clips according to the new, improved dates. You've just rewritten history.

---

this information eats up screen space, but is very helpful if your Events list isn't already sprawling off the screen.

To make it so, choose iMovie→Preferences, and then turn on "Show date ranges for Events." As shown in Figure 5-8, you now see little date ranges for your movies.

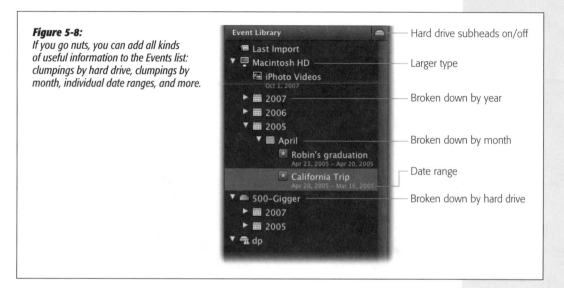

Figure 5-8:
If you go nuts, you can add all kinds of useful information to the Events list: clumpings by hard drive, clumpings by month, individual date ranges, and more.

Hard drive subheads on/off

Larger type

Broken down by year

Broken down by month

Date range

Broken down by hard drive

Splitting Events

Very often, you might want to split one Event into two. After all, a MiniDV tape holds an hour of footage; a hard drive camcorder holds five hours or more. On any given day, what you're importing to iMovie is probably made up of video you shot on different days. It will all wind up in one Event—unless you manually split it apart into different ones.

Figure 5-9:
To split an Event, inspect the video clips within it by skimming and playing. When you find a clip that was obviously shot on a different day, as part of a different real-life event, click it. Then choose File→Split Event Before Selected Clip. iMovie places that clip, and all later ones, into a new Event. (The Event browser is shown here swapped to the top of the screen for clarity; see Figure 5-12.)

To split an event, click its name in iMovie, and then proceed as shown in Figure 5-9.

Merging Events

You can combine Events, too. For example, if you import from your camcorder after each day at Disney World, you might want to combine it all into one Event at the end of the three-day vacation.

To do that, see Figure 5-10.

Figure 5-10:
To merge two Events, simply drag the name of one onto the name of another (top). iMovie asks what you want to name the newly merged Event; type a name, and then click OK.

(Once again, the Event library is shown here swapped to the top of the screen.)

Renaming an Event

You rename an Event the same way you rename a project—that is, double-click its existing name. The renaming rectangle appears, so you can edit or replace the name.

Deleting an Event

You delete Events the same way you delete projects—highlight an Event's name, and then press ⌘-Delete (or choose File→Move Event to Trash).

iMovie gets rid of the event and moves it to the Macintosh Trash. (You can even click the Trash icon on your Dock and *see* it inside the iMovie Temporary Items folder.)

Be careful, though. When you delete an Event, you're also deleting *all the video inside it!* All of those clips you so carefully imported are now sitting in the Trash, poised for extinction.

In a pinch, you can rescue them. Just open the Trash, open iMovie Temporary Items, and drag the Event's folder back into your Home→Movies→iMovie Events folder. The procedure is almost identical to what's depicted in Figure 5-3.

If you do decide you're really finished with those clips, return to your Desktop, choose Finder→Empty Trash, and then click OK. Now they're really, truly gone.

Four Ways to Remodel Your Workspace

iMovie '08 is refreshingly respectful of your screen real estate. It offers a bunch of different ways to maximize your working area without the hassle of buying a whole new monitor.

Hide the Projects or Events List

Once you're well into working on a movie, you probably don't need the list of projects staring you in the face. Chances are, you'll be working on only *one* project for the next few hours. By hiding the list of projects, you gain more space for the storyboard itself.

To hide the Projects list, choose Window→Project Library, or just click the Hide/Show Project List button identified in Figure 5-11. The list goes away, and the storyboard area expands to fill the larger area.

You can hide the Events list the same way, and for the same reason: because when you're editing your Disney vacation video, you probably don't need to be staring at the list of other vacation footage. This time, choose Window→Event Library, or click the Show/Hide Events List button (Figure 5-11). The list goes away, and the video-clip area expands.

To bring either list back, repeat the procedure. A checkmark appears next to Projects or Events in the Window menu when the list is visible.

Tip: Don't forget that you can also make the *font* bigger in these two lists; see page 114.

Make the Clips Smaller

In iMovie '08, your video clips are represented by *filmstrips*—multiframe horizontal strips whose lengths are proportional to the clip duration. You can read more about filmstrips in Chapter 6.

For now, it's enough to note that you can adjust the size of these filmstrips, both vertically and horizontally. Making them smaller gives you less information about what's in a clip, of course, but also makes more clips fit your screen.

See Figure 5-11 for instructions on making these adjustments.

Tip: Note that when you drag the flimstrip-length slider to its extreme-right position (as shown in Figure 5-11, top), every video clip is represented by *one* frame. The filmstrips' relative lengths are no longer represented; every clip has just one icon. This arrangement makes clips very easy to move around, resequence, and so on. It also makes iMovie more familiar if you're used to working in previous versions of the program.

Adjust the Viewer Size

The *Viewer*, in iMovie, is the playback window at the upper-right corner of the screen. It's always locked into the iMovie window—you can't drag it around freely—but you can change its size.

To do that, choose from the Window→Viewer submenu: either Small, Medium, or Large. Or better yet, learn the keyboard shortcuts for these so you can flip between them while you work: ⌘-5, ⌘-6, and ⌘-7.

Hide/show Project list   Filmstrip length (Projects)

Hide/show   Thumbnail
Event list   size

Filmstrip length
(Events)

Figure 5-11:
You can change the look of iMovie rather radically. You can hide the lists at the left side. To adjust the height of your filmstrips, drag the Thumbnail Size slider; it affects the filmstrips both in the Event browser and in the storyboard. To adjust the horizontal size of your film-strips, drag the slider at the lower-right of the storyboard or Event browser. At its far-left setting, each frame of a filmstrip represents a half-second of video. At its far-right setting, each clip is represented by a single frame.

The advantage of a large Viewer is, of course, that you get the best view of your movie as you work. The disadvantage is that a large Viewer eats up screen space; on smaller screens, it squishes down the Events area so much that you have to do more scrolling.

Tip: For more gradations of size and control, you can also resize the viewer by dragging the central, horizontal iMovie toolbar up or down. Use any blank spot as a handle.

Swap the Two Clip Areas

When you first fire up iMovie, the storyboard area, where you actually build your movie, is fairly small. It's wedged in between the Project Library and the Viewer.

The source-clips area, on the other hand, gets far more space, because it doesn't have the Viewer to contend with.

As you work on your movie, therefore, you may wish that you could *swap* these two areas. You may wish that the *storyboard* could be the one with room to run, especially in the later stages of editing.

In that case, choose Window→Swap Events and Projects, or click the Swap *button* shown in Figure 5-12.

Tip: It probably goes without saying—but the first and most important step you can take to avoid having to use iMovie's scroll bars is to make the iMovie window itself as big as it can go! To do that, choose Window→Zoom, or click the little round, green Zoom button in the upper-left corner of the window.

Figure 5-12:
When you hit the Swap button), iMovie swaps the storyboard and Event browser areas, complete with an animated "funneling" effect to make sure you understand how you've just flopped the iMovie layout upside-down. (For even more fun, press the Shift key while you click the Swap button. It's the only form of slow motion that iMovie '08 can do.)

Building the Movie

W hether you're working on your Mac or in a multimillion-dollar Hollywood professional studio, film editing boils down to three tiny tasks: selecting, trimming, and rearranging *clips*. Of course, that's like saying that there's nothing more to painting than mixing various amounts of red, yellow, and blue. The art of video editing lies in your decisions about *which* clips you select, *how* you trim them, and *what* order you put them in.

When you get right down to it, iMovie boils down to two big storage places for video clips. There's the *Event browser,* usually the bottom half of the screen, where all your raw, unedited video shots live. And there's the *storyboard,* usually the top half, which is where you assemble and edit your masterpiece.

At its simplest, then, iMovie editing is all about this three-step process:

1. **Review your video in the Event browser; find the good parts.**

2. **Add those chunks to the storyboard, where iMovie plays them in one seamless pass, from left to right.**

3. **Add crossfades, titles (credits), music, and effects.**

This chapter is dedicated to showing you the mechanics of the first two tasks: selecting raw footage and adding it to your movie. The following chapters cover the last step.

Phase 1: Review Your Clips (Skim + Play)

Video editing always starts out with a pile of raw, unedited footage. In iMovie's case, that's the bunch of clips in the Event browser. Click an Event's name to see what video is inside.

Filmstrips

In iMovie '08, every imported camcorder shot is represented by a *filmstrip*—a horizontal bar whose length represents the duration of the clip. The filmstrip is made up of individual sample frames from the clip.

Note: If a filmstrip is too wide for the iMovie window, it wraps around to the next line. A ragged filmstrip edge tells you that it's been wrapped in this way. Think of that ragged edge as the video version of a hyphen.

Each of these frames represents, for example, 5 seconds of actual video. So a 30-second video clip would appear as a filmstrip that's six frames long (Figure 6-1).

Figure 6-1:
Top: This filmstrip is 12 seconds long. So with the slider set to "2 seconds," each frame stands in for 2 seconds of video. That's why there are six frames.

Bottom: But if you adjust the slider, you can change how many seconds of video each frame represents. Here, each frame represents a 10-second video chunk (or a part thereof), which is why there are now only two.

Using the slider at the lower-right corner of the window, you can adjust the relative lengths of the filmstrips in your Event browser area. An identical slider appears beneath the project storyboard area, meaning that you can adjust the filmstrip lengths independently for these two clip display areas.

So what's the right setting for these sliders? That's totally up to you, but here are some suggestions:

- At the slider's extreme-right position, every video clip is represented by *one* frame. The filmstrips' relative lengths are no longer represented; every clip appears as an icon. This arrangement makes clips very easy to move around, resequence, and so on. It makes a very long movie fit on your screen without scrolling.

  It also makes iMovie a lot more familiar if you're used to working in previous versions of the program.

- At the slider's extreme-left position, each frame of the filmstrip represents a *half second* of video. At this position, you can actually make frame-by-frame edits; see the box on page 128.

- As you work, you can fiddle with the slider, zooming in and zooming out as necessary. When you need to tweak the precise starting point of a piece of audio, for example, you might want to zoom in (drag the slider to the left); when you want to get a good overview of a long movie, you might want to zoom out (drag the slider to the right).

Skimming

At this point, you're about to learn the two iMovie skills you'll use most of all: *skimming* and *playing*. Practice them, commit them to memory, make them automatic, and you'll absolutely fly through the editing process.

Skimming means *moving* your cursor across a filmstrip. Do not *drag*, which would mean pressing the mouse button. Just *point* with the mouse. Move the cursor across a filmstrip without clicking or dragging.

The *Playhead*—a vertical line, the height of the filmstrip—moves along with your cursor. And as you skim, the Viewer window shows the underlying video playing back at high speed—or medium speed, or slow speed, depending on your cursor speed. (You also see the same video playing within the filmstrip itself, beneath your cursor.)

Tip: Skimming also plays the *sound* of whatever clip you're examining—fast or slow, forward or reverse. Usually, that's helpful. But if the audio is driving you crazy, you can shut it up. Click the Audio Skimming button, shown in Figure 6-2, so that it turns yellow. Or choose View→Audio Skimming (⌘-K) so that the checkmark disappears.

Repeat the process to turn audio skimming back on.

Skimming might take some getting used to, because it's such an unusual computer technique; it's probably the first time in history that moving the mouse without clicking has done *anything* besides, well, moving the cursor to a new spot. But it means that

---

BEHIND THE SCENES

Secrets of the Filmstrip

When you stop and think about it, a filmstrip behaves just like a miniature QuickTime movie—and, in fact, that's precisely what it is.

You know how, after you import video, iMovie grinds to a halt and displays a message for several minutes that says, "Generating thumbnails"?

What it's actually doing is creating a little, tiny QuickTime movie, 190 by 60 pixels, for use as the filmstrip for that clip. When you skim by moving your pointer, all you're really doing is playing back that QuickTime movie.

You can even see these "thumbnail movies." They're sitting right there in your Movies→iMovie Events→[Name of the event]→Movie Thumbnails folder. (Look, but don't touch. Leave these miniatures alone.)

iMovie's most impressive stunt, in other words, is the way it lets you work with these miniatures as a representation for the enormous, full-frame clips—and plays the big ones back on command.

---

you can control not only the speed of the playback, but also the direction—forward or reverse—in real time, almost effortlessly.

Skimming works anywhere fine filmstrips are found—either in the Event browser or in the project storyboard (Figure 6-2).

Tip: You might sometimes wish that you could use the cursor as, well, a *cursor* instead of always making stuff play back. You might wish, for example, that you could freeze the frame as you skim—"Stay on this frame for just a sec"—while you go off to do something else with the cursor.

You can. When you get to the spot you want to freeze, hold down the Control key. iMovie turns off skimming (leaves the same video frame on the screen) until you release the Control key.

Skimming audio on/off

Move the mouse without clicking

Figure 6-2:
When you skim, you move the cursor across the face of a filmstrip without clicking. It's a fast, simple way to find out what's in a clip without having it sit through a full playback. Click the Audio button to turn off the audio-scrubbing sound, which can be annoying.

GEM IN THE ROUGH

Playhead Info

One nice thing about working with *digital* video is that every frame of every shot is, behind the scenes, date- and time-stamped. (This presumes, of course, that you set your camcorder's internal clock when you bought it!) Years later, you can return to some captured video and see when, exactly, you filmed it.

Ordinarily, iMovie hides this information, on the assumption that the screen is quite busy enough already. (Besides, you

may already have asked it to show the dates of your imports right in the Events list, as described on page 114.)

To see the dates of your video, choose View→Playhead Info, or just press ⌘-Y. Now when you skim, a handy info balloon floats above your play-head that says, for example, "Sunday, February 10, 2008, 4:35 PM." It also shows how many seconds into the clip your pointer is.

Press ⌘-Y again to hide the balloon.

Playback

Skimming is great for quickly getting the gist of what's in your captured clips. But unless you're some kind of quasi-mechanical cyborg, you'll find it very difficult to skim at exactly the right speed for *real-time* playback.

Fortunately, iMovie can also play back clips all by itself, at the proper speed. To do that, use the Space bar on your keyboard as the start/stop control. Hitting Space always begins playing video at the position of your cursor. And it always stops when you press Space again.

Once you've mastered that difficult technique, you're ready for the real gem: using skimming and playback *together*.

It works like this: Point at a filmstrip with your mouse, skimming as you scan around, looking for the part you want to watch. When you get close to the right spot, tap the Space bar. Playback begins from the precise position of your mouse.

Tap Space to stop playback, then move your mouse to another spot, and tap the Space bar again. In this way, you can jump around, spot-inspecting your clips, or even *pieces* of your clips, without ever touching the mouse button—and without ever having to wait.

Tip: Instead of point-and-tap, point-and-tap, here's an alternative system: double-click. Wherever you double-click a filmstrip in iMovie, playback begins at that spot.

You can stop playback with another click, or with a tap of the Space bar.

Actually, there are four other ways to play back a source clip or your movie in progress, complete with corresponding keyboard shortcuts. Page 136 has details on all four:

- Play the selected chunk (/ key).

- Play from the beginning (\ key).

- Play the 2 or 6 seconds around your cursor ([or] key).

- Play full screen (⌘-G).

GEM IN THE ROUGH

The Mighty Undo

As programs go, iMovie is a forgiving one. Its Edit→Undo (⌘-Z) command is an *unlimited* Undo command, meaning that you can retrace (undo) your steps, one at a time, working backward all the way back to the moment when you opened iMovie. (You can even unimport a clip from your camcorder!)

There's an Edit→Redo command, too (Shift-⌘-Z), so you can undo your undoing.

Phase 2: Select the Good Bits

The reason you're reviewing the clips in the Event browser, of course, is to find the good parts—the highlights, the pieces you want to include in your finished movie. Once you've selected a chunk, you can drag it into the storyboard to make it part of your movie.

Selecting comes in handy for other purposes, too. As you'll read in the next chapter, you can designate part of a clip as either a Favorite (a snippet you know you'll want to come back to later) or as a Reject (a worthless shot). These steps, too, require that you first *select* the piece of clip that you want to flag.

Since selecting is such a critical step in iMovie moviemaking, Apple made sure you had all kinds of different ways to make a selection. The following pages review them one by one.

Select by Dragging

The first selection method is the one you'll probably use the most often: dragging. That is, slide the cursor across some footage while pressing the mouse button, just the way you'd select text in a word processor.

iMovie indicates which part of a clip you've selected by surrounding it with a yellow rectangle (Figure 6-3). The bottom edge of the iMovie window shows you how many seconds' worth of video you've highlighted, relative to the original clip. Once you've made a selection this way, you can adjust it; see page 129.

Figure 6-3:
You can highlight a piece of a clip by dragging across it. iMovie shows you what you've selected by enclosing it with a yellow boundary.

Select 4-Second Chunks

iMovie makes it easy to build your movie from video snippets that are all exactly the same length—4-second chunks, for example. The iMovie online help says, over and over again, that using chunks of the same duration throughout your movie creates "an evenly paced project."

Unless you're creating a music video of snowboarders, however, using all 4-second chunks also creates "an artificially limiting project." Real-life events don't unfurl in consistent lengths.

Still, having the ability to select tidy 4-second (or 2-second, or 10-second) chunks is occasionally handy—when you want to make the video match the chord changes in the background music, for example.

To choose a 4-second chunk, just click a filmstrip in the Event browser (without dragging). Your click marks the starting point; iMovie instantly selects the following four seconds of video.

Tip: You can change the factory setting, 4 seconds, to any length between 1 and 10 seconds. To do that, choose iMovie→Preferences, and drag the "Clicking in Event browser selects:" slider (Figure 6-4).

Figure 6-4:
What does a single click on a filmstrip in the Event browser mean? That's up to you. Out of the box, it means "Select 4 seconds" (or whatever duration you choose using the slider). But you can have it mean, "Select the whole clip" if you prefer.

Selecting Entire Clips

In some cases, you might find that all of this dragging or 4-second-clicking business is just too much fussiness—that you really want to select *entire clips* from the Event browser.

Depending on the situation, you can select an entire clip in any of three ways:

- *Option-click* a filmstrip to highlight the whole thing.

- Click to select *part* of a clip, and then choose Edit→Select Entire Clip (⌘-A).

- Finally, if you *never* use that 4-second-clip selection feature, you can tell iMovie that one click on a filmstrip *always* selects the whole thing, even without the Option key.

To do that, choose iMovie→Preferences. Click "Clicking in Event browser selects entire clips" (Figure 6-4) and then close the Preferences window.

Note: These instructions apply only to selections in the Event browser. When you click a clip in your project storyboard, you *always* select the entire clip.

Selecting Multiple Clips

It's often useful to be able to select *more* than one clip at a time. Imagine how much faster it can be to work with clips—delete them, drag them, cut and paste them, mark them as Favorites or Rejects, apply keywords to them—all at once.

That dream became a reality with the iMovie 7.1 update.

Clips in the storyboard now behave just like icons in the Finder. For example:

- **To highlight all the filmstrips.** Press ⌘-A (the equivalent of the Edit→Select All command).

- **To highlight random icons.** If you want to highlight, for example, only the first, third, and seventh clips in the storyboard, start by clicking icon No. 1. Then ⌘-click each of the others.

POWER USERS' CLINIC

Frame-Accurate Editing

When iMovie '08 first appeared, there was an outcry from veterans of the previous iMovie version. A long list of iMovie 6 features seemed to be missing.

That's true, of course. But not all of the "missing features" are indeed missing. One of them is *frame-accurate* editing.

Modern digital video flashes about 30 pictures per second to create the illusion of motion. If you wanted to be able to edit down to a specific frame, then, you'd need to be able to zoom in close enough to see those 30 individual frames per second. It sure looks at first as though iMovie works in much larger chunks.

But you can indeed make those more precise adjustments. First, zoom way in, using the "Frames per thumbnail" slider

at the lower-right corner of the window. In fact, if you drag this slider all the way to the left, each frame of the filmstrip represents a *half second* of video.

Then, if you drag the end of the yellow selection boundary carefully and slowly, you can actually feel it snap against *individual frames* of the recording—15 times for every filmstrip frame, in fact.

Let's see—each frame of your filmstrip represents half a second, and there are 15 snaps per frame. Sure enough, that's true frame-accurate editing.

(The Shift-arrow key tip that appears on page 130 offers another method—that doesn't require zooming in first.)

• **To remove a clip from the selection.** If you're highlighting a long string of icons and click one by mistake, you don't have to start over. Instead, just ⌘-click it again, so that the highlighting disappears. (If you do want to start over, you can deselect all selected clips by clicking any empty part of the window.)

The ⌘ key trick is especially handy if you want to select *almost* all the icons in a window. Press ⌘-A to select everything in the storyboard, then ⌘-click any unwanted icons to deselect them.

• **To highlight consecutive clips.** Click the first clip you want to highlight, and then Shift-click the last one. All the clips in between are automatically selected, along with the two you clicked. (This one works in both the storyboard *and* the Event browser.)

Adjusting a Selection

Once you've highlighted a portion of a filmstrip, you're not stuck with that yellow boundary just the way it is. You can adjust it within the filmstrip in any of four ways:

• Drag the vertical end handles of the yellow border to the right or left to select more or less of the clip.

• Shift-click another spot in the filmstrip. The nearest edge of the yellow border jumps to the location of your click, which makes the selection longer or shorter. Pressing Shift-arrow key (right or left) does the same thing.

• Drag the top or bottom edge of the yellow border to move the *entire* border, sliding it around without changing its length, on the filmstrip. This technique selects a new chunk of footage.

Figure 6-5:
Top: You can adjust the start or end points of a selection by dragging the side handles.

Middle: You can Shift-click to extend, or shrink, the right or left edge of the border. (iMovie adjusts whichever end of the border is closest to your Shift-click.)

Bottom: You can use the top or bottom edge of the yellow border as a handle to slide the entire selection area horizontally, without changing its duration. (You can also press the left or right arrow keys.)

• Press the right or left arrow keys to slide the selection border right or left one frame at a time.

Figure 6-5 shows these techniques.

Playing a Selection

As you know, tapping the Space bar always begins playing a video clip *at the position of the cursor*. But when you're making a selection, fiddling with that yellow border, that's not always what you want.

In fact, it's probably *not* what you want.

A much more useful keystroke would be one that means, "Play what I've selected." And that's what the / key is for. (That's the slash next to the period key.)

Tap it once to play whatever is selected; tap a second time to stop playback.

Deselecting

To *deselect* whatever's selected—that is, to take away the yellow border entirely—use any of these three techniques:

• Click anywhere in the dark gray background.

• Choose Edit→Select None.

• Press Shift-⌘-A.

Actually, there's another way, too, but it involves a little backstory; see the box on the facing page.

GEM IN THE ROUGH

The Arrow-Key Trick

By tapping the right or left arrow keys, you can "walk through" a clip, frame by frame, as though you're watching the world's least interesting slideshow. You'll even hear "one frame" of the audio, if you've got the audio turned on.

Hold down these arrow keys steadily to make the frame-by-frame parade go by faster—on a fast Mac, in fact, you get real-time playback when you hold down the arrow keys.

If you add the Shift key when you press the arrow, you make the nearest yellow selection border snap to your Playhead

position. That's handy when you want to fine-tune a selection. You can slap the yellow border around a certain clip, walk with the arrow keys to see if there might be a better ending point, and—when you're about to land on just the right frame—press *Shift*-arrow. The closest vertical end of the yellow border snaps to the current frame.

In time, you can get extremely good at finding or selecting exact frames in a particular piece of footage just by mastering the arrow-key shortcuts. (These shortcuts work only when the clip isn't playing.)

Phase 3: Build the Storyboard

The project storyboard is the large work area that starts out at the top of the screen, as shown in Figure 6-6. The key to building a movie is moving your selected video bits from the Event browser into this storyboard.

Adding to the End of the Storyboard

Most people, most of the time, build a movie by reviewing the raw footage from left to right—from beginning to end—and choosing bits, in sequence, to include in the edited masterpiece. In such cases, you'll want to add your selected clip or clips to the *end* of your storyboard.

iMovie offers two ways to do that. Select some video in the Event browser, and then do one of these things:

- Press the letter E key.
- Click the Add Selection button (identified in Figure 6-6).

In either case, you'll see the selected chunk(s) of video fly from the Event browser to the *end* of your storyboard.

Note: It's perfectly legal to add multiple clips to the storyboard at once; just Shift-click to select several filmstrips in the Event browser first. But if you do so, iMovie will scold you: "You may achieve better results by individually adding only the best segments of your video." Yeah, yeah, we get it—less is more.

WORKAROUND WORKSHOP

When One Click Means "Deselect"

The way iMovie comes from the factory, *one click* on any clip in the Event browser selects a piece of it. Four seconds of it, to be exact.

That's a pretty unusual behavior, if you think about it. After all, one click in a word processor doesn't select four words; one click in Photoshop doesn't select four inches of a photo; and so on.

In fact, what one click *usually* means in a creative program—word processor, Photoshop, and so on—is, "Deselect everything."

Apple's programmers must have had quite a discussion about this point: What should a single click do in the Event browser?

In the end, they went with the "4-second selection" thing,

remaining true, as always, to the overarching goal of rapid movie assembly.

But at least they've acknowledged the weirdness of that choice. And for anyone who's a little freaked out by the appearance of that 4-second yellow border every time they click, Apple has built in a way out.

Choose iMovie→Preferences. In Preferences, turn on "Clicking in Event browser deselects all." Close the Preferences dialog box.

From now on, one click anywhere in the Event browser (except inside a yellow selection border) deselects everything. Of course, you can still select portions of clips (by dragging across them) or entire clips (by Option-clicking them); you just won't be surprised by the yellow border when you *don't* expect it.

To check the result, point to the storyboard (without clicking) just before the spot where the new video has landed, and then press the Space bar.

Add Selection button

Figure 6-6:
When the storyboard area is fresh and new, the message "Drag media here to create a new project" appears. (It means "drag movies here," of course.)

But clicking the Add Selection button, or pressing the letter E, works just as well.

Adding to the Middle

You don't *have* to add selected video to the end of the storyboard. You can also place it between two existing clips, or even right smack in the middle of an existing clip.

To do that, just drag the selected clip (using anything inside the yellow border as a handle) right up into the storyboard, and release the mouse when it's where you want it. Figure 6-7 shows the effect.

Once again, you'll probably want to inspect the insertion immediately afterward. Point (without clicking) just before the inserted video and tap the Space bar for a quick playback.

The Orange Stripe

Each time you add some source video to your edited movie, iMovie slaps an orange stripe across the bottom of the original clip in the Event browser. That's a reminder that you've *used* this segment in your project. As your work proceeds, you'll be able to tell, with a glance at your Event browser, what proportion of the original video you've used in the finished opus.

Now, remember that all of your edited movies—your *projects*—draw upon the same well of source video on your computer. What's cool, therefore, is that iMovie memorizes the orange striping differently for every project. If you've used a different set of Little League footage in each of three projects, then you'll see the stripes jump around in the Event browser as you click each project in turn.

Figure 6-7:
Once you've highlighted some video (top), you can drag it into position anywhere in the storyboard—in the gap between two existing clips, for example, or even right in the middle of an existing clip. In that case, iMovie splits the existing clip in half, and puts the new footage between the split pieces.

Don't Remember to Save

You don't have to save your work. iMovie '08 automatically saves as you go. (It doesn't even have a Save command.)

Phase 2-3 (Alternate): Paint-to-Insert

Having slogged this far into the chapter already, you might think that iMovie offers quite enough ways to drop footage into your movie. But believe it or not, there's yet another method.

This one makes throwing together a movie *crazy* fast. It turns your cursor into a sort of magic paintbrush. As you drag across filmstrips in the Event browser, any segment that you "paint across" with your mouse instantly becomes part of your movie. You'll never see any yellow borders. It's not select-and-then-place; it's *selectandplace*. One step, not two.

Here's how to set up this advanced technique:

1. **Choose iMovie→Preferences.**

   The Preferences dialog box appears.

2. **Turn on "Show advanced tools." Close the Preferences dialog box.**

   You might not notice at first, but there are now several additional buttons in the toolbar across the center of the iMovie window (Figure 6-8).

Edit (paint-to-insert) button

Figure 6-8:
In paint-to-insert mode, the second toolbar icon (to the right of the standard arrow cursor tool) is permanently selected. Now you can just drag across bits of footage at high speed, each time adding it to the end of your storyboard.

3. **Make sure that no video is selected in iMovie.**

   If you have video somewhere, then some of the toolbar icons appear in washed-out light gray. In that case, try tapping the Esc key, and/or choose Edit→Select None. When nothing is selected, the toolbar tools are black and gray, ready to be used.

4. **Click the Edit tool, or press the letter E key.**

The Edit tool, better described now as the Paint-to-Insert tool, is identified in Figure 6-8.

All that is setup. Now you're ready to go to work.

From now on, forget everything you've read about (1) selecting a chunk of video and then (2) adding it to the storyboard. Instead, any time you drag the mouse across a filmstrip, iMovie adds it *instantly* to the end of the storyboard. If you know what you're doing, you can whip together a movie made of 15 shots with only 15 swipes of the mouse.

This trick takes some getting used to. You have to train yourself never to touch the mouse button except when you're prepared to commit something to the finished movie.

You should still use the skim-and-play technique to identify the chunks you want to add; performed correctly, skimming and playing doesn't involve the mouse button at all. (Point and tap the Space bar; point and tap the Space bar.) When you've found a worthy chunk, *then* drag across it with the mouse button down.

Or, faster still, Option-click a filmstrip to add the entire thing to the project.

If you add something by mistake, or if you undershoot or overshoot, remember iMovie's all-powerful Undo command. Hit ⌘-Z to rewind your last step and try again.

To turn off paint-to-insert mode, press the letter E key (or click the Edit Tool icon) again. You're back in yellow-border mode.

Phase 4: Fine-Tune the Edit

Once you've got a rough cut of your storyboard, you may consider the Event browser a lot less necessary. Your work focus will probably shift to the storyboard from here on in. Now, in other words, might be a good time to hide the Projects list and move the whole storyboard to the wider space at the *bottom* of the iMovie window, as described in the previous chapter.

The rest of this chapter explores a few of the ways you can fine-tune the movie in progress.

Storyboard Playback

You can use instant playback to spot-check your storyboard work in the Viewer window. Since you'll probably be doing a lot of this, iMovie offers multiple techniques:

• **Anyplace playback.** Point (without clicking) to any spot; press the Space bar, or double-click, to begin playback. Press Space again to stop.

Tip: As you near completion of your movie, you might want to make the Viewer bigger, so you see your work closer to full size. See page 117.

- **Selection playback.** Make a selection. (Either click a clip once to select the whole thing, or drag across it to choose just part.) Then press the forward slash key (/, next to the period key) to play back *just that selection* from the beginning. Press / again to stop.

- **Two-second (or six-second) playback.** Here's a supremely handy new feature that debuted in iMovie '08 version 7.1: You can tap the [or] keys to play back the 3 or 6 seconds, respectively, immediately before and after the position of your cursor. It's sort of like a skim-and-play all at once.

  If some video is highlighted with the yellow boundary, then these keystrokes play back either the *first* second (or 3 seconds) of the selection, or the *last* second (or 3 seconds), depending on which is closer to your cursor.

Tip: You can press these bracket keys even when your mouse button is down in the process of making a selection. That's a fantastic way to gauge whether you've selected exactly the right bit.

- **Whole-storyboard playback.** Press the backslash key (\, above the Return key) to play the *entire* storyboard from the beginning. Press \ again (or the Space bar) to stop.

Note: There are menu equivalents for all three of these commands in the View menu: Play, Play Selection, and Play from Beginning. But it's far more efficient to use the keyboard shortcuts.

No matter how you started playback, you can always stop by clicking in the iMovie window or tapping the Space bar.

Full-Screen Playback

You can make the Viewer window bigger to get a more detailed view of your video using the ⌘-5, ⌘-6, and ⌘-7 keystrokes; see page 117. But eventually, you'll want to treat yourself to iMovie's IMAX mode: *full-screen* playback. That's when all the controls and menus of iMovie itself disappear, and the video fills your entire monitor.

Here again, iMovie offers different approaches:

- **Play from the pointer.** Point without clicking to any spot in the storyboard. Then press ⌘-G to begin *full-screen* playback of that selected video.

- **Play the entire storyboard.** Click the Full-screen Playback button (identified in Figure 6-9) to play your storyboard from the beginning. Choosing View→Play Full Screen does the same thing.

Note: In theory, ⌘-G is the keyboard equivalent for the View→Full Screen command. But they are not, in fact, equivalent.

The ⌘-G is the *only way* to begin full-screen playback from a specific spot. If you choose View→Full Screen from the menu, iMovie begins playing the storyboard from the *beginning*. (It has to—since you moved your mouse to the menu, you're no longer pointing to a certain spot in the video!)

Figure 6-9:
Top: Click the Full Screen button to begin playback of your entire storyboard from the beginning.

Bottom: During full-screen playback, if you wiggle your mouse, you get the navigation filmstrip shown here at bottom. Click the filmstrip, then skim it or drag the mouse to jump to a new spot without exiting full-screen mode.

Once full-screen playback is underway, just moving your mouse produces the navigation strip shown in Figure 6-9. Its behavior is a little quirky, but here are the basics:

• Press the Space bar to start and stop playback without exiting Full Screen mode. Or click the **❙❙/▶** button at the left end of the navigation filmstrip.

• During playback, click another spot in the navigation filmstrip to jump there and pause.

• During playback, *double-click* another spot in the filmstrip to jump there *without* pausing.

• When you've paused playback, you can skim the navigation filmstrip (point without clicking) to explore the movie. Press the Space bar to begin playback from any spot.

When you're finished with full-screen playback, click the ⊗ button, or press the Esc key, to return to the iMovie window. (Or, if you wish that iMovie would exit Full Screen automatically after each playback, turn on that option in iMovie→Preferences.)

Tip: Usually, your camcorder's video has lower resolution than your Mac's screen. To fill your screen for playback, then, iMovie *stretches* the picture, which lowers its quality slightly.

In a few other cases (for example, high-def video on a small laptop), the video may actually be too *big* for the screen. In that case, iMovie has to scrunch it *down* to fit.

If you choose iMovie→Preferences, however, you can control all of this stretching and scrunching. The "Fullscreen playback size" pop-up menu lets you change the Entire Screen setting to Actual Size (the cleanest settings for video that's smaller than your screen) or Half Size (best-looking if the video is bigger than the screen).

Rearranging Video

Unless your last name is Spielberg or Scorsese—and maybe even if it is—the first place you put a clip in the storyboard won't *always* be the best spot for it. Sooner or later, you'll wish you could move shots around in the film.

You can, if you know the secret.

1. **Select the part you want to move.**

   If it's an entire clip, simply click it in the storyboard. iMovie highlights the entire clip.

   If it's just part of a clip, drag to select the chunk you want. Fine-tune it with the arrow keys as described on page 129.

Tip: At this point, consider adjusting the storyboard's zoom level (page 117) so you'll have finer control over where you're about to place the moved video.

2. **Drag the selection to its new location.**

   Click carefully inside the outlined yellow-border area before you drag. When your cursor reaches the approximate destination, keep your finger on the mouse button, but move the cursor from side to side to find the precise target frame. Yes, you're actually skimming with the mouse button down, but don't let that confuse you.

   You can drop the dragged clip either in between two clips in the storyboard, or even right in the middle of a clip. In that event, iMovie splits the target clip into pieces to make room (Figure 6-10).

Copying and Pasting Video

Dragging isn't the only way to move footage around in iMovie; the Copy, Cut, and Paste commands can feel more precise. These commands are also the *only* way to copy edited footage from one project to another.

Tip: When you copy and paste clips, you're never duplicating files on your hard drive. So don't worry about eating up free space.

Figure 6-10:
Rearranging scenes in the storyboard is a two-step process.

Top: Select what you want to move, whether it's a full clip or just part of one.

Bottom: Drag it where you want it to go, whether it's in between two clips or right in the middle of another clip.

You already know how to indicate *what* you want to cut or copy; just use the selection techniques described on page 128.

Then use the Edit→Cut or Edit→Copy command (⌘-X or ⌘-C). Point where you want to paste the copied material (do not click), and then choose Edit→Paste (⌘-V).

Presto! The cut or copied material appears at the position of your cursor, and shoves the rest of the movie to the right to make room.

Shortening or Lengthening Clips

Almost nobody hits the camcorder's Record button at the precise instant when the action begins and stops recording the instant it stops. Life is just too unpredictable, not to mention animals, geysers, and children.

Most of the time, of course, you'll trim out the boring stuff in the Event browser before you add it to the storyboard. Sometimes, though, you'll discover only *after* you've put the clips into the storyboard that the clip-shortening process isn't quite right. Maybe the shots are still too languorous, and should be shorter. Or the shots are *too* quick, and it's going to be hard for your audience to figure out what's going on.

In both cases, it would be nice to be able to lengthen or shorten a clip even after it's been placed in the storyboard.

Note: "Lengthen a clip?" That's right. iMovie is a *nondestructive* editing program. No matter how much editing you do, iMovie never, ever changes the original imported video on your hard drive.

For example, after you've shortened a clip by hacking a piece off the right end, you can later change your mind, even three Presidential administrations later. You can restore some or all of the missing footage, using the techniques described on these pages.

Fortunately, iMovie is crawling with ways to perform these adjustments, even after the clips are in the storyboard. They boil down to these approaches:

- Shorten a clip by selecting the part you want to *delete*.

- Shorten a clip by selecting the part you want to *keep*.

- Shorten, lengthen, or re-edit a clip in iMovie's oddball Trim window.

- Lengthen a clip by clicking iMovie's hidden Extend buttons.

Note: When you *shorten* a clip, all subsequent clips slide to the left to close up the gap. (That's called *ripple* editing.) On the other hand, when you lengthen a clip, exposing previously hidden footage, iMovie shoves all subsequent clips to the *right* to make room. Your movie, as a result, gets longer.

The following pages cover all four methods.

Select a Piece to Delete

Suppose a clip is running too long in your edited movie. Fortunately, having mastered the art of selecting a portion of a clip, as described earlier, you're ready to put it to work. You can shave off some footage from only one end of your clip, or even right from the middle.

All you have to do is highlight the footage you want to delete, and then choose Edit→Cut (or press ⌘-X).

iMovie promptly trims away whatever was inside the yellow border. As a bonus, your invisible Clipboard now contains the snipped piece, which you're welcome to paste right back into the storyboard (at the position of your pointer) using the Edit→Paste command, in case you might need it again.

Tip: You can also press the Delete key to get rid of the selected video. The difference is that the Delete key doesn't put the cut material onto the Clipboard, ready for pasting, as the Cut command does.

On the other hand, the Delete/Clear command doesn't replace what's *already* on the Clipboard, unlike the Cut command.

If you're not prepared for it, the results can be startling. If you cut a chunk out of the middle of the clip, iMovie throws back at you the *two end pieces*—as two separate clips, side by side in the storyboard.

Select the Piece to Keep

If you want to trim some footage off *both* ends of a clip, it's quicker to highlight the part in the middle that you want to *keep*. That is, highlight the part you want, and then choose Edit→Trim to Selection. (Or press ⌘-B. Why B stands for "trim to selection" is left for you to figure out.)

When you use this command, what used to be the selected part of the clip becomes, in effect, the *entire* clip. The clip is shorter now, as a tap on the Space bar proves.

Use the Trim Window

All right, the Delete and Trim to Selection commands—mirror images of each other—are both quick, efficient ways to *shorten* a clip in the storyboard. But what if you decide you've cropped out *too much,* and you want to restore some? Or what if you can't even grasp what you're looking at, and wish you could see the entire original clip?

That's what the Trim window is all about.

You can open it in either of two ways:

- Point to a clip without clicking. Click the tiny clock icon that appears at its lower-left corner (Figure 6-11, top).

- Click the clip in question and then choose Edit→Trim (⌘-R).

Tip: The meaning of the ⌘-R keystroke changes depending on what's highlighted—a still photo, a title, a clip—but one thing remains constant: It always means "change this thing's duration."

---

iMovie replaces the entire storyboard area with a new display, labeled Trim Clip. You can see it at bottom in Figure 6-11.

In essence, what you're seeing here is the full-length clip, just as it originally appeared in the Event browser. The yellow border indicates which part you originally selected to include.

You can use all the usual tricks to play back what's here, including skimming, hitting the Space bar, or double-clicking. Or, in case you were just struck by a girder and have forgotten all of that, you can click the Play button that appears right in the Trim window.

Your main business here is to readjust the selection border. Make it longer if you want to include more of the clip in your project, shorter if you want less. Or grab the top or bottom edge of the yellow boundary and slide the entire thing horizontally to include an earlier or later portion (of the same duration). Page 129 details all the fun you can have with the yellow border.

Tip: Press Option-left arrow or Option-right arrow to add one frame at a time to the video selection in the Trim window. (You're shifting either the beginning or the end of the yellow border, whichever is closest to your cursor.)

When you're finished with your reselection, click Done.

Figure 6-11:
Top: To open the Trim window, click the tiny clock button that appears when you point to a clip. (The number above it tells you how many seconds long the clip is at the moment.)

Bottom: In the Trim window, the yellow border shows which piece of the clip you're currently using in your movie. The darkened portions are the ones you've so far eliminated.

Fine-Tuning with the Extendo Buttons

The Trim window is a handy way to rechop a clip—especially if you want to *extend* the amount you're including in the project. But having to open a special editing window just to snap a few more frames onto a clip is a hassle.

There is, fortunately, another way to extend a cropped clip without having to bother with the Trim window: Use the Extendo buttons (what Apple calls the Fine Tuning buttons), which debuted in iMovie's 7.1 update. To make them appear, you can use either the mouse or the keyboard:

- **Point to a clip** to make the tiny double-arrow icons appear in the corners (Figure 6-12) and then click one of them. (If you don't see the icons, they may have been turned off in Preferences.)

- **Point to either end of a clip,** and press ⌘-Option.

In either case, the ends of the selection border turn orange, and nearby filmstrips scoot away to make a little room. At this point, you can drag the orange handle to the left *or* right, either shortening the clip or (by revealing previously hidden footage) lengthening it by up to 1 second. To trim more than that, you can either open the Trim window—or just click and use the Extendo buttons again. And again. And again.

Tip: You can also *fine*-fine tune a clip's length with a secret keyboard shortcut. Press Option-left arrow or Option-right arrow. Each press makes the clip one frame shorter or longer. (You're changing either the beginning or the end of the clip, whichever is closest to your cursor.)

Figure 6-12:
Buttons appear in the corners of any storyboard clip that you've previously shortened from either end. Click one of these buttons to make the orange end-adjustment handles appear.

Extendo button

Splitting a Clip

The techniques described in the previous section work well when you want to remove some footage from a clip. Sometimes, however, it can be useful to split a clip *without* deleting footage in the process. For example, in a clip of a young snowboarder heading rapidly toward a ramp and then sailing into space, you could insert a quick shot of his horrified parents' faces.

Or you might just want to break off one piece of a clip to use somewhere else in the movie.

The Split Clip command is exactly what you need in that case. Just make a selection in any storyboard filmstrip:

- **To chop the clip into two pieces.** Select from the desired split point to the end (or beginning) of the clip.

Figure 6-13:
After you split a clip, you wind up with two or three pieces. (You can tell where these clips were split by examining the filmstrip corners; they're sharp rather than rounded.)

Split: Sharp corners

Normal: Rounded corners

- **To chop the clip into three pieces.** Select whatever piece of it that you want to wind up as the center piece. The end pieces will wind up as separate clips.

Either way, you can use the Shift-arrow technique described on page 130 to find exactly the right spot.

Then choose Edit→Split Clip. The results are shown in Figure 6-13.

Tip: If you change your mind immediately, you can always use the Undo command to take back that step. But if you split a clip and change your mind *much later,* after you've done a lot of other editing, iMovie can still accommodate you. Click the first part of a split clip and choose Edit→Join Clip; iMovie reunites it with the section to its right, assuming that it's still adjacent.

Video Chunks: Keywords, Favorites, and Rejects

I n iMovie '08, all the imported footage on all your hard drives is sitting there, like paints on a palette, to inspire your editorial brilliance. But that blessing is also a curse, because it's such a huge pile of video to manage—and a lot of it's dreck.

Fortunately, iMovie comes with a set of tools—unusual in a video editing program— that are specifically designed to help you sort and manage these vast chunks of video. Working in the Event browser, you can:

- Flag pieces of clips as your favorites, to make them easy to find.

- Flag pieces of your clips as rejects—bad footage that you'll either *probably* or *definitely* never want to incorporate into an edited project.

  The "probably" stuff you can just hide from view. The "definitely" stuff you can tell iMovie to delete, freeing up space on your hard drive, even if that entails snipping off only portions of clips.

- Flag pieces of clips with **keywords** of your choosing—your children's names, adjectives, characterizations like "action" or "moody," whatever you like. Later, you can summon all matching keywords with a single click.

This short chapter explores these clip-flagging tools, and also describes the proper way to get rid of bad shots forever.

Marking Favorites and Rejects: Two-Step Method

Most people, most of the time, flag a clip, or a piece of one, as a favorite or a reject using this technique:

1. **In the Event browser, select the video you like (or don't like).**

   You can use any of the selection techniques described on page 128. That is, you can select an entire clip, multiple clips, or only part of one.

2. **Flag it.**

   To flag the selection as a favorite, click the black star icon (Figure 7-1), or just press the letter F on your keyboard.

   To flag it as a reject, either click the X icon, press the letter R key, choose Edit→Reject Selection, or press the Delete key.

Tip: You can also choose Edit→Reject Entire Clip (or press Option-Delete) to flag the *entire* clip as worthless. This method can save you a little time, because it means that you can select any old sloppy slice of the clip first, rather than highlighting the entire thing.

If you're flagged something as a favorite, it sprouts a green line across the top edge (Figure 7-1).

If you've marked something as a reject, it sprouts a *red* line across the top edge—and promptly disappears from view. (If it doesn't disappear, you must have changed the pop-up menu shown in Figure 7-3 to say Show: All Clips.)

Figure 7-1:
Select some video, and then click the black star button identified here. iMovie adds a green stripe, which designates a favorite shot.

Mark Selection as Favorite – F

Marking Favorites and Rejects: One-Step Method

The usual method of flagging your best and worst footage takes only two steps. But believe it or not, even that's excessive in the eyes of Apple's Faster Editing team.

Hidden in the motley assortment of options known as the iMovie Advanced Tools lies another method, which reduces the favoriting and rejecting process down to *one* step.

To set up this method, choose iMovie→Preferences. Turn on "Show advanced tools," and then close Preferences.

Now have a look at the horizontal toolbar that divides the iMovie screen. It has sprouted a few additional tools, as shown in Figure 7-2. But you're not interested in the new icons. You're interested in the new behavior of three *original* buttons, the ones near the center—solid star, hollow star, and X. They now represent virtual *paintbrushes* that turn anything you touch with your cursor into a favorite or a reject.

Figure 7-2:
The three icons identified here let you "paint" portions of your Event browser filmstrips with green highlighting (meaning "favorite") or red highlighting ("reject"). You don't have to select and then click the button.

Unmark

Mark as Favorite   Mark as Reject

For example, here's an amazingly fast way to zoom through a freshly imported pile of footage, marking favorite scenes as you go:

1. **Click the Favorite button (the black star), or press the letter F key.**

   The black star icon darkens to show that you've selected it. Your cursor is now loaded with green Favorite paint, so be careful.

   Take a moment to skim (move your cursor over the filmstrip without clicking) and play (tap Space) to identify the good parts, and then:

2. **Drag across the filmstrip to indicate the good stuff.**

   The green "favorite" strip appears instantly. Instead of "select, then flag as favorite," you've managed to select and flag-as-favorite all in one stroke.

Marking sections as rejects is just as easy, except you press the letter R key in step 1 (or click the X button). Now, when you drag across filmstrips in step 2, they instantly become rejects, which usually means that they disappear from view.

Tip: To mark an *entire* clip as a favorite or a reject, Option-click it. That's a lot faster than dragging.

For best results, then, you should plow through your footage, riding the F and R keys (favorite and reject modes), painting across good and bad sections of video as you go. Later, this prescreening process will make assembling your movie a heck of a lot easier and faster.

Tip: If you mark something as a reject or a favorite by mistake, you can unmark it quickly: hold down the ⌘ key. iMovie switches temporarily to the Unmark tool described below, just long enough for you to paint over (or Option-click) the mismarked footage.

Release the ⌘ key to return to the tool you were using.

Unmarking

No matter which method you used to mark favorites or rejects, it's easy to change your mind later. Just repeat the original process, but use the hollow star (or the letter U key) as your paintbrush.

- To use the "select, then flag" method, select the piece of filmstrip that you want to unmark, and then click the hollow-star icon (or press the letter U).

- If you prefer the Advanced-tools, "paintbrush" method, turn on the Advanced tools (page 146, bottom). Then click the hollow-star icon (or press the letter U), and begin painting. When you drag your cursor across a piece of filmstrip, you remove *all* colored strips from it—both the favorite and the reject strips.

Note: Of course, you can't unmark rejected footage unless you can *see* it on the screen. The following section shows you how to bring hidden footage back into view.

Selecting Marked Footage

In time, your Event footage will be twinkling with green, red, blue, and even orange bars, corresponding to the various ways you've flagged or used your footage.

But these colored stripes aren't just labels; they're also handles. Carefully double-click directly *on* one of the colored stripes, and presto: iMovie neatly selects just the piece of filmstrip that's marked by that bar, ready for unmarking, cutting, deleting, placing in your project, or whatever.

Hiding and Showing Favorites and Rejects

Flagging clips as favorites and rejects wouldn't save you any time if all it did was draw colored stripes on your filmstrips. The real payoff comes when you tell iMovie to *hide* everything except your favorites or rejects, making it exceptionally easy to work with a big pool of extraordinary footage, or to review all the lousy footage before you delete it for good.

You can access these various hide/show modes in two places: in the View menu, or in the "Show" pop-up menu on the bottom edge of the iMovie window.

- **Show only favorites.** Choose Favorites Only, either from the View menu or the "Show" pop-up menu (Figure 7-3).

- **Show everything except rejects.** Choose "Favorites and Unmarked," either from the View menu or the "Show" pop-up menu.

  This is what you see most of the time: iMovie shows you everything that you've marked as favorite *and* everything you haven't marked either way. Only the rejects are hidden.

Tip: Since this is the view Apple expects you'll use most often, it has a keyboard shortcut all its own: ⌘-L.

Figure 7-3:
When you choose Favorites Only from this pop-up menu, the Event browser hides all your rejects and all footage that you haven't marked at all. This feature should translate into even faster movie-building time, since you're working exclusively with clips you already know you love.

- **Show everything.** Choose All Clips, either from the View menu or the "Show" pop-up menu.

  Now you're seeing everything: favorites, rejects, and unmarked. This can be a handy anti-desperation view when you can't find a certain shot that you're sure you had before. It rules out the possibility that you've flagged it as a favorite or a reject and then hidden it.

- **Show only rejects.** Choose Rejected Only, either from the View menu or the "Show" pop-up menu.

  Now you're seeing *only* the bad stuff. Everything else is hidden.

  You'd summon this view when hunting for a clip you can't seem to find among the good stuff (maybe you rejected it by mistake), or when reviewing your rejected footage before deleting it for good, as described on page 153.

Keywords

In iPhoto, iMovie's sibling in the iLife suite, *keywords* play an important role in helping you manage tens of thousands of photos.

A keyword is a text label that you can slap on a picture, a tag that will help you pluck that photo (and ones like it) out of a haystack later. Some people make keywords for the people in the pictures: "Casey," "Mom," "Robin," and so on; others use them to identify what's going on in the photo: "Vacation," "Home," "Kids." Either way, the point is that if you're consistent in using keywords, you can later round up *all* photos bearing a certain keyword ("Robin") with one click.

Well, don't look now, but keywords have come to iMovie. Actually, *do* look now; you probably won't see them, though, because they're hidden at first. iMovie keywords belong to the handful of miscellaneous efficiency features that Apple calls the Advanced tools, so most people don't even know that they exist.

To make them appear, choose iMovie→Preferences. Turn on "Show advanced tools," and then close Preferences.

Now, if you look carefully, you'll see that a new button has appeared on iMovie's central toolbar—one that looks like an old-fashioned key. Click it to open the Keywords window (Figure 7-4).

Figure 7-4:
Top: When the Advanced Tools are turned on, the Keywords button appears. Click it to open the Keywords window (bottom). You can now "paint" a selected keyword, or several, onto a filmstrip, using the Auto-Apply tab. Or, on the Inspector tab, you can select some video first on the filmstrip, and then turn on the relevant keyword checkboxes.

You can see that Apple has started you out with several sample keywords: Indoor, Outdoor, Landscape, People, Pets, and so on. You can also see that the Keywords window has two tabs at the top, Auto-Apply and Inspector. They correspond to the two ways that you can apply keywords to your filmstrips: by "painting" across them, or using the select-then-apply method.

Note: You can apply keywords to your filmstrips either in the storyboard or the Event browser.

Editing the Keyword List

To make up new keywords, click the Auto-Apply tab. Click in the Keyword box (lower-left), type a keyword, and press Enter. Type the next keyword, and press Enter. And so on.

To edit a keyword name, double-click it.

Tip: Be careful—keywords are case-sensitive. iMovie treats *kids* and *Kids* as two different keywords.

You can also rearrange the keyword list—to put the most common ones at the top, for example. (The top nine keywords get numeric keyboard shortcuts.) Just drag the keywords themselves up or down the list.

To remove keywords that you're not using, click the Auto-Apply tab, click the keyword you want to eliminate (*not* its checkbox), and then click Remove. If that keyword is actually in use—if you've applied it to some footage—iMovie warns you in a confirmation box. Click Yes to proceed with the keyword vaporization.

"Painting" Keywords onto Clips

This method is wicked fast. It's especially good if you want to apply the *same* set of keywords to a slew of different filmstrips. When you get back from your Disney World vacation, for example, chances are good that a lot of your video will fall into the categories "Vacation," "Family," and "Kids." Using this method, you can leave those keyword checkboxes turned on and then whip through the clips, "painting on" the keywords as necessary.

Start by opening the Keywords window, and then:

1. **Click the Auto-Apply tab.**

   If you want to add a new keyword to the list, type it into the box at the bottom of the list and then click Add (or press Enter).

2. **Turn on the checkboxes for the relevant keywords.**

   As noted above, you can turn on as many as you like.

Tip: See the little numbers 1, 2, 3, and so on, at the right side of the list? You can press these keys on your keyboard to turn keyword checkboxes on and off, for added speed.

3. **Drag across the filmstrip sections that should have those keywords.**

   As always, you can skim and play to review a clip before you paint the keywords onto it.

   As you drag, a blue line appears at the top of the filmstrip, indicating that you've applied keywords to it.

Tip: *Option*-click a filmstrip to apply the selected keywords to the whole thing.

The Select-then-Apply Method

When you have a more motley assortment of video and you'll be applying a lot of different keywords as you go, it might make more sense to use this second method. Here, you highlight some video first and *then* turn on the keyword checkboxes.

Start by opening the Keywords window, and then:

1. **Click the Inspector tab.**

   The keyword list appears.

2. **Select some video.**

   You can use any of the techniques described on page 128. Of course, you can skim and play to see what you've got before you apply a keyword.

3. **Turn on the appropriate keyword checkboxes.**

   Click to select the checkboxes—or press the number keys on your keyboard that correspond to the numbers in the keyword list.

   Once again, a blue line appears at the top of the filmstrip, indicating that you've applied keywords to it.

   If you see a hyphen (-) in one of the checkboxes, it's because *part* of the selected video has that keyword, and part doesn't. Click that checkbox once to apply the keyword to the *entire* selection, or twice to remove the keyword from the entire selection.

Tip: To apply a keyword that's not yet in the list, type the new keyword into the "Keyword" text box, and then click Add to Clip (or press Enter). iMovie simultaneously adds the new keyword to the list *and* applies it to whatever's selected.

Now you can repeat steps 2 and 3, selecting, then applying keywords; selecting, then applying keywords.

Removing Keywords from Filmstrips

It's easy enough to strip away keywords that you've already applied. Just highlight the clip and then, on the Inspector tab, turn off the keywords you don't want. Or, if you don't want *any* keywords on this selection, click Remove All.

Note: Whatever keywords are applied to a certain clip are visible in all projects. In other words, keywords are not project-specific.

The Keyword Filter

The payoff for painstakingly categorizing your footage with keywords comes when you need just the right clip, and you don't have time to review the 6 hours of footage you took during your 11-day cruise. You want to see all the footage of museums (or beaches, or shipboard fake Broadway shows), *now*.

That's easy. Choose Window→Keyword Filter. iMovie opens up a strange little keyword panel, wedged in between the Events list and the Event browser (Figure 7-5).

The minutes:seconds display down the right side is a cumulative tally of all the video in your library that bears each keyword.

What's even handier is the checkboxes down the *left* side. When you turn on one, the Event browser changes. It hides all your filmstrips *except* the snippets bearing that keyword.

Tip: You can double-click a keyword, or indeed anywhere on its row, to turn the corresponding checkbox on or off. A bigger target means more efficiency.

Figure 7-5:
As long as the master switch is turned on ("Filter by Keyword"), the checkboxes hide or show the video with matching keywords. When "Filter by Keyword" is off, the Event browser shows everything, regardless of keywords.

At least, that's what it does fresh from the factory. By clicking the buttons below the list, you can manipulate what's hidden and what's visible in several creative ways:

- **Any** means "show me video with *any* of the keywords I've selected." If you turn on Vacation and Kids, you'll see footage that has *either* of those keywords applied.

- **All** means "show me only the video that has *all* of these keywords." If you turn on Vacation and Kids, you'll see *only* footage to which you've applied *both* those keywords.

- **Include** and **Exclude** mean "show" and "hide." If you turn on the Funny keyword checkbox when Include is turned on, you'll see *only* the footage that's Funny. If Exclude is turned on, you'll see all footage *except* the Funny stuff. (That includes video with no keywords at all.)

Deleting Footage for Good

When you mark a shot as a reject, iMovie generally hides it from you, so that you can spend less time wading through mountains of video as you build your project.

But marking shots as rejects has another payoff, too: It's the gateway to iMovie's video *deletion* feature. If a shot is really bad, and you're sure you'll never need it again, you can delete it from your Mac completely, thereby reclaiming a substantial amount of hard drive space.

iMovie '08 can even delete *part* of a clip on the hard drive, leaving the rest for you to work with. Technically speaking, that's quite a trick. (See the box on page 155.)

To purge your rejected clips and clip portions, do this:

1. **Choose View→Rejected Only.**

   As shown in Figure 7-6 (top), the Rejected Clips window appears. Skim or play these clips to double-check their worthlessness. The point is to review the rejects to make sure you're not about to nuke anything you'll regret.

Tip: If you spot an *orange* stripe on any of these clips, then you've actually used that video in a project—you must have marked it as rejected *afterward*—and iMovie won't let you delete it. Remove it from your project first, or unmark it as a reject.

2. **Click Move Rejected to Trash.**

   You'll find this button in the upper-right corner of the Rejected Clips window. iMovie immediately asks if you're sure (Figure 7-6, bottom).

Figure 7-6:
Top: The Rejected Clips window shows you everything you've indicated is destined for the cutting-room floor. Here's your last chance to look it over before deleting it forever.

Bottom: When you click "Move Rejected to Trash," this confirmation box appears. Click "Move to Trash."

3. **Click Move to Trash.**

   After a moment of processing, iMovie places all of the rejected footage in your *Macintosh* Trash. The filmstrips disappear from the window before you.

Tip: At this point, the video isn't yet gone from your hard drive. You have one last, desperate chance to resurrect it. Click the Trash icon on your Dock, and then open the iMovie Temporary Items folder within. There you'll find both the deleted clip and the mini filmstrip movie thumbnail that iMovie '08 generated for it.

To rescue some video, drag it out of this Trash folder and back into the appropriate folder in your Movies→ iMovie Events folder. The next time you open iMovie, you'll see it listed in the Event browser.

4. Empty your Macintosh Trash.

In other words, switch to the Finder (click the first icon on your Dock), and choose Finder→Empty Trash. Or, if you can see the Trash icon on your Dock right now, hold down your cursor on it; from the shortcut menu, choose Empty Trash.

Space Saver

Now you know how to permanently vaporize all the footage you've flagged as useless. But as it turns out, iMovie offers an additional tool for reclaiming hard drive space—a little something called Space Saver.

It's a little complicated, thanks to the double-negative wording of its options ("Reject if a clip is *not* this"), but here goes:

Space Saver's function is to mark *all* unused, unfavorited, or unkeyworded video in an Event as rejects, all in one fell swoop. That way, you can use the previous steps to empty your Rejected Clips window and get a *lot* of hard drive space back.

The most useful application of this powerful command is to purge your Event of leftover footage after you're really, truly finished editing a project. Space Saver can help you throw away *all* of the imported video that didn't wind up being used in the project. In essence, you're locking down your project in its current form, removing any chance of expanding the clips you've used in it—but you're getting a lot of hard drive space back.

Tip: If you have a tape camcorder, and you still have the original tape, this is a no-lose, no-risk proposition. If you're ever desperate to re-edit your movie years from now, you can always re-import the original clips from the tape. In the meantime, you're not filling up your hard drive with a lot of video deadwood.

GEM IN THE ROUGH

Deleting Partial Clips: The Mixed Blessing

iMovie '08's ability to delete *pieces* of clips from your hard drive certainly seems, at first glance, like a refreshing change from the previous versions of iMovie.

In iMovie 5 and 6, you'd reclaim hard drive space only if you deleted an *entire* clip. If you'd incorporated even one second of a clip into your project, iMovie retained the entire clip on your hard drive, even if it was many minutes (and megabytes) long. As a result, even short iMovie projects could occupy many gigabytes of disk space.

Apple's justification for this behavior was, "Well, you might want to change your mind. You might want to re-edit this movie later and use *more* of that clip in your project." And

that was true; it's frequently convenient to tinker with your edit by dragging the outer edges of already-placed clips to bring more of those shots into view. That trick's possible only if you haven't *deleted* the hidden part of a clip.

All of this history is printed here for one purpose: To remind you that partial-clip deletion is a mixed blessing. iMovie '08 can save you an *enormous* amount of hard drive space if you diligently reject, and then delete, the footage that you're certain you'll never want anyone to see.

But keep in mind that when you do that, you lose the flexibility to change your mind.

To get started, choose File→Space Saver. The dialog box shown in Figure 7-7 appears. It's offering to mark *everything* as a reject unless it's:

- **Part of a project.** This is the example described above. Turn on "Not added to any project" if you want to get rid of all video clips in this Event that you haven't used in any movie project.

- **One of your favorites.** If you've been using the Favorites feature religiously, and have marked *all* usable video as Favorite, then you can turn on "Not marked as Favorite." Anything you did *not* mark as a favorite now becomes a reject. (Pretty harsh!) The only footage left in this Event will be your favorites.

- **Categorized with a keyword.** This option is for people who categorize *everything* useful with one keyword or another, as described on page 149. Turning on "Not marked with a keyword" marks *everything else* as a reject, and puts it on the road to deletion.

There probably aren't very many people who always keyword *everything* that's useful, which is why the factory setting for this checkbox is off.

Figure 7-7:
iMovie can save you time and disk space if you let it reject whole categories of clips at a time.

Once you've made your selections, click Reject and Review. You arrive in the Rejected Clips window (Figure 7-6, top), where you'll see all the clips that Space Saver has marked for termination.

If you're puzzled by what's here and what's not, keep these eccentricities in mind:

- Space Saver marks a clip as a reject only if *the entire thing* meets the criteria you selected. If part of it is flagged as a favorite, for example, and you've selected "Not marked as Favorite," then no part of the clip will be moved to the Rejected Clips window.

- The checkboxes are cumulative. You can turn on as many of the Space Saver checkboxes as you like. But in keeping with Space Saver's double-negative thinking, turning on *more* checkboxes rejects *fewer* clips. That is, if you turn on all three boxes, a clip won't be deleted unless it's unused in a project *and* not a favorite *and* doesn't have a keyword. This quirk, too, may explain why some clips don't wind up in the Rejected Clips window when you expected them to.

Once you've skimmed or played the filmstrips in the Rejected Clips window, and you've assured yourself that they're all expendable, you can delete them just as you'd delete any rejected clips. Page 154 has the full details, but the gist is this: Click "Move Rejected to Trash," click "Move to Trash" in the confirmation box, and then empty the Macintosh Trash.

Transitions

This chapter and the next describe two iMovie tools—Transitions and Video Effects—that can make your raw footage look even better than it is. Both of these tools involve hidden panels of options that you don't ordinarily see in iMovie. Impressively enough, there's no *rendering time* required by iMovie—no delay while the program computes the effect you're creating—as there is in most other video editing programs. You see the effect instantly.

About Transitions

What happens when one clip ends and the next one begins? In about 99.99 percent of all movies, music videos, and commercials—and in 100 percent of camcorder movies before the Macintosh era—you get a *cut*. That's the technical term for "nothing special happens at all." One scene ends, and the next one begins immediately.

Professional film and video editors, however, have at their disposal a wide range of *transitions*—special effects that smooth the juncture between one clip and the next. For example, the world's most popular transition is the *crossfade* or *dissolve*, in which the end of one clip gradually fades away as the next one fades in. (See Figure 8-1.) The crossfade is so popular because it's so effective. It gives a feeling of softness and grace

Figure 8-1:
The world's most popular and effective transition effect: what iMovie calls a Cross Dissolve.

to the transition, and yet it's so subtle that the viewer might not even be conscious of its presence.

Like all video editing programs, iMovie offers a variety of transitions, of which crossfades are only the beginning. You'll find a catalog of them starting on page 170. iMovie makes adding such effects incredibly easy, and the results look awesomely assured and professional.

When Not to Use Transitions

When the Macintosh debuted in 1984, one of its most exciting features was its *fonts.* Without having to buy those self-adhesive lettering sets from art stores, you could make posters, flyers, and newsletters using any typefaces you wanted. In fact, if you weren't particularly concerned with being tasteful, you could even combine lots of typefaces on the same page—and thousands of first-time desktop publishers did exactly that. They thought it was exciting to harness the world of typography right on the computer screen.

You may even remember the result: a proliferation of homemade graphic design that rated very low on the artistic-taste scale. Instead of making their documents look more professional, the wild explosion of mixed typefaces made them look amateurish in a whole new way.

In video, transitions present exactly the same temptation: If you use too many, you risk telegraphing that you're a beginner at work. When you begin to polish your movie by adding transitions, consider these questions:

- **Does it really need a transition?** Sometimes a simple cut is the most effective transition from one shot to the next. Yes, the crossfade lends a feeling of softness and smoothness to the movie, but is that really what you want? If it's a sweet video of your kids growing up over time, absolutely yes. But if it's a hard-hitting issue documentary, then probably not, as those soft edges would dull the impact of your footage.

  Remember, too, that transitions often suggest the *passage of time.* In movies and commercials, consecutive shots in the same scene never include such effects. Plain old cuts tell the viewer that one shot is following the next in real time. But suppose one scene ends with the beleaguered hero saying, "Well, at least I still have my job at the law firm!"…and the next shot shows him operating a lemonade stand. (Now *that's* comedy!) In this case, a transition would be especially effective, because it would tell the audience that we've just jumped a couple of days.

  Learn taste in transitions. They should be done *for a reason.*

- **Is it consistent?** Once you've chosen a transition-effect style for your movie, stick to that transition style for the entire film (unless, as always, you have an artistic reason to do otherwise). Using one consistent style of effect lends unity to your work. That's why interior designers choose only one dominant color for each room.

- **Which effect is most appropriate?** As noted earlier, the crossfade is almost always the least intrusive, most effective, and best-looking transition. But each of the other iMovie transitions can be appropriate in certain situations.

  The catalog on page 170 gives you an example of when each might be appropriate. Most of them are useful primarily in music videos and other situations when wild stylistic flights of fancy are more readily accepted by viewers.

Tip: The Fade Through Black transition in iMovie is exempt from the stern advice above. Use it the beginning of *every* movie, if you like, and at the end. Doing so adds a fade in and fade out, lending a professional feeling to your film. But it's so subtle, your audience will notice it subconsciously, if at all.

Two Ways to "Transish"

You can insert iMovie's transition effects one by one, placing them between scenes only where appropriate, and hand-tailoring each one. That's the way you do transitions in most programs, including the old iMovie.

But lurking one millimeter beneath iMovie's surface at all times is its primary mission: letting you assemble edited video *fast,* automating *everything.* For that reason, iMovie '08 also lets you turn on *automatic, global* transitions. (Great for slideshows!)

The following sections cover both methods.

Creating Individual Transition Effects

To see the 12 transitions iMovie offers, click the Transitions button, which is identified in Figure 8-2. Point to a transition's name (like Cross Dissolve) without clicking to see a small animated preview of it.

Once you've found a good effect, drag its icon *out* of the Transitions panel and directly into the storyboard area, in the vertical gap between the two filmstrips that you want transitioned. Figure 8-3 shows the technique.

Tip: Most people think of putting transitions *between* two clips. But if you drag one to the *beginning* of your storyboard, the transition works just as well—except that it transitions out of blackness. "Fade Through Black" and "Circle Open" work especially well to begin a movie.

The same happy surprise awaits if you drag a transition to the *end* of the movie. iMovie wipes, fades, or ripples from the final shot into blackness.

Once you've dropped a transition into place, you can look over the result easily.

- To watch just the transition itself, click its icon in the storyboard (it sprouts a yellow border to show that it's highlighted) and then press the / key. That's on the bottom row of the keyboard, and it always means "play the selection" in iMovie.

- It's a good idea to watch your transition by "rewinding" a few seconds into the preceding footage, to get a sense of how the effect fits in the context of the existing footage. To watch the transition *and* the clips that it joins together, point to a spot just before the transition, and then hit the Space bar.

- If you think the scene seam looked better without the transition, choose Edit→Undo (⌘-Z).

Show/Hide Transitions

Figure 8-2:
When you point to a transition's icon, you get to see a small preview right on its icon. Click to pause the tiny playback loop at any point, or double-click to reset the animation to its first frame.

Transitions

Circle Open Circle Close Cross Dissolve

Cube Fade Through Black Fade Through White

Page Curl Ripple Wipe Down

Wipe Left Wipe Right Wipe Up

You'll discover that the audio from the clips on either side of a transition still plays—you hear the sounds overlapping for a moment—but iMovie gradually crossfades the two.

Tip: If you want transitions on *most* of your scene seams, turn on the Automatic Transitions feature described on page 166. Then, using the Tip on page 169, you can turn all those iMovie-generated transitions into manually editable ones—in other words, you can delete just the ones you don't want.

Changing or Deleting a Transition

If you like the *idea* of a transition but you just don't like the one you put there, drag a different one out of the Transitions panel right on top of the old one.

To get rid of a transition, even months or years later, highlight its icon and then press the Delete key. Your original clips return instantly, exactly as they were before you added the transition.

Figure 8-3:
Insert a transition by dragging its icon out of the Transitions palette and in between two clips (or at either end of your movie). In the storyboard, a transition shows up as a tiny icon. You can even tell what kind of transition it is by the little logo on that icon.

Transition icon

A Long Discussion of Transition Lengths

In the old iMovie, you specified how long each transition effect lasted before you even put it into your movie. The new iMovie thinks that *that*—choosing durations each time—is a nuisance. iMovie '08 really, *really* wants all of your transitions to have exactly the same length.

Here are three ways to adjust the durations of your transitions. All three of them involve a visit to the Project Properties dialog box (see Figure 8-4). Here, you'll find a Transition Duration slider (whose settings range from .5 seconds to 4 seconds) and several options that affect it.

- **Change all transition durations at once.** If you select "Applies to all transitions," then the Duration slider affects all transitions simultaneously. Taking this road ensures consistency and minimizes the amount of effort you have to expend. For best results, choose something between 1 and 2 seconds.

Note: If you've manually set the durations of individual transitions, as described in the following paragraphs, be careful. Using "Applies to all transitions" wipes out all of the handwork you've done.

• **Change transition durations from here on.** The weird little option labeled "Applies when added to project" actually means "Whatever duration you choose on the Duration slider applies to the *next* transition you drop into the storyboard—and all future ones."

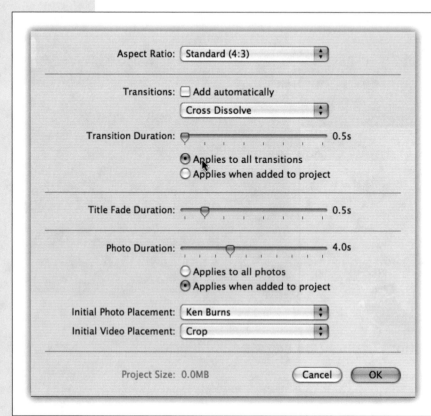

Figure 8-4:
Choose File→Project Properties. In this dialog box, drag the slider to indicate how long you want each transition effect to last. If "Applies to all transitions" is selected, then, by golly, this slider affects all transitions in your project at once.

So you choose this option, you adjust the Duration slider, and finally you click OK. You've just preserved the durations of all *existing* transitions in your project, but changed the standard timing for all *incoming* transitions.

Here again, iMovie is trying to enforce a standard duration, albeit a different one, and trying to remove all necessity for you to manage your durations one by one.

• **Change individual transitions.** Fortunately for control freaks, you can also change transition durations on a one-at-a-time basis. Click a transition icon to select it, and then choose Edit→Set Duration (⌘-R).

Now the Set Duration dialog box appears (Figure 8-5). Type in the number of seconds you want for the transition. Whereas iMovie's automatic Duration slider limits your transitions to lengths between .5 and 4 seconds, this time, you have much greater creative latitude. You can type in anything between .25 (one-quarter second) and 60 (a whole minute, although, frankly, transitions longer than a couple of seconds are excruciating to watch).

Tip: You can type decimals here. If you want a 2.1-second transition, then, by all means, type *2.1.*

Figure 8-5:
Type in the number you want, and then click OK. (This box, as you can see, offers a second way to change the durations of all transitions in your project so far.)

Why You Don't Always Get What You Want

Even after you've mastered all of the transition-duration permutations described on the previous pages, you may find yourself thwarted by iMovie itself. You may indicate that you want a 2-second transition, but iMovie may give you a half-second one, no matter how many things you try.

That's because iMovie enforces its own Law of Reasonable Durations, which states that *no transition effect may consume more than half the length of a clip.* Figure 8-6 shows the problem, and the result.

Note: If you can't manually change the durations of *any* transition, it's probably because you've got Automatic transitions turned on (page 166).

Figure 8-6:
Top: One of the clips involved in the transition is only 3 seconds long. You try to add a 2-second transition.

Bottom: iMovie gives you only a 1.5-second transition, because that's half of the clip's 3-second length—and iMovie won't let you add a transition longer than half the clip's length.

How Transitions Affect the Length of Your Movie

As you can see by the example in Figure 8-7, transitions generally make your movie shorter. To superimpose the ends of two adjacent clips, iMovie is forced to slide the right-hand clip to the left, making the overall movie end sooner.

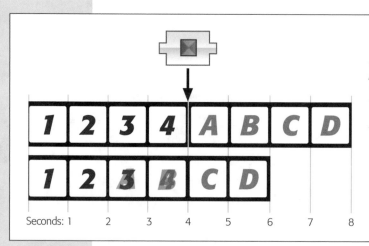

Figure 8-7:
When you insert a 2-second transition (top) between two clips, iMovie pulls the right-hand clip 2 seconds to the left so that it overlaps the end of the left-hand clip. The result (bottom): The entire movie is now 2 seconds shorter.

Under most circumstances, there's nothing wrong with that. After all, that's why, when importing your clips, you wisely avoided trimming off *all* of the excess "leader" and "trailer" footage (known as *trim handles*) from the ends of your clips. By leaving trim handles on each clip—which will be sacrificed to the transition—you'll have some fade-in or fade-out footage to play with.

Sometimes, however, having your overall project shortened is a serious problem, especially when you've been "cutting to sound," or synchronizing your footage to an existing music track. Suppose you've spent hours putting your clips into the storyboard, carefully trimming them so that they perfectly match the soundtrack. And now, as a final touch, you decide to put in transitions. Clearly, having these transitions slide all of your clips to the left would result in chaos, throwing off the synchronization work you had done.

In iMovie '08, there's no good solution to this problem if you've opted for manual control over transitions. (The *automatic* transition feature, which puts a transition in between every single scene seam in the entire movie, offers a semisolution; see below.)

That's why it's a good idea to edit your video *before* you start mucking around with background music.

Automatic Transitions

If you're really in a hurry to crank out your edited movie, like the now-legendary Apple programmer who wound up writing iMovie '08 so he could whip out highlight reels without hand-tweaking everything, then you're in luck. You don't have to bother placing transitions one at a time. Using the Automatic feature, you can tell iMovie to put the same, identical, fixed-length transition effect between *all* clip seams. Figure 8-8 shows the idea.

Figure 8-8:
The Automatic feature takes your rough edit (top) and inserts identical transitions everywhere (bottom), masking the divider between every pair of clips.

This feature is OK *if* all of this is true:

- You choose a nontacky transition effect, like the cross dissolve.

- You set the duration to something short, like 1 second.

- You're creating a highlight reel, a sequence of shots that aren't intended to tell a story.

If you're not careful, these frequent transitions can get annoying or cloying, and they'll lose their impact in a hurry.

You should also note that turning on the Automatic feature *removes* any customization you've done using the individual-transition feature described on the preceding pages. All of your duration adjustments are wiped away.

Tip: There is, however, a way to turn all of these automatic transitions into *individual* transitions that you can edit separately; see page 169.

Still interested? Then proceed like this:

1. **Choose File→Project Properties.**

   Alternatively, press ⌘-J. Either way, the Project Properties screen appears (Figure 8-4).

---

2. **Turn on "Add transitions automatically." From the pop-up menu, choose the transition style you want.**

   This time, you don't get the handy self-illustrating icons that show you what the effect will look like. It doesn't matter; the only one you'd ever use without looking amateurish is the Cross Dissolve. (Right?)

3. **Use the Transition Duration slider to specify the length of the transition itself.**

   One second or less is a good bet.

4. **Click OK.**

   Now a weird little question pops onto the screen (Figure 8-9). It's asking how you want these transitions to affect the overall timing of your movie.

Figure 8-9:
Of course, the "Extend" feature may wind up revealing something that you most distinctly do not want to see or hear, something that you originally edited out for a good reason—a swear word or a wardrobe malfunction, for example.

The factory setting is "Overlap ends and shorten clip." As the discussion on page 166 makes clear, your movie will get shorter. iMovie slides every clip slightly to the left so that it can overlap the one to its left. That's usually fine *unless* you've got the whole thing carefully timed to a music track, which will now be totally out of sync with the video.

The alternative is "Extend ends and keep duration the same (where possible)." Here, iMovie is proposing *not* shortening your movie. You'll still see every frame of the clips that you're seeing now.

But to provide "trim handles" for the transition, iMovie automatically *lengthens* the clips in your storyboard. It reveals footage on either end that you had, in the process of choosing excerpts from the raw footage, previously hidden.

"Where possible" means that if iMovie encounters a clip that was *not* edited down from a longer one, it can't help you. It has no choice but to add a transition that eats into the clip, using up some of its frames, and shortening your movie overall.

5. **Choose either "Overlap…" or "Extend…" and click OK.**

You return to your project, where the icons for iMovie's automatic transitions now appear in place. Play back the movie to enjoy the effect, keeping in mind that you can't edit, change, or delete them *individually*, only en masse.

Note: If you add any new clips to your movie, iMovie adds transitions to them automatically.

Adjusting the Automatic Transitions

You can change the uniform length or uniform style of *all* those auto-transitions, but you can't edit them individually.

Just choose File→Project Properties again (⌘-J). In the dialog box (Figure 8-4), you can change the Duration slider or, using the pop-up menu, the transition style. Any change you make here affects *all* of the transitions.

Turning off Automatic Transitions

If you decide that the all-at-once approach is a bit much, you can turn off the automatic-transitions feature. Choose File→Project Properties again (⌘-J), and just turn off "Add transitions automatically."

When you click OK, iMovie has one more bit of business to take care of: what to do about that messy overlapping-ends affair. A message now appears to ask what you want to do:

• **Remove transitions and extend clip ends.** This option leaves in place whatever footage is now being used by the transition. For example, if you had an 8-second clip with a 1-second transition at the end, the clip will wind up being about 9 seconds long.

• **Remove transitions and keep clip duration the same.** If you've spent a lot of energy working out timings, maybe to match a soundtrack, you'll probably want this choice. Now, that 8-second clip will still be 8 seconds long after the transitions are removed. The video that *was* being used in the transitions is hidden once again.

• **Leave transitions in current locations.** This handy option turns off automatic transitions, but leaves the actual transition icons in place. They've now turned into *individual* transitions, which you can now delete or edit on a one-at-a-time basis.

Tip: This option can be a terrific help when you want transitions on *most* of your clips, but not all. You can turn Automatic Transitions on, and then choose this option as you turn them off again. Now you have a storyboard full of *manual* transition icons; just delete the ones you don't need.

Transitions: The iMovie Catalog

Here, for your reference, is a visual representation of each transition, and what editing circumstances might call for it.

Circle Open, Circle Close

This effect, called *iris close (iris open)* or *iris in (iris out)* in professional editing programs, is a holdover from the silent film days, when, in the days before zoom lenses, directors used the effect to highlight a detail in a scene.

It creates an ever-growing (or opening) "porthole," with the first clip inside and the second clip outside. It's useful at the beginning or end of the movie, when the second clip is solid black and the subject of the first clip is centered in the frame. In that setup, the movie begins or ends with a picture that grows or shrinks away to a little dot. (If the subject in the center waves goodbye just before being blinked out of view, this trick is especially effective.)

Circle Opening

Cross Dissolve

The crossfade, or dissolve, is the world's most popular and effective transition. The first clip gradually disappears, superimposed on the beginning of the second clip, which fades in. If you must use a transition at all, you can't go wrong with this one.

Tip: You can use a very short cross dissolve to create what editors call a "soft cut." When the footage would jump too abruptly if you made a regular cut, put in a 10-frame cross dissolve, which makes the junction of clips *slightly* smoother than just cutting. Soft cuts are very common in interviews where the editors have deleted sections from a continuous shot of a person talking.

Cube

Here's an Applehead favorite, one that first appeared in Apple's Keynote presentation program. It makes your scenes look like they're playing simultaneously on adjacent sides of a cube; the transition makes this cube seem to rotate outward toward the camera from one facet to another. It calls more attention to itself than most transitions, but it sure is cool-looking.

Cube

Fade Through Black, Fade Through White

Use this effect at the beginning and end of every movie, for a handsome, professional fade in/fade out. Or use it at the start of any scene that begins in a new place or time. In that situation, it makes the first scene fade to black momentarily, and then the next one fades in.

"Fade Through White" is the same thing, with one big difference: It fades out to, and then in from, *white* instead of black.

Fading in and out to white, an effect first popularized by Infiniti car commercials in the early 1980s, lends a very specific feeling to the movie. It's something ethereal, ghostly, nostalgic. In today's Hollywood movies (including *The Sixth Sense*), a fade to white often indicates that the character you've been watching has just died.

The fade through white is an extremely popular technique in today's TV commercials, when the advertiser wants to show you a series of charming, brightly colored images. By fading out to white between shots, the editor inserts the video equivalent of an

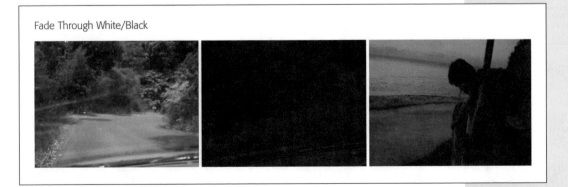

Fade Through White/Black

ellipsis (…like this…), and keeps the mood happy and bright. (Similar fade-outs to black seem to stop the flow with more finality.)

Tip: If you'd rather fade to black and then *hold* on the black screen for a moment, use the transition between your video and a *black clip.* See page 197 for details on making a black clip.

Page Curl

Here's another slightly tacky transition: the page curl. It makes the upper-right corner of the video frame appear to curl inward and toward you, and then peel down and to the left, as though it's a giant Post-it note being ripped off a pad. The following clip is revealed underneath.

Page Curl

Ripple

This effect is gorgeous, poetic, beautiful—and hard to justify.

Ripple invokes the "drop of water on the surface of the pond" metaphor. As the ripple expands across the screen, it pushes the first clip (the pond surface) off the screen to make way for the incoming new clip (the expanding circular ripple). It's a soothing, beautiful effect—but unless you're making mascara commercials, it calls a little too much attention to itself for everyday home movies.

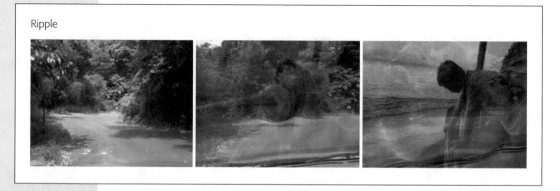

Ripple

Wipe Down, Up, Left, Right

In this transition, the incoming clip *covers up* the outgoing clip, as though it's being shoved into the frame on a cookie sheet. (A cookie sheet with a soft, slightly blurry leading edge, that is; iMovie doesn't *do* hard transition edges.)

You could use it to simulate an old-style projector changing slides, or when filming a clever, self-aware documentary in which the host (who first appears in the second clip) "pushes" his way onto the screen.

Wipe

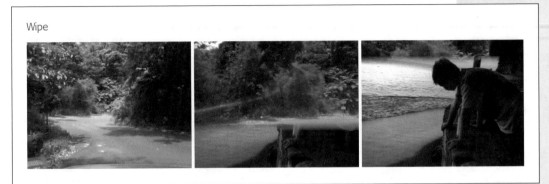

Color Fixes, Cropping, and Rotating

The old iMovies, the versions before iMovie '08, were big on *special effects*. The software came with a panel full of video effects that you could apply directly to your footage. Some were mainstay effects like slow motion, backward, black-and-white, and so on. Lots more were actual special effects that simulated fog, rain, earthquakes, lightning, flashbulbs, and bleary-eyed bad LSD.

All those "special effect" effects are pretty much gone in iMovie '08. Let us honor their demise with a moment of silence. (And let us skip to page 301 to see where a handful of them still lurk.)

But iMovie '08 replaces them with something that might be more useful, more often: a Video Adjustments panel just like the one in iPhoto.

Plenty of video needs no help at all, and looks fantastic right out of the camcorder. But every now and then, you'll find a shot that came out too dark, or washed out, or with a yellowish or bluish color cast. The new Video Adjustments panel lets you make slight or gigantic changes to the brightness, contrast, white balance, saturation, and other image qualities of any clip.

For example, if a shot looks too dark and murky, you can bring details out of the shadows without blowing out the highlights. If the snow in a skiing shot looks too bluish, you can de-blue it. If the colors don't pop quite enough in the prize-winning soccer goal shot, you can boost their saturation levels.

In addition, the new program offers two features that the old iMovie versions couldn't even fantasize about:

• **Cropping.** *Cropping* video means to use only a portion of the frame, like an artificial zoom.

• **Rotation.** You can turn the entire video image 90 degrees, or even upside-down.

Coolest of all, iMovie does all of this—picture adjustment, cropping, and rotating—*instantaneously and nondestructively.* That is, there's no waiting around while iMovie renders (processes) the changes you make, which makes joyous, real-time experimentation possible. Furthermore, you're never actually making changes to the original clips. You can restore the original video any time you like.

This chapter introduces you to all of iMovie '08's video effects.

Phase 1: Select the Clip, Find the Frame

iMovie can apply these impressive effects only to an entire clip at once. You can't make the effect fade in or out, you can't apply it to just a portion of a clip, and you can't apply it to multiple clips at once (although you *can* copy and paste the adjustments you make).

Before you apply an effect, therefore, you might want to start by isolating the piece you want. You can always chop up a clip into smaller pieces (page 417).

Then click the clip that needs help. You can click a filmstrip anywhere:

• **In the Event browser.** If you click a raw source clip here, then the changes you make appear in *every project* that incorporates that clip.

• **In the project storyboard.** If you click a clip you've already placed into the storyboard, the changes you make affect that video *only in this movie.* The original, underlying source clip in the Event browser remains unchanged.

(Of course, the truth is, you're never *really* changing anything at all. You can remove all your changes and revert to the original camcorder-captured clip at any time, even months or years from now.)

Once you've selected a clip, you see a still image of it in the Viewer window.

Phase 2: The Video Adjustments Panel

Now you're ready to open the Video Adjustments panel. Do that by pressing the V key on your keyboard, by clicking the Adjust Video button (Figure 9-1), or by clicking the tiny, faint sunshine icon that appears on every filmstrip when you point to it (also identified in Figure 9-1).

If you've ever adjusted the colors of a picture in iPhoto, these controls should look familiar. They affect your video here exactly as they affect a digital photo in iPhoto.

Don't overlook the tiny red dot on the filmstrip itself (Figure 9-2). Using this dot, you can move around *within* the clip to find a better representative frame as you work. (That's important, because once the Video Adjustments panel is open, you can no longer skim in the usual way.)

Introduction to the Histogram

Learning to use the Video Adjustments panel effectively involves learning about its *histogram*, the colorful little graph at the top of the panel (visible in Figure 9-1).

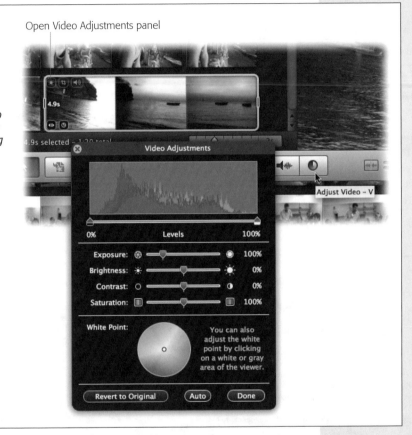

Figure 9-1:
The Video Adjustments panel is a see-through, floating entity that lives on a plane of its own. You can drag it anywhere on the screen, and–here's the part that might not occur to you–you can move on to a different clip without having to close the panel first. (Click another clip among your filmstrips.) Also note that you can drag the tiny red dot to move around in the clip as you work.

Open Video Adjustments panel

The histogram is a self-updating visual representation of the dark and light tones that make up your video clip. If you've never encountered a histogram before, this all may sound complicated. But the histogram is a terrific tool, and it'll make more sense the more you work with it.

Within each of the superimposed graphs (red, blue, green), the scheme is the same: The clip's darker shades appear toward the left side of the graph; the lighter tones are graphed on the right side.

Therefore, in a very dark clip—a coal mine at midnight, say—you'll see big mountain peaks at the left side of the graph, trailing off to nothing toward the right. A shot of a brilliantly sunny snowscape, on the other hand, will show lots of information on the right, and very little on the left.

The best-balanced shots have some data spread across the entire histogram, with a few mountain-shaped peaks here and there. Those peaks and valleys represent the really dark spots and bright spots. Those mountains are fine, as long as you have some visual information in other parts of the histogram, too.

The histogram for a *bad* shot, on the other hand—a severely under- or overexposed one—has mountains all bunched at one end or the other. Rescuing those pictures involves spreading the mountains across the entire spectrum, which is what the Video Adjustments palette is all about.

Three Channels

As you can see, the histogram actually displays three superimposed graphs at once. These layers—red, green, and blue—represent the three "channels" of color video.

When you make adjustments to a clip's brightness values—for example, when you drag the Exposure slider just below the histogram—you'll see the graphs in all three channels move in unison. Despite changing shape, they essentially stick together. Later, when you make color adjustments using, say, the Saturation slider, you'll see those individual channels move in different directions.

Tip: As you work, don't forget to spot-check your adjustments by moving the tiny red dot on the filmstrip itself; see Figure 9-2.

Figure 9-2:
The red dot lets you choose the representative frame you want to see in the Viewer—and you should check a number of different frames within each clip to make sure that the change you're making looks good all the way through the shot.

Exposure

Most of the sliders in the Video Adjustments panel affect the histogram in some way. But where do you begin?

Here's a general suggestion: Make exposure adjustments first. In the simplest terms, the Exposure slider makes your video lighter when you move it to the right and darker when you move it to the left.

Watch the data on the histogram as you move the Exposure slider. Make sure you don't wind up shoving any of the "mountain peaks" beyond the edges of the Histogram box. If that happens, you're discarding precious image data; you'll see a loss of detail in the darks and lights.

The first step in fine-tuning a clip, then, is to drag the Exposure slider until the middle tones of the footage look acceptable to you. You can't add details that simply aren't there, but brightening a dark, shadowy image, or deepening the contrast on a washed-out shot, can coax out elements that were barely visible in the original.

If the dark and light areas aren't yet perfect, don't worry; you'll improve those areas next with the Levels control.

Adjusting the Levels

After you've spent some time working with the middle tones of your clip, you can turn your attention to the endpoints on the histogram, which represent the darkest and lightest areas of the clip.

If the mountains of your graph seem to cover all the territory from left to right, you already have a roughly even distribution of dark and light tones in your picture, so you're probably in good shape. But if the graph comes up short on either the left (darks) or the right (lights) side of the histogram, you might want to make an adjustment.

To do so, drag the right or left pointer on the Levels slider *inward*, toward the base of the "mountain." If you're moving the right indicator inward, for example, you'll notice that the whites become brighter, but the dark areas stay pretty much the same; if you drag the left indicator inward, the dark tones change, but the highlights remain steady (Figure 9-3).

Figure 9-3:
Left: There's something wrong with the exposure of this clip.

Right: Drag the handles of the histogram inward to brighten the brights and darken the darks. Avoid moving the handles inward beyond the outer edges of the mountains. You'll throw away data outside the handles, which degrades the image quality.

Brightness and Contrast Sliders

Once you've massaged the Exposure and Levels controls, the overall exposure for a clip usually looks pretty good. In effect, you've managed to create a full range of tones from dark to light.

So why, then, does Apple include Brightness and Contrast sliders, which govern similar aspects of the video's appearance?

Because they're not quite the same as Exposure and Levels.

- **Brightness.** When you move the Brightness slider, you're making the *entire* image lighter or darker. You're literally sliding the entire histogram to the left or right without changing its shape. (Remember that the Exposure and Levels controls affect the midtones, highlights, and shadows independently.)

  In other words, if the shot's contrast is already exactly as you want it, but the whole clip could use darkening or lightening, Brightness should be your tool of choice.

- **Contrast.** The Contrast slider, on the other hand, *does* change the shape of the histogram. Contrast is the difference between the darkest and lightest tones in your clip. If you increase the contrast, you "stretch out" the shape of the histogram, creating darker blacks and brighter whites. When you decrease the contrast, you're scrunching the shape of the histogram inward, shortening the distance between the dark and light endpoints. Since the image data now resides in the middle area of the graph, the overall tones in the video are duller. Video pros might call this look "flat" or "muddy." (See Figure 9-4.)

Figure 9-4:
Here's another way to fiddle with the darks and lights of your video—use the Brightness and Contrast sliders manually. The somewhat washed-out vista at left looks a lot better with the contrast goosed and the brightness toned down a tad.

Automatic Correction

Dragging the Levels, Exposure, and Brightness sliders by hand is one way to address color imbalances in a clip. But there's an easier way: iMovie can also adjust all three sliders *automatically*.

Just click the Auto button at the bottom of the Video Adjustments palette. Watch the results in the Viewer.

Amazing, isn't it? You'd be stunned at how much better a lot of camcorder video can be made to look with this one-click trick (Figure 9-5).

Tip: To compare the Before and After looks of your clip, press ⌘-Z and then Shift-⌘-Z, which correspond to the Undo and Redo commands. For added fun, go back and forth a few times.

Figure 9-5:
The Before (left) and After shots of a clip that needed help. The only difference between the two is one click on the Auto button. (It affects only the brightness, contrast, and exposure–it does not attempt to fix color problems.)

Color Balance

Camcorders don't always capture color very accurately. You might encounter scenes with a slightly bluish or greenish tinge, dull colors, lower contrast, or sickly-looking skin tones. And you might wish you could fix it.

Or maybe you just want to take color adjustment into your own hands, not only to get the colors right, but also to create a specific mood for an image. Maybe you want a snowy landscape to look icy blue, so friends back home realize just how freakin' cold it was.

The Video Adjustments panel offers three controls that wield power over this sort of thing: Saturation, White Balance, and individual sliders that control the intensity of red, green, and blue.

- **White Balance.** Different kinds of light—fluorescent lighting, overcast skies, and so on—lend different color casts to video footage. White balance is a setting that eliminates or adjusts the color cast according to the lighting.

  If you find a clip with such a color cast, it's easy to fix. Move your cursor into the Viewer window and find a spot that's *supposed* to be pure white or gray. (It might help to press ⌘-6 or ⌘-7 to enlarge the frame first.) The instant you click that white point, iMovie suddenly understands exactly what the nature of the color cast is—and adjusts *all* the colors accordingly. Often, that one click does the trick and fixes the entire clip (Figure 9-6).

  Other times, you have to click around a few more times until you find a spot that makes the color cast go away.

  As a last resort, you can try clicking inside the White Point color wheel *manually,* watching the results in the Viewer as you go.

• **Saturation.** Once you're happy with the color tones, you can increase or decrease their intensity with the Saturation slider. Move it to the right to increase the intensity and to the left for less saturation.

Figure 9-6:
In the Viewer, the cursor is a tiny eyedropper. (When you click a spot that's supposed to be white, the whole scene's color tint changes. You'll also see the tiny circle in the White Point color wheel shift to a new location, indicating its new understanding of the color cast.

When you increase the saturation of a clip's colors, you make them more vivid; essentially, you make them "pop" more. You can also improve clips that have harsh, garish colors by dialing *down* the saturation, so that the colors end up looking a little less intense than they appeared in the original footage. That's a useful trick in shots whose *composition* is so strong that the colors are almost distracting.

Individual Channel Sliders

It's hard to imagine that any iMovie aficionado would need any more control over the colors in a shot than what's provided by the White Point and Saturation controls—especially in a program that's so simple and limited in so many other ways.

But believe it or not, iMovie can also offer you three individual sliders for red, green, and blue. You can use these to correct color-tint problems manually, or you can use

---

GEM IN THE ROUGH

The Return of Black-and-White

You don't have to write Apple to complain about the removal of the Black-and-White effect from iMovie. It's still there—it's just not called Black-and-White anymore.

To give a clip the look of black-and-white, just drag the Saturation slider all the way to the left—and presto, black-and-white. After all, what is black-and-white but video with no color at all?

(At that point, you can give the scene a lot more punch and crunch with a little assistance from the Contrast slider. Old films have high contrast levels, primarily because the film used in those days was less capable of capturing fine differences of light. For most videos, a 50 percent Contrast boost should do the trick.)

them to create crazy special effects like "Kids on Mars" or "I'm Feeling Really, Really Blue."

So how come you don't see these sliders? Because they're hidden. And the switch to make them appear is in a place where you'd least expect to find it.

Choose iMovie→Preferences. At the bottom of the dialog box, turn on "Show advanced tools." As you know from Chapter 5, the "advanced tools" are a motley assortment of hidden editing features. What the dialog box *doesn't* tell you is that it makes these three sliders magically appear in the Video Adjustments panel: Red Gain, Green Gain, and Blue Gain (Figure 9-7).

Figure 9-7:
In Preferences, you can turn on the secret on/off switch for the three color Gain sliders. These new, bonus sliders control the amount of each color present in the clip. (Compare with the standard Adjustments panel shown in Figure 9-1.)

Use these sliders to adjust the color mix of the clip. For example, if a scene is too bluish (because it was shot under fluorescent lighting, for example), you can nudge the Blue Gain slider a bit to the left.

Move the Red Gain slider to the right to warm up the tones, making them more orangeish—a particular handy technique for breathing life back into skin tones that have been bleached white with a spotlight or flashlight.

Removing or Adjusting Adjustments

Whenever you unleash the awesome powers of the Video Adjustments panel on a clip, you leave that clip branded—with a tiny sun icon in the upper-left corner of its filmstrip. That's to remind you, "Hey, I didn't always look like this."

Note: That little badge appears faintly on *any* clip when you point to it, as a shortcut to open the Adjustments panel. But after you apply adjustments, the badge is whiter and remains visible at all times.

None of the changes you make in the Video Adjustments panel are permanent. You can return at any time—minutes, days, or years later—and adjust them or remove them entirely.

- **Adjust them.** Click a clip, open the Video Adjustments panel, and make any changes you'd like.

- **Remove them.** If you click a clip and then click Revert to Original (at the bottom of the Video Adjustments panel), you're saying, "Throw away *all* the changes I've made. Bring back my original, unmodified clip." iMovie instantly reinstates the original clip.

Copying and Pasting Adjustments

All of the fun you might be having in the Video Adjustments panel comes to a crashing halt the minute you realize one massive bummer in iMovie '08: You can't select more than one clip at a time. You might have just spent 15 minutes tweaking the color of your opening ski-school clip into submission—but what about the other 25 skiing shots in your montage? Are you condemned to repeating all of that handwork 25 more times?

Fortunately, no. While you can't choose multiple clips at once, you *can* copy and paste *just* the video adjustments between clips. Once you've got the blue cast worked out of the first skiing shot, you can wipe it out of each additional shot with a single command. Figure 9-8 shows the drill.

Figure 9-8:
Click the clip that you've already got looking good. Then choose Edit→Copy (⌘-C). Now click the next clip that needs the same touch and choose Edit→Paste Adjustments→Video (or press Option-⌘-I). Proceed through all the clips that were filmed under the same lighting conditions: Paste, paste, paste. You've just saved a heck of a lot of time.

Tip: If you're the kind of person who plans ahead, consider this: If you intend to excerpt several clips from a single, long, master clip in the Event browser, you'll save time by fixing *that original clip* before you start adding clips to your storyboard.

The reason: If you make color adjustments to the master clip *before* you grab chunks of it, they inherit the fixes. If you adjust the master clip *after* you've placed some pieces of it into the storyboard, then the pieces won't change. (You can always use the Paste Adjustments command at that point, of course, but that's still more steps.)

Cropping Video

The Video Adjustments panel is only one example of the incredibly sophisticated, pro-level features that you stumble across in this supposedly simple, idiotproof program. Another one is the cropping tool, which was previously relegated to the stratosphere of professional, $1,000 video editing programs like Final Cut Pro.

This tool lets you crop a video clip just the way you'd crop a photo; that is, you can chop off the edges of the video frame. Figure 9-9 shows the idea.

Cropping isn't something you'll do every day. But it can be handy in situations like these:

- **You're adding a clip that's got the wrong aspect ratio to a project (page 109).** For example, you're creating a regular, squarish, standard-definition movie, but you want to place a widescreen clip into it. The Cropping tool lets you lop off the sides of that widescreen clip so it fits perfectly into the squarish frame without any black bars.

- **There's something at the margins of the picture that you want to get rid of.** Maybe your finger was in the lens. Maybe there's some ugly pipe or wire that you didn't notice. Maybe a telephone pole appears to be sticking out of your interviewee's head. Or maybe you just want to crop out the bonehead who kept trying to get on camera.

- **The scene is off-center.** Maybe the camera was on a tripod, self-running, when you and a buddy did your comedy schtick, but the whole thing wasn't framed right. By cropping away the empty part of the frame, you can recenter the whole thing.

- **The subject of the shot isn't prominent enough.** This happens often with accidental footage: That is, you were filming your Uncle Ned reminiscing about his days working for the National Guard when, *bam!*, there's a three-car collision in the intersection behind him. By cropping away Uncle Ned, you can isolate the car-crash portion of the frame. It now fills the screen; in effect, you've created an artificial zoom.

Now, whenever you crop out some video, you're leaving fewer pixels behind. You're therefore losing resolution and creating a less sharp picture. If you crop away a *huge* amount—more than half of the frame—you might wind up with noticeable pixellation and graininess.

If that happens, you can either live with it—or use Undo.

In any case, here's how you crop in iMovie:

Figure 9-9:
Top: Suppose you were too far away from the subject, or your zoom wasn't powerful enough.

Middle: Adjust the green rectangle so that it encloses the portion of the video you want to keep. The rectangle is either squarish or wide, depending on whether your project has the standard 4:3 aspect ratio or is widescreen. (See page 109 for details on aspect ratios.)

Bottom: After the cropping, the smaller portion of the frame expands to fill the entire frame. You lose some resolution in the process, of course, but you won't notice any graininess unless you crop out a lot of the original image.

1. **Select the clip you want to edit, and the frame.**

   If the clip is in the Event browser, then your crop applies to this clip every time you use it in a project from now on. If the clip is already in the storyboard, then you're cropping it only there.

Also find a good representative frame of the clip to work with in the Viewer. Do that by dragging the red dot across the filmstrip itself (Figure 9-2). Remember, you're working with video here, so things do tend to move around on the screen—but the iMovie cropping area does not move. You don't want to crop the clip in a way that centers your subject nicely on frame 50, but cuts it out completely on frame 100.

Tip: This will all be a lot easier if you magnify the image. Choose Window→Viewer→Large, or press ⌘-7.

---

2. **Press the letter C key on your keyboard, or click the Crop button on the toolbar, or click the faint crop *badge* that appears when you point to a clip (Figure 9-10).**

   Now the Viewer window sprouts a few new controls at the top, like Fit and Crop (Figure 9-10). The Crop button is already selected.

Figure 9-10:
Top: Click the Crop icon, or press the letter C, or click the tiny Crop badge on any clip. Bottom: A little icon appears on the filmstrip to show that it's been cropped.

Open Crop window

Crop, Rotate and Ken Burns - C

iMovie – Coyote

Crop badge

3. **Drag across the Viewer window to indicate what you want to keep.**

   As you drag, you create a green rectangle. Everything outside it will be thrown away when the cropping is over.

   As you work, you can drag inside the rectangle to move it around on the video. And you can drag any of the four corners to make the rectangle bigger or smaller. (You can't crop away more than half of the video area.)

Don't forget to move that little red dot on the filmstrip itself to spot check different places in the video, to make sure you're not cropping out anything important somewhere else in the clip. Or just click the Play button, or press your Space bar, to play the clip from the beginning.

4. Press Enter (or click Done).

The cropping is complete.

The tiny Crop icon that used to appear in the upper-left corner of the clip only when you pointed to it (Figure 9-10) now remains visible at all times, reminding you that this clip isn't what it used to be.

Adjusting or Removing the Crop

Cropping, like any iMovie edit, is nondestructive. That is, you haven't done anything permanent to the video on your hard drive, and you can adjust or remove the cropping at any time.

To do that, just click the Crop badge on the clip (Figure 9-10), or select the clip and then click the Crop tool (or press the letter C), and redo the cropping in the Viewer. For example, you can adjust the green boundary rectangle.

To remove the cropping altogether, click the Fit button in the Viewer. Then press Enter (or click Done).

Rotating Video

If there's any iMovie feature you'll use even less often than cropping, it's rotating. But sure enough, iMovie lets you rotate a clip by 90 degrees, or even upside-down.

When would you use this? OK, the answer is "almost never," but here are a couple of remote possibilities:

- Somebody actually filmed the scene with the camera turned 90 degrees. (This sometimes happens when people record video with a digital *still* camera, which they're used to turning 90 degrees for capturing tall subjects. Sometimes people forget that they can't rotate the camera that way when they're shooting *video.)*

- You shot a kid crawling along the rocks and want to make it look like he's mountain-climbing, vertically, straight up a cliff.

- You're making some strange, avant-garde film, and you're hoping to intentionally disorient your audience.

Anyway, if you're reading this, then you must have your reasons. Here's how you do the rotation:

1. Select the clip you want to edit, and the frame.

As usual, if the clip is in the Event browser, then the rotation applies to this clip every time you use it in a project from now on. If the clip is already in the story-board, then you're rotating it only there.

You can also move the red dot in the filmstrip itself (Figure 9-2) to find a good representative frame of the clip to watch in the Viewer.

2. **Press the letter C key on your keyboard, or click the Crop icon.**

So far, this is exactly like the cropping procedure.

3. **Click one of the Rotate buttons at the top of the Viewer (Figure 9-11).**

With each click, the entire video image rotates by 90 degrees in the corresponding direction. If you click twice, you flip the whole picture upside-down.

If you rotate the image only 90 degrees, of course, the video no longer fits in the frame; black bars appear on either side. At this point, you have two options: You can either leave it like that, or you can crop it so that it fills the frame.

To do that, click the Crop button in the Viewer, and then drag the green rectangle exactly as described in the previous section.

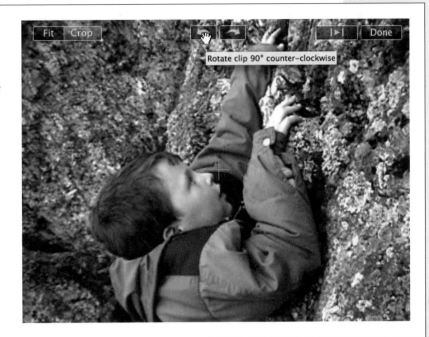

Figure 9-11:
With each click of the rotation arrows, you rotate the image 90 degrees. Use for special effects, or just for fun.

Rotate clip 90° counter-clockwise

4. **Press Enter (or click Done).**

The rotation is complete.

The little Crop icon appears in the upper-left corner of the clip's filmstrip (Figure 9-10). OK, you haven't necessarily *cropped* the video, but in iMovie's head, rotation is close enough for cropping for icon purposes.

Adjusting or Removing the Rotation

When you rotate your video, you're not changing the underlying footage. You can adjust or remove the rotation at any time.

Just click the clip, click the Crop tool (or press C), and click those rotation arrow buttons again until the video looks the way you want it. Then press Enter (or click Done).

QuickTime Video Filters

The old iMovie effects haven't all disappeared; some just went into hiding.

In Chapter 16, you can read about exporting iMovie projects as *QuickTime* movies—digital movie files on the hard drive. During that exporting process, you'll have the opportunity to apply the special effects that are still around. These *filters*, as they're called, can process your footage in ways like these:

Blur softens the look of the video;

Edge Detect creates outlines of the subjects in your footage;

Emboss makes your footage look like it was carved into a sheet of metal;

Sharpen makes blurry footage sharper (as much as is possible anyway);

Color Tint makes your footage turn black-and-white, sepia tone, cobalt, or negative image;

Film Noise adds scratches, dust, and rot to otherwise modern footage;

Lens Flare adds a cool-looking light flare that progresses across your footage as though caught in the lens of your camera.

Unfortunately, you have to apply these filters at the moment you export a project as a Quicktime movie—and that means that the filter will have to apply to your *entire* movie.

So what if you want to apply one of these filters just *one* clip within a movie? The trick: Create a separate project containing only that one clip. Export the one-clip project using the steps on page 308.

When it's all over, you'll have a QuickTime file on your hard drive, which you can bring right back into iMovie using the File→Import Movies command. Once the filtered footage is back in your Event library, just add it to your main project.

Titles, Subtitles, and Credits

T ext superimposed over footage is incredibly common in the film and video worlds. You'd be hard-pressed to find a single movie, TV show, or commercial that doesn't have titles, captions, or credits. In fact, one telltale sign that you're watching an *amateur* video is the *absence* of superimposed text.

In iMovie, the term *title* refers to any kind of text: credits, titles, subtitles, copyright notices, and so on. You don't need to be nearly as economical in your use of titles as you are with, say, transitions. Transitional effects interfere with something that stands perfectly well on its own—the footage. When you superimpose text, on the other hand, the audience is much more likely to accept your intrusion. You're introducing this new element for its benefit, to convey information you couldn't transmit otherwise.

Moreover, as you'll see, most of iMovie's text effects are far more focused in purpose than its transition selections, so you'll have little trouble choosing the optimum text effect for a particular editing situation. For example, the Scrolling Credits effect rolls a list of names slowly up the screen—an obvious candidate for the close of your movie.

Setting Up a Title

Adding some text to your movie requires several setup steps:

1. Choose a title style (centered, scrolling credits, or whatever).

2. Drag it into position in the storyboard.

3. Type the text.

4. Choose a font, color, and type size.

Here are these steps in more detail.

Choose a Title Style

Start by choosing Window→Titles (⌘-3), or click the T button just below the Viewer. The Titles panel appears (Figure 10-1).

Figure 10-1:
The icons here represent the various title styles in iMovie. There are really only a handful: centered, scrolling, and many variations of subtitles.

Figuring out what each title style is for isn't rocket science, but here's a quick run-down:

- **Centered.** The Centered Title may be the most useful of all iMovie text effects. It produces a single line of text (or two lines, if you take advantage of the subtitle option), fading in, staying onscreen for a moment, then fading out, making this effect ideal for displaying the title of your movie. This is a tasteful, professional, powerful effect.

Tip: You can always string together several consecutive Centered titles to imitate the way a movie's major stars' names appear at the beginning of a typical Hollywood movie.

- **Lower Third.** That's what it's called in the TV business—meaning the lower third of the TV screen—but the common name for this is *subtitle*. On TV, they usually use a "lower third" title to identify the talking head on the screen ("Harold P. Higgenbottom, GrooviTunes CEO"). You can use it that way, or to identify the location of a scene, or to translate what the person or baby is saying.

- **Scrolling Credits.** This effect produces two columns, like *Director…Steven Spielberg* and *Writer…Robert Towne,* or *character name…actor name* (Figure 10-2).

  Be careful when using this effect, for two reasons. First, iMovie automatically adjusts the speed of scrolling to fit all the names you've typed into the duration you've specified. If the title effect is too short, they'll scroll by too fast to read.

  Second, the type is fairly small, which could be a problem if you intend to save your movie as a QuickTime file.

Note: Setting up this title style requires special instructions, which appear on page 198.

Figure 10-2:
Top: The Scrolling Credits title style is the only iMovie text effect that's actually animated. You control its speed by controlling the length of the title strip in your storyboard.

Bottom: These subtitle variations all include an opaque or semi-opaque background to make your text stand out against the video. You can change the color of that background bar by simply clicking it.

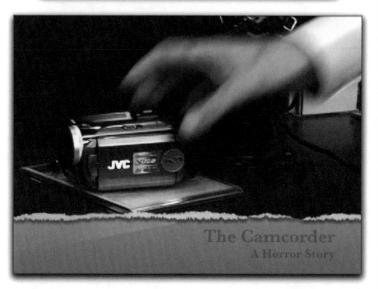

- **Gradient, Transparent, Formal, Torn Edge, Paper.** These are all variations on the Lower Third style. The only difference is what's *behind* the text; you have a choice of various semi-opaque backgrounds to make the text more readable, to make it stand out more from the video playing behind it.

Tip: In these styles, the background behind the text–the transparent bar, the torn-edged paper, and so on–starts out black, white, or tan. You can, however, choose *any* color for this background bar.

When you're editing the text, click anywhere *on* that background bar to open the Color Picker. (The Color Picker is described on page 204.)

- **Echo.** This unusual title style features a title, a subtitle—and an *echo* of the main title. An enormous, semitransparent, all-caps version of the main title also appears *behind* the text, almost as a graphic element.

Drag It into Position

Once you've chosen a title style, drag its icon directly into the storyboard. While you're still dragging (and the mouse button is down), you see purple highlighting on the filmstrip that will be covered by the text (Figure 10-3). That's iMovie's way of helping you pinpoint where the text will *first appear*.

As you'll soon see, knowing where the title is going to land in your storyboard is extremely important. You'll feel it snap into four places as your cursor moves:

- **Between clips.** Under normal circumstances, iMovie text gets superimposed over the video picture. Particularly when you're creating opening or closing credits,

Figure 10-3:
As you drag a title onto a clip, the purple highlighting shows how long the title will last. It snaps into three positions relative to the clip, shown in these three examples.

Top: If you drag toward the beginning of the clip, the title covers the first third of it.

Middle: If you drag over the middle, the title covers the entire clip.

Bottom: if you drag toward the end of the clip, the title covers the final third of it. Of course, you can adjust any of this later.

however, you may want the lettering to appear on a black screen—a striking and professional-looking effect.

In those cases, drag the title to the gap *between* filmstrips. You wind up with a title *over black* (rather than superimposed over your video). There's no longer a checkbox for "Over black," as in previous iMovie versions; you must simply drag the title between two clips, or to the very beginning or end of the storyboard (Figure 10-4).

This option is attractive for three reasons. First, it looks extremely professional. Second, the high contrast of white against black makes the text very legible. Third, the audience will *read* it, instead of being distracted by the video behind it.

Note: When you create a title over black, you *add* to the total length of your movie. You force the clips to the right of your title to slide further rightward to accommodate the credit you just inserted. That's just a reminder to anyone who's editing a video to be in sync with music. (When you insert text over video, by contrast, you don't change the overall length of your movie.)

Figure 10-3:
Top: If you drag a title in between two filmstrips, you wind up creating a black clip that's four seconds long (bottom). You can adjust the title's time on the screen by dragging the ends of its blue stripe; you can adjust the black clip's timing by clicking it and then choosing Edit→Set Duration (⌘-R).

- **At the beginning of the clip.** As the purple highlighting illustrates (Figure 10-3), iMovie proposes covering the *first third* of the filmstrip with the title.

- **Over the middle of the clip.** If your cursor winds up here, the title covers *the entire clip*, beginning to end.

- **At the end of the clip.** If your cursor falls here, the title stretches over the *final third* of the clip.

These are, of course, just starting points; you can always adjust a title's placement or duration after you've placed it.

Adjusting the Timing

Once you've dropped the title into place, it turns into a blue stripe over the filmstrip. (This, as it turns out, will become a familiar element in iMovie; audio such as background music is represented with draggable strips, too.)

The stripe indicates how long the text appears on the screen. As you can see in Figure 10-5, this stripe can straddle part of a clip, a whole clip, or many clips, which gives you a huge amount of flexibility.

Tip: iMovie won't let you overlap titles. You can, however, have more than one title on the same clip. Drag one onto the front third and another on the back third of the clip, for example. Then move those away from the ends and add even more titles, always using the ends of the clip as landing spots.

The only rule is that titles can't overlap.

Figure 10-5:
When your cursor approaches either end of a title stripe, it changes to a double-headed arrow. That's your cue that it's OK to start dragging the stripe's endpoint horizontally to make it longer or shorter.

You can adjust this stripe in three ways:

- **Adjust the starting point** by dragging the left edge of the stripe, as shown in Figure 10-5.

- **Adjust the ending point** by dragging the *right* end of the stripe.

  Adjusting either the left or right end of the stripe also changes its duration.

- **Move the entire title in time** by dragging horizontally *anywhere else* on it.

As you do that, take into account your viewers' reading speed. There's only one thing more frustrating than titles that fly by too quickly to read, and that's titles that sit there

---

onscreen forever, boring the audience silly. Many video editors use this guideline: Leave the words onscreen long enough for somebody to read them aloud twice.

Also consider the location of your title carefully. If you're superimposing it on a solid-colored background or a still image, no problem. But if you're planning to superimpose it on moving video, choose a scene that's relatively still, so that the video doesn't distract the audience from the words onscreen.

Be particularly careful not to superimpose your titles on an unsteady shot; the contrast between the jiggling picture and the rock-steady lettering on the screen will make your audience uncomfortable.

Note: The beauty of titles in iMovie '08 is that there's no rendering (computing) time. They appear instantly. So you can freely adjust the placement and timing of your titles as often as you like.

Type the Text

Unless the name of your movie is, in fact, "Title Text Here," you'll probably want to edit the dummy placeholder text of your newly born title.

To edit the text, click the blue stripe in the storyboard to select it. In the Viewer, text boxes appear, ready to edit.

Tip: Enlarge the viewer (Window→Viewer→Large, or ⌘-7) for easier access to these text boxes.

In most styles, you'll actually see *two* text boxes: a main title and a subtitle. Just click inside one of these boxes to edit the dummy text.

Tip: You don't have to type text into both of these boxes. The subtitle box underneath is there solely for your convenience, for those occasions when you need a second, smaller line of type underneath the larger credit. If you don't need text there, just delete the placeholder text.

All of the usual Mac OS X text-editing tricks apply in the text boxes. For example:

FEATURE HUNT

Return of the Black Clip

In iMovie 6 and previous versions, you could easily create a solid black clip, a moment of darkness, that could serve as a visual pause or a moment of silence in your video. You could even make it a solid *white* clip, or amber, or puce.

When that feature disappeared from iMovie '08, old-timers cried foul.

As it turns out, you can still create black clips in iMovie '08—you just have to know the secret.

The trick is to create a title *over black*—that is, drag a title icon into the space between two filmstrips in the storyboard. Then just click the blue title stripe to select it, and press your Delete key.

Presto—the title's gone, but the black clip remains. You can adjust its timing by selecting it and then choosing Edit→Set Duration (⌘-R).

- Double-click a word to highlight it.

- Triple-click inside the text box to select the entire title; at this point, you can just begin typing to replace the placeholder text.

- Press Option-arrow key (left or right) to jump one word at a time.

- Press Control-arrow key to jump to the beginning or end of the text box.

- Add Shift to those keystrokes to jump *and* select the intervening text simultaneously. For example, Shift-Option-right arrow highlights the word to the right of your insertion point.

- Cut, Copy, and Paste all work the way you'd expect.

- Press Tab to jump between text boxes.

When you're finished editing (and formatting, as described next), click Done in the Viewer.

Special notes on scrolling credits

When you click the blue stripe representing this kind of title, you see placeholder text snippets like the one shown in Figure 10-6.

To replace the dummy text with the actual names of your actors and characters, heed these notes:

- First, double-click where it says "Starring." Now you can type something new in its place, like "Featuring" or "Cast."

- When you see a dotted red underline, iMovie is warning you of a misspelling. Control-click (or right-click) the word to see spelling alternatives

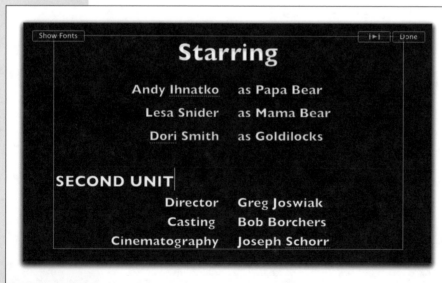

Figure 10-6:
Press Tab between names for one big scrolling list. Press Enter after a row to create a left-justified heading. After you type the heading, either press Tab (to list another name on the same row) or Enter, then Tab (to leave the heading on a row by itself). .

- Next, drag diagonally through the scrolling list of placeholder names. Once they're highlighted, you can begin typing your own cast list: the character name (*Raymond,* for example), then press Tab, then type the actor's name (*Dustin Hoffman,* for example). Press Tab to go to the next row. Type the next character name, press Tab, then add that actor's name. And so on.

- As you go, you can create headings like the ones shown in Figure 10-6 by pressing the Enter key at the end of a row. iMovie places the insertion point at the *left* side of the frame, so that you can type the heading (like *CREW* or *SECOND UNIT*).

- You can create a blank line in the credits by pressing Enter, Enter, Tab.

Tip: Using the Font panel, you can control the spacing between the lines of credits. See the Tip on page 204.

If you have too many names to fit on one screen, don't worry; the list scrolls automatically when you reach the bottom of the frame. You can keep typing until you've given credit to every last gaffer, best boy, and caterer. (You can scroll back up again by holding down the up arrow key.)

Font, Size, and Style

iMovie's creators are rather fond of Gill Sans; that's the typeface used in most of the title styles. It looks great, but it also looks like everyone *else's* iMovie '08 videos.

Fortunately, you have a surprising amount of typographical flexibility at your command. Which might come as a surprise, considering that *no* font, size, style, or justification controls are visible when you create a title.

The most basic style options are available in the Text menu.

Start by highlighting the text you want to change. That is, click the blue stripe of a title you've already placed. Then drag through some of the text in the text boxes in the Viewer.

Tip: iMovie '08 doesn't limit you to a single font and size; you can use different fonts within a single text block, if you must. You can even use a different font for *every letter,* if you so desire (or if you're making a ransom-note video).

Now you can choose a style from the Text menu. Your options include:

- **Bold, Italic, Underline, Outline.** Avoid Underline; it looks cheesy.

  In a document, Outline usually looks cheesy, too. But in iMovie, it's a terrific help; it means that each letter has a fine hairline around it, to help set it off against the video background. If the lettering is white, for example, it would otherwise disappear against white parts of the background.

- **Bigger, Smaller.** Here's a quick way to enlarge or shrink the highlighted text.

- **Align.** This submenu refers to the horizontal alignment of the text within its text block. You can choose Left (against the left side), Center (centered), or Right (against the right side). (The final choice, Justified, does nothing in iMovie.)

- **Kern.** *Kerning* is the typographical process of squishing characters closer together. Sometimes doing that can make a title more readable, more artistic, or just fit better in a small space. The commands in this submenu let you either tighten or loosen the spacing a tiny bit at a time.

- **Ligature.** *Ligatures* are character pairs, usually beginning with the lowercase *f,* that are artistically fused into a single symbol. For example, the word "*figure,*" with ligatures turned on, becomes *figure.*

  To turn ligatures on, highlight the text that contains the ligature-able pair (fl, fi, oe, or ae) and then choose Text→Ligature→Use All. To turn ligatures off, highlight the text and choose Text→Ligature→Use None.

- **Baseline.** The *baseline* is the invisible horizontal line on which text sits. Using this control, you can raise or lower some text, like this, or even create superscript (2^2) or subscript (H_2O) characters. ("Use Default" restores the text to the original baseline.)

- **Justification.** Press Shift-⌘-[to align the text with the left side of the text box, Shift-⌘-] for the right side, or Shift-⌘-\ to center it.

Figure 10-7 shows examples of many of these styles in use at once in a single, truly hideous opening credit.

Tip: Most of the commands in the Text menu have easy-to-remember keyboard shortcuts. It's always Shift, ⌘, and the first letter—B for bold, I for italic, + for bigger, - for smaller, and so on.

Figure 10-7:
You would never use all of iMovie's typography variations in a single title. But you could.

The Font Panel

Handy as the Text menu may be, it's missing a few important options—like text color and a choice of *fonts*.

For that purpose, iMovie also gives you full access to the Fonts panel, a standard Mac OS X feature that puts all typographical controls into a single place.

Suppose you've just highlighted a title block, and now you want to choose an appropriate typeface for it. Open the Fonts panel (Figure 10-8) by choosing Text→Show Fonts (⌘-T). Here's what's waiting for you there:

- **Collections.** The first column lists your *collections*—canned sets of fonts. Apple starts you off with collections called things like PDF (a set of standard fonts used in PDF files) and Web (fonts you're safe using on Web pages—that is, fonts that are very likely to be installed on the Macs or Windows PCs of your Web visitors).

Tip: *You can also create your own collections called, for example, Headline or Sans Serif, organized by font type. Then you can switch these groups of fonts on or off at will, just as though you'd bought a program like Suitcase. You use Mac OS X's Font Book program for this purpose.*

- **Family, Typeface.** The second column shows the names of the actual fonts in your system. The third, Typeface, shows the various style variations—Bold, Italic, Condensed, and so on—available in that type family. (Oblique and Italic are roughly the same thing; Bold, Black, and Ultra are varying degrees of boldface.) Just click the font you want to use in your iMovie title.

Figure 10-8:
The Fonts panel, available in many Mac OS X programs, offers elaborate controls over text color, shadow, and underline styles. It also contains some of the genetic material of old-style programs like Suitcase and Font Juggler. See the handy font sample shown here above the font lists? To get it, choose Show Preview from the Action (gear-shaped) pop-up menu at the bottom of the panel. Or use the mousy way: Place your cursor just above the headings (Collections, Family, and so on) and drag downward.

- **Size.** The last column lists a sampling of point sizes. You can use the size slider, choose from the point-size pop-up menu, or type any number into the box at the top of the Size list.

Underline, strikethrough, color, shadow

At the top of the Font panel are five rectangular buttons. Each is a pop-up menu that gives you an even more ridiculous amount of typography control:

- **Underline.** You can choose how you want the selected text to be underlined: with one underline, two, or none. If you choose Color, then the Mac OS X Color Picker appears (Figure 10-9), so that you can specify what *color* you want the underlines to be.

Figure 10-9:
Some of the typographical options can get ridiculous. When you request a different color for an underline or strikethrough, you get the Mac OS X Color Picker dialog box, which gives you a million different ways to dial up a precise shade.

- **Strikethrough.** This option draws a line through your text, as though you'd crossed it out. These days, there's really only one situation when you might find it useful: the way bloggers indicate a correction, either a real one or a fake one done for humorous purposes. You know: "Cellphone Companies Are ~~Greedy Slimebags~~ Profitable."

- **Text color.** The third pop-up rectangle opens the Color Picker dialog box. Here, you can specify what *color* you want the highlighted text to be. (See the box on page 204.) The important thing is to choose a color that *contrasts* with the footage behind the lettering. Use white against black, black against white, yellow against blue, and so on.

Note: iMovie doesn't limit you to TV-safe colors. But be careful. If colors are too bright (saturated), the edges of the letters can smear and tear when played back on a TV.

- **Document color.** The next pop-up rectangle is supposed to let you choose a background color for your text, but it doesn't work in iMovie.

- **Drop shadow.** The rightmost pop-up button is responsible for the shadow that iMovie adds to your titles to help them stand out from the background (Figure 10-10).

Figure 10-10:
The four tiny controls to the right of the Shadow button control the shadow itself: its opacity, degree of "spread," distance from the main characters (controls how far away the "page" looks from the text), and the angle of the light that's casting the shadow.

Secondary controls

At the bottom of the Fonts panel are controls for Bold, Italic, Underline, and Outline; Alignment; Kerning; and Baseline height. All of these duplicate the equivalent commands in the Text menu.

There are, however, two controls here that are *not* in the Text menu, and they can sometimes be very useful:

- **Line Spacing.** In a word processor, this slider would affect the distance between lines of text in a single paragraph. iMovie doesn't let you create paragraphs, of course—each text block contains only a single line of type—but this slider can still be helpful. It governs the distance between the main title and its *subtitle*, so that you can add some space between the two.

Tip: In the Scrolling Credits title style, this control lets you adjust the amount of vertical space between the rows of credits. Cool!

- **Outline.** This slider governs the thickness of the outline (when you're using the Outline font style). Make it thick enough, and you can create some truly, er, *unforgettable* effects.

Tip: Once you've got a piece of text formatted just the way you like it, you're not condemned to repeating all that work to format the *next* title.

Instead, highlight some of the text that already looks good. Choose Text→Copy Style (Option-⌘-C). Then highlight the text that you want to match, and choose Text→Paste Style (Option-⌘-V). The second title now changes to match the formatting of the first one.

The Color Picker

Here and there—not just in iMovie, but also in System Preferences, TextEdit, Microsoft Office, and many other programs—Mac OS X offers you the opportunity to choose a *color* for some element, like your desktop background, a window, and so on.

The Colors dialog box (Figure 10-9) offers a miniature color lab that lets you dial in any color in the Mac's rainbow. *Several* color labs, actually, arrayed across the top, are each designed to make color-choosing easier in certain circumstances:

Color Wheel. Drag the scroll bar vertically to adjust the brightness, and then drag your cursor around the ball to pick the shade.

Color Sliders. From the pop-up menu, choose the color-mixing method you prefer. *CMYK* stands for Cyan, Magenta, Yellow, and Black. People in the printing industry will feel immediately at home, because these four colors are the component inks for color printing. (These people may also be able to explain why *K* stands for *black*.)

RGB is how a TV or computer monitor thinks of colors: as proportions of red, green, and blue. And **HSV** stands for Hue, Saturation, and Value—a favorite color-specifying scheme in scientific circles.

In each case, just drag the sliders to mix up the color you want, or type in the percentages of each component.

Color Palettes presents canned sets of color swatches. They're primarily for programmers who want quick access to the standard colors in Mac OS X.

Image Palettes offers the visible rainbow arrayed yet another way—cloudy, color-arranged streaks.

Crayons. Now *this* is a good user interface. You can click each crayon to see its color name: "Mocha," "Cayenne," "Fern," and so on. (Some interior decorator in Cupertino had a field day naming these crayons.)

In any of these color pickers, you can also "sample" a color that's *outside* the dialog box—a color in the video shot, for example, or one that you found on a Web page. Just click the magnifying-glass icon and then move your cursor around the screen. You'll see the sliders and numbers automatically change inside the dialog box when you click.

Finally, note that you can store frequently used (or frequently admired) colors in the mini-palette squares at the bottom. To do that, drag the big rectangular color swatch (next to the magnifying glass) directly down into one of the little squares, where it will stay fresh for weeks.

General Guidelines

As you choose fonts and type effects for the various credits in your movie, consider these guidelines:

- **Be consistent.** Using the same typeface for all of the titles in your movie lends consistency and professionalism to the project.

- **Remember the QuickTime effect.** If you plan to distribute your finished movie as a QuickTime file—an electronic movie file that you can distribute by email, network, CD, disk, or Web page—use the biggest, boldest, cleanest fonts you have. Avoid spindly, delicate fonts or script fonts. When your movie is compressed down to a 3-inch square, what looks terrific in your Viewer will be so small it may become completely illegible.

Come to think of it, you might want to choose big, bold, clean fonts even if you're going to play the finished movie on a TV whose resolution is far lower than that of your computer screen. Be especially careful when using one of the text effects that includes a subtitle, as iMovie subtitles often use an even smaller typeface than the primary title font, and may lose legibility if the font has too much filigree.

Finally, favor *sans serif* fonts—typefaces that don't have the tiny *serifs*, or "hats and feet," at the end of the character strokes. The typeface you're reading now is a serif font, one that's less likely to remain legible in a QuickTime movie. The typeface used in the Tip below is a sans serif font.

UP TO SPEED

Title Fade-In/Fade-Out Timing

Apple isn't into *hard edges* on things. When you listen to a 30-second sample of a song on the iTunes music store, it fades in and out. When you answer a call on the iPhone, the music gracefully fades out first. Even the upper-right corners of your Mac screen are gently rounded.

In the same way, iMovie text never just *pops* onto the screen—it always fades in, hangs around for the specified time, and then fades out.

Title Fade Duration: ⟞———◯————⟝ 0.5s

You do, however, have some say in how *long* it takes to fade in and out. In a fast-moving, hard-hitting video, a slow, graceful fade-in can sap some of the energy away;

but in a languorous, wordless retrospective of someone's life, a more gradual appearance and disappearance would be appropriate.

To change the fade timing, choose File→Project Properties, or press ⌘-J. In the Properties dialog box, use the Title Fade Duration slider to specify how long titles in this movie should take to appear and disappear. You can make them pop on in a quarter of a second, or take their sweet time (2 seconds).

You can't control the fade-ins and fade-outs separately. And you can't change the fade timing of any *one* title; this slider affects all titles in the movie simultaneously.

Tip: Some of the standard Mac fonts that look especially good as iMovie fonts are Arial Black, Capitals, Charcoal, Chicago, Gadget, Helvetica, Impact, Sand, Techno, and Textile.

Some of the fonts whose delicate nature may be harder to read are Monaco, Courier, Old English, Swing, Trebuchet, Times, Palatino, and Verdana.

The beauty of iMovie's titling feature is that the fonts you choose become embedded into the actual digital picture. In other words, when you distribute your movie as a QuickTime file, you don't have to worry that your recipients might not have the same fonts you used to create the file. They'll see on their screens exactly what you see on yours.

Tip: Don't forget that you can superimpose text on a *still* image (Chapter 12), too—such as a photo or some gradient fill you've created in, say, Photoshop Elements.

Add a Backdrop

Using the Titles feature isn't the only way to create text effects. Using a graphics program like Photoshop or Photoshop Elements, you can create text "slides" with far more flexibility than you can in the Titles feature. For example, the built-in Titles feature doesn't give you any way to create little music-video text blocks in the lower-left corner of the frame. But using a "title card" that you import as a graphic, you're free to use any text color and any font size. You can even dress up such titles with clip art, 3-D effects, and whatever other features your graphics software offers. Figure 10-11 (bottom) shows the idea.

Creating a title like this involves creating an *alpha-channel TIFF* file. A little Photoshop experience is helpful, but here's the gist:

Use the text tool to type and format the text in Photoshop. In the Layers palette, ⌘-click the text layer's thumbnail to select it (see the picture on page 244). Then, in the Channels palette, click the Save Selection as Channel button at the bottom of the Channels palette. Finally, choose File→Save As. Choose TIFF as the format, turn *off* the Layers checkbox, and leave Alpha Channels turned on. Name the title and save it to your desktop.

Now just drag the title graphic off your desktop and onto a title, as shown in Figure 10-11 (top).

Checking the Result

As you're editing the title, you can see how it looks in context by clicking the Play button (upper right of the Viewer).

Or, once your title is complete, point to a spot in the storyboard just before the title and then press the Space bar to view the title in the context of the movie. Or just move your cursor back and forth across the title without clicking to see how it looks.

If the title isn't quite what you wanted—if it's the wrong length, style, or font, or if there's a typo, for example—you can change its settings as described in the next section. If the title wasn't *at all* what you wanted—if it's the wrong title style, for example—you can undo the entire process by highlighting the blue title strip and pressing the Delete key (or choosing Edit→Undo, if you added the title recently).

Figure 10-11:
Top: Drag your alpha-channel TIFF title graphic right off the desktop and into a filmstrip.

Bottom: iMovie recognizes it instantly as a traditional title, and superimposes it on your video. You can adjust the timing or placement by dragging the title strip, just as you would with any other title.

Editing or Deleting a Title

Making changes to a title is easy.

• **Change the starting or ending points** by dragging the endpoints of the blue stripe in the storyboard.

- **Move the entire title earlier or later** in the storyboard by dragging its stripe left or right.

- **Edit the text or its typography** by clicking the title's blue stripe in the storyboard. The text boxes appear immediately in the Viewer. Press ⌘-T to open the Font panel if you need to change the color, font, or other typographical niceties.

- **Delete a title** by clicking its blue stripe and then pressing the Delete key.

Narration, Music, and Sound

I f you're lucky, you may someday get a chance to watch a movie whose soundtrack isn't finished yet. You'll be scanning channels and stumble across a special about how movies are made, or you'll see a tribute to a film composer, or you'll rent a DVD of some movie that includes a "making of" documentary. Such TV shows or DVDs sometimes include a couple of minutes from the finished movie as it looked *before* the musical soundtrack and sound effects were added.

At that moment, your understanding of the film medium will take an enormous leap forward. "Jeez," you'll say, "without music and sound effects, this $100 million Hollywood film has no more emotional impact than...my home movies!"

And you'll be right. It's true that the *visual* component of film is the most, well, visible. The household names are the directors and movie stars, not the sound editors, composers, *foley* (sound effects) artists, and others who devote their careers to the audio experience of film.

But without music, sound effects (called SFX for short), and sound editing, even the best Hollywood movie will leave you cold and unimpressed.

Two Kinds of Audio

iMovie '08's audio features are completely and totally different from what was in previous versions. You can no longer view audio tracks as waveforms beneath the video, there's no way to make manual volume adjustments within an audio clip, and all the audio filters and effects are gone. (Apple hints that restoring these features are a priority.)

What you *can* do in iMovie '08 is plunk down music or audio files into your storyboard in either of two ways, so that it plays along with your video:

- **Background music** is a solid block of music that plays from the beginning of the movie, no matter how you shuffle the video clips around. You can even line up a "playlist" of several songs; they play consecutively, crossfading nicely between songs.

- **Sound effects.** In this case, you attach an audio file to a specific spot in the video. It goes along for the ride as you rearrange your clips.

Now, the following gets confusing, so read it slowly: There's no difference at all between the *kinds* of audio that you can use in these two ways. *Any* audio, including sound effects, can be background audio; and *any* audio, including songs, can behave like a sound effect. Details later in this chapter.

Audio Sources

Much like traditional film cameras, iMovie separates the audio and video into separate tracks, which you can view and edit independently. In iMovie, audio shows up as a colored stripe under or behind the filmstrips.

You can incorporate sound from any of these sources:

- **Camcorder audio.** You can extract the audio from a camcorder video clip to use as an independent sound clip, for use somewhere else in the movie.

- **iTunes tracks.** This, of course, is an example of what makes iLife a suite and not just a handful of separate programs: iMovie's integration with the other Apple programs. As described later in this chapter, iMovie displays your complete iTunes music collection, playlists and all. Adding background music to your flick is easy as can be.

- **Narration.** This can be anything that you record with your microphone.

- **Sound effects.** Choose these from iMovie's Audio palette (gunshots, glass breaking, applause, and so on).

- **MP3, WAV, AIFF, and AAC files.** iMovie can directly import files in these popular music formats. You can drag them in from the Finder or bring them in from iTunes.

LOST TREASURE

Importing Music from a CD

For several versions of iMovie, you could import songs from a CD directly into iMovie. You could just insert your favorite music CD (Carly Simon, Rolling Stones, the Cleveland Orchestra, or whatever), choose the track you want to swipe, and the deed was done.

That feature mysteriously disappeared, starting in iMovie 6. Now you're supposed to switch into iTunes, import the CD into your music collection there, and then return to iMovie to import it. (You may have to quit and reopen iMovie to make it "discover" the changes in the iTunes list.)

This chapter covers all of these sound varieties.

Adding Audio to the Storyboard

Nothing adds emotional impact to a piece of video like music. Slow, romantic music makes the difference between a sad story and one that actually makes viewers cry. Fast, driving music makes viewers' hearts beat faster—scientists have proven it. Music is so integral to movies these days that, as you walk out of the theater, you may not even be aware that a movie *had* music, but virtually every movie does—and you were emotionally manipulated by it.

Home movies are no exception. Music adds a new dimension to your movie, so much so that some iMovie fans *edit to music.* They choose a song, lay it down in the audio track, and then cut the video footage to fit the beats, words, or sections of the music.

Tip: Even if you don't synchronize your video to the music in this way, you might still want to experiment with a music-only soundtrack. That is, set the volume for your camcorder clips to zero (page 227), so your movie is silent except for the music. The effect is powerful, and often used in Hollywood montage sequences.

The Music and Sound Effects Browser

Here's how you go about choosing a piece of music, or a sound effect, for your movie:

1. **Choose Window→Music and Sound Effects (or press ⌘-1).**

   Alternatively, click the musical-notes icon just beneath the Viewer. Either way, the lower-right chunk of your iMovie window is now filled with the Music and Sound browser (Figure 11-1).

2. **Find just the right song (or other sound).**

   The panel is filled with useful controls to help you find the right sound. Its listings include:

   iMovie '08 Sound Effects. This list includes about 100 handy sound effects like doors closing, trains passing, and animal sounds.

   iLife Sound Effects represents another enormous collection of sound effects, organized into folders. Don't miss, in particular, the Jingles folder; it contains 200 pieces of terrific, professionally recorded, *royalty-free* background music in every style.

   GarageBand. Here's a nice perk of having an integrated suite of programs like iLife: You can share the output of each program and touch it up in the others. For example, any musical compositions you've worked up in GarageBand show up here.

Note: Actually, you see in this list only the compositions you've saved with what Apple calls an iLife preview. To make sure your piece has this preview attached, open GarageBand→Preferences, click General, and then turn on "Render an audio preview when saving." This option makes saving a GarageBand song take longer, but it's necessary if you want your musical masterpieces to show up in iMovie.

iTunes. If you keep your music collection in the free iTunes software, you're in luck; the entire assortment shows up right here, in the iTunes category. In fact, if you've organized your iTunes music into *playlists* (subsets), you can scroll through them right in the list. You can also use the Search box at the bottom of the list, as shown in Figure 11-2, right.

Figure 11-1:
Welcome to the Music and Sound browser, which reveals your iTunes music collection, your GarageBand masterpieces, and several hundred sound effects. (If you don't see the category you want, click the corresponding flippy triangle at the top of the list.)

To listen to a piece of audio in *any* of these categories (GarageBand, iTunes, and so on), click its name, and then click the ▶ button beneath the list. Or, if you think life is too short already, just *double-click* a song name. (To interrupt playback, either double-click a different song, double-click the same one, or click the round ▶ button again.)

You can sort the list alphabetically by song name, artist name, or song length, just by clicking the appropriate heading above the list. (Ordinarily, you wouldn't think that it would be very useful to sort the list by track length. But remember that in the context of a video editing program, finding a song that's exactly the right length for your video might wind up being more important than which band plays it.)

Tip: The playback controls on the Audio pane are independent of the playback controls in the Monitor window. You may find it useful, therefore, to play your movie in progress *as* you listen to the different songs, so that you can preview how the music might sound when played simultaneously with the video.

The easiest way to experiment in this way is to click ▶ in the Music and Sound browser at precisely the same instant that you press the Space bar to begin the movie playback.

3. Drag the music into your storyboard.

Using the song's name as a handle, drag it directly out of the list and into the storyboard. Release the mouse when the song looks like it's in the right place.

POWER USERS' CLINIC

Adding or Removing Sound Effects

The list of sound effects in the Music and Sound Effects panel isn't magical. It's simply a listing of the sound files that came with iMovie. If you know the secret, you can delete, move, or rename your sound effects—or even install new ones. Here's how.

First, quit iMovie. In the Finder, open your Applications folder. Control-click (or right-click) iMovie's icon; from the shortcut menu, choose Show Package Contents.

The iMovie *package window* appears. You've just discovered, if you didn't already know, that many Mac OS X program icons are, in fact, thinly disguised folders (called *packages*) that contain dozens or hundreds of individual support files. You've just opened up iMovie for inspection.

Open the Contents→Resources folder. Welcome to the belly of the beast. Before you sit hundreds of individual files, most of them the little graphics that make up the various iMovie buttons, controls, and so on. (If you're really feeling ambitious, you can actually open up these graphics and edit them, completely changing the look of iMovie.)

The icon you want is the folder called iMovie '08 Sound Effects. It's a folder full of individual sound files—in MP3 format—that make up the list you see in the Audio pane (Figure 11-2).

Feel free to reorganize these files. For example, you can throw away the ones you never use, or rename the ones you do. You can add new MP3 files to this list. You can even make new folders to categorize the selection; later, you'll see them show up as subfolders of the iMovie '08 Sound Effects heading in the Music and Sound Effects browser.

(Looking for even more sound effects? The Internet is filled with downloadable MP3 files that you can use in your iMovie projects. You might start your search at *www.google.com*. Perform a search for *free sound effects*. Many are already in MP3 format; many others are in AIFF format, which you can convert to iMovie-friendly MP3 files using iTunes.)

Close all the windows. When you return to iMovie, you'll see, under the iMovie '08 Sound Effects heading, the updated list of MP3 sound-effects files.

And what, you may ask, is "the right place?" It turns out that where you drop the music is extremely important.

Figure 11-2:
Choose any of your playlists to navigate your massive music collection. You can also click in the Search box. As you type a song or performer's name, iMovie hides all songs whose names don't match, so that you can quickly home in on a certain song or group of songs from among thousands. (To restore the entire list and delete what you've typed, click the little X button at the right end of the Search box.)

If you release the mouse when the *entire background* of the storyboard has turned green (Figure 11-3), then you're creating what iMovie calls background music; see the next page for details.

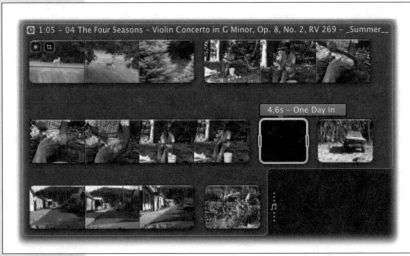

Figure 11-3:
Background music turns into a huge green puddle behind your filmstrips. Try skimming/ playing the movie after you've placed the music. If it doesn't have quite the effect you thought it would, press ⌘-Z (Edit→Undo) and try another experiment.

Tip: If your intention is to add background music like this, then you can actually drag *more than one* song from the Music and Sound Effects browser simultaneously. (To select more than one, click the first one, and then ⌘-click each additional one in the list.)

This presumes, of course, that there's enough video to "cover" them all. If there's not, you could wind up with stacked, superimposed background audio bubbles. If that happens, you can delete one at a time (page 220) until they're no longer stacked.

If you release the mouse when the pointer is on a filmstrip, then you're creating what iMovie calls a "sound effect"; page 220 has more information.

Adding Audio from the Finder

The Music and Sound Effects browser is a great way to find music and effects for your movie—*if* they're listed there. You may very well have folders full of audio files that *didn't* come from iTunes, GarageBand, or Apple.

Fortunately, they're easy to incorporate; see Figure 11-4. Just keep in mind that *how* you drag files in from the desktop determines whether they become background audio (big green bubble) or "sound effects" audio (horizontal stripes)—just exactly as described above.

Figure 11-4:
If you have audio files on your Mac that aren't listed in the iMovie audio browser, make the iMovie window smaller (drag its lower-right corner inward) so you can see the desktop behind it. Open the desktop window that contains your audio clips, and then drag them into your storyboard.

Background Music

If you drag a piece of music into the *background well* of your storyboard—basically, anywhere *except* onto a clip—the background of the entire storyboard area develops a broad green bubble. That's your clue that you've just installed a piece of what Apple calls "background music."

Understanding what, exactly, Apple means by this term—and figuring out how it's different from the *sound effects*–style music—is not especially easy. This much, though, is clear:

- **Background music appears in the storyboard** as a huge green or purple background bubble behind your filmstrips. (Sound-effects audio, on the other hand, appears as a skinny horizontal stripe over the filmstrip.)

- **The music ends at the end of your video, even if the song isn't over yet.** If the song is *longer* than the movie, a special vertical indicator bar appears after the last filmstrip to let you know—a vertical dotted line with two musical notes. And if you then add *more* video to the project, the background music auto-expands to include it. It's stretchy that way.

- **Background music generally plays from the beginning of your movie.** You can drag it into a different spot, however, as described on the next page.

- **If you place two pieces of background music right up against each other, iMovie plays them consecutively, with a crossfade in between.** You can add another piece the same way you added the first one: by dragging its name from the Music

---

FREQUENTLY ASKED QUESTION

Fun with Copyright Law

Don't I break some kind of law when I copy music from a commercial CD, or use iTunes Music Store music in one of my movies?

Exactly what constitutes stealing music is a hot-button issue that has tied millions of people (and recording executives) in knots. That's why some iMovie fans hesitate to distribute their iMovie films in places where lawyers might see them—like the Internet.

Frankly, though, record company lawyers have bigger fish to fry than small-time amateur operators like you. You're perfectly safe showing your movies to family and friends, your user group, and other limited circles of viewers. In fact, Apple *encourages* you to use iTunes Music Store purchases in your movies; after all, Apple is the one who made them available right in iMovie.

You'll risk trouble only if you go commercial, making money from movies that incorporate copyrighted music.

Still, if your conscience nags you, you could always use one of your GarageBand compositions. And even if you're not especially musical, the world is filled with royalty-free music—music that has been composed and recorded expressly for the purpose of letting filmmakers add music to their work without having to pay a licensing fee every time they do so.

Some of it's even free. You'll find 200 free musical pieces in the Jingles folder of your Music and Sound Effects browser, for example, ready to use.

Or check out *www.freeplaymusic.com*, a Web site filled with prerecorded music in every conceivable style, that you're welcome to use in your movies at no charge for noncommercial use.

If that's not enough for you, visit a search page like *www. google.com*, search for *music library* or *royalty-free music,* and start clicking your way to the hundreds of Web sites that offer information about (and listenable samples of) music that you can buy and use without fear. (Many of these sites require a RealAudio plug-in, an add-on for your Web browser that you can download and install from *www.real.com*.)

---

and Sound Effects browser. (Two pieces of background music can never overlap, though.)

Pinning and Un-pinning Background Music

When you drag music into the background of your storyboard, it starts out being *unpinned.* It's called unpinned because it's not attached to the video. You can add or delete chunks of video, but that good ol' music pad stays right where it is, unaffected. It's a steady stream of music that plays from the beginning of your movie. Unpinned background music has a green bubble.

There are times, however, when unpinned music can be a real pain. You might have a situation where you want to line up a certain video moment (like Bill-Gates-getting-hit-with-a-pie footage) with a particular audio moment (like a cymbal crash). You'll find that when you insert or delete some video footage *after* lining up audio with specific video moments, everything goes out of alignment. This syndrome can rear its ugly head in many video editing programs.

POWER USER'S CLINIC

The Music Trimmer

Most people treat background music in iMovie as a set-it-and-forget-it affair. You drop it into the storyboard, it plays as long as necessary to cover your video, end of story.

Truth is, though, you have a little more control than that. Exhibit A: You can start any piece of music playing from someplace *other* than its beginning (and stop it before its end). If you have an iTunes track that begins with an annoying 35-second drum solo, for example, you can lop it out, so that the music (and your movie) begins with the actual hook of the song—the main part.

To edit background audio in this way, click anywhere on the green background bubble to select it (a yellow outline appears on it). Now choose Edit→Trim Music, or press ⌘-R, or click the tiny clock icon in the upper-left corner of the background audio bubble.

Suddenly, the storyboard filmstrips disappear. They're replaced by the Music Trimmer window, which looks a lot like the Clip Trimmer described on page 141.

You're seeing the soundwaves that represent the background music. The soundwaves you'll actually hear are light pink; if the music is longer than the video, the soundwaves you *won't* hear (because they would play after the video is over) are black.

Your job here is to adjust the position of the yellow vertical end handles. Drag the first one to the right if you want the music to begin at a point that's later in the song; drag the final one to the left if you want the music to end before the official end of the song. You can skim or play to hear where you are in the piece.

Click Done when you're finished adjusting the beginning and ending points.

Incidentally, this trick also works on "sound effects" audio (page 220), narration, and so on. In those situations, begin with one click on the corresponding colored stripe in the storyboard, and then choose Edit→Trim Music (⌘-R).

You may wind up playing a frustrating game of find-the-frame, over and over again, all the way through the movie, as you try to redo all of your careful audio/video alignments.

The solution is to *pin* the audio. Click carefully on the *name* of the background audio bubble, and drag it horizontally (Figure 11-5).

When you release the mouse, you'll see that the background audio bubble has now turned purple. iMovie has now locked the audio to the video at that frame, as indicated by the little pushpin (Figure 11-5, bottom). Even if the video later gets moved around in its track, or even if you later trim away some footage from the beginning of the video clip, the music will still begin at that point in the video.

Figure 11-5:
Top: These two consecutive green background songs are unpinned. They're floating, completely unaffected by your video editing.

Bottom: If you drag one of the bubbles to the right, you pin it to a particular video frame—which you'll know because of the purple coloring and the pushpin. You can add new video clips or take some away, but this audio will always begin playing at this spot in the video.

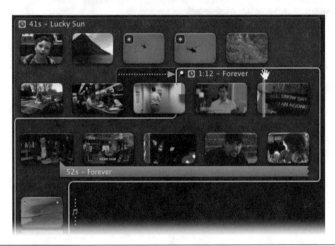

Once you've locked an audio clip to its video, you no longer have to worry that it might lose sync with its video when you edit your video clips.

By the way, pinning an audio clip doesn't prevent *you* from shifting it. Dragging the audio clip does *not* drag the "attached" video clip along with it. You're still welcome to slide the audio clip left or right in its track, independent of any other clips. Doing so simply makes iMovie realign the clip with a new video frame, lining up the pushpin accordingly. (If you *cut* the video clip, the background audio disappears entirely.)

Note: Pinning an audio clip also cuts off any background audio that's playing at that point, whether it's pinned or not. If you want overlapping audio tracks, you must implement them as sound effects; see page 220.

To *un-pin* an audio clip, restoring it to its free-floating status, click it, and then choose Edit→Un-Pin Music Track. The audio bubble turns green again, and slams against the left side of the storyboard area (or against the whatever background audio bubble is to its left). It's no longer attached to the video.

Rearranging Unpinned Background Music

If you understand the concept of unpinned, free-floating background audio (and you're forgiven if you don't), then you realize that these songs play consecutively, one after another. Unless you've dragged and pinned them, they stack up against each other, left to right in your storyboard, and play sequentially, with a 1-second crossfade between them.

Now suppose that you want to rearrange them. How are you supposed to do that? Certainly not by dragging them—as you now know, dragging in iMovie means "pin this music to the video."

The trick is to choose Edit→Arrange Music Tracks. The weird little dialog box shown in Figure 11-6 appears.

Figure 11-6:
The Edit→Arrange Music Tracks command is available only when you've added at least two background audio clips to your project. It opens this dialog box.

Pinned Music Tracks	Duration
A Walk in the Sun	9.2s
Forever	7s

Un-Pin Track

Floating Music Tracks	Duration
The Vow	51s
Lucky Sun	41s
Come Clean	7.5s
Lucky Sun	41s

Drag music items up or down to change the order that they are heard in your project.

Cancel   OK

It's a master list of all the background audio clips you've added. Two master lists, actually, helpfully color-coded to match the background audio bubbles in the storyboard:

- **Pinned Music Tracks (purple).** This is a list of all the audio you've pinned to specific moments in the storyboard, complete with their durations.

  You can't do anything in this upper list *except* to click a song, and then click Un-Pin Track. Doing so makes the song leave the purple list and jump down to the green list of Floating Music Tracks. (Meanwhile, back in the storyboard, that bit of audio turns green and slams against the next available piece of green, floating background audio.)

Note: In all, there are three ways to un-pin a piece of music. You can use the Un-Pin Track button described here; you can use the Edit→Un-Pin Music Track command; or you can Control-click (right-click) a piece of pinned, purple music, and, from the shortcut menu, choose Un-Pin Music Track.

- **Floating Music Tracks (green).** Here are all the background audio pieces that you *haven't* pinned to your video. These are the ones that "float" from the left side of your storyboard, playing sequentially, without any connection to the video.

  And here's the main idea behind this dialog box: You can drag the names of the floating tracks up or down in the list to rearrange them. (Music at the *top* of this list appears at the *beginning* of your project.)

When you're finished, click OK.

Deleting Background Audio

To remove a piece of background audio from your project, click its green or purple bubble once; when the yellow border appears, press the Delete key.

Sound Effects (Pinned Music)

As you now know, iMovie has two kinds of audio. What Apple calls background music is represented by a big green bubble *behind* your filmstrips. It's mean to play continuously as a background pad, regardless of the video that's playing. (Yes, yes, it's true, you *can* "pin" this type of audio to a specific video frame, but for the sake of clarity, let's ignore that.)

Apple calls the other type of audio *sound effects* audio, and it's specifically intended to be attached, or pinned, directly to a particular frame of a particular clip. If that clip gets pushed around in the storyboard during editing, the audio goes along for the ride.

There are three interesting things about sound-effects audio (Figure 11-7). First, it's represented as a green horizontal stripe above the filmstrip. Second, you can attach more than one of these stripes, stacking them up as high as necessary. (That is, you can overlap these audio tracks, which you can't do with background music tracks.)

And finally, you can move, shorten, or delete the sound-effect stripes by simply dragging.

Sound FX (Pinned Music)

Tip: Actually, there are two ways to adjust the length of a sound-effect stripe. You can drag its right end with your mouse, which is quick and direct. You can also click the stripe (to select it), and then choose Trim Music (⌘-R). For details on using the Music Trimmer window, see the box on page 217.

Figure 11-7:
You can attach multiple sound effects to a single clip; they all move when the video clip moves. To delete a sound effect, click its stripe, and then press the Delete key. To move it, drag the stripe horizontally. And to shorten the clip, drag either end inward.

Recording Narration

If anyone ever belittles iMovie for being underpowered, point out an iMovie feature that isn't even available in most expensive video editing programs: the ability to record narration while you watch your movie play. If your Mac has a microphone, you can easily create any of these effects:

FREQUENTLY ASKED QUESTION

Music Beyond the Video

How the heck do I make the music start before the video—or play on for a few seconds past the end of the video?

You're on to something here. There is no way to drag audio, of any type, to the *left* of the first filmstrip in your storyboard. And there's no way to make one extend to the *right* of the last one. Therefore, there doesn't seem to be any way to make the music begin before the movie, or play past the end of it.

Ah, but that's what workarounds are for.

The solution, in this case, is simple: Create a *black clip* at the beginning or end of your movie. Fill the screen with nothingness. Your music will play happily, since it *thinks* that it's playing under video—but your audience will see a black screen as the music plays.

Details on creating a black clip appear on page 197.

- **Create a reminiscence.** As the footage shows children playing, we hear you saying, "It was the year 2007. It was a time of innocence. Of sunlight. Of children at play. In the years before the Great Asteroid, nobody imagined that one 6-year-old child would become a goddess to her people. This, then, is her story."

This technique of superimposing an unseen narrator's voice over video is called a *voiceover.* It's incredibly popular in TV, commercials, and movies (such as *Saving Private Ryan, Sin City,* and of course, the *Look Who's Talking* movies).

- **Identify the scene.** Even if your movie isn't one with a story line, iMovie's narration feature offers an extremely convenient method of identifying your home movies. Think about it: When you get photos back from the drugstore, the date is stamped across the back of each photo. In years to come, you'll know when the photos were taken.

Video cameras offer an optional date-stamp feature, too—a crude, ugly, digital readout that permanently mars your footage. But otherwise, as they view their deteriorating VHS cassettes in 2025, most of the world's camcorder owners will never know where, why, or when their footage was shot. Few people are compulsive enough to film, before each new shot, somebody saying, "It's Halloween 2007, and little Chrissie is going out for her very first trick-or-treating. Mommy made the costume out of some fishnet stockings and a melon," or whatever.

Using iMovie, though, it's easy to add a few words of shot-identification narration over your establishing shot. (To find out the time and date when the footage was shot, just double-click the clip.)

- **Provide new information.** For professional work, the narration feature is an excellent way to add another continuous information stream to whatever videos or still pictures are appearing on the screen. Doctors use iMovie to create narrated slideshows, having created a storyboard filled with still images of scanned slides. (See Chapter 12.) Real estate agents feature camcorder footage of houses under consideration, while narrating the key features that can't be seen. ("Built in 1869, this house was extensively renovated in 1880…").

And it doesn't take much imagination to see how *lawyers* can exploit iMovie.

To create a *voiceover* (a narration), follow these steps.

1. **Click the Voiceover button (Figure 11-8, top), or press the letter O key.**

   The Voiceover window appears (Figure 11-8, bottom).

2. **Choose a sound source, like your Mac's microphone.**

   Your Mac's microphone takes one of two forms: built-in or external. The built-in mike, a tiny hole in the facade of the iMac, eMac, or MacBook, couldn't be more convenient—it's always with you, and always turned on.

   If your Mac doesn't have a built-in microphone, you can plug in an external USB microphone, an old external iSight camera, or a standard microphone with an adapter (like the iMic, *www.griffintechnology.com*).

The Record From pop-up menu lists all the audio sources that the Mac knows about—Built-in Microphone, Built-in Input (meaning the audio-input jack on the back or the side), USB Microphone, or whatever you've got connected.

Note: The selection you make here is independent of the input that's currently selected in System Preferences. That's a welcome change from the old iMovie.

Figure 11-8:
Click the Voiceover button (top) to open the Voiceover window (bottom), where you set up the voice recording to come. Test your setup by speaking into the microphone; if the live VU meter twitches in response, and has a decent level, you're ready to record. When it's all over, your recording will look like the purple stripe below the filmstrip (top). It behaves just like the green stripes of other "sound-effects" audio.

3. **Set the input level.**

   That is, move close to the microphone and practice your spiel. If the level meter bars are dancing, but only partway across the graph (Figure 11-8), then your narration isn't loud enough. On playback, it'll probably be drowned out by the camcorder audio track.

   If they're hitting the right end of the graph, on the other hand, those bars turn bright red to get your attention. In that case, the sound source is too loud, and the recording will have an ugly, "overdriven" distortion.

   To increase the recording volume, drag the Input Volume slider to the right. (You can learn tricks for boosting the volume of audio tracks later in this chapter, but it's much better to get the level right the first time.)

4. **Adjust the Noise Reduction and Voice Enhancement controls, if you like.**

   The Voice Enhancement checkbox is supposed to make your voice "electronically altered to sound more smooth." The Noise Reduction slider is supposed to screen out ambient background noise. Neither one produces an earth-shaking effect, but you can experiment with them to see how you like the result.

5. **Turn the "Play project audio" checkbox on or off.**

   The question you're answering here is: Do you want to hear the audio from your movie playing back while you record?

   Usually, the answer is "Yes." That way, you can avoid talking over somebody's on-camera conversation, and you can time your own utterances to perfection. The problem is, your microphone *hears* the movie playback coming out of your Mac's speakers—and records a second copy of it, or even triggers squealing feedback.

   Therefore, turn on "Play project audio" only if you're wearing headphones to monitor the playback.

6. **Find the spot where you want the narration to begin.**

   You can use all the usual navigational techniques to navigate your clips: skim (point without clicking), press the Space bar to play the movie, and so on. Don't click the mouse; just skim and play.

7. **When you've found the spot, click the mouse there.**

   Big red letters in the Viewer say, "Get ready…", and a big 3-2-1 countdown timer appears, accompanied by attention-getting countdown beeps. You even see "pre-roll"—the Viewer shows the 3 seconds of video that *lead up* to the point you clicked. All of this is intended to help you get ready to speak at the spot you clicked.

8. **When the Viewer says Recording, start talking. Press the Space bar (or click any-where) to stop.**

   Now a new, purple stripe appears below your filmstrip, already highlighted, bearing the name Voiceover Recording 1 (or 2, or 3), as shown in Figure 11-8. Point to a spot just before the beginning of the new recording, and then press the Space bar, to listen to your voiceover work.

9. **Close the Narration window.**

If the narration wasn't everything you hoped for, it's easy enough to record another take. Just hit ⌘-Z (Undo) or click the purple stripe, and then press Delete. Then repeat the process.

You can record as many overlapping narration takes as you like; the purple stripes just pile up.

They behave exactly like the sound-effects stripes described on page 220. That is, you can:

- **Delete one** by clicking it and then pressing the Delete key;

- **Shorten one** by dragging its endpoints (or by clicking the purple stripe, and then using the Edit→Trim Audio command as described on page 217); or

- **Move one** by dragging the stripe to a new spot, using the middle of it as the handle.

When you're finished, click the Voiceover button again, or hit the letter O again, to return to normal editing.

Extracting Audio from Video

iMovie is perfectly capable of stripping the audio portion of your footage apart from the video. The recorded audio suddenly shows up as an independent audio clip; its pushpins indicate that it's locked to whatever spot on the video you've selected. Figure 11-9 shows the process.

Figure 11-9:
Top: Highlight part of a filmstrip, either in your Event browser or your storyboard. (See page 128 for selection tricks.) Then Shift-⌘-drag the selection into your storyboard. (Hold down those keys until you release the mouse.)

Bottom: The camcorder audio appears as an independent clip, which you can manipulate exactly as though it's any ordinary audio clip: delete it, shorten it, trim it, move it, and so on. You can create a reverb or echo effect by overlaying the same extracted audio several times.

This command unleashes all kinds of useful new tricks that are impossible to achieve any other way:

- **Create cutaways.** You're interviewing Grandpa on camera about his childhood. He shares a funny story about a day down at the old swimming hole. You happen to have a picture of him and his friends posing in front of the water; you want to *cut away* to that shot while Grandpa's narration continues (Figure 11-10). That's exactly what you can do with extracted audio.

  To make this work, you have to do some careful planning—and make some frame-accurate selections (page 128). Select the frames that will be occupied by the cutaway; extract the audio by dragging it to another spot; *delete* those frames;

drag the cutaway shot into the gap; and then drag the extracted audio clip carefully underneath it.

- **Make an echo.** This is a cool one. Park the extracted audio clip a few frames to the right of the original, as shown at bottom in Figure 11-9. Use the Audio Adjustments panel (page 228) to make it slightly quieter than the original. Repeat a few more times, until you've got a realistic echo or reverb sound.

Figure 11-10:
You can extract the audio from an interview to keep the narration going as you cut away to a shot of what's being described.

"What did I love about Edenville? Well, not the odor, that's for sure. And not the plant. No, what I loved most was the

old canoe lake. Oh, sure, it was all foamed up with nitrates, and you didn't dare touch the water. But without a doubt, those were

some of the happiest days of my life. I'd give almost anything to take one more look at that old lake."

- **Reuse the sound.** You can put the extracted audio elsewhere in the movie. You've probably seen this technique used in dozens of Hollywood movies: About 15 minutes before the end of the movie, the main character, lying beaten and defeated in an alley, suddenly pieces together the solution to the central plot mystery, as snippets of dialog we've already heard in the movie float through his brain, finally adding up.

- **Grab some ambient sound.** In real movie editing studios, it happens all the time: A perfect take is ruined by the sound of a passing bus just during the tender kiss moment—and you don't discover it until you're in the editing room, long after the actors and crew have moved on to other projects.

You can eliminate the final seconds of sound from the scene by cropping or splitting the clip, of course. But that won't result in a satisfying solution; now you'll have 3 seconds of *silence* during the kiss. The real world isn't truly silent, even when there's no talking. The air is always filled with *ambient sound,* such as breezes, distant traffic, the hum of fluorescent lights, and so on.

Even inside in a perfectly still room, there's *room tone.* When you want to replace a portion of the audio track with "silence," what you usually want, in fact, is to replace it with ambient sound.

Professionals always record about 30 seconds of room tone or ambient sound just so they'll have material to use in case of emergency. You may not need to go to that extreme; you may well be able to grab some sound from a different part of the same shot. The point is that by extracting the audio from another part of the scene (when nobody was talking), you've got yourself a useful piece of ambient-sound "footage" that you can use to patch over unwanted portions of the originally recorded audio.

• **Add narration.** The technique described on page 222 is ideal for narration that you record at one sitting in a quiet room. But you can add narration via camcorder, too. Just record yourself speaking, import the footage into iMovie, extract the audio, and then throw away the video. You might want to do this if you're editing on a mikeless Mac, or if you want the new narration to better match the camcorder's original sound.

It's important to note that iMovie never *removes* the audio from the original video clip. You'll never be placed into the frantic situation of wishing that you'd never done the extraction at all, unable to sync the audio and video together again (which sometimes happens in "more powerful" video editing programs).

Instead, iMovie places a *copy* of the audio into the storyboard. The original video clip retains its original audio. As a result, you can extract audio from the same clip over and over again, if you like. iMovie simply spins out another copy of the audio each time.

Volume Adjustments

Ah, yes: volume adjustments…one of the most controversial aspects of iMovie '08.

It's true: There's no manual volume adjustments in iMovie '08. No "rubber-banding," no little graph that represents the way a clip's volume rises and falls over its length, no way to make the music get softer at a point you select.

The following pages provide instructions, workarounds—and even a blank book page, to hold the how-to information for the audio-volume editing tools that Apple will *surely* add in a free iMovie update.

Adjusting Overall Clip Volume

In the initial releases of iMovie '08, you can't make manual changes to a clip's volume level along its length. You can, however, make the *entire* song louder or softer, raising or lowering all of its peaks and valleys simultaneously.

To do that, click the clip. It can be any kind of audio: a background audio bubble, a purple narration stripe, a green sound effect stripe. In fact, you can even click a *video* clip, with the understanding that you're about to adjust the camcorder audio's volume.

Tip: The clip can even be one that's still in your Event browser, not even placed in a project yet. In that case, the audio changes you're about to make will affect that video selection in *every* project from now on.

Now click the Adjust Audio button (shown in Figure 11-11), or press the letter A. Immediately, the Audio Adjustments dialog box appears.

Tip: When you point to a video clip, a tiny, faint speaker badge appears in the top-left corner; you can click that to open the Audio Adjustments panel, too. After you make a change, that little badge is visible *all* the time, as a reminder that you've fooled around with the audio.

Adjust Audio button

Figure 11-11:
Click the Adjust Audio button to open the Audio Adjustments dialog box. (If your Audio Adjustments dialog box doesn't look like this, then you may not have yet installed the 7.1 iMovie update.)

There are four items of interest here:

- **Volume slider.** By dragging the Volume slider, you can adjust the overall volume level of the selected clip. You can mute it entirely (drag the slider all the way to the left) or make it twice as loud (all the way to the right).

At this point, you *can't* skim your filmstrips to hear the changes you're making. Instead, to spot-check your work, click the filmstrip corresponding to the audio change you're making. Drag the little red dot handle to position the Playhead, and then press the Space bar to start playback.

- **Ducking.** Apple's response to, "Hey, you took away manual audio controls!" is, "You don't need them. We'll do your mixing *for* you!"

And that's the purpose of this intriguing checkbox. When you turn it on, you're saying, "The selected audio clip is the most important audio. I want to hear it above any other audio that's going on." This checkbox, in other words, makes all other simultaneous audio clips play softer. And using the slider, you can specify how *much* softer they get.

In the film business, lowering the music volume so that you can hear the spoken dialogue is called *ducking*. What Apple is offering here is *automatic* ducking.

For example, suppose you've cluttered up your storyboard with so many back-ground songs, crowd noises, and sound effects that you can no longer hear the dialogue in the original video. You can apply this option to the *video itself* (not one of the colored audio stripes or bubbles) to bring out the original filmed talking.

Note: You can't use this checkbox to boost the volume of background audio; it's dimmed and unavailable for background tracks. If you want to duck everything *but* the background track, you'll have to do it the old-fashioned way: Use the volume sliders to lower the volume on *other* tracks, and/or to raise the volume on the background audio track.

Overall, auto-ducking is not as good as having manual volume controls, but it's better than nothing.

- **Fade In, Fade Out.** Ordinarily, you hear the audio for a sound or video clip immediately. But if you click Manual, you can create a graceful audio *fade-in* or *fade-out* for the selected clip—even if it's a *video* clip from the camcorder. Use the slider to indicate how long you want that fading to take, in seconds (up to 2 seconds).

Note: The fade controls are available only for clips in your storyboard—not for clips in the Event browser.

- **Normalize Clip Volume.** You may not have much call for this button, but it can be handy now and then. It's designed for situations when the clips in your project were recorded at different volume levels, resulting in some jarring unevenness during playback.

iMovie can *normalize* the clips, so that all of them have roughly the same volume. Just click the clips whose volume is out of whack, and then click Normalize Clip Volume. (For tips on selecting multiple clips, see page 128.)

iMovie takes a moment to compute the clip's new audio level. And then, just as a reminder that you've messed around with that clip, iMovie displays a tiny speaker icon near the beginning of it (Figure 11-12).

When you're finished fiddling, click Done. The dialog box goes away, and you return to the movie.

Copying and Pasting Audio Adjustments

It's very, very cool that with the 7.1 update, Apple gave iMovie the ability to select more than one clip at a time. Yay, Apple!

Unfortunately, that's of no help when it comes to audio. You can still select only one clip at a time to make volume adjustments. Boo, Apple!

So if you've got an interview with a 100-year-old man, interspersed with footage of the old town where he grew up, and his audio needs boosting *every single time* he's on camera, you might suppose that you're in for a bit of work. You'll have to click those clips, one at a time, and fix their audio. Right?

Click to adjust audio

Figure 11-12:
Top: In the iMovie scheme, faint little corner-of-the-clip badges appear on any filmstrip when you point to it. They're intended to provided quick access to iMovie's color, cropping, and audio tools.

Bottom: The upper clip's audio has been made louder or softer (the badge is now permanent, and shows round sound waves). The lower clip's audio has been normalized (straight sound waves). It might sound truly abnormal, but at least its audio levels are roughly even with the rest of the movie.

Volume has been adjusted

Volume has been normalized

Not quite. Fortunately, you can make the changes only once, and then *copy and paste* those changes to all the other clips.

Begin by boosting the overall clip volume, or applying the "Reduce volume of other tracks" option, or using the Normalize button, to *one* clip.

Now highlight that clip, and then choose Edit→Copy (or press ⌘-C).

At this point, you can select all of the other clips that need a change (see page 128 for multi-clip selection tips), and then choose Edit→Paste Adjustments→Audio (or just press Option-⌘-U). The appearance of the little icons shown in Figure 11-12 lets you know that all of those other clips have now taken on the audio adjustments of the first.

Or you can plow through your storyboard, clicking and hitting Option-⌘-U, to apply the same settings to each additional clip. Either way, you can breathe a sigh of relief that at least you don't have to work through the Audio Adjustments dialog box each time.

Removing Audio Adjustments

As with all iMovie editing tools, the changes you make in the Audio Adjustments dialog box are nondestructive, meaning that you're never actually changing the underlying clips. You can undo or adjust your changes at any time, even years later.

Just click the clip you edited; click the Adjust Audio button (or press the letter A, or click the tiny audio badge shown in Figure 11-12); and then click Revert to Original. The clip now has its original audio levels back. (Finally, click Done.)

Editing Audio in GarageBand

Why do you suppose the audio-editing features in iMovie '08 are so much weaker than they were in iMovie 6?

One possibility is that Apple said to itself, "Well, sheesh—if they want to edit audio, let them use an audio-editing program—like the one that comes on *the same DVD as iMovie!*"

That would be a reference to GarageBand, the music composition program included with iLife. It offers all of the tools that iMovie lacks: rubber-band volume levels, multiple overlapping audio tracks, a convenient timeline, audio processing effects like reverb and a graphic equalizer, and much more.

Fortunately, you can export your movie into GarageBand to edit its soundtrack with these much more powerful tools. Don't read any further, however, until you've absorbed these two warnings:

- Your movie arrives in GarageBand with only a single, boiled-down audio track. You can't adjust the camcorder audio and the iMovie music independently. (That's a good argument for avoiding adding *any* music in iMovie. Wait until you're in GarageBand to add all music and sound effects.)

- The iMovie→GarageBand train goes only one way. Once you've worked with a movie in GarageBand, you can no longer return to iMovie for further edits. You *can* return to iMovie, edit the video, and re-export the thing, but of course then you lose all the audio work you'd done in GarageBand the first time.

GarageBand Basics

GarageBand is a music composition program, containing dozens of powerful tools. It lets you combine dozens of audio tracks, giving you fine control over each track's sound effects, volume, and even stereo panning.

But if you're like most people, you've never even set foot in GarageBand. (Apple says that GarageBand is the second least-used iLife program, second only to iWeb.) Here's a crash course:

1. **Export your movie from iMovie.**

   Either send it to the Media Browser (page 282) or save it as a QuickTime movie (page 308) in your Home→Movies folder. (GarageBand can import from either of these locations—the Media Browser or your Movies folder—without any digging around on your part.)

2. **Open GarageBand.**

   GarageBand's icon looks like an electric guitar; it's in your Applications folder.

3. **Create a new project.**

   If this is your first time in GarageBand, you're greeted by a welcome screen with four choices. If you *have* worked in GarageBand before, it opens the last project you worked on. Choose File→New.

   In either case, click the option called "Create a New Podcast Episode."

Note: GarageBand '08 no longer offers the movie-score project option of its predecessor, but the essential features are still there. To edit your movie's audio tracks, you'll just use the Podcast project type.

   You're asked to name your project and save it *before* you start editing. Then click Create.

4. **Add your movie from the Media Browser.**

   Choose Control→Show Media Browser. Find your movie on the Movies tab, either under the "iMovie" or "Movies" heading. Drag the movie into the GarageBand timeline, right into the podcast track.

   (You can also drag a movie file in from the Finder.)

   Once you do, you get the message shown in Figure 11-13.

Figure 11-13:
Don't worry about the change from podcast to movie. A movie is what you're making, right?

A project can contain either a podcast track or a movie track. Do you want to replace the podcast track with a movie track?

If you replace the podcast track, all existing markers and artwork will be lost. This cannot be undone.

Cancel   Replace

5. **Click Replace.**

   GarageBand creates its own thumbnails to represent your movie.

6. **Edit your movie's audio track.**

Once GarageBand has imported your movie, you'll see, directly under the video track, an audio track. This is the audio from your exported movie. It contains *all* of your movie's audio, all merged into one track.

Now that it's in GarageBand, you can manipulate the audio in a multitude of ways. At the left edge of the window, under the words Movie Sound, tiny icons let you mute, isolate, lock, and pan the audio (shift the stereo sound right or left). You can also make the volume rise and fall at particular points, as shown in Figure 11-14.

Figure 11-14:
To show the rubber band tool, click the ▾ button (A) to expand the volume graph (B). Drag any point on the graph to make the volume rise or fall. Using the pop-up menu (C), you can also plot a graph for the panning, reverb, and other sophisticated audio effects over time.

7. **Add audio tracks.**

Add additional tracks, if you like, by choosing Track→New Track (Option-⌘-N), or by clicking the **+** button on the toolbar. You might use these new tracks to create a custom score. (Read on.) In GarageBand, you can create have as many parallel audio tracks as you like, although a huge number bring your Mac to a crawls.

You can also drag songs from the Media Browser (for example, from iTunes) right into a blank area of the GarageBand window. GarageBand automatically creates a new track and places the song in it.

8. **Export your movie.**

Once you have finished the audio editing, send the movie out into the world using the commands in the Share menu. For example, you can send the movie directly to iWeb, iTunes, or iDVD.

Or, if you choose Share→Export to Disk, you can create a standalone QuickTime movie file on your hard drive. In theory, you could actually import *that* movie *back* into iMovie, although the shuttling back and forth might be getting a little ridiculous at that point.

Scoring in GarageBand

Because GarageBand is a music program, its greatest strength is its ability to help you create a custom musical score for your movie. You can actually record or compose music that runs along with the video, turning you into a regular John Williams. (Actual musical ability may vary.) GarageBand shows the movie in the timeline, frame by frame, so you know exactly where to add the cymbal crash or guitar riff.

Here's a supercondensed review of the different tools for scoring:

- **Use prerecorded loops.** Click the eyeball icon to see all the different categories of prerecorded *loops* (musical building blocks) that you can drag directly upward into new tracks beneath your video. Once it's installed, you can drag the upper-right corner of a loop to make it repeat over and over, for as long as you drag to the right. (This works well with drum parts.)

- **Record a MIDI instrument.** If you have a MIDI instrument connected to your Mac (usually a musical keyboard or synthesizer), choose Track→New Track, click Software Instrument, and then click Create. Now you can choose an instrument sound from the list that appears at lower right, and then click the round red Record button to begin recording as you play. You can even use the Tempo control (hold your mouse down on the digits) to make the movie play back more slowly, so that you have a better chance at a perfect performance. After you're finished playing, you can crank the tempo back up to its original speed.

- **Record a live instrument or voice.** GarageBand can record live sounds, like your own singing or saxophone playing. Choose Track→New Track, click Real Instrument, and then click Create; next, choose a reverb preset from the list at lower right (like Female Basic or Male Rock Vocals). Click the round red Record button to begin recording.

When the musical soundtrack is complete, export the result using the methods described on the previous page. With enough practice, you might eventually wind up on Steven Spielberg's speed dial.

THESE PAGES INTENTIONALLY LEFT BLANK
so that when Apple adds manual audio-volume editing,
we'll have somewhere to describe it.

THESE PAGES INTENTIONALLY LEFT BLANK
so that when Apple adds manual audio-volume editing,
we'll have somewhere to describe it.

Photos

Y ou might think that iMovie's primary purpose is working with video. But the truth is, it's quite handy with still photos, too. You can bring in still images from iPhoto or from your hard drive, for use as slideshows. You can also turn individual frames of your movie *into* still images, for use as freeze-frames. And, if you know the secret, you can even *export* individual frames as graphics files to your hard drive, suitable for emailing or Web posting.

This chapter tells all there is to tell.

Importing Still Images

You might want to import a graphics file into iMovie for any number of reasons. For example:

- You can use a graphic, digital photo, or other still image as a backdrop for iMovie's titling feature (Chapter 10). A still image behind your text is less distracting than moving footage.

- You can use a graphics file *instead* of using the iMovie titling feature. As noted in Chapter 10, iMovie's titling feature offers a number of powerful features, but it also has a number of serious limitations. For example, you have only rudimentary control over the title's placement in the frame. (See Figure 12-1.)

  Preparing your own title "slides" in, say, Photoshop Elements or Photoshop gives you a lot of flexibility that the iMovie titling feature lacks. You get complete control over the type size, color, and placement, and you can also add graphic touches to your text or to the "slide" on which it appears.

• One of the most compelling uses of video is the *video photo album*: a smoothly integrated succession of photos (from your scanner or digital camera), joined by crossfades, enhanced by titles, and accompanied by music. Thanks to iMovie's ability to import photos directly—either from your hard drive or from your iPhoto collection—creating this kind of video slideshow is a piece of cake.

Note: Of course, *iPhoto* can create video photo albums, too. And in iPhoto, you can opt to loop a slideshow (which iMovie can't do); rearranging and regrouping your photos is much easier than in iMovie, too.

But building them in a movie has several advantages. First of all, your audio options are much greater; you can record narration as you watch the slideshow, for example. You have a full arsenal of tools for creating titles, credits, and special effects, too.

Figure 12-1:
Preparing your "title cards" in a graphics program gives you far more typographical and design flexibility than iMovie's own titling feature gives you. Using separate graphics software, for example, you can enhance your titles with drop shadows, a 3-D look, or clip art.

As your life with iMovie proceeds, you may encounter other uses for the picture-importing feature. Maybe, when editing a home movie of your kids tussling in the living room, you decide it would be hilarious to insert some *Batman*-style fight-sound title cards ("BAM!") into the footage. Maybe you need an establishing shot of, say, a storefront or apartment building, and realize that you could save production money by inserting a still photo that passes for live video in which there's nothing moving. And maybe you want to end your movie with a fade-out—not to black, but to maroon (an effect described later in this chapter).

You have a delicious choice of two methods for bringing still photos into a project. The first and most convenient method is to choose the photo from among those you've organized in iPhoto, using iMovie's window into your picture collection. If you're not using iPhoto to organize your digital photos, you can also use the older method of importing pictures directly from the hard drive.

The Photos Browser

The more you work with iMovie and iDVD, the more you appreciate the convenience of the way Apple has linked them to the other i-programs, like iTunes and iPhoto. Here's a classic case:

When you open the Photos browser (Figure 12-2), or choose Window→Photos, or press ⌘-2, you're shown what amounts to iPhoto Lite: a scrolling panel of thumbnail images reflecting the contents of your entire iPhoto Library. Using the navigation panel just above the thumbnails, you can browse your photos by event, album, folder, or according to the other iPhoto presets (like flagged photos or photos added in your last import). If you use Aperture, Apple's pro photo-organization program, its library shows up here, too.

Tip: Events in iPhoto are a lot like Events in iMovie. That is, iPhoto groups all the photos taken on the same day into an Event.

Albums are the category "containers" that you can create in iPhoto by choosing File→New Album (or by clicking the + button at the lower-left corner). You can drag a single picture into as many of these albums as you like. Folders are simply larger structures that let you group albums together. Complete details are in *iPhoto '08: The Missing Manual.*

Figure 12-2:
The Photos browser shows all the pictures you've imported into iPhoto (or Aperture, if you have it). Use the navigation panel to limit the photo display to those in a certain album or folder. (The white lettering at the lower right tells you how many pictures are in that album or folder—or in your entire library, if that's what you're seeing.)

Note the Search box. As you type into it, iMovie smoothly hides all photos except the ones whose names or keywords contain matching text. It's an amazingly quick way to pinpoint one photo out of several thousand. To clear the search box and return to viewing all photos, click the ⊗ at the right end of the box.

iPhoto albums, events, and groups   Photos browser

Thumbnail size

Here are four other handy Photos browser tips:

- iMovie starts out showing you rows of photo thumbnails. You can control their size by dragging the slider below the browser.

- iMovie offers an alternative, and very useful, way to view your photos. Control-click (or right-click) anywhere in the Photos browser; from the shortcut menu, choose Display as List.

Figure 12-3:
The List view shows each photo, the day it was taken, and its size. An additional right-click lets you add even more columns that show the photo dimensions and file type. To return to icon view, right-click (Control-click) again and choose "Display as Icons."

iMovie changes the Photos browser's display into columns, as shown in Figure 12-3.

- If you want to edit a photo before adding it to your movie, you don't have to fire up iPhoto manually. Just Control-click (or right-click) the photo; from the shortcut menu, choose Open in iPhoto. iPhoto opens and takes you directly to the photo you clicked. Once you make the necessary changes, iMovie returns and uses the updated version of your photo.

- Double-click a thumbnail to make that photo fill the *entire* Photos browser for a much closer look. Then press the left and right arrow keys to walk through the adjacent photos at this larger size. Click a photo once to return to the thumbnails.

Photos from the Finder

If you haven't added the image you need to your iPhoto library, you can still add it to your movie project. All you have to do is locate it in the Finder and drag it into your project window.

Tip: iMovie can import graphics in any format that QuickTime can understand, which includes PICT, JPEG, GIF, PNG, Photoshop files, and even PDF files, for when an IRS form is exactly what you want to illustrate in your movie. Avoid the GIF format for photos, which limits the number of colors available to the image; otherwise, just about any format is good still-image material.

Once you've added a photo to iMovie, you don't have to keep track of the original. iMovie actually socks away a *copy* of any image that you import. Even if you delete a photo file from iPhoto or the Finder, iMovie still keeps a copy of it. (Just don't try this with video clips—iMovie treats them very differently!)

Two Ways to Add Photos

Adding photos to your project is a lot like adding music, in that there are two ways to go about it. If you're using photos from your iPhoto library or from the Finder, adding photos in iMovie behaves almost identically to adding titles, as described in Chapter 10. That is, there are two placees to drag photos: between clips, or onto them. The results are quite different.

Photo Filmstrips

If you drag a photo *between* two filmstrips in your storyboard, you create a new *photo filmstrip* (Figure 12-4, top).

Figure 12-4:
Top: Here's a photo you dragged between two other filmstrips. It turns into a photo filmstrip, which behaves in almost every way like a video filmstrip. (You can identify a photo filmstrip by the tiny badges that appear when you point to it without clicking. If it's a photo, there's no audio icon, and the Crop icon is white and unfaded.)

Bottom: If you drag onto part of an existing filmstrip, you produce a photo stripe like the one shown here.

A photo filmstrip

Click to crop, rotate, or add Ken Burns effect

A "blue-stripe" photo

A "blue-stripe" photo being placed

Tip: You can add more than one photo at a time in this way—a handy trick if you're creating a slideshow. Select multiple photos in the iPhoto browser just as you'd select multiple icons in the Finder. For example, you can click the first one, then Shift-click the last to select a group, or ⌘-click individual thumbnails.

You can even just drag an entire album from the album list.

In most regards, it now behaves exactly like a video filmstrip. You can crop it, rotate it, and make color adjustments to it, for example, exactly as described in Chapter 9. You can superimpose titles and credits on it, just as described in Chapter 10. You can even duck audio running under it, as described in Chapter 11, even though the photo doesn't have any audio of its own.

Key differences: You can't adjust a photo's timing by dragging the clip ends or by using the Fine Tuning controls (page 142). Instead, you have to use the Set Duration command, described on page 245. And you can't use the Split or Trim commands on a photo, either.

Photo Stripes

Alternatively, you can drag a photo *on top of* a video clip (or photo filmstrip). At that point, it behaves exactly like a title (Chapter 10). That is, blue highlighting appears on the first third of the clip, the last third, or the entire clip as you drag, indicating what part of the filmstrip the photo will "cover" (Figure 12-4).

At that point, the photo is represented by a blue stripe across the top of the affected clip. As with titles, you can span multiple clips with your photo, but you can't cross another blue flag, be it a photo or a title; they can never overlap.

When you create a photo stripe, it *covers up* the video in the filmstrip beneath it. So if the photo blocks the video, what good is it? Why not just create a photo filmstrip?

Actually, a photo stripe has three advantages over a photo filmstrip:

- **It's much easier to adjust.** You can slide it left or right, earlier or later in the movie, with the touch of the mouse. And you can shorten or lengthen it just by dragging its ends.

- **It might not cover up the *whole* video underneath.** If the photo doesn't have the same aspect ratio as the movie frame, then you'll get letterbox bars, as you'd expect—with one key difference. Instead of black letterbox bars, you get *video* letterbox bars (Figure 12-5).

- **Cutaways are incredibly easy to create.** You've seen it a million times on TV. Someone starts talking; as the narration continues, the camera *cuts away* to a photo or another video clip; and then we return to the original person speaking.

  Page 225 describes one way to create this effect. But if you intend to cut away to a *photo,* creating a photo stripe is infinitely easier. Instead of having to extract audio from your video clip and then create a still clip to plug in the middle, you just drop a photo over the video. The result is a cutaway with a cross dissolve that looks like it took a lot more work than it actually did.

- **You can see through it.** This tip is for Photoshop (or Photoshop Elements) mavens, but it's wicked cool. It lets you create see-through *pieces* of a photo—and the video behind it plays through the holes. The steps for creating this fantastic effect appear in Figure 12-6.

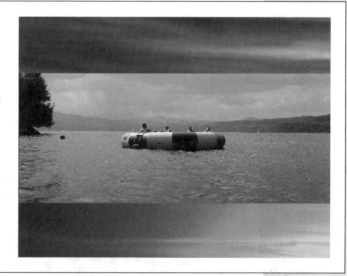

Figure 12-5:
If a photo doesn't match the project's aspect ratio, then you can actually see the video playing inside the letterbox bars that bracket the photo. Here, the horizontally cropped photo fills most of the frame, but the sunrise from the video behind it creates a living border.

This trick opens up a host of effects that iMovie can't do with its built-in tools. You could make a black image with two holes; they'll show up in iMovie as though you're peering through a pair of binoculars. (A great way to pump up your ten-year-old's spy movie!)

Or use this trick to put a pair of nose glasses or a funny hat on someone. Or create text titles, like *Batman*-style "BAM!"s and "KAPOW!"s superimposed on your footage. As long as you use an image format that recognizes transparency (TIFF or PNG, for example), then a little creativity can lead to all sorts of cool effects.

Timing Changes

The way you change the duration and position for a photo depends on what kind it is.

Photo filmstrips

A still image doesn't naturally have a *duration,* as a movie clip might. (Asking "How many seconds long is a photograph?" is like asking, "What is the sound of one hand clapping?")

Still, it's working like a clip, so iMovie has to assign it *some* duration. iMovie turns every filmstrip photo into a 4-second clip. If you prefer a different default timing, choose File→Project Properties (⌘-J), and then adjust the Photo Duration slider. You can change the default timing to as little as 1 second or as long as 10 seconds.

Actually, there are *three* ways to adjust filmstrip photos' durations:

• **Change all photo durations at once.** If, in the Project Properties dialog box, you select "Applies to all photos," then the Duration slider affects all photos simultaneously.

Figure 12-6:
This effect pops up often in opening credits for TV shows (at least ones from the 1970s) and the occasionally cheesy movie.

Top: Make a graphic in Photoshop that contains cutouts. Select the pieces that you don't want to be transparent; ⌘-click the "Save selection as channel" button on the Channels palette; and save the result as a TIFF graphic with an alpha channel. Drag the resulting file right off the desktop onto any filmstrip in iMovie. (Page 207 shows the effect.)

Bottom: Once it becomes a photo stripe in iMovie, the underlying video plays through the holes!

• **Change photo durations from here on.** The weird little option labeled "Applies when added to project" actually means "Whatever duration you choose on the Duration slider applies to the *next* photo you drop into the storyboard—and all future ones." It preserves the durations of all *existing* photos in your project, but changes the standard timing for all *incoming* photos.

- **Change individual photo durations.** You can also change photo durations on a one-at-a-time basis. Click a photo to select it, and then choose Edit→Set Duration (⌘-R). Or click the tiny clock badge on the filmstrip, visible in Figure 12-4.

In the Set Duration dialog box, type in the number of seconds you want for the photo. You can make your photo appear on the screen for as little as .25 of a second (a favorite of subliminal advertisers) or as long as 60 seconds (a favorite of all other advertisers).

Tip: When you get right down to it, 60 seconds is plenty of time for looking at one particular photo, no matter how good it is. Still, if you need it to last longer—perhaps because you're using it as a background for a series of opening credits—you can always overcome the 60-second limit by placing the same photo into your project over and over again, side by side, each for 60 seconds.

Photo stripes

As noted earlier, changing the duration of a superimposed photo stripe is much easier. Just drag the ends of its blue stripe to make it longer or shorter. (You can even span more than one filmstrip.)

Note: You've probably have noticed that superimposed photos fade in and out just like titles. That's because in Project Properties (⌘-J), the slider for "Title Fade Duration" *also* governs the fade duration of superimposed photos!

You can change this slider to change the fade length of your superimposed photos, but be aware that it affects the fade duration of all your titles simultaneously.

The Dimensions of an iMovie Photo

If you're designing a custom image for your movie, you'll generally want it to have the same dimensions as your video dimensions. Otherwise, iMovie crops the photo or inserts black bars to make it fit.

iMovie offers three standard aspect ratios for your videos—Standard (4:3), iPhone (3:2) and Widescreen (16:9); see page 109 for a complete discussion. For now, here's how big to make your photos so that they fit these movie frames:

- **Standard 4:3.** Make your image 640 pixels wide and 480 pixels tall. (Be aware that the outer edges may get chopped off on standard-definition TVs, as explained on page 329.)

- **iPhone 3:2.** Make the photo 480 pixels wide and 320 pixels tall to fit the iPhone screen.

- **Widescreen 16:9.** Your imported photo should be at least 960 pixels wide and 540 pixels tall. (True high definition is more than that—1920 pixels wide and 1080 pixels tall—but Apple doesn't think you'll see much difference.)

Note: Previous editions of this book included a lengthy discussion on getting the dimensions of your images right, because iMovie had a funny way of fitting them in the video frame. In the past, if you imported a 640 x 480 photo into iMovie, you'd wind up with black bars on either side, even though a standard TV *is* 640 x 480 pixels!

Fortunately, iMovie '08 has kicked this bad habit. A 640 x 480 image now fits perfectly into a standard-def movie frame.

If you have an image that wasn't born with the right dimensions, don't worry. The powerful Crop tool and the Ken Burns effect can help you compensate.

Crop, Fit, Rotate

One of iMovie's greatest virtues is its resolution agnosticism. You can combine widescreen footage from your new HD camcorder with standard-def footage from your old DV camera in the same movie; iMovie gracefully handles their different dimensions.

This adaptability also extends to photos. Chapter 9 contains a detailed discussion of cropping *video* to fit the frame (or to draw emphasis to a certain part of the picture), making it fit the frame (by adding letterbox bars), and even rotating it.

Well, surprise, surprise: *Exactly* the same features are available for photo filmstrips. See the writeups beginning on page 185 for the full discussion.

Note: You can crop, fit, and rotate only photo *filmstrips,* not the blue-stripe photos. (The blue-stripe ones are automatically scaled to fit the frame, and there's nothing you can do about it.)

UP TO SPEED

Avoiding Pixellated Images

You may have tried adding an image to iMovie and found that it looked pretty rotten. Blurry, pixellated, or jaggy images are ugly and quite jarring when they appear in a movie surrounded by pristine video footage.

Sloppy-looking images like these usually result from using a photo file whose resolution is too low to begin with. For example, you might have taken a hilarious little shot with your cameraphone—emphasis on little. Images downloaded from the Web often have very low resolution, too.

iMovie, thinking it's doing you a favor, stretches that photo larger than its original size to make it fit the movie frame—and ugly-looking coarseness results.

If you absolutely must use a small image, consider framing your picture inside a larger image of the proper dimensions. iMovie shows the small picture with the "frame" surrounding it, preventing the jagged, blurry resizing you would otherwise see.

The Ken Burns Effect

The only problem with using still photos in a movie is that they're *still*. They just sit there without motion or sound, wasting much of the dynamic potential of video.

For years, professionals have addressed the problem using special sliding camera rigs that produce gradual zooming, panning, or both, to bring photographs to life.

But this smooth motion isn't just about adding animation to photos for its own sake. It also lets you draw the viewer's attention where you want it, when you want it. For example: "Little Harry graduated from junior high school in 1963"—slow pan to someone else in the school photo, a little girl with a ribbon in her hair—"little suspecting that the woman who would one day become his tormentor was standing only a few feet away."

Among the most famous practitioners of this art is Ken Burns, the creator of PBS documentaries like *The Civil War* and *Baseball*—which is why Apple named the feature after him.

Applying the Ken Burns Effect

iMovie '08's Ken Burns controls are totally different from what was in iMovie before. Here's how you use them:

1. **Click a photo filmstrip.**

   A yellow border appears.

2. **Press the letter C key, or click the Crop icon on the toolbar, or click the tiny Crop** *badge* **that appears when your cursor approaches the upper-left corner of the filmstrip.**

   All three of these techniques open up the Crop/Fit/Rotate/Ken Burns window in the upper-right corner of the iMovie window.

3. **Click the Ken Burns button.**

   Now you see the outlines of two rectangles over your photo, one green and one red. They represent the framing of your photo during its short moment in the sun: the way it will first appear (the green box) and the way it will conclude (red). Basically, you're setting up the start frame and the end frame; iMovie automatically produces the animation required to smoothly pan and/or zoom between them.

4. **Set up the photo's starting point.**

   That is, select the green box by clicking on it. Drag its corners to resize it and drag in the middle to move it.

Tip: Getting your hands on those boxes isn't always easy, since they're hugging the outer edges of the Viewer. Here's a tip: Try clicking the *word* Start or End. Then drag inside the frame, anywhere, just to pull the box boundaries into view. Now you can drag the corners to make the box smaller.

You're setting up the green box so it frames the photo as you'll want it to *start out*—the part that your viewers will see first. For example, if you want to zoom in on the photo, make the green box big. (Drag its corners to resize it.) If you want to pull back from the photo, make the green box small. See Figure 12-7.

Note: In previous versions of iMovie, you could adjust your start or end points so that the picture slid into or out of the frame. Unfortunately, you can't do that in iMovie '08; a photo *must* begin and end in the frame.

Click "End" to adjust   Swap start/stop
stopping point   settings

Drag corners
to resize

Figure 12-7:
Top: In this some-what confusing display, you adjust the green box and then the red one, to show iMovie how you want to pan and zoom across the photo. A yellow arrow shows the current direction of iMovie's pan, from the green box to the red one, to help you visualize the motion of the shot.

Bottom: This three-frame sample shows a representation of the pan and zoom out that will be produced by the setup at top.

5. **Adjust your end point (the red box).**

   Click the red box, or the word End, to select it. Move and resize it just as you did with the green box.

   If you don't want your shot to zoom (but only to move), make sure that the red box is the same size as the green one. Line them up, match their sizes, then move each where you want it. With the start and end points the same size, iMovie just pans from one to the other.

6. **Preview your effect and make adjustments.**

Click the |▶| button to preview your Ken Burns effect. If you don't like what you saw, adjust your green and red boxes accordingly.

If you decide that you want to *reverse* what you've set up—you want to zoom out instead of in, or pan left instead of right—click the very tiny Swap button identified in Figure 12-7. That turns your green box into the red one, and vice versa.

7. **Click Done.**

You can always adjust the Ken Burns effect by selecting the photo filmstrip and pressing the letter C again.

Tip: If you drag a group of photos into your project all at once, iMovie creates automatic, *varied* Ken Burns effects, subtly panning and zooming in different directions for each one. Add a sweet little crossfade to all of them simultaneously (page 159), and you've got a gorgeous little slideshow.

(If you're a killjoy, you can always turn off the automatic Ken Burns feature in Project Preferences.)

Creating Still Images from Footage

iMovie doesn't just accept still photos; it can also *create* them for its own purposes. To do this, it can pluck a frame out of any footage, whether it's in the storyboard or the Event browser.

And why would you want to create a still from your video? Let us count some ways:

- **Create cool titles.** One of the best reasons to get to know iMovie's still-image feature is to supplement iMovie's built-in titling feature. Using still images as titles gives you the freedom to use any colors, type sizes, and positions you want.

POWER USERS' CLINIC

The Fade-to-Black (or Fade-to-Puce) Secret

As noted in Chapter 8, it's easy to create a professional-looking fade-out at the end of your movie. But unlike professional movies, which fade to black and then hold for a moment, iMovie fades to black at the end of the movie and then stops playing, sending your viewers back to iMovie, your desktop, the football game, or whatever was on the computer or TV screen before you played the movie.

The solution is very simple, and well worth making a part of your regular iMovie repertoire. Here's the drill:

Just after the final fade-out, create a black clip. (Page 197 has the instructions.)

Then, use the Cross Dissolve transition. iMovie fades smoothly from the final footage of the clip into your black frame—and holds.

Choose Edit→Set Duration to make your black frame last as long as you desire.

Nor should you be content to fade to black. In fact, you can cross-dissolve to whatever color you want—white, blue, gray, anything. Instead of adding a black frame, insert a solid-colored image of your own creation.

Now that you know about Ken Burns, in fact, you can even animate them (if they're filmstrip-style photos); now that you know about alpha channels (Figure 12-6), you can make video play behind them (if they're blue stripe–style photos).

- **The freeze-frame effect.** One of the most obvious uses of a still frame is the *freeze-frame* effect, in which the movie holds on the final frame of a shot. It's a terrifically effective way to end a movie, particularly if the final shot depicts the shy, unpopular hero in a moment of triumph, arms in the air, hoisted onto the shoulders of the crowd. (Fade to black; bring up the music; roll credits.)

- **Credits sequences.** If you were a fan of 1970s action shows like *Emergency!*, you may remember how the opening credits looked: You'd be watching one of the starring characters frantically at work in some lifesaving situation. As she looked up from her work just for a moment, the picture would freeze, catching her by lucky happenstance at her most flattering angle. At that instant, you'd see her credit flashed onto the screen: "JULIE LONDON as Dixie McCall, RN."

  That's an easy one to simulate. Just create a freeze-frame as described in the next section, and then add a superimposed title image.

- **The layered effect.** In many cases, the most creative use of still-image titles comes from using *several* of them, each building on the last. For example, you can make the main title appear, hold for a moment, and then transition into a second still graphic on which a subtitle appears.

  If you have more time on your hands, you can use this trick to create simple animations. Suppose you were to create 10 different title cards, all superimposed on the same background, but each with the words in a different size or position. If you were to place each title card on the screen for only half a second (15 frames), joined by very fast crossfades, you'd create a striking visual effect. Similarly, you might consider making the *color* of the lettering shift over time. To do that, create two or three different title cards, each with the text in a different color. Insert them into your movie, join them with slow crossfades, and you've got a striking, color-shifting title sequence.

Creating a Still Frame

Here's how you go about extracting a still frame from your video (a feature that debuted in iMovie '08 version 7.1).

1. **Position the Playhead on the frame you want frozen.**

   You can choose from any filmstrip, either in the Event browser or on the storyboard.

Tip: If you want to create a still from the first or last frame of a clip, point to a spot near that end of the filmstrip, and then hit the left or right arrow key. The Playhead jumps to the first or last frame of the clip.

---

2. **Control-click (or right-click) the filmstrip at the spot from which you want to extract the still. From the shortcut menu, choose Add Still Frame to Project.**

   This command directs iMovie to place a new photo clip at the end of the storyboard. See Figure 12-8.

Figure 12-8:
This command is one of the very few iMovie commands that's available only in the shortcut menu—not in any of the main menus.

Note: If you generate a still image from a filmstrip in your Event browser, iMovie applies a subtle Ken Burns effect to the still image. If you captured the still from your storyboard, however, iMovie assumes that you wanted a freeze-frame effect. The still image will be still—unanimated.

3. **Drag the still clip into the right place in your storyboard.**

   If your goal was to freeze a frame of video, you'll have to put the newly hatched photo clip at exactly the spot from which you captured it. If you grabbed the still from the beginning or ending of a clip, that's easy.

   But it came from the *middle* of a clip, finding precisely the same frame can be challenging. That's a good argument for splitting the filmstrip at that spot *before* you create the still. (See page 143.)

4. **Adjust the still's duration, cropping, color, and so on.**

   Your still frame behaves like any other photo. You can use the Ken Burns effect, for example, to zoom in on a meaningful part of the shot. (Ever seen a suspense movie, where the director zooms in on the once-vanquished villain watching the hero from the middle of a crowd? Works every time.)

Figuring out how to handle the *audio* in such situations is up to you, since a still frame has no sound. That's a good argument for starting your closing-credits music *during* the final clip and making it build to a crescendo for the final freeze-frame.

Exporting a Still Frame

The still-frame feature is primarily designed for adding freeze-frames within iMovie. But you may sometimes find it useful to export a frame to your hard drive as a graphics file—for emailing to friends, installing on your desktop as a background picture, posting on a Web page, and so on. An exported frame also makes a neat piece of "album art" that you can print out and slip into the plastic case of a homemade DVD.

The Resolution Problem

It's worth noting, however, that the maximum *resolution* for a standard-definition digital video frame—the number of dots that compose the image—is 640 across, 480 down. As digital photos go, that's pretty pathetic, on a par with the photos taken by some cameraphones. That's one-third of a megapixel—a pretty puny number compared with the shots from today's five- and eight-megapixel cameras. High-def video produces better stills, but it's still nothing like what you'd get from a digital camera.

The low resolution of the video frame is only half the reason your captured pictures look so bad. Most camcorders capture images the same way television displays images: as hundreds of fine horizontal stripes, or *scan lines*. You don't actually see all of the scan lines at any one instant; you see odd-numbered lines in one frame, even-numbered lines in the next. Because the frames flash by your eyes so quickly, your brain smoothes the lines together so that you perceive one continuous image.

This system of *interlacing* may work fine for moving video images, but it presents an unpleasant problem when you capture just one frame. Capturing a still image from this footage gives you, in essence, only half of the scan lines that compose the image. QuickTime does what it can to fill in the missing information. But as shown in Figure 12-9, the horizontal scan lines still cause a jaggedness problem.

Figure 12-9:
Digital still frames you export from your DV footage suffer from two disadvantages. First, the resolution is comparatively low. Second, the horizontal scan lines of the original video may sometimes create subtle stairstepped, jagged edges in the still.

Exporting a Frame

Now that your expectations have been duly lowered, here's how you export a frame in iMovie:

1. **Create a new project.**

   You'll be exporting to QuickTime for this task, and iMovie can export only an *entire project* at a time. So you'll have to isolate the frame you want in a new, separate project.

Tip: Rather than creating another project every time you want to export a frame, consider creating a single project called "Image Export." Use this project every time you want to export a still frame.

---

2. **Add the video frames you want to export.**

   Here's where you get to practice your frame-accurate editing skills. In the Event browser, select only the frame—yes, you can select a single frame—that you want to export as a still image. (See page 128 for details.) Actually, you can select a *several-frame* stretch of footage; you'll wind up with each frame as a separate graphic.

   Add the selection to your new project by dragging it there or hitting the E key on your keyboard.

Figure 12-10:
Use this handy dialog box to specify the still-image format you want, and how many frames you want per second.

3. **Choose Share→Export Using QuickTime.**

   The QuickTime export window appears, allowing you to adjust the myriad settings that come with a QuickTime export (Chapter 16).

   As iMovie creates your pile of stills, it uses, as its naming scheme, whatever you type into the Save As box (Movie Frame 1, Movie Frame 2, and so on).

---

4. **From the Export pop-up menu, choose Movie to Image Sequence.**

This setting tells iMovie to save a separate image for every frame. You might want to save these in a special folder; if you're exporting a lot of frames, they'll clutter your desktop pretty quickly.

5. **Click Options. In the next dialog box, click Settings.**

You now arrive at the mighty Export Image Sequence Settings box (Figure 12-10).

6. **From the Format pop-up menu, choose the graphics format you want for the exported frames.**

All the usual suspects are here: JPEG (great for Web posting and email), TIFF (higher quality, larger files, better for printing), and so on.

Also choose how *many* stills you want iMovie to pull from each second of video. For the greatest freedom in choosing just the right expression, you'd want to extract *every single frame* of the video. In that case, type *29.97* (to match standard North American video), *30* (for high-def video), or *25* (European video).

6. **Click OK, then Save.**

Head over to your destination folder, where you'll find all of the images you exported, named and ready to be used in other applications.

Tip: If you plunked down the $30 for QuickTime Player Pro (Chapter 17), you can export a still with much greater efficiency.

Find the source footage in the Finder. (Control-click a clip; from the shortcut menu, choose Reveal in Finder.)

Double-click it to open it in QuickTime Player Pro. Set the Playhead on the frame of video you want, and choose File→Export. The resulting dialog box looks much the same, but the Export pop-up menu offers a "Movie to Picture" option. You'll wind up exporting only the one frame you wanted.

Advanced Editing

S tumble around long enough with iMovie '08, and you might be able to figure out most of its workings. But in this chapter, you can read about another entire level, another realm of power and professionalism, that would never occur to most people.

This chapter covers two advanced topics:

- **Advanced editing theory.** Where the preceding chapters have covered the *technical* aspects of editing video in iMovie—where to click, what keys to press, and so on—the first part of this chapter is about the *artistic* aspects of video editing. It covers when to cut, what to cut to, and how to create the emotional impact you want.

  Put another way, this chapter is a continuation of the film-theory crash course that began in the first three chapters of this book. Chapter 2, for example, describes filmmaking techniques that you must think about at the time you're *shooting*. This chapter offers some tricks for *editing*.

- **Back and forth with iMovie 6.** It's a fact of life: iMovie '08 is not in any way a relative of iMovie 6. They're two different programs, designed for different purposes, with different kinds of people in mind. Each offers long lists of features that aren't in the other.

  The older iMovie is still available to you, however (page 3), complete with all of its goodies. There's no reason you can't use *both* programs, swinging deftly back and forth, using each for what it's good for.

  In this chapter, you'll find out how and why.

The Power of Editing

The editing process is crucial in any kind of movie, from a home movie to a Hollywood thriller. Clever editing can turn a troubled movie into a successful one, or a boring home movie into one that, for the first time, family members don't interrupt every 3 minutes by lapsing into conversation.

You, the editor, are free to jump from "camera" to "camera," angle to angle, to cut from one location or time to another, and so on. Today's audiences accept that you're telling a story; they don't stomp out in confusion because one minute, James Bond is in his London office, but shows up in Venice a split second later.

You can also compress time; that's one of editing's most common duties. (That's fortunate, because most movies tell stories that, in real life, take days, weeks, or years to unfold.) You can also *expand* time, making 10 seconds stretch out to 6 minutes—a familiar effect to anyone who's ever watched a final sequence involving a bomb connected to a digital timer (and heroes racing to defuse it).

Editing boils down to choosing which shots you want to include, how long each one lasts, and in what order they should play.

Modern Film Theory

When you're creating a rock video or an experimental film, you can safely chuck all the advice in this chapter—and in this book.

But if you aspire to make good "normal" movies, designed to engage or delight your viewers rather than shock or mystify them, then you should become familiar with the fundamental principles of film editing that shape virtually every Hollywood movie (and even most student and independent films) of the last 75 years. For example:

Tell the story chronologically

Most movies tell the story from beginning to end. This part is probably instinct, even when you're making home movies. Arrange your clips roughly in chronological order, except when you're representing your characters' flashbacks and memories or deliberately playing a chronology game, as in *Pulp Fiction.*

Try to be invisible

These days, an expertly edited movie is one where the audience isn't even aware of the editing.

This principle has wide-ranging ramifications. For example, the desire to avoid making the editing noticeable is why the simple cut is by far the most common joint between film clips. Using, say, the Circle Open transition between alternate lines of the vows at somebody's wedding would hardly qualify as invisible editing.

Within a single scene, use simple cuts and no transitions. Try to create the effect of seamless real time, making the audience feel as though it's witnessing the scene in its entirety, from beginning to end. This kind of editing is more likely to make your viewers less aware that they're watching a movie.

Develop a shot rhythm

Every movie has an editing *rhythm* that's established by the lengths of the shots in it. The prevailing rhythm of *Dances with Wolves,* for example, is extremely different from that of *Natural Born Killers.* Every *scene* in a movie has its own rhythm, too.

As a general rule, linger less on closeup shots, but give more time to establishing and wide shots. (After all, in an establishing shot, there are many more elements for the audience to study and notice.) Similarly, change the pacing of the shots according to the nature of the scene. Most action scenes feature very short clips and fast edits; most love scenes include longer clips and fewer changes of camera angle.

Maintaining Continuity

As a corollary to the notion that the audience should feel that they're part of the story, professional editors strive to maintain *continuity* during the editing process. This continuity business applies mostly to scripted films, not home movies. Still, knowing what the pros worry about makes you a better editor no matter what kind of footage you're working with.

Continuity refers to consistency in:

- **The picture.** Suppose we watch a guy with wet hair say, "I'm going to have to break up with you." We cut to his girlfriend's horrified reaction—but when we cut back to the guy, his hair is dry.

  That's a continuity error, a frequent by-product of having spliced together footage that was filmed at different times. Every Hollywood movie, in fact, has a person whose sole job it is to watch out for errors like this during the editing process.

- **Direction of travel.** In the effort to make the editing as seamless as possible, film editors and directors try to maintain continuity of direction from shot to shot. That is, if the hero sets out crawling across the Sahara from right to left across the scene to be with his true love, you better believe that when we see him next, hours later, he'll still be crawling from right to left. This general rule even applies to much less dramatic circumstances, such as car chases, plane flights, and even people walking to the corner store. If you see her walk out of the frame from left to right in Shot A, you'll see her approach the corner store's doorway from left to right in Shot B.

- **The sound.** In an establishing shot, suppose we see hundreds of men in a battle-field trench, huddled for safety as bullets and bombs fly and explode all around them. Now we cut to a closeup of two of these men talking—but the sounds of the explosions are missing.

  That's a sound continuity error. The audience is certain to notice that hundreds of soldiers were issued a cease-fire just as these two guys started talking.

- **The camera setup.** In scenes of conversations between two people, it would look really bizarre to show one person speaking only in closeup, and his conversation partner filmed in a medium shot. (Unless, of course, the first person were filmed in *extreme* closeup—just the lips filling the screen—because the filmmaker is trying to protect his identity.)

- **Gesture and motion.** If one shot begins with a character reaching down to pick up the newspaper from her doorstep, the next shot—a closeup of her hand closing around the rolled-up paper, for example—should pick up from the exact moment where the previous shot ended. And as the rolled-up paper leaves our closeup field of view, the following shot should show her straightening into an upright position. Unless you've made the deliberate editing decision to skip over some time from one shot to the next (which should be clear to the audience), the action should seem continuous from one shot to the next.

Tip: For this reason, when filming scripted movies, directors always instruct their actors to begin each new scene's action with the same gesture or motion that *ended* the last shot. Having two copies of this gesture, action, or motion—one on each end of each take—gives the editor a lot of flexibility when it comes time to piece the movie together.

This principle explains why you'll find it extremely rare for an editor to cut from one shot of two people to another shot of the *same* two people (without inserting some other shot between them, such as a reaction shot or a closeup of one person or the other). The odds are small that, as the new shot begins, both actors will be in precisely the same body positions they were in as the previous shot ended.

When to Cut

Some Hollywood directors may tell their editors to make cuts just for the sake of making the cuts come faster, in an effort to pick up the pace.

The more seasoned director and editor, however, usually adopts a more classical view of editing: Cut to a different shot when it's *motivated*. That is, cut when you *need* to cut, so that you can convey new visual information by taking advantage of a different camera angle, switching to a different character, providing a reaction shot, and so on.

Editors look for a motivating event that suggests *where* they should make the cut, too, such as a movement, a look, the end of the sentence, or the intrusion of an off-camera sound that makes us *want* to look somewhere else in the scene.

Choosing the Next Shot

As you've read elsewhere in this book, the final piece of advice when it comes to choosing when and how to make a cut is this: Cut to a *different* shot. If you've been filming the husband, cut to the wife; if you've been in a closeup, cut to a medium or wide shot; if you've been showing someone looking off-camera, cut to what she's looking at.

Avoid cutting from one shot of somebody to a similar shot of the same person. Doing so creates a *jump cut,* a disturbing and seemingly unmotivated splice between shots of the same subject from the same angle.

Video editors sometimes have to swallow hard and perform jump cuts for the sake of compressing a long interview into a much shorter sound bite. Customer testimonials on TV commercials frequently illustrate this point. You'll see a woman saying, "Wonderglove changed … [cut] our lives, it really did … [cut] My husband used to be a drunk and a slob … [cut] but now we have Wonderglove." (Often, a fast cross dissolve is applied to the cuts in a futile attempt to make them less noticeable.)

As you can probably attest if you've ever seen such an ad, however, that kind of editing is rarely convincing. As you watch it, you can't help wondering exactly *what* was cut out and why. (The editors of *60 Minutes* and other documentary-style shows edit the comments of their interview subjects just as heavily, but conceal it better by cutting away to reaction shots—of the interviewer, for example—between edited shots.)

Popular Editing Techniques

Variety and pacing play a role in every decision the video editor makes. Here are some common tricks professional editors use, which you can also use in iMovie editing.

Tight Editing

One of the first tasks you'll encounter when editing your footage is choosing how to trim and chop up your clips, as described in Chapter 6. Even when editing home movies, consider the Hollywood guideline for tight editing: Begin every scene as *late* as possible, and end it as *soon* as possible.

In other words, suppose the audience sees the heroine receiving the call that her husband has been in an accident, and then hanging up the phone in shock. We don't really need to see her putting on her coat, opening the apartment door, locking it behind her, taking the elevator to the ground floor, hailing a cab, driving frantically through the city, screeching to a stop in front of the hospital, and finally leaping out of the cab. In a tightly edited movie, she would hang up the phone—and then we'd see her leaping out of the cab (or even walking into her husband's hospital room).

You might keep this principle in mind even when editing your own, slice-of-life videos. For example, a very engaging account of your ski trip might begin with only three shots: an establishing shot of the airport; a shot of the kids piling on to the plane; and then the tumultuous, noisy trying-on-ski-boots shot the next morning. You get less reality with this kind of tight editing, but much more watchability.

Variety of Shots

Variety is important in every aspect of filmmaking—variety of shots, locations, angles, and so on. Consider the lengths of your shots, too: In action sequences, you might prefer quick cutting, where each clip in your Movie Track is only a second or two long. In softer, more peaceful scenes, longer shots may set the mood more effectively.

Establishing shots

Almost every scene of every movie and every TV show—even the nightly news—begins with an *establishing shot:* a long-range, zoomed-out shot that shows the audience where the action is about to take place.

Now that you know something about film theory, you'll begin to notice how often TV and movie scenes begin with an establishing shot. It gives the audience a feeling of being there, and helps them understand the context for the medium shots or closeups that follow. Furthermore, after a long series of closeups, consider showing *another* wide shot, to remind the audience of where the characters are and what the world around them looks like.

As with every film editing guideline, this one is occasionally worth violating. For example, in comedies, a new scene may begin with a closeup instead of an establishing shot, so that the camera can then pull back to *make* the establishing shot the joke. (For example, closeup on main character looking uncomfortable; camera pulls back to reveal that we were looking at him upside down as he hangs, tied by his feet, over a pit of alligators.) In general, however, setting up any new scene with an establishing shot is the smart, and polite, thing to do for your audience's benefit.

Cutaways and cut-ins

Cutaways and *cut-ins* are extremely common and effective editing techniques. Not only do they add some variety to the movie, but they let you conceal enormous editing shenanigans. By the time your movie resumes after the cutaway shot, you can have deleted enormous amounts of material, switched to a different take of the same scene, and so on. Figure 13-1 shows the idea.

The *cut-in* is similar, but instead of showing a different person or a reaction shot, it usually features a closeup of what the speaker is holding or talking about—a very common technique in training tapes and cooking shows.

Reaction shots

One of the most common sequences in Hollywood history is a three-shot sequence that goes like this: First, we see the character looking offscreen; then we see what he's looking at (a cutaway shot); and finally we see him again so that we can read his reaction. This sequence is repeated so frequently in commercial movies that you can feel it coming the moment the performer looks off the screen.

From the editor's standpoint, of course, the beauty of the three-shot reaction shot is that the middle shot can be anything from anywhere. That is, it can be footage shot on another day in another part of the world, or even from a different movie entirely. The ritual of character/action/reaction is so ingrained in our brains that the audience believes the actor was looking at the action, no matter what.

In home-movie footage, you may have been creating reaction shots without even knowing it. But you've probably been capturing them by panning from your kid's beaming face to the petting-zoo sheep and then back to the face. You can make this sequence look great in iMovie just by snipping out the pans, leaving you with crisp, professional-looking cuts.

Figure 13-1:
Top: You've got a shot of your main character in action.

Middle: We cut away to a shot of what he's looking at or reacting to.

Bottom: When you cut back to the main character, you could use a different take on a different day, or dialog from a much later part of the scene (due to some cuts suggested by the editor). The audience will never know that the action wasn't continuous. The cutaway masks the fact that there was a discontinuity between the first and third shots.

Parallel cutting

When you're making a movie that tells a story, it's sometimes fun to use *parallel editing* or *intercutting*. That's when you show two trains of action simultaneously; you keep cutting back and forth to show the parallel simultaneous action. In *Fatal Attraction*, for example, the intercut climax shows main character Dan Gallagher (Michael Douglas) downstairs in the kitchen, trying to figure out why the ceiling is dripping, even as his psychotic mistress Alex (Glenn Close) is upstairs attempting to murder his wife in the bathtub. If you're making movies that tell a story, you'll find this technique an exciting one when you're trying to build suspense.

Back and Forth to iMovie 6

Owning iMovie '08 also means that you get a free copy of iMovie 6. (If you already had iMovie 6, it's now in your Applications→Previous iMovie folder. If not, you can download your free copy from Apple's Web site.)

That's lucky, because iMovie 6 offers a lot of features that are gone in iMovie '08. They include:

- **Audio rubber-banding.** As shown in Figure 13-2, this term refers to manual volume adjustments on an audio track. It's like iMovie '08's *automatic ducking* feature (page 228), except that it's not automatic; you get complete control.

  Of course, when you export your iMovie '08 movie to iMovie 6, your audio gets mashed down into a single track. So passing off the project to iMovie 6 doesn't mean you'll be able to do elaborate mix adjustments of the camcorder audio, the background music, and so on.

  But you *can* do most of the editing in iMovie '08, using what *it's* good for: quick selection of shots, better-looking titles, superior color-correction tools, cropping and rotation of video, and so on—and then add your music and sound effects in iMovie 6.

Figure 13-2:
In iMovie 6, you can adjust the audio volume manually along the length of a clip just by drawing in its volume graph, also known as "rubber-banding" because of the way the line snaps to the control points you create.

- **Audio effects.** iMovie '08 doesn't offer any audio effects at all. You can't add reverb or echo, adjust the pitch, change the audio speed, or tweak the sound with a graphic equalizer. But all of that *is* available in iMovie 6.

  Here's another reason to do your *video* work in iMovie '08, and then export the result to iMovie 6 for audio editing and fine-tuning.

- **Video special effects.** iMovie '08 doesn't have any visual effects, either—not even such essentials as Slow Motion, Fast Motion, and Reverse Motion.

  iMovie 6, on the other hand, is absolutely outstanding at special effects. A partial list of these great-looking effects includes Aged Film, Fog, Lens Flare, Mirror, Crystallize, Glass Distortion, Sepia Tone, Water Color, Rain, Sharpen, and Soft Focus.

  iMovie 6 can also accommodate *add-on* effects from other companies. (iMovie '08 can't.) At *http://geethree.com,* for example, you can buy some really powerful stuff for iMovie 6, like picture-in-picture, split picture, a camcorder-jitter stabilizer, and much more.

So there's no reason you can't get your rough edit done in iMovie '08, and then send the whole thing back to iMovie 6 to apply these effects.

• **Export to tape.** This one's *huge.*

When you're finished with an iMovie '08 project, you can export it to the Web, burn it to a DVD, or export it as a QuickTime movie. Unfortunately, *all* of those involve some degradation of video quality. (Yes, even a DVD compresses the video somewhat.)

In iMovie 6, there's an easy solution. You can preserve the really important videos, the ones you wanted to save forever with 100 percent of the original quality, on tape. iMovie 6 can play your finished masterpiece directly into a DV camcorder at full original quality—a great way to archive your masterpiece where not even a hard drive crash can affect it.

By exporting your movie from iMovie '08 into iMovie 6, you can grant yourself the freedom to back up your best work onto tapes in just this way.

Transferring Your Project, iMovie '08→iMovie 6

In all of the examples described above, it makes sense to begin your project in iMovie '08, and then to finish it up in iMovie 6.

Here's how you go about it. (For more explanation of what you're doing here, see Chapter 18, which goes into more detail about exporting iMovie projects as Quick-Time movies.)

1. **When you've gone as far as you can go in iMovie '08, choose Share→Export using QuickTime.**

   The "Save exported file as" dialog box appears. Type a name for the intermediate transfer file you're going to create. In this example, suppose you call it *Transfer Movie.*

   Choose a location for the exported movie, as shown in Figure 13-3, top.

2. **Make sure the Export pop-up menu says "Movie to QuickTime Movie." Then click Options.**

   Now the Movie Settings dialog box appears (Figure 13-3, bottom).

3. **Click the top Settings button.**

   The Video Compression Settings dialog box appears.

4. **From the Compression Type pop-up menu, choose Apple Intermediate Codec.**

   You can read more about this important format on page 100. In essence, it's a file format that's understood by all of Apple's video editing programs, past and present, and retains 100 percent of the video quality of the original.

5. **Click OK. Click OK in the next dialog box. Click Save.**

   iMovie takes a few moments to export the video.

You now have on your desktop a QuickTime movie version of your project, named "Transfer Movie" or whatever you called it in step 1.

6. Open iMovie 6.

It may be in your Applications→iMovie (Previous Version) folder. Or, if you downloaded it from the Apple Web site, it's wherever you saved it. Oh, and it's probably called iMovie HD. (And yes, it's perfectly OK to have iMovie '08 and iMovie 6 open at the same time.)

Note: Apple is schizophrenic in its naming scheme. The icons for both iMovie 5 and iMovie 6 were named "iMovie HD."

---

7. In iMovie 6, create a new, empty project. Name and save it. Choose File→Import (Shift-⌘-I). In the Open dialog box, find and double-click the exported movie file you created in step 5 ("Transfer Movie").

Figure 13-3:
Top: In this first dialog box, your job is to type a name for the exported movie. It doesn't really matter what you call it. Choose your desktop as the save location, but don't click Save yet.

Bottom: Here's where you specify a format for your exported QuickTime movie. Click Settings.

Incidentally, you can also pass your iMovie '08 projects off to Final Cut Pro or Final Cut Express; page 419 has the details. That way, you can use iMovie for what it's good at (importing video from tapeless camcorders, quickly choosing the best shots)—and then use Final Cut for what it's good for (everything else).

It shows up in iMovie 6 on the Clips shelf, as shown in Figure 13-4.

8. **Drag the Transfer Movie icon down to the Timeline at the bottom of the window.**

   You're ready to edit it!

Note: iMovie 6, of course, is an entirely different ball of wax. Not to be totally mercenary here, but the best way to learn it is to read *iMovie 6 and iDVD: The Missing Manual.*

Figure 13-4:
Your partially finished iMovie '08 movie is now safely ensconced in iMovie 6. It's represented by a single icon on the Clips shelf. Drag it down to the Timeline and start editing.

Transferring Your Project, iMovie 6→iMovie '08

As noted above, most people will probably go from iMovie '08→iMovie 6. But you may very well want to go the other direction. Maybe you want to begin in iMovie 6, and then finish up in iMovie '08, because:

- **You want to send the finished movie to YouTube.** Only iMovie '08 has that feature built right in.

- **You want to crop, rotate, or color-correct some scenes.** iMovie '08 is clearly the superior tool for these functions.

- **You want to use iMovie '08's titles.** The newer version offers better-looking text over video, not to mention far greater typographical control. (For example, only iMovie '08 lets you create different fonts, sizes, and colors *within* a single title.)

Actually, the process of transferring an iMovie 6 project to its successor is almost the same as going the other way. Here's what you do:

1. **When your iMovie 6 project is ready to export, choose Share→QuickTime.**

The Share dialog box appears.

2. **From the pop-up menu, choose Expert Settings. Click Share.**

You arrive at the dialog box shown in Figure 13-3 (bottom).

3. **Follow steps 2 through 5 on page 263.**

Creating the transfer movie is exactly the same no matter which direction you go.

4. **Open iMovie '08. Choose File→Import Movies.**

The Open dialog box appears (Figure 13-5).

5. **Locate and open your Transfer Movie.**

The former iMovie 6 movie is now safely ensconced in iMovie '08, in the Event you specified. You can add it to a project and begin your final surgery on it.

Tip: There's no reason you can't go back and forth between the two iMovies, repeating the process as necessary. You're not losing any video quality with each trip.

Figure 13-5:
Before you find and open your Transfer Movie, specify whether you want it to become part of an existing Event or a new one. (See pages 86 and 87 for details on this process.)

Part Three:
Finding Your Audience

3

Exporting to iPod, iPhone, Apple TV, or Front Row

A pple, as you may have noticed, is really into the electronic presentation of video. In iMovie '08, all the other possibilities of sharing your finished movies have been demoted (like sending to a DVD) or removed altogether (recording back to tape). What Apple *really* wants you to do with your finished masterpiece is to post it on the Web (see Chapter 15) or transfer it to another Apple machine, like an iPod, iPhone, Apple TV, or Front Row (to play on your Mac from across the room).

That's what this chapter is all about: sending your finished masterpiece to another fine piece of Apple merchandise.

Exporting the Movie to iTunes

As it turns out, the steps for exporting a movie to Apple's four video-playing machines (iPod, iPhoto, Apple TV, Front Row) are nearly identical. All of them involve exporting the movie to iTunes, which is the loading dock for iPods, iPhones, Apple TVs, and even Front Row. The only difference is the size of the movie you're creating.

So, for the sake of saving the Brazilian rainforest, the instructions appear here only once, with the necessary variations written out along the way:

1. **When your project is ready for prime time, choose Share→iTunes.**

   The "Publish your project to iTunes" dialog box appears (Figure 14-1). You've probably never seen a dialog box quite like this one.

   In essence, it's offering you various screen sizes for exporting your finished movie. The faint gray dots indicate which sizes are appropriate for which kinds of gadgets.

For example, the **iPhone's** screen is 480 by 360 pixels, which is precisely the dimensions of the Mobile option here. A standard-definition TV set has 640 by 480 pixels, which is why that's an option for the **Apple TV**. That's also why **iPods** prefer 640 by 480 videos: just in case you connect them to a TV for playback. (The **iPhone** has both a screen-size recommendation and a Tiny option—176 by 144—which is for those iPhone-wielding fans who attempt to watch your videos over a cellular connection.)

2. **Turn on the checkboxes that correspond to the sizes you want to export.**

   You can actually turn on *more than one* of these checkboxes. You'll wind up with *several* copies of this video.

Tip: If you point to the ❶ button without clicking, a tooltip appears. As shown in Figure 14-1, it tells you more about the exported movie file you're about to create. For example, you'll see the file format (H.264); the number of frames per second; the Internet speed required to watch the video from the Web (in megabits per second—for comparison, a typical cable-modem connection is 2 megabits per second); and the file size (in megabytes).

Figure 14-1:
This unusual-looking dialog box is just Apple's way of offering you some ready-made compression settings for typical playback gadgets. Point to the ❶ button to see some techier details.

3. **Click Publish.**

   Now the time-consuming exporting and compression process begins. Feel free to switch into other programs—check your email or surf the Web, for example—while iMovie crunches away in the background. A progress bar lets you know how much farther iMovie has to go.

When it's all over, iTunes opens by itself. If you click the Movies folder, you'll see the new exported movies nestled there (Figure 14-2). They're named after the project and the size you exported. For example, you might see "Birthday Party – Mobile" and "Birthday Party – Medium."

From iTunes to iPod, iPhone, Etc.

Once your movies are in iTunes, getting them onto your iPod, iPhone, Apple TV, or copy of Front Row works just like it always does:

- **iPod, iPhone.** Connect the iPod or iPhone to your Mac. Its icon shows up in the column at the left side of iTunes. Click the Movies tab and select the movies you want copied over to your i-gadget when they sync (Figure 14-3).

Figure 14-2:
Here, tucked in among your other movies, are the exported ones from iMovie. To watch one, double-click it; it starts playing in the lower-left corner of the screen. Click that area, once, to make the movie play bigger, in a window of its own.

- **Apple TV.** Same deal here. The Apple TV's name and icon show up in the left-side column of iTunes. Click it, then click the Movies tab and turn on the movies you want synced to the Apple TV, so you can enjoy your iMovie productions on the big screen.

- **Front Row.** Front Row, of course, is the built-in movie/music/DVD player that's built into every current Mac model (except the Mac Pro). It's designed to be operated and enjoyed from a couch across the room—all the fonts and menus are presented in huge, razor-sharp text—which is why all Front Row computers come with a tiny white remote control.

Tip: If you lose the remote, you can also open Front Row by pressing ⌘-Escape or, on some models, F1.

The catalog of movies and music presented by Front Row is simply whatever you've got in iTunes. All you have to do to see your videos, therefore, is to use the remote to choose Videos. Your exported iMovie masterworks appear right there, ready to watch (Figure 14-4).

Figure 14-3:
When iTunes notices that you have an iPod, iPhone, or Apple TV, the corresponding icon appears in the Source list (left). Click the gadget's name to make the tabs appear (main window), where you can specify what music, movies, and other stuff you want to copy to your i-gadget at the next sync. On the Movies tab, you'll find all of your iMovie '08 exports.

Figure 14-4:
Here's the Front Row listing of your videos. Lo and behold, here are all the movies you've exported from iMovie, ready to enjoy!

Exporting to YouTube and the Web

I f you ask Apple—or Steve Jobs, anyway—the DVD has had its day in the sun. The format is 10 years old. *Nobody* puts their movies on DVD anymore. Plastic shiny discs that have to be—ugh—*mailed?* That's such an old-fashioned, clumsy, *physical* way to share video.

No, the real action is on the Internet. This billion-seat megaplex is where the action is, where unknown independent filmmakers get noticed, and where it doesn't cost you a penny to distribute your work to a vast worldwide audience.

It's all about YouTube, baby. One hundred million videos watched per day. It costs nothing to sign up and nothing to post your videos there.

Or put your videos up on your .Mac account. It costs $100 per year, but man, do videos look fantastic on your own .Mac home page. They're available at multiple frame sizes, to accommodate visitors with Internet connections of different speeds. Your fans can even skim your iMovie '08 movies, just like you can on your own Mac.

Or, what the heck—post videos on your own Web site.

This chapter covers all three ways of making your opus visible on the Web.

Method 1: iMovie→YouTube

By far the easiest way to post your movies on the Internet is to use iMovie '08's new YouTube command.

YouTube, of course, is the insanely popular video-sharing Web site, filled to the brim with hundreds of millions of funny home videos, TV excerpts, amateur short films, memorable bloopers—and, now, your iMovie projects. Once you've posted your iMovie there, other people can find it by Web address, by searching for your name, by searching for videos by description, and so on.

As it turns out, the steps for posting your movie on YouTube are longer the *very first time* you do it. After that, it's a breeze. Observe:

Posting to YouTube (First Time)

Suppose your movie is now ready for the masses.

1. Choose Share→YouTube.

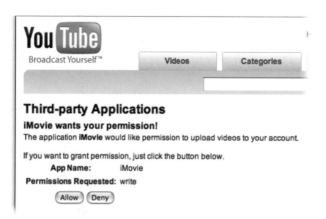

Figure 15-1:

Top: The first stop on the YouTube Express is signing up for a free YouTube account. Later, you'll be able to sign in to edit or delete the movies you've posted.

Bottom: You can't post movies to YouTube unless, um, you give permission for iMovie to post movies to YouTube.

A *sheet* (dialog box attached to the window) appears. Since you're a YouTube virgin, it probably looks something like Figure 15-1—empty.

2. **If your YouTube account name doesn't already appear in the pop-up menu, click Add.**

On the next screen, click Sign In.

You're taken into your Web browser, to the YouTube site. Here, you can either sign in with your existing YouTube name and password (if you have one), or sign up for a free account (if you don't).

In that case, on the Create an Account screen, make up a name and password, fill in your vital statistics, and so on. When it's all over, YouTube sends an email to the address you specified. (Not always immediately, however. The path to YouTubeness is not always instant.)

The email message, when it finally arrives, contains a link that says "Confirm your email address." What it really means is, "Click me to confirm that you're a real person with a real email account and not one of those annoying software robots that tries to set up thousands of bogus YouTube accounts in hopes of spreading spam."

When that great moment arrives, your YouTube account will be official. Return to iMovie and click Confirm Sign-in. You go back to YouTube again.

3. **On the Third-Party Applications screen, click Allow.**

This, too, is a blockade meant to stop the Internet bad guys. It's saying, "Are you sure it's OK for iMovie to upload movies to your account? Just checking, in case this thing requesting permission is actually a nasty piece of spyware written by one of the Internet's evildoers and designed to overrun your account with random gibberish behind your back."

4. **When the "you have given permission" screen appears, close the Web browser window. Return to iMovie. Click Confirm Sign-In.**

Now you arrive at the original sheet (Figure 15-1), where your YouTube account name finally appears in the pop-up menu.

5. **Fill in the name, description, and keywords for your movie (Figure 15-2).**

The name and description will appear right beside the movie when it appears on YouTube.

6. **Specify what size you want the movie to be.**

YouTube can play movies in either of the two sizes listed here: Mobile or Medium. For details on this table-like dialog box, see page 270; for now, it's enough to note that YouTube can play back both of these sizes. The Medium size will look bigger and better, but will play only over fast Internet connections. If you expect that your audience will be connecting over dial-up modems, choose the Mobile option.

7. Turn on "Make this movie private," if you like.

Most YouTube movies are available to the entire universe of people on the Internet. If you'd rather control who gets to see your epic, though, turn on this checkbox. Now, *nobody* will be able to see it unless you specifically invite people by sending them its Web address.

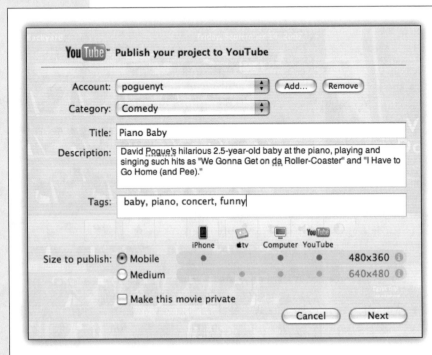

Figure 15-2:
The Tags are keywords to ensure that your video will come up when other YouTubers search for such flag words. (Sorry about the ugly see-through background of this shot. But that's what you actually see, since the sheet is semitransparent.)

8. Click Next.

A dialog box appears, reminding you that it's naughty to upload TV shows, movies, or anything else that you don't have the copyright for.

9. Click Publish.

iMovie springs into action, compressing and uploading your video. This part can take awhile. Feel free to switch into another program while iMovie crunches away. Check your email.

When the upload is finally complete, you see the message shown in Figure 15-3.

10. Tell a friend, or view the movie, or just return to iMovie.

If you click Tell a Friend, your email program opens. The Mac thoughtfully opens a new, outgoing message; types "My Great iMovie!" in the Subject line; and fills in the body with a message that alerts your fans to the presence—and the YouTube address—of your new video.

Note: Well, sort of. If you use Apple's own Mail program, the outgoing message includes the correct click-able address for your movie (such as *http://www.youtube.com/watch?v=tdcark_siiU*). If you use another program, like Microsoft Entourage, the address includes only *"http://www.youtube.com/watch"* and doesn't take your fans directly to the movie. It seems to be a bug.

Figure 15-3:
Newly posted YouTube videos aren't available to the masses immediately.

Your video has been uploaded to YouTube. It may be several minutes or hours before your video is processed and viewable, depending on YouTube's server load.

Your video can be viewed at: http://www.youtube.com/watch?v=vZNsziqL0fo

(Tell a Friend)   (View   )   (OK)

Posting to YouTube (After the First Time)

Once you've done all that account setting-up, the posting-to-YouTube process is much simpler.

Once the finished project is open on the screen, choose Share→Publish. The dialog box shown in Figure 15-2 appears.

Then follow the preceding instructions from step 5.

Tip: If you upload a movie that's *exactly* the same length as one that you uploaded earlier, YouTube may reject the new video, claiming that it's a duplicate.

The solution is to humor it. Make the new video a fraction of a second longer or shorter.

After the Movie Is Up

Once you've successfully posted a video on YouTube, you won't forget it, thanks to the new icons and labels that identify it in the Projects list (Figure 15-4).

At this point, you have several movie-management options:

- **Tell another friend about the movie.** Click the project's name, and then click the "Tell a friend" link that appears above the storyboard (visible in Figure 15-4).

- **Watch the YouTube video yourself.** Click the project's name, and then click the "View" link above the storyboard (also visible in Figure 15-4).

- **Edit the movie and re-publish it.** As soon as you start making changes to the published project, all hell breaks loose. A yellow exclamation-point icon appears at the top of the storyboard, along with the notation "out of date." And just in case you didn't get the point, a warning box appears, too.

  Click OK to dismiss the warning box. Finish making your changes, and then choose Share→YouTube again. Repeat the process from step 5 on page 275.

Note: Actually, this process doesn't *update* or even *replace* the original version of the video. It just uploads another copy of it.

~~You'll have to delete the original manually—and you can't even use iMovie's Remove from YouTube command~~ to do that. You have to go to YouTube, sign in to your account, and delete the bad version by hand.

Published online but out of date

Figure 15-4:
After you've published a project to YouTube, iTunes, or .Mac, the Projects list reminds you—and lets you know which of iMovie's four standard export sizes you used. If you see the yellow exclamation point, beware! Your version of the project no longer matches what you shared on YouTube/iTunes/.Mac!

Published online   Quality indicators

- **Delete the movie from YouTube.** Once you feel that a movie has outlived its useful-ness (or become an embarrassment), you can remove it from YouTube. Just click the project's name in iMovie and then choose Share→Remove from YouTube.

Getting a .Mac Account

.Mac, Apple's subscription online service, provides everything you need to put a collection of your movies online. A .Mac membership will set you back $100 per year.

Mac OS X makes it easy to sign up for an account, and a two-month trial account is free.

If you don't already have an account, start by choosing →System Preferences. Click the .Mac icon, and then click

Sign Up. Now you go online, where your Web browser opens up to the .Mac sign-up screen. Follow the steps.

When you return to System Preferences, you'll see that the Mac has filled in your account name and password automatically. You're now ready to use your .Mac account—and to post iMovie masterworks to it.

Method 2: iMovie→.Mac Web Gallery

YouTube is certainly the people's video-sharing service. It's got the most videos and the most eyeballs watching them, and it offers buttons that let your audience leave fan mail (or hate mail) in the comments and rate your work on a five-star scale.

YouTube does not, however, have the best quality. The videos are fairly small and blurry.

If you publish your masterwork to a .Mac account, though, it's a whole different world. The presentation is classy and glamorous, and the movie itself is nice and big (Figure 15-5).

Figure 15-5:
Movies you post to .Mac look quite a bit better than they do on YouTube. The background is dark and classy; the scroll bar and volume controls are easy to figure out; and the My Gallery button takes you back to the full "table of contents" for the movies and iPhoto slideshows on your site.

.Mac, of course, is Apple's $100-per-year suite of Internet services and conveniences: electronic greeting cards, synchronizing of calendars and Web bookmarks among the different Macs in your life, a backup program, an antivirus program, the ability to check your email online—and HomePage, which lets you generate your own Web pages.

Here's how you get your movie to your .Mac gallery:

1. **With your project on the screen before you, choose Share "Publish to .Mac Web Gallery."**

   The dialog box shown in Figure 15-6 appears.

2. **Fill in the title and a description for your movie. Then choose what frame size you want for your movie: Mobile, Medium, or whatever.**

   Medium is a great size if your viewers have high-speed Internet connections (like cable modems or DSL). If they're using dial-up or slow DSL, choose Mobile.

   Tip: You can choose *more* than one size, if you like. See page 270 for details on these size options.

   Incidentally, iMovie keeps track of which sizes of each project you've exported to your .Mac gallery. If you see some of the Size checkboxes dimmed, it's because you've *already* posted versions of this project in those sizes.

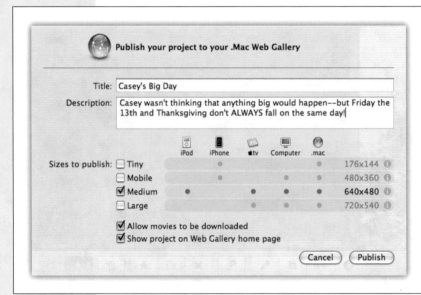

Figure 15-6:
If you've ever published a video to YouTube, this one should look distinctly familiar. Once again, you're supposed to specify a title, description, and frame size for your Web movie.

3. **Turn on "Allow movies to be downloaded," if you like.**

   In other words: Do you want people to be able just to watch your movie *online*—to stream it, in other words?

   Or do you want to permit them to download the movie as a file to their hard drives? That would mean that they can play the movie when they're not online. It would also mean that they could, if they were so inclined, edit your movie themselves, incorporate it into their own presentations, and so on. It's all up to you.

4. **Hide the video from the unwashed masses by turning off "Show project on Web Gallery home page," if you like.**

   If you do that, then nobody will see the movie's icon on your .Mac gallery home page. The only way they'll be able to watch your movie is through a personal invitation from you—that includes the movie's Web address.

This, in other words, is precisely what you should do for movies that you don't want the whole world to see.

5. Click Publish.

iMovie begins the time-consuming process of compressing and uploading the movie. When it's finished, you get a message much like the one in Figure 15-3.

6. Click "Tell a Friend," "View," or OK.

The first button opens a new, outgoing email message, ready to address and send to your adoring public. The second takes *you* to the .Mac Gallery to enjoy the online version of your flick. And OK just takes you back to iMovie.

After the Movie Is Up

Once you've successfully hung a new movie in your .Mac Gallery, the project takes on new icons and labels within iMovie (Figure 15-4).

As with YouTube, you can now manage the online movie in any of several ways:

- **Tell another friend about the movie.** Click the project's name, and then click "Tell a friend" above the storyboard (visible in Figure 15-4).

- **Watch the video yourself.** Click the project's name, and then click View above the storyboard (also visible in Figure 15-4).

- **Edit the movie and re-publish it.** Once you edit the project, iMovie makes it very clear that the online version no longer matches the master version. You see a yellow exclamation-point icon, the words "out of date," and a warning dialog box (Figure 15-4).

    Click OK to dismiss the warning box. Finish making your changes, and then choose Share→"Re-publish to .Mac Web Gallery." Repeat from step 2 of the previous instructions.

Note: This time, iMovie actually does *replace* the originally published movie. You don't wind up with two versions, as you do with YouTube.

- **Delete the movie from your Web gallery.** To take down a movie—perhaps because of rampant picketing from special-interest groups who declare your film to be offensive, despite never even having seen it—click the project's name in iMovie, and then choose Share→Remove from .Mac.

Custom Web Pages: Three Roads

What's amazing about the .Mac Web Gallery is that it's so perfectly tailored for the presentation of movies. The black screen, the high-tech scroll bar, the absence of text…it's just awesome.

Unless, of course, you *want* to control the background, the look, the text on the Web page. Why can't you embed a movie into a *normal* Web page, just like any ordinary person?

Actually, you can. In fact, you can embed your iMovie movies onto your own custom Web pages in any of three different ways:

- **The iWeb way.** Use iWeb, which is one of the other iLife '08 programs. It's a Web-design program that requires zero hand coding in the HTML language of the Web. You just pick a design template, type new text, slap in some pictures or movies, and you're done. iMovie can hand off a movie to iWeb with only a couple of mouse clicks; from there, you can incorporate them into the Web pages that you design.

Note: Once you've designed a Web site in iWeb, you can post it on your .Mac account (if you're paid up) *or* post it on the Web using space provided by, for example, your Internet provider. In other words, it doesn't have to be a .Mac page.

- **The iDisk way.** Copy an exported QuickTime movie to the Movies folder of your iDisk (an Internet-based "virtual hard drive" that comes with a .Mac account). Then use the HomePage features at Apple's Web site (instead of the layout tools in iWeb) to set up your pages. (HomePage is another template-based Web-page creation program that came before iWeb.)

- **The freehand way.** Suppose you're a savvy, Webmastery kind of person, and you design your own Web pages, and post them on the Web, without any help from sissy templates like iWeb and .Mac HomePage. In that case, you can embed *any* movie into *any* of your Web pages—without paying Apple *any* money every year.

Meet the Media Browser

The *Media Browser* is a common, central multimedia library for your Mac, designed to facilitate sharing of photos, music, and movies between Apple programs.

You can open the Media Browser in programs like Keynote, iDVD, GarageBand, iWeb, and iMovie. (The Media Browser is shown in Figure 15-7.)

And here's what you'll see there: **music** from iTunes (complete with your playlists) and GarageBand; **photos** from iPhoto (complete with your albums) and PhotoBooth; and **movies** from iMovie, iPhoto, iTunes, and the Movies folder in your Home folder.

The Media Browser is especially important to iMovie, because it provides by far the easiest way for you to hand

off your videos to use in iWeb, Keynote, or—most important of all–iDVD. (You'll read more about *that* subject in Chapter 18.)

In fact, iMovie even uses the Media Browser when you upload videos to YouTube or your .Mac gallery. If you watch the progress bars closely, you'll see that these are actually two-step procedures. First, iMovie creates a compressed QuickTime version of your movie and puts it *in the Media Browser;* second, it uploads that movie to the Web.

The movie you uploaded, however, *remains* in the Media Browser. That's how iMovie always seems to know which size versions of each project you've sent to the Web (Figure 15-4)–because they're still sitting right there on your hard drive!

The rest of this chapter covers all three of these methods of creating your own Web pages with movies on them.

Method 3: iMovie→iWeb

This isn't a book about iWeb, of course, but here's enough information to get your movie onto a Web page of your own design—and hang the whole thing on the Internet for the masses to see.

1. **With the finished iMovie project open, choose Share→Media Browser.**

   In any case, the dialog box shown in Figure 15-7 appears. At this point, it should look familiar. See page 270 for a description of its options. In this case, though, you're about to hand off the movie to the Media Browser. (See the box on the facing page.)

Figure 15-7:
The Media Browser is your one-stop shopping center for all the music, photos, and movies on your computer. You're about to load it up with even more movies to share with your other Apple programs.

2. **Choose the size(s) you'll want for the movie on your Web page.**

   Word to the wise: In general, choose Tiny or Mobile. Use Medium only if all of your fans use high-speed Internet connections.

   You can choose multiple sizes to send to the Media Browser, if you like, although, of course, you're using up more hard drive space.

3. **Click Publish.**

   iMovie cranks away, compressing your project down to an exported QuickTime movie file in the size you specified.

Note: iMovie actually keeps track of which sizes of each project you've exported to the Media Browser. If you see some of the Size checkboxes dimmed, it's because the Media Browser *already* has versions of this project in those sizes.

---

4. **Open iWeb (Figure 15-8).**

5. **Open the Web page you want to edit, or choose File→New Page to create a new one. Click the Media button at the bottom of the screen (or choose View→Show Media Browser).**

The Media button (bottom of the window, second from right in Figure 15-8) opens—what else?—the Media Browser.

Figure 15-8:
Welcome to iWeb, a what-you-see-is-what-your-Web-site-will-look-like editing world for Web sites. The left-side column lists the Web pages you've made so far. The links at the top connect to them. The small Inspector palette (here labeled Metrics) lets you tweak the characteristics of your movie and your page.

6. **Find the movie you exported in step 3, and drag it wherever you want it on the page.**

If you drag it on top of one of the sample photos, it snaps nicely into alignment. Finish editing your page as usual in iWeb.

7. **Edit the page title, subtitle, and description text.**

Don't be concerned by the presence of all the Latin ("Lorem ipsum dolor amet…"); that's intended to be placeholder text. Drag your cursor through it and type new stuff to replace it.

8. **Edit the design of the page, if you like.**

Choose View→Show Inspector. The Inspector window's seventh tab, labeled Metrics, is a palette of movie-frame options. You can control its name, dimensions, and so on. (First, click the movie itself.)

9. In the lower-left corner of iWeb, click Publish. In the confirmation box, click OK.

This is the big moment: iWeb connects to the .Mac Web site, and then transfers the video and its page to the server. This magic requires, of course, that you already have a .Mac account. It can also take a *very* long time.

When the upload is complete, a dialog box appears, offering three buttons: Announce (email the site address to your friends), Visit Site Now, and OK.

Congratulations—you've just published your own Web site with a movie in it.

Note: You don't need a .Mac account to use iWeb. If you maintain your own Web site, for example, choose File→Publish to a Folder in this step. You wind up with a folder of correctly linked HTML documents and folders on your hard drive. All you have to do is upload them manually to your Web site.

What you get when you're done

When you see what you've created with iWeb, you'll be impressed: It's a professional-looking, stylishly titled Web page with thumbnails neatly arranged in a grid. Clicking the ▶ button under your movie starts playback.

Tip: In the URLs for your .Mac-hosted Web sites (such as *http://web.mac.com/casey/iWeb/Site/Summertime .html*), capitalization counts. If your friends type one of these addresses into a Web browser with incorrect capitalization, they may get only a "missing page" message.

Then again, maybe it's better to send your friends a much shorter, easier to remember address. You can convert long URLs into shorter ones using a free URL redirection service. At *www.tinyurl.com,* for example, you can turn that long address into something as short as *http://tinyurl.com/bus4.*

Editing or deleting the Web page

Within iWeb, make your changes and then click the Publish button again at the bottom of the screen. iWeb sets about updating the movie page online.

To delete a page, click its name in iWeb's left-side panel (the Site Organizer) and press the Delete key. Then click Publish at the bottom of the window, meaning, "OK, make the online version of my site match what I now have in iWeb."

Deleting a movie page like this also deletes all of the online movie files, which frees up space on your iDisk.

Method 4: HomePage

Although using iWeb is incredibly simple, it entails a lot of sitting and waiting for the program to compute and upload things. HTML aficionados complain, too, that iWeb's behind-the-scenes HTML code can be a tad unorthodox.

Fortunately, there's yet another way to go about creating, editing, and managing your video galleries online: Visit your .Mac Web site and use HomePage. The advantage here is that you can make changes to your movie pages even when you're far from home, using any Web-connected computer.

To get started with HomePage, you first must export the video from iMovie as a Quick-Time movie with modest dimensions and frame rate, as described in Chapter 16.

Then copy the movies you want to publish to the Movies folder of your iDisk, as shown in Figure 15-9.

Figure 15-9:
To summon your iDisk icon to the screen, choose its name from the Go menu in the Finder (top left). At last, it appears on your desktop, bearing your member name (top right). Double-click it—and wait—to see its contents (bottom). Copy the movies that you want to post online into the Movies folder.

Once your movie's in the iDisk's Movies folder, you're ready to create your Web pages. Go to *www.mac.com*, sign in, click the HomePage button, and then click one of the "Create a page" tabs on the HomePage screen to view the styles of pages you can create. Some of the formatting options available are shown in Figure 15-10.

The tab called iMovie offers special movie-showcase layouts in a far wider range of styles than iWeb offers. But you're free to use your movies on the other Web page designs here, too, like the baby announcements, writing samples, invitations, and so on.

Click the miniature image of the design you want. HomePage next asks which movie in your Movies folder you want to place on your new Web page, as shown in Figure 15-10. Select a movie, and then click Choose. After a few moments, your new video page appears with the movie already inserted.

Figure 15-10:
The HomePage home page offers a gallery of predesigned Web pages. The iMovie category offers special designs intended exclusively for QuickTime movie playback, but you're welcome to choose a design from any other category; just stick a movie anyplace Apple left a space for a photo. Your movie occupies only a small rectangle in the center of your visitors' screens; the rest is graphic fluff to fill up the window.

To finish the project, edit the chunks of dummy text on the page, as shown in Figure 15-11. (Make an effort to avoid misspellings and typos, unless you want an audience of 400 million to think you slept through fourth-grade English.)

Finally, click Preview to see how the Web page will look. When everything is just the way you want it, click Publish. The page goes live, as indicated by a confirmation dialog box.

Tip: You can create as many Web pages as your iDisk will hold. When you return to the main HomePage screen, a list of your existing Web pages appears, complete with New Page, Edit Page, and Delete Page buttons.

Corporations and professional Web designers may sniff at the simplicity of the result, but it takes *them* a lot longer than 2 minutes to do their thing.

Editing your Web page

To make changes to your Web site using the .Mac tools, log back into *www.mac.com*. On the main .Mac page, click HomePage. You're back at Figure 15-11.

At the top left of the page is the list of Web pages you've created so far. Click the name of the movie you want to edit, and then click the small Edit button beneath it. You're ready to proceed as shown in Figure 15-11.

Figure 15-11:
Here's where you edit your movie page before unleashing it on the Web—for example, adding or editing a title and a description. To choose a different movie, click the tiny Choose button beneath the movie scroll bar. When everything looks good, click Publish. You've just updated your Web page.

Behind the screens

Behind the scenes, iMovie builds your movie Web site by placing new Web page (HTML) documents in the Sites folder of your iDisk (Figure 15-9). If you know how to use a Web-page creation program like Dreamweaver or even Microsoft Word, you can make changes to your Web page by editing these documents.

Method 5: Posting a Movie on Your Own Web Site

In some cases, you might prefer the control and the freedom of putting movies onto your *own* Web page, designed the way you like it, without any hand-holding from Apple's templates and without having to sign up for a .Mac account.

If you already have a Web site, you can export a QuickTime version of your flick (see Chapter 16) and upload it to your Web site, no matter what the Web-hosting service. (Most Internet accounts, including those provided by AOL, Earthlink, or your cable-modem or DSL company, come with free space for Web pages uploaded in this way.)

Method 5: Posting a Movie on Your Site

This is the most labor-intensive route, but it offers much more flexibility if you know how to work with HTML to create more sophisticated pages. It's also the route you should take if you hope to incorporate the resulting movie into an existing Web site (that is, one in which the movies aren't the only attraction).

This isn't really a book about Web design. But to get you started, a free PDF appendix to this chapter, called "Movies on Custom Web Sites," awaits on this book's "Missing CD" page at *www.missingmanuals.com*. It provides the HTML code you need to post a movie on your Web page, make it pop up in a window or play embedded, looking into QuickTime Streaming Server, and other advanced topics.

From iMovie to QuickTime

For the best and most cinematic viewing experience, play your finished iMovie productions on TV, from a tape or DVD, or at high resolution on a big computer screen. That way, your public gets to see the full-sized picture that your camcorder captured. (iMovie '08 can't play your movie on a tape or export the finished project to a tape for archiving and viewing—but iMovie 6 can. See Chapter 13 for details.)

But when you want to distribute your movies electronically, convert them into QuickTime files instead. Both Mac and Windows machines can play these files right on the screen with little more than a double-click.

Your distribution options for QuickTime files are far greater than for videocassette or DVD, too. You can email a QuickTime file to somebody or post it on the Web for all the world to see (Chapter 15). You can put bigger QuickTime files onto a disk, like a recordable CD, DVD, external hard drive, or an iPod, to transport them. You can export only the *audio* portion of your movie—or only the video portion.

This chapter covers all of these techniques, step by step.

Understanding QuickTime

A computer displays video by flashing many still images in rapid succession. But if you've ever worked with graphics, you know that color graphics files are data hogs. A full-screen photograph file might occupy 5 or 10 MB of space on your hard drive and take several seconds to open up.

Most computers today are fast enough to open and flash 30 full-screen, photographic-quality pictures per second. Problem is, movies of that size and quality consume hundreds of megabytes of disk space, requiring many hours to download from the Web or by email—a guaranteed way to annoy citizens of the Internet and doom your moviemaking career to obscurity.

That's why most QuickTime movies *aren't* full-screen, photographic-quality films. In fact, most QuickTime movies are much "smaller"—in three different dimensions:

- **The window is much smaller.** It's rare to see a QuickTime movie that, when played back, fills the computer screen. Instead, most QuickTime movies today play in a much smaller window (Figure 16-1), therefore requiring far less data and resulting in far smaller files.

Figure 16-1:
Here's the same movie in two playback sizes. Movies designed for playback from the hard drive are often 640 pixels wide, 480 tall (640 x 480). Movies intended for the Web and email are often smaller—like 320 x 240. (Movies sent by email are often as tiny as 160 x 120.) The common denominator: Most QuickTime movies have the same aspect ratio as standard-definition TV (4:3). Widescreen movies are only slowly popping up.

- **The frame rate is lower.** Instead of showing 30 frames per second, many QuickTime movies have far lower frame rates; even 15 frames per second produces smooth motion. On the Web, especially during live QuickTime "broadcasts," still lower frame rates are common, such as two or five frames per second. This kind of movie is noticeably jerky, but sends so little data that people using telephone-line modems can watch live events in this format.

- **The video is *compressed*.** This is the big one—the technical aspect of QuickTime movies that gives you the most control over the resulting quality of your movie. In short, when iMovie uses QuickTime to compress your video, it discards information that describes each frame. True, the picture deteriorates as a consequence, but the resulting QuickTime movie file is a tiny fraction of its original size. The following section describes this compression business in much greater detail.

The bottom line is that by combining these three techniques, iMovie can turn a 10-gigabyte digital movie into a *3-megabyte* file that's small enough to email or post on your Web page. The resulting movie won't play as smoothly, fill as much of the screen, or look as good as the original footage. But your viewers won't care. They'll be delighted to be able to watch your movie at all, and grateful that the file didn't take hours to download. (And besides, having already been exposed to QuickTime movies, most know what to expect.)

Tip: The newer the QuickTime version your Mac contains, the better and faster the movie-exporting process becomes. Mac OS X's Software Update feature is supposed to alert you every time a new version becomes available (if you have it turned on in System Preferences).

A Crash Course in Video Compression

The following discussion explores some technical underpinnings of QuickTime technology. It may take you a few minutes to complete this behind-the-scenes tour of how a computer stores video. But without understanding the basics, iMovie's QuickTime-exporting options will seem utterly impenetrable.

Spatial compression

Suppose you overhear a fellow Mac fan telling her husband, "Would you mind running to the grocery store? We need an eight-ounce box of Cajun Style Rice-A-Roni, and an eight-ounce box of Cajun Style Rice-A-Roni, and also an eight-ounce box of Cajun Style Rice-A-Roni."

You'd probably assume that she's enjoyed a little too much of that new-computer smell. Why didn't she just tell him to pick up three boxes of it?

When it comes to storing video on a hard drive, your Macintosh faces the same issue. When storing a picture file, it must "write down" the precise color of *each pixel* of each frame. It could, of course, store the information like this:

- *Top row, pixel 1:* Beige

- *Top row, pixel 2:* Beige

- *Top row, pixel 3:* Beige

…and so on. Clearly, this much information would take a lot of space and a lot of time to reproduce.

Fortunately, when Apple engineers were designing QuickTime in the 1980s, it occurred to them that the individual dots in solid-colored areas of the picture don't need to be described individually. That top row of pixels could be represented much more efficiently, and take up a lot less disk space, if the Mac were simply to write down:

- *Top row:* 60 consecutive pixels of beige

This simplified example illustrates the power of *compression software,* whose job it is to make graphics files smaller by recording their pixel colors more efficiently. This kind of compression explains why a JPEG file always takes up far less space on your hard drive (and less time to download by email) than, for example, the Photoshop document that created it; the JPEG file has been compressed.

This form of file-size reduction is called *spatial* or *intraframe* compression. iMovie analyzes the picture on each individual frame and reduces the amount of information needed to describe it.

Temporal compression

But there's another way to reduce the size of a QuickTime file. Not only is there a lot of redundant color information from pixel to pixel in a single frame, but also from *frame to frame.*

Suppose, for example, that you've captured some footage of a man sitting behind a desk, talking about roofing materials. Picture the first pixel of the back wall in that piece of footage. Chances are good that this pixel's color remains absolutely consistent, frame after frame, for several seconds at least, especially if the footage was shot using a tripod. Same thing with the rug, the color of the desk, the fern in the pot beside it, and so on. These elements of the picture don't change at all from one frame to the next.

Here again, if it were your job to record what's on each frame, you could choose the slow and laborious method:

- *Frame 1:* The upper-left pixel is beige.

- *Frame 2:* The upper-left pixel is still beige.

- *Frame 3:* The upper-left pixel is *still* beige.

... and so on. This time, however, a clever QuickTime movie would record the details of only the *first frame.* "The upper-left pixel on the first frame is beige," it might begin. In filmmaker terminology, that first, completely memorized image is called the *key frame.*

Thereafter, rather than memorizing the status of every pixel on the second frame, the third frame, and so on, the Mac might just say, "On the next 60 frames, pixel #1 is exactly the same as on the first one." That more efficient description just made the resulting QuickTime file a *lot* smaller, as shown in Figure 16-2. (The subsequent, shorthand-recorded frames are often called *delta frames* by the geeks.)

This kind of shorthand is called *temporal* or *interframe* compression, because it refers to the way pixels change over time, from one frame to the next.

About Codecs

When you save your QuickTime movie, you'll be asked which of several schemes you want to use for compressing your footage. To use the technical terminology, it asks you to choose a *codec* from a long list. That term is short for compressor/decompressor, the software module that translates the pixel-by-pixel description of your footage into the more compact QuickTime format—and then *un*translates it during playback.

Figure 16-2:
When iMovie saves a QuickTime movie, it doesn't bother writing down the description of every pixel on every frame. If a lot of areas remain identical from frame to frame, the QuickTime movie doesn't remember anything more than, "Same as the previous frame." In this example, the faded portions of the picture are the areas that the QuickTime movie data doesn't describe—because they're the same as on the first (key) frame. (At last you understand why, as you may have read in Chapter 2, using a tripod for your footage doesn't just give your movies a more professional look. By ensuring that most of the picture stays exactly the same from frame to frame, a tripod-shot video helps to produce smaller QuickTime files.)

Each QuickTime codec works differently. Some provide spatial compression, some temporal, some both. Some are ideal for animations, and others for live action. Some work well on slower computers, others on faster ones. Some try to maintain excellent picture quality, but produce very large QuickTime files on the disk, and others make the opposite tradeoff. Later in this chapter, you can read about each of these codecs and when to use them.

In the meantime, all of this background information should help explain a few phenomena pertaining to converting DV movies into QuickTime files:

- **Saving a QuickTime movie takes a long time.** It's nothing like saving, say, a word processing document. Comparing every pixel on every frame with every pixel on the next frame involves massive amounts of number crunching, which takes time. (Some codecs take longer than others, however.)

- **QuickTime movies don't look as good as the original video.** Now you know why: In the act of shrinking your movie down to a file size that's reasonable for emailing, copying to a CD-ROM, and so on, a codec's job is to *throw away* some of the data that makes a movie look vivid and clear.

- **QuickTime is an exercise in compromise.** By choosing the appropriate codec and changing its settings appropriately, you can create a QuickTime movie with excellent picture and sound. Unfortunately, it will consume a lot of disk space. If you want a small file on the hard drive *and* excellent picture and sound, you can make the QuickTime movie play in a smaller window—320 x 240 pixels, for example, instead of 640 x 480 or something larger—or at a slower frame rate. The guide in this chapter, some experimentation, and the nature of the movie you're making all contribute to helping you make a codec decision.

The Export Pop-up Menu

After you've finished editing your iMovie production, the first step in exporting it as a QuickTime movie is to choose **Share→Export using QuickTime.**

The "Save exported file as" dialog box appears (Figure 16-3). Here, you'll eventually type a name and choose a folder location for the file you're about to save. But for now, resist the temptation.

Figure 16-3:
This is the first dialog box of many that you'll encounter as you crawl down Alice's rabbit hole of QuickTime compression options.

The real power lies in the buttons and pop-up menus elsewhere in this little box. For starters, the Export pop-up menu (visible in Figure 16-3) offers a wealth of conversion options. This is your opportunity to save your film as:

- **An AVI file to give to your Windows PC-using friends.** (Choose **Movie to AVI.**)

- **A huge folder full of still images, one per frame of your movie.** (Choose **Movie to Image Sequence.** Click Options to specify the file format—like JPEG or Photoshop—and how many stills per second you want.)

- **A soundtrack.** Here's a great opportunity to convert the audio tracks of your movie into standalone sound files. (Choose **Sound to AIFF, Sound to Wave,** or whatever format you want.)

  You'll find this feature very handy every now and then. For example, certain troubleshooting situations, described in Chapter 11 and elsewhere, call for exporting and reimporting your finished soundtrack—in essence, temporarily splitting it apart from the video. (You can even edit the soundtrack file in GarageBand or another program along the way, if you're so inclined. That's one way to get rid of the occasional pop or crackle.)

- **A movie that's formatted for the iPod, iPhone, or Apple TV.** Of course, there are easier ways to go about these tasks; see Chapter 14.

But most of the time, you'll ignore this Export pop-up menu. Most of the time, you'll want to leave it set to "Movie to QuickTime Movie," and then click the Options button to make some settings changes.

Figure 16-4:
When you click Options, you get the Movie Settings box. It's just a summary screen for the dialog boxes that hide behind it: Settings, Filter, Size, and so on.

That Options button opens a very important dialog box: the Movie Settings box (Figure 16-4). Here's where you can export your finished product with *exactly* the size-smoothness-speed compromise you want.

You'll notice that this box offers three buttons for video: Settings, Filter, and Size. Below that, you get one Settings button for Sound; at the bottom of the box, you get options for *Internet streaming.* All of these settings are covered in the next few pages.

The Settings Button

The Settings button takes you to the powerful Compression Settings dialog box (Figure 16-5), the heart of the entire Options software suite. Here's what the controls do:

Figure 16-5:
Top: This dialog box gives you point-by-point control over the look, size, and quality of the QuickTime movie you're exporting. Not all of these controls are available for all codecs. Furthermore, only some of the codecs offer an Options button in the middle of the dialog box.

Bottom: Here's where you can specify the dimensions of the movie you're saving, in pixels. (This box appears when you click the Size button shown at the bottom of Figure 16-4.)

Compression Type pop-up menu

The Compression Type pop-up menu at the top lets you choose one of several dozen codecs—or None, which means that iMovie won't compress your project at all. Each codec compresses your footage using a different scheme that entails different compromises. You can read "The Video Codecs: A Catalog" later in this chapter for details. For now, note that for live video that will be played on modern computers, the H.264 codec almost always produces the highest quality at reasonably small file sizes.

Quality slider

This slider offers another tradeoff between the size of the resulting QuickTime file and the quality of its picture. In general, the proposed value (usually Medium or High) offers the best balance between file size and picture quality. But on important projects, by all means experiment. Export a representative sample of your movie several times, moving the slider each time, so that you can compare the results.

Frames per second

The number you specify here makes an enormous difference in the smoothness of the QuickTime movie's playback. As always, however, it's a tradeoff—the higher the number, the larger the QuickTime file, and the more difficult it is to email, store, or transfer.

You can type any number between 1 and 29.97 in this box, or you can use the pop-up menu to the right of the "Frames per second" box. Here's what you can expect from these settings:

- **8, 10.** These movies are very compact, and make good candidates for transmitting over the Internet. They also look very jerky.

- **12,15.** These are the most common frame rates for today's QuickTime movies on the Internet. By playing only half as many frames as you'd see on a TV show, the QuickTime movie saves a lot of data, making itself smaller on the disk and more likely to succeed when played over slower connections. And yet this many frames per second tricks the eye into perceiving satisfying, smooth motion; most people

---

RARELY ASKED QUESTION

30 fps Drop-Frame

OK, I'll bite. Why on earth did the USA, which is supposed to be so technically advanced, settle on a TV standard that plays at such an oddball frame rate? Why is it 29.97—why couldn't it be rounded off to 30?

The 29.97 frame rate, known in the TV business as 30 fps drop-frame, dates back to the dawn of color TV. As they prepared to launch color TV broadcasts in January 1954, network engineers wanted to make sure that the expensive black-and-white TV sets of the day could receive the color shows, too. (Talk about backward-compatible software!)

Trouble was, when they tried to broadcast a color signal at the then-standard 30 frames per second, the extra color information wound up distorting the audio signal. Eventually, they hit upon a discovery: If they slowed down the frame rate just a hair, the distortion disappeared. The video, meanwhile, looked just as good at 29.97 frames per second as it did at 30.

A standard was born.

---

can sense that they aren't seeing quite the motion quality they'd see on TV, but don't miss the other 15 frames each second.

- 24, 25. An actual Hollywood movie plays at 24 frames per second, and the European television signal (PAL) plays at 25. These settings, in other words, are provided for situations where you want excellent motion quality, without going all the way to the extreme of 29.97 frames per second of the American TV standard (NTSC). You save a little bit of disk space, while still showing as many frames as people are accustomed to seeing in motion pictures.

- **29.97.** If you're wondering how this oddball number got into the pop-up menu, you're not alone. As it turns out, every source that refers to television broadcasts as having 30 frames per second (including other chapters in this book) is rounding off the number for convenience. In fact, a true television broadcast plays at *29.97*

FREQUENTLY ASKED QUESTION

Oddly Shaped Movies

I'm doing a project where I need my movie to be perfectly square, not in a 4:3 width-to-height ratio. But every time I try to specify these dimensions in the QuickTime Settings dialog box, I get a distorted, squished iMovie movie. What can I do?

What you're really asking is how to crop your movie.

iMovie '08, of course, is capable of cropping your video—but only in the standard 4:3 or 16:9 aspect ratios (see page 109).

Unfortunately, neither iMovie nor QuickTime Player Pro (Chapter 19) offers any simple method of cropping the picture in any other aspect ratio.

There is software that can do so, however: Cleaner 6.5 (*www.discreet.com*), the $475 professional QuickTime-compression software. As shown

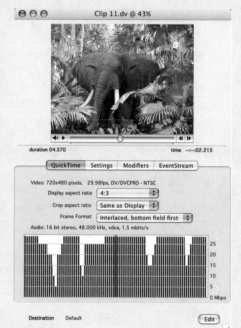

here, it lets you draw a dotted-line rectangle that indicates how you'd like the picture to be cropped.

Apple's professional video editing programs, Final Cut Pro and Final Cut Express, can freely crop video, too.

If you're using iMovie for professional purposes, a program like one of those is a worthwhile investment. Think of it as a much more powerful and flexible version of the Settings dialog box (Figure 16-5). Its sole purpose is to compress movies, using much more efficient and intelligent software than that built into iMovie.

And if you have more expertise than cash, the freeware program ffmpegX can crop video, too. You have to do it by typing in coordinates (rather than adjusting a visual cropping frame), but it works. (You can download ffmpegX from this book's "Missing CD" page at *www.missingmanuals.com*.)

---

frames per second. iMovie can reproduce that rate for you, if it's important to do so. In fact, this is iMovie's top frame rate.

- **30.** This is the proper setting for full-quality high-definition footage.

Note: If you're not working with high-def video, then ignore this choice; it's for suckers. *Standard*-definition video, at least in North America, is itself 29.97 frames per second. So asking iMovie to save a QuickTime movie with an even *higher* rate is like thinking you'll be wealthier if you exchange your dollar bills for quarters.

If you *do* try choosing 30 from this pop-up menu, when you click OK, you'll be scolded, told you're out of line, and then returned to the dialog box to make another choice.

As described under "Quality slider" in the previous section, you don't have to export your movie in its entirety just to see the effects of different frame-rate settings. Create a dummy project that contains only a few seconds of movie, and try exporting it at each frame rate. Then play back the short QuickTime movies. You'll get a self-taught course in the effects of different frames-per-second settings.

Key frame every __ frames

You can read about *key frames* earlier this chapter—they're the full frames that get "memorized" in your QuickTime movie, so that the QuickTime file can store less data for subsequent frames. (See Figure 16-2.)

In most cases, one key frame per second is about right. In movies that will be played back from beginning to end and never rewound or scrolled, it's safe to increase the number in this box.

Limit data rate

Each delivery mechanism—a CD-ROM, a cable modem, a 56 K modem, and so on—delivers information at a different rate. If you want to ensure that no frame-skipping or jerkiness occurs when somebody plays your movie, turn this checkbox on and type a number into the box.

The precise number to type depends on your goals for the movie you're exporting. In other words, it depends on what kind of gadget will be playing the movie data. Here are some guidelines:

If the movie will be played by:	Use this maximum data rate:
56 K modem	5 K/second
T1 or cable modem	20 K/second
CD-ROM	100 K/second
Hard drive	250 K/second

iMovie automatically adjusts the picture quality as necessary, on a moment-by-moment basis, so that the QuickTime movie never exceeds this rate.

The Filter Button

As noted in Chapter 9, iMovie '08 doesn't offer any of the special effects that were present in iMovie 6. But unbeknownst to nine out of ten iMovie fans, you still have access to an enormous range of visual effects, which you can apply to your movie on its way *out* of iMovie. Simply click the Filter button (shown in Figure 16-4) as you export a QuickTime movie.

The dialog box shown in Figure 16-6 appears. By opening the various flippy triangles, you'll find a lot of favorite effects that were in the old iMovie (color balance, brightness and contrast, lens flare, fake old-film grain)—and a few that weren't (blur or sharpen, emboss).

Figure 16-6:
The Filter dialog box offers special effects that let you adjust the color, brightness, or contrast of the footage; sharpen or blur it; add a phony "lens flare;" or even add fake "film noise" like scratches and dust. Using the Load and Save buttons, you can even save an effects configuration you've created onto your hard drive, so you'll be able to apply exactly the same settings to another clip at another time. (Unfortunately, you can apply only one effect at a time.)

The list of effects appears in the scrolling list at top left; a preview of the result appears at lower left. Use the controls on the right side of the dialog box to affect the intensity and other settings of the effect.

As you work, remember that whatever filter you apply here applies to the *entire movie* you're about to export. You might be inclined to pooh-pooh this whole feature, in that case. Really, when would you ever want to apply the same degree of blur to an entire movie?

But with a little forethought, you can still apply an effect to just one clip. The trick is to create a new iMovie project containing *only that clip*. Export it using the DV/DVCPRO-NTSC or DV-PAL compressor to make sure that you retain all your digital-video size and quality—and apply the filter you want in the process. Save this exported chunk somewhere easy to find—on your desktop, for example.

When it's all over, you can reimport your exported, processed clip into the original iMovie project.

Who *says* iMovie '08 doesn't have special effects?

Caution: iMovie preserves your Options settings from export to export, even if weeks or months elapse in between. That's an especially treacherous feature when it comes to these filters; you may sit through a 45-minute export the next time, only to find that the resulting movie is all embossed and color-shifted because those are the settings you used last time. The only way to escape this nightmare is to reopen the Filter dialog box and choose None.

The Size Button

And now, back to your tour of the dialog box shown in Figure 16-4.

The Size button summons the dialog box shown at bottom in Figure 16-5, where—after clicking "Use custom size"—you can specify the dimensions for the playback window of your QuickTime movie. Of course, the larger the window you specify, the longer the movie will take to save, the slower it will be transmitted over the Internet, and the larger the resulting file will be.

Keeping the dimensions you specify here in a width-to-height aspect ratio of 4:3 (for standard video) or 16:9 (for high-def video) is important. The QuickTime software plays back most smoothly if your movie retains these relative proportions. Furthermore, if the width and height you specify *aren't* in one of those ratios, iMovie has to squish the picture accordingly, which may lend a funhouse-mirror distortion effect to your film.

Most QuickTime movies play in at one of several standard sizes, such as 320 x 240 or 640 x 480—both examples of the 4:3 aspect ratio. Still, there are dozens of other possible sizes that maintain the correct proportions.

Audio Settings

At the bottom of the dialog box shown in Figure 16-4 is a *second* button called Settings. This one lets you specify how—and how much—your soundtrack is compressed in the exported QuickTime movie (Figure 16-7).

Format

When most people think of codecs—those who've even *heard* of codecs, that is—they think of *video* compression. But iMovie offers a choice of audio codecs, too. This pop-up menu lets you specify which one you want to use.

Many of them aren't, in fact, appropriate for movie soundtracks. Remember that these codecs are provided by QuickTime, not by iMovie, and that QuickTime is designed to be an all-purpose multimedia format. It's supposed to be just as good at creating pictureless sound files as it is at creating movies.

It's also supposed to recognize every format that ever trudged through the music industry—including plenty that nobody uses anymore. The ones you might conceivably care about are these:

- **AAC.** If you choose this audio codec, you'll save your soundtrack in AAC format—the same one used for songs you buy from the iTunes music store.

The sound quality is superb, although it depends on the settings you make when you click Options. (For example, choose 128 kbits/second from the Bit Rate pop-up menu to match the quality of iTunes songs.) The file size, meanwhile, is only a fraction of the original. It's a welcome and useful choice for movies not intended to be played over the Internet.

Figure 16-7:
It probably goes without saying that the better the audio quality you specify, the larger your QuickTime movie will be. In any case, this is the dialog box where you make such decisions. Audio isn't nearly as data-greedy as video, so compressing it isn't quite as urgent an issue (unless you want your movie to play over the Internet).

- **AMR Narrowband.** This item stands for Adaptive Multi-Rate, and it's intended for movies in the 3GPP format (a standard developed for cell phones). Use it if you have a 3GPP-compatible phone. For other phones, use the Qualcomm PureVoice codec (described below), click Options, and then turn on the Half Rate option.

- **Apple Lossless.** This item is a truly *lossless* audio compression option. "Lossless" means that although this codec cuts the audio track's file size in half, it doesn't lose *any* of the sound quality in the process. The resulting files are too big for the Web or emailing, but Apple Lossless is great when you're saving a movie for best-quality playback from a hard drive.

- **IMA 4:1.** This codec was one of the first QuickTime movie audio compressors. It provides excellent audio quality—you *can't* change it to a sample size less than 16-bit—and plays back equally well on Windows and Macintosh.

  It's great for movies that will be played from a hard drive or CD or over a fast Internet connection.

- **QDesign Music 2.** This is an aging sound codec that's still useful for online or emailed movies. It maintains terrific audio quality, but compresses the sound a great deal, producing files small enough to deliver over dial-up modems. Apple's favorite example: One minute of music from an audio CD requires 11 MB of disk space, but after compression by this codec, it consumes only 150 K and sounds almost as good.

Rate, Size

A computer captures and plays back sound by capturing thousands of individual slices, or snapshots, of sound per second. As though describing somebody at a wine tasting, computer nerds call this process *sampling* the sound.

The two controls here let you specify *how many samples* you want the Mac to take per second (the sampling Rate) and *how much data* it's allowed to use to describe each sample (the sampling Size).

Even if that technical explanation means nothing to you, the principle is easy enough to absorb: The higher the Rate and Size settings (see Figure 16-7), the better the quality of the audio and the larger the size of the resulting QuickTime file. Here are a few examples of the kind of file-size increase you can expect for each of several popular rate and size settings. (Note that the information here is *per channel*. If you're going for stereo, double the kilobyte ratings shown here.)

- **11 kHz, 8 bits.** Sounds like you're hearing the audio track over a bad telephone connection. Tinny. Use it only for speech. 662 K per minute.

- **11 kHz, 16 bits.** Sounds a lot better. Roughly the sound quality you get from the built-in Mac speaker. 1.3 MB per minute.

- **22 kHz, 16 bits.** Starting to sound very good. Suitable for playing on a computer equipped with external speakers. 2.6 MB per minute.

- **44.1 kHz, 16 bits.** This is the real thing, the ultimate audio experience. CD-quality audio. Suitable for listening to with headphones. The ultimate storage and transmission headache, too—this much data requires 5.3 MB per minute, mono. But of course, you'd never go this far without also including the stereo experience, so make that 10.6 MB per minute in stereo.

Use: Mono/Stereo

These radio buttons let you specify whether or not your movie's soundtrack is in stereo.

Exporting your QuickTime movie with a stereo format is often a waste of data. Many computers that might play back your movie, including Power Macs, Mac Pros, and Mac Minis, don't *have* stereo speakers.

Furthermore, even though most camcorders include a stereo microphone, there's virtually no separation between the right and left channels, thanks to the fact that the microphone is mounted directly on the tiny camcorder. Nor does iMovie let you edit the right and left audio channels independently. Even if people are listening to your movie with stereo speakers, they'll hear essentially the same thing out of each.

Therefore, consider using the Mono setting when you're trying to minimize the amount of data required to play back the soundtrack.

The Video Codecs: A Catalog

When you decide to export your iMovie production as a QuickTime movie, you can exert a great deal of control over how the Mac produces the resulting movie file by clicking Options in the dialog box shown in Figure 16-3, and then clicking Settings (Figure 16-4). You get access to a long list of codecs.

Few of these codecs are very useful for everyday use. Many of them are intended for:

- **Saving still frames (not movies).** Examples: BMP, PNG, Photo-JPEG, JPEG 2000, TGA, TIFF, Planar RGB.

- **Keeping around for old times' sake, despite having been technologically surpassed.** Examples: Cinepak, Component Video, Sorenson.

- **Professional cameras and high-end production firms.** Examples: Apple Pixlet Video, Apple ProRes, MPEG IMX, HDCAM.

Most of the time, the compressor called H.264 will make you and your audience the happiest.

Note: The list of codecs in your dialog boxes may not match what you see here. Your codecs reflect the version of QuickTime that you have installed, which may be older or newer than version 7, described here.

Here are some of the ones that *aren't* totally useless:

- **Animation.** This codec is significant because, at its Best quality setting, it maintains *all* of the original picture quality, while still managing to convert files so that they're smaller than files with no compression at all. (As the name implies, this codec was originally designed to process video composed of large blocks of solid colors—that is, cartoons.) The resulting file is huge when compared with the other codecs described here, but not as huge as it would be if you used the None choice in this pop-up menu.

- **Apple Intermediate Codec.** You can read all about this clever, sneaky codec on page 100. It's how Apple makes it possible for iMovie to handle high-definition video and AVCHD video at standard-video speeds: by first *converting* it into this intermediate format for use on the Mac. Your primary interest in this codec is for transferring videos back and forth between iMovie versions.

- **DV/DVCPRO-NTSC.** Suppose you've just completed a masterful movie, and the thought of compressing it to a much smaller, image-degraded QuickTime movie breaks your heart. You can use this codec to turn your finished, effect-enhanced, fully edited iMovie production into a new, raw DV clip, exactly like the DV clips that iMovie captures when it imports from a tape camcorder.

You might do so if, for example, you wanted to send a full-quality DV clip to somebody electronically, or as an alternative to the Apple Intermediate Codec for moving video between editing programs. (*DV*, of course, means digital video; NTSC is the format used in the Western Hemisphere and Japan. DVCPRO50 is a high-end variation used in professional TV cameras.)

- **DV-PAL, DVCPRO-PAL.** These options are here so that you can export your iMovie masterpiece in the European video format (PAL), while retaining full size and frame rate. (DVCPRO and DVCPRO50 are slight variants of the DV format, intended for use with expensive professional broadcast TV video gear.)

Unfortunately, the quality of the video suffers when you make this kind of conversion, especially in action scenes.

- **H.264.** This is it—Apple's favorite. It's also the format of satellite TV, high-definition DVD, iPod and iPhone video, .Mac Web gallery video, newer YouTube videos, and other quality-dependent video uses. Technically speaking, it's a flavor of *MPEG-4*, described later. It looks spectacular, compresses relatively well, and it scales beautifully from cellphone screens all the way up to high-definition TVs.

It's not, however, the fastest codec on earth. If the client is standing beside you, tapping his foot, the MPEG-4 Video codec takes less time to export.

- **HDV.** Here's the format captured by high-definition consumer tape camcorders. You won't have much use for it, since iMovie converts it automatically into Apple Intermediate Codec anyway; but you could one day encounter another video program that can edit this stuff without conversion.

- **Graphics.** Uses a maximum of 256 colors to depict each frame. The result is grainy and blotchy. Use it only if your movie contains nothing but solid-colored images, such as cartoons, pie charts, or other computer-generated simple images. Even then, this aging codec doesn't compress the video very much.

- **Motion JPEG A, Motion JPEG B.** These codecs don't perform any temporal (frame-to-frame) compression. Each movie frame is saved as an individual, full-sized color picture. The disadvantage is, of course, that the resulting files are extremely large. In fact, you need to buy a special circuit board for your computer just to play back this kind of movie. In other words, motion JPEG is occasionally useful when editing video, but never for distributing it.

So what good is it? Motion JPEG is the format used by many professional DV-editing machines (such as those from Avid, Accom, and Discreet). Because there's no key-frame business going on, editors can make cuts at any frame. (Doing so isn't always possible in a file created by a codec that stores only the *difference* between one frame and the next. A particular frame might contain data that describes only new information.)

- **MPEG-4 Video.** MPEG-4 is an older version of the H.264 codec described above. (By the way, AAC, the audio format of the iTunes music store, is an audio version of MPEG-4). It compresses your movie much more quickly, although the files aren't as small and the quality isn't as good as H.264.

- **None.** If quality is everything to you, and disk space and Internet-ability are nothing, you can use this option, which (like the DV codecs) doesn't compress the video at all. The resulting QuickTime file may contain so much data that your computer can't even play it back smoothly. You can, however, put it in a cryogenic tank in anticipation of the day when superfast computers come your way.

Saving a QuickTime Movie

All right—having read all of that theory of QuickTime and compression, you're ready to do the actual exporting.

1. **Choose Share→Export using QuickTime.**

   The "Save exported file as" dialog box appears (Figure 16-3).

2. **Type a name for your movie.**

   Unless, of course, you want to name your movie whatever the current project is called, as iMovie suggests.

   Don't remove the letters *.mov* from the end of the file's name, especially if it might be played on Windows computers. That suffix is a requirement for machines who aren't savvy enough to know a movie file when they see one.

3. **Navigate to the folder where you'll want to store the resulting QuickTime file.**

   You can simply press ⌘-D if you want your QuickTime Movie saved onto the desktop, where it'll be easy to find.

4. **Make sure the Export pop-up menu says "Movie to QuickTime Movie." Click Options. Click Settings at the top of the next dialog box.**

   The dialog box shown in Figure 16-5 at top appears.

5. **Choose your compression options, and then click OK.**

   You return to the "Save exported file as" dialog box.

6. **Click Save.**

   Now the time-consuming compression process begins. Compression can take a long time to complete—from a minute or two to an hour or more, depending on the settings you selected, the length of your movie, and the speed of your Mac.

Feel free to switch into other programs—check your email or surf the Web, for example—while iMovie crunches away in the background.

A progress bar lets you know how much farther iMovie has to go.

When the exporting is complete, the progress bar disappears. Switch to the Finder, where you'll find a new QuickTime movie icon (Figure 16-8). Double-click it to see the results.

Tip: You can click Stop during the export process, but you'll wind up with no exported movie at all.

Figure 16-8:
When you double-click the resulting QuickTime movie on your hard drive (left), it opens into your copy of QuickTime Player, the movie-playing application described in Chapter 17. Press the Space bar to make the movie play back (right).

QuickTime Player

I f iMovie is the program on your hard drive that's the master of *DV* files, its sibling software, the corresponding master of traditional *QuickTime* movies, is QuickTime Player, a small, free program that comes with every Macintosh. (It's in the Applications folder.) It does three things very well: show pictures, play movies, and play sounds (Figure 17-1).

If you're willing to pay $30, you can upgrade your copy of QuickTime Player to the Pro version. Doing so grants you a long list of additional features, most notably the ability to *edit* your QuickTime movies, not just watch them.

There are two reasons QuickTime Player is worth knowing about. First, if you turn your iMovie projects into QuickTime movies (Chapter 16), QuickTime Player is the program you'll probably be using to play them on your screen. Second, the Pro version acts as an accessory toolkit for iMovie, offering you the chance to perform several tricky editing maneuvers you couldn't perform with iMovie alone.

This chapter covers both versions of the program, using QuickTime 7 for illustration purposes.

QuickTime Player (Free Version)

The free version of QuickTime Player is designed exclusively to *play* movies and sounds. You can open a movie file by double-clicking it, by dragging it onto the QuickTime Player icon, or by opening QuickTime Player and then choosing File→ Open. As shown in Figure 17-1, a number of controls help you govern the movie's playback:

- **Audio level meters.** This tiny graph dances to indicate the relative strength of various frequencies in the soundtrack, like the VU meters on a stereo. If you don't see any dancing going on, then you've opened a movie that doesn't have a soundtrack.

- **Resize handle.** Drag diagonally to make the window bigger or smaller.

Tip: When you drag the resize handle, QuickTime Player strives to maintain the same *aspect ratio* (relative dimensions) as the original movie, so that you don't accidentally squish it. If you want to squish it, however (perhaps for the special effect of seeing your loved ones as they would look with different sets of horizontal and vertical genes), press Shift as you drag.

If you press Option while dragging, meanwhile, you'll discover that the movie frame grows or shrinks in sudden jumping factors of two—twice as big, four times as big, and so on. On slower Macs, keeping a movie at an even multiple of its original size ensures smoother playback.

- **Scroll bar.** Drag the diamond (or, in the Pro version, the black triangle) to jump to a different spot in the movie.

Tip: You can also press the right and left arrow keys to step through the movie one frame at a time. If you press *Option*-right or -left arrow, you jump to the beginning or end of the movie. In the Pro version, Option-arrow also jumps to the beginning or ending of a selected stretch of the movie.

Figure 17-1:
When QuickTime Player's "stainless steel" look debuted in version 4, it inspired a firestorm of criticism on the Internet. Among other design limitations, its title bar didn't have a collapse box, zoom box, or stripes that told you when a window is active.

The newer QuickTime Player 7, shown here, addresses all of those concerns and removes many confusing controls.

- **Play/Stop button.** Click once to start, and again to stop. You can also press the Space bar, Return key, or ⌘-right arrow for this purpose. (Or avoid the buttons altogether and double-click the movie itself to start or stop playback.)

Tip: You can make any movie play automatically when opened, so that you avoid clicking the Play button. To do so, choose QuickTime Player→Preferences→Player Preferences, and turn on "Automatically play movies when opened."

- **Selection handles.** These tiny black triangles appear only in the $30 Pro version. You use them to select, or highlight, stretches of footage.

- **Volume.** If you like, you can make the soundtrack louder or softer by dragging this slider with your mouse or clicking in its "track." You may find it easier, however, to press the up or down arrow keys.

Tip: To mute the sound, click the little speaker icon, or press Option-down arrow. Press Option-up arrow to make the volume slider jump to full-blast position.

- **Counter.** In hours:minutes:seconds format, this display shows how far your diamond cursor has moved into the movie.

  If you have QuickTime Pro, the counter reveals the position of the selection handle you've most recently clicked (if any).

FREQUENTLY ASKED QUESTION

QuickTime Player vs. QuickTime Player Pro

What's with all of these dimmed menu commands that say PRO beside their names?

That's Apple's subtle way of saying, "Just *look* at all you'd get if you upgraded your free player to the Pro version! All of these features await you!"

If you're convinced, then for $30, Apple will sell you a password that turns your copy of QuickTime Player into QuickTime Player Pro. (To obtain this password, call 888-295-0648, or click the Upgrade Now button to go online to *www. apple.com/quicktime/buy.*)

To record your password, choose QuickTime Player→ Registration. Your password gets stored in your Home folder→

Undo	⌘Z
Redo	⇧⌘Z
PRO Cut	⌘X
Copy	⌘C
PRO Paste	⌘V
PRO Delete	
PRO Select All	⌘A
PRO Select None	⌘B
PRO Trim to Selection	
PRO Add to Movie	⌥⌘V
PRO Add to Selection & Scale	⌥⇧⌘V
Find	▶
Special Characters...	⌥⌘T

Library→Preferences folder, in a file called QuickTime Preferences. (Remember that when you upgrade to a new Mac.)

Once you've upgraded, you gain several immediate benefits—not the least of which is the permanent disappearance of the "upgrade now" advertisement. Now QuickTime Player is QuickTime Player Pro, and it's capable of editing your movies, as described later in this chapter. It can also import many more sound and graphics formats, and—via the File→Export command—convert sounds, movies, and graphics into other formats.

Oh—and all of those dimmed commands come back to life and lose the little PRO logos.

- **Rewind, Fast-Forward.** By clicking one of these buttons and keeping the mouse button pressed, you get to speed through your movie backward or forward, complete with sound. This is a terrific way to navigate your movie quickly, regardless of whether you're using QuickTime Player or QuickTime Player Pro.

- **Jump to Start, Jump to End.** These buttons do exactly what they say: scroll to the beginning or end of your movie. In the Pro version, they can also jump to the beginning and ending of the selected portion of the movie (if any). All of this, in other words, is exactly the same as pressing the Option-left arrow or -right arrow keys.

Tip: Try minimizing a QuickTime Player window while a movie is playing. It shrinks to the Dock—and *keeps on playing.* Do this enough times, and you'll know what it's like to be Steve Jobs on stage.

Hidden Controls

Don't miss the Window→Show A/V Controls command. As shown in Figure 17-2, this is where you can fine-tune the video and audio you're experiencing.

Figure 17-2:
Here's where you can adjust a QuickTime movie as though it's a TV set. Boost the brightness, turn up the treble, correct the color, and so on.

Oddly enough, the two Playback sliders at the bottom aren't settings at all. Rather, they're real-time controls. Dragging the Jog Shuttle handle, for example, actually triggers forward or reverse playback at high speed, and dragging the Playback Speed handle makes playback proceed at the indicated multiple of real time.

(Be careful, though. This one is also a setting. If you leave the slider at 3X and close the window, your movie will always play back at 3X and you probably won't know why.)

Fancy Playback Tricks

Nobody knows for sure what Apple was thinking when it created some of these additional features—exactly how often do you want your movie to play backward?—but here they are. Some of these features are available only in the unlocked Pro version of QuickTime Player, as indicated below:

- **Change the screen size.** Using the View menu commands, such as Double Size and Full Screen, you can enlarge or reduce the actual "movie screen" window. Making the window larger also makes the movie coarser, because QuickTime Player simply doubles the size of every dot that was present in the original. Still, when you want to show a movie to a group of people more than a few feet away from the screen, these larger sizes are perfectly effective.

- **Play more than one movie.** You can open several movies at once and then run them simultaneously. (Of course, the more movies you try to play at once, the jerkier the playback gets.)

As a sanity preserver, QuickTime Player plays only one soundtrack—that of the movie you most currently clicked. If you really want to hear the cacophony of all the soundtracks being played simultaneously, choose QuickTime Player→ Preferences, and turn off "Play sound in frontmost player only." (The related checkbox here, "Play sound when application is in background," controls what happens when you switch out of QuickTime Player and into another program.)

Tip: If you have QuickTime Player Pro, you can use the View→Play All Movies command to begin playback of all open movies at the same instant. It's a handy way to compare the quality of two or more copies of the same exported movie, each prepared with a different codec.

- **Play the movie backward.** You can play the movie backward—but not always smoothly—by pressing ⌘-left arrow, or by Shift-double-clicking the movie itself. (You must keep the Shift button pressed to make the backward playback continue.) There's no better way to listen for secret subliminal messages.

- **Loop the movie.** When you choose View→Loop and then click Play, the movie plays endlessly from beginning to end, repeating until you make it stop. (Loop Back and Forth makes it loop backward again, from end to beginning.)

- **Play Selection Only (Pro only).** View→Play Selection Only, of course, plays only what you've highlighted on the scrubber bar.

- **Play All Frames (Pro only).** If you try to play a very large movie that incorporates a high frame rate (many frames per second) on a slow Mac, QuickTime Player skips individual frames of the movie. In other words, it sacrifices smooth motion in order to maintain synchronization with the soundtrack.

But if you choose View→Play All Frames and then play the movie, QuickTime Player says, "OK, forget the soundtrack—I'll show you every single frame of the movie, even if it isn't at full speed." You get no sound at all, but you do get to see each frame of the movie.

QuickTime Player Pro

If you've spent the $30 to upgrade to the Pro version of QuickTime Player, you've unlocked a number of additional features. Some of these are playback tricks described in the previous section; others are especially useful for iMovie work. Read on.

Presenting Your Movies

After going to the trouble of editing down your footage (as described in Part 2) and exporting it as a QuickTime movie (as described in Chapter 16), what you may want to do most of all is to *show* the movie to other people. Even the non-Pro version of QuickTime Player can play movies, of course, but the Pro version offers a much better showcase for your work: the View→Present Movie command.

"Presenting" your movie is the best possible way to view a QuickTime movie on your screen. When you use this command (Figure 17-3), QuickTime Player blacks out the screen, automatically magnifies your monitor image (by choosing a lower resolution) so that the movie fills more of the screen, and devotes all the Mac's power to playing the movie smoothly. (To interrupt the movie, press ⌘-period.)

Figure 17-3:
The Present Movie command makes the movie fill your screen (although enlargement makes the movie grainier and coarser, which is why Apple gives you a choice here).

Editing Movies

The most powerful feature you gain in the Pro version is its ability to *edit* QuickTime movies. You can rearrange scenes, eliminate others, and save the result as a new movie with its own name.

All of this is perfectly possible within iMovie itself, of course, but sometimes you'll want to edit one of the QuickTime movies you've already exported from iMovie—to make it shorter for emailing, for example.

Tip: QuickTime Player can open all of iMovie's favorite formats (page 100). In fact, you can find all of the clips that iMovie knows about—every last shred of video in your Event browser—tucked away in your iMovie Events folder (see page 108), ready for double-clicking to examine in QuickTime Player. This trick may come in handy if you want to edit a clip you've already imported, using some feature that's available only in QuickTime Player but not in iMovie.

Selecting footage

Before you can cut, copy, or paste footage, QuickTime Player needs to provide a way for you to specify *what* footage you want to manipulate. Its solution: the two tiny L-shaped handles beneath the horizontal scroll bar, visible in Figure 17-4. These are the "in" and "out" points, exactly like the crop handles in iMovie. By dragging these handles, you're supposed to enclose the scene you want to cut or copy.

Tip: You can gain more precise control over the selection procedure by clicking one of the L-shaped handles and then pressing the right or left arrow key, exactly as when using the Scrubber bar under iMovie's Monitor window. Doing so expands or contracts the selected chunk of footage by one frame at a time.

You may also prefer to select a piece of footage by Shift-clicking the Play button. As long as you hold down the Shift key, you continue to select footage. When you release the Shift key, you stop the playback, and the selected passage appears in gray on the scroll bar.

Figure 17-4:
QuickTime Player Pro has a little-known subtitling feature, complete with freedom of type style. Copy some formatted text from a word processor; highlight a slice of footage in QuickTime Player; and choose Edit→Add to Movie. The copied text appears as a subtitle on a black band, beneath the picture, as shown here.

Once you've highlighted a passage of footage, you can proceed as follows:

- Jump to the beginning or end of the selected footage by pressing Option-right or -left arrow key. (This doesn't work if one of the handles is highlighted.)

- Deselect the footage by dragging the two triangles together again.

- Play only the selected passage by choosing View→Play Selection Only. (The other Movie menu commands, such as Loop, apply only to the selection at this point.)

- Drag the movie picture out of the Player window and onto the desktop, where it becomes a *movie clipping* that you can double-click to view.

- Cut, copy, or clear the highlighted material using the commands in the Edit menu.

Tip: If you paste some copied text directly into QuickTime Player Pro, you get a 2-second title (such as an opening credit) at the current frame, professionally displayed as white type against a black background (Figure 17-4). QuickTime Player automatically uses the font, size, and style of the text that was in the text clipping. You can paste a graphic image, too; again, you get a 2-second "slide" of that still image.

If you find it easier, you can also drag a text or picture *clipping file* directly from the desktop into the QuickTime Player window; once again, you get a two-second insert. To make the text or picture appear longer than 2 seconds, drag or paste it several times in a row.

In either case, you specify the fonts, sizes, and styles of your low-budget titling feature by formatting the text that way *before* you copy it from your word processor. (This feature requires a word processor that preserves such formatting on the Clipboard. Most modern text processors, including Stickies, TextEdit, and Word, and most email programs, are all examples.)

Pasting footage

After cutting or copying footage, you can move it elsewhere in the movie. Specify where you want the pasted material to go by first clicking or dragging in the horizontal scroll bar, so that the black Playhead marks the spot; then choose Edit→Paste. The selection triangles (and their accompanying gray scroll bar section) show you where the new footage has appeared. (That makes it easy for you to promptly choose Edit→Cut, for example, if you change your mind.)

There are several variations of the Paste command at your disposal, too. They work like this:

- The Edit→Trim to Selection command is like the Trim to Selection command in iMovie, in that it eliminates the outer parts of the movie—the pieces that *aren't* selected. All that remains is the part you first selected.

- The Edit→Add to Movie command adds whatever's on the Clipboard so that it plays *simultaneously* with the selected footage—a feature that's especially useful when you're adding a *different kind* of material to the movie. (See Figure 17-4.)

- If you highlight some footage and then choose Edit→Add to Selection & Scale, whatever you're pasting gets stretched or compressed in time so that it fits the highlighted region, speeding up or slowing down both audio and video. The effect can be powerful, comical, or just weird. (Can you say, "Alvin and the Chipmunks"?)

Tip: You can edit sounds exactly as you edit movies, using precisely the same commands and shortcuts. Use the File→Open command in QuickTime Player Pro to locate a sound file you want to open. It opens exactly like a QuickTime movie, except with only a scroll bar—no picture.

Exporting Edited Movies

After you've finished working on a sound or movie, you can send it back out into the world in any of several ways.

The Save As command

If you choose Edit→Save As, you're offered only two options, both of which can be confusing:

- **Save as a reference movie.** You'll almost never want to use this setting, which produces a very tiny file that contains no footage at all. Instead, it's something like an alias of the movie you edited. It works only as long as the original, unedited movie remains on your hard drive. If you try to email the newly saved file, your unhappy recipient won't see anything at all.

- **Save as a self-contained movie.** This option produces a new QuickTime movie—the one you've just finished editing. Although it consumes more disk space, it has none of the drawbacks of a "reference movie" file.

The Export command

Usually, your primary interest in using QuickTime Pro will be to export its edited clip, either for use in iMovie or to use in other programs (PowerPoint, Web pages, and so on).

When you find yourself in that situation, choose File→Export. The resulting dialog box should look familiar: It's the Save As dialog box that appears when you save an iMovie project as a QuickTime movie. This is your opportunity to specify the size, frame rate, color depth, special effects, and many other aspects of the movie you're about to spin off.

This is also where you can convert the QuickTime movie into some other format: AVI (Windows movie) format, Image Sequence (which produces a very large collection of individual graphics files, one per frame), and so on—or convert only the soundtrack to AIFF, System 7, or WAV (Windows) formats, for example.

How to Use QuickTime Player with iMovie

But as an iMovie fan, what you'll probably want to do the most is open your iMovie clips in QuickTime Player Pro, make changes to them, and then save them for further use in iMovie.

In that case, you'll probably adopt a routine like this:

1. **In iMovie, Control-click the clip you want to edit. From the shortcut menu, choose Reveal in Finder.**

   You switch to the desktop, where the movie file's icon is highlighted and waiting in whatever window it calls home.

2. **Option-drag the movie icon to your desktop to make a copy of it. Double-click the copy.**

   The movie clip opens before you in QuickTime Player. Edit it as described in this chapter. (The following pages walk you through some rather spectacular special-effect edits.)

When you're finished editing, go on:

3. **Choose File→Save.**

You now have an edited version of the clip on your desktop.

5. **Switch back to iMovie. Choose File→Import Movies, then navigate to the desktop and open the edited movie.**

After you indicate which Event you want it to join, the edited video becomes a new iMovie clip, which you can use to replace the original in your project, if you like. After the import, you can delete the one you saved to the desktop in step 2.

So why did you edit a copy, and not just save changes to the original clip?

Because if you edited one of iMovie's clips behind its back, iMovie wouldn't be able to update the tiny filmstrip movie that it uses to represent your video while you're editing. (It creates that filmstrip movie only when you import video the official way.)

And if the clip and its filmstrip don't match, you can't export the results—they're locked in iMovie forever.

Advanced QuickTime Pro: Track Tricks

As far as QuickTime Player is concerned, a piece of footage is nothing more than par-allel *tracks* of information: audio and video. Most movies have only two tracks—one video and one audio—but there's nothing to stop you from piling on multiple audio tracks, overlapping video tracks, and even specialized layers like a text track or an animation track.

The key to understanding the multiple simultaneous tracks in a QuickTime movie is the Movie Properties dialog box (Figure 17-5). It opens when you choose Window→Show Movie Properties (⌘-J).

Here's some of the fun you can have at this point:

• **Turn off tracks.** Turn off the Enabled checkbox for any track you want to hide/mute. This fascinating command highlights an intriguing feature of QuickTime Player Pro—its ability to embed more than one audio or video track into a single movie. If you really wanted to, you could create a movie with six different soundtracks, all playing simultaneously.

Or maybe you've created two different versions of a movie—one with throbbing, insistent background music, and one with New Age noodling. Using this option, you can quickly and easily try watching your movie first with one soundtrack, and then with the other.

• **Extract Tracks.** Click a track name and click the Extract button (top left). "Extract" actually means *copy and separate* into a new Player window. (If you double-click a soundtrack, it appears as nothing but a scroll bar with no picture.) At this point, you can copy some or all of the extracted track, in readiness to paste it into another movie.

• **Delete Tracks.** As the name implies, this button removes the selected track from the movie. For example, after experimenting to see which of several soundtracks you prefer (as described above), you'll want to delete the rejected versions before you save the final movie.

Now that you know the general workflow, here are a few recipes that illustrate how iMovie + QuickTime Player Pro = Fun and Creativity.

Figure 17-5:
The Movie Properties dialog box shows you all the parallel streams that go by when you play a movie: the various video, sound, and even text tracks.

The Visual Settings tab is particularly useful for iMovie fans, because it lets you do things you can't do in iMovie (like flipping a movie 90 degrees).

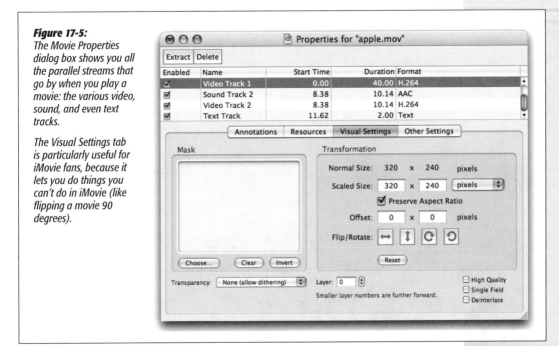

Flip a Clip

So you're making a gag movie of your buddy at work. You have a shot of him leaving the starting line in a potato-sack race at the office retreat. You want to splice in some old footage of Olympic track star Carl Lewis breaking through the tape, making it look like that's your buddy at the finish line. Only one problem: Your buddy is running from left to right in the shot, and Carl Lewis, in his shot, is running from right to left. How will you ever make that look right?

By fixing it first:

1. **Open the clip in QuickTime Player Pro.**

   See the steps on the previous two pages.

2. **Choose Window→Show Movie Properties (⌘-J).**

The Properties dialog box appears (Figure 17-5).

3. **Click Video Track, and then click Visual Settings.**

You can now apply all kinds of freaky changes to this video track. The simple Rotate commands are available in iMovie itself—but not the *Flip* commands.

4. **Click the first Flip button (the first arrow button visible in Figure 17-5).**

As you watch, your entire video picture flips, mirror image.

5. **Save the edited movie. Switch back into iMovie and import the QuickTime file as described on page 320.**

Suddenly, you're a master at comedy.

Picture-in-Picture

Ever wonder how news channels manage to show a video *inset*—a little TV picture floating in the corner of the bigger TV picture, just over the anchorperson's shoulder (Figure 17-6)?

Figure 17-6:
QuickTime Player can create very fancy picture-in-picture effects.

For example, after copying footage from a second movie (upper left), paste it over the first movie (bottom), and then use the Properties dialog box (top right) to shrink it enough to reveal what's underneath.

It's a piece of cake in more advanced programs like Final Cut Express and Final Cut Pro. But in iMovie? No way. But the following steps show you how to simulate that effect in QuickTime Player:

1. **Open the newscaster clip in QuickTime Player Pro.**

   See page 319 for instructions. (Of course, you can put *any* video on top of *any* video. This newscaster thing is just an example.)

2. **Choose File→Open File. Open the second clip, the one that will appear in the smaller, picture-in-picture frame.**

   It appears in its own window.

3. **Copy as much of it as you want.**

   If you want the whole thing, choose Edit→Select All, then Edit→Copy.

4. **Switch back to the newscaster window. Click in the scroll bar where you'll want the video insert to appear.**

   If you want it to occupy only a certain number of seconds, use the triangles beneath the scroll bar to highlight that stretch.

5. **Choose Edit→Add to Movie.**

   Or, if you chose a stretch of footage in step 4, choose Edit→Add to Selection & Scale instead. (Keep in mind that QuickTime Player stretches or shortens the pasted material to fit the selected region.)

   Either way, the pasted video now appears on top of the newscaster, covering him up. (Your Playhead is at the end of it; press the left arrow a few times to back up so that you can see it.) In the next steps, you'll shrink this overlaid video track so that it's no longer obscuring the main character.

6. **Choose Window→Show Movie Properties (⌘-J).**

   The Properties dialog box appears.

7. **Click Video Track 2, and then click Visual Settings. From the Scaled Size pop-up menu, choose Percent. Then type 50 into the first box.**

   You've just made the pasted footage appear at one-quarter its original size (reduced 50 percent in each dimension). (Because "Preserve Aspect Ratio" is turned on, you didn't have to type 50 into the second box.)

   The inset is now hugging the top-left corner of the newscaster window. If you like, you can type numbers into the Offset boxes to shove it away from that corner; keep in mind that there are about 72 pixels per inch.

8. **When the inset looks the way you like it, close the Properties palette. Export your clip back to iMovie as described on page 320.**

The Video Wall

QuickTime Player isn't fussy. It's perfectly happy to accept two, three, four, or more videos, all pasted into the same clip. You can move, scale, and shrink them independently, creating a video-wall effect like the one shown in Figure 17-7.

To create this effect, just repeat the preceding steps, over and over again. The trick, of course, is keeping track of which videos are on top, so that you can control the overlapping.

Actually, it's not terribly difficult if you have good concentration and an assistant with a notebook; see Figure 17-7.

Figure 17-7:
Each time you paste another layer of video, it becomes a new track, listed independently in the Properties palette. (You might want to rename each track to help you keep them straight. Do that by double-clicking a track's name.)

To specify the front-to-back layering of your videos, choose a layer's name, and then click Visual Settings. Use the Layer control, circled here, to move this video track closer to the front of the stack. (Lower-numbered tracks cover up higher-numbered ones.)

Part Four: iDVD '08

4

iDVD Basics

iDVD—the program, the legend—turns iMovie movies and iPhoto slideshows into Hollywood-style DVDs that people can watch on TV sets. iDVD is where you design DVDs' main menu screens, add playback controls, and otherwise dress up iMovie movies, resulting in dynamic, interactive DVDs that look amazingly professional. iDVD handles the technology; you control the style.

Not only are there lots of pro-style features and effects, but you can even burn widescreen DVDs—that is, ones with wide, rectangular, cinematic proportions that fit today's plasma and LCD digital TV screens.

The software requirement is iDVD. The hardware requirement is a DVD recorder, inside, or connected to, your Mac.

Why iDVD?

Don't look now, but Apple thinks that the era of the DVD has passed. iDVD '08, according to Steve Jobs, is "for people who still want to make DVDs." (His subtext: "Those losers!")

The real action, he believes, is on the Internet.

But don't tell that to the 120 million U.S. families who don't have high-speed Internet access—or any Internet access at all—and therefore can't see online video. These people aren't on YouTube. They can't see your .Mac gallery.

They almost certainly have DVD players, though. And producing your movies on DVD offers a wealth of benefits: They're small, light, and easy to mail. DVDs can last a long time—a century, if you believe the manufacturers—if you stick to brand-name blanks like Verbatim and Imation, and keep the burned discs in a cool, dry place.

Getting iDVD '08

If you own iMovie '08, you also have iDVD '08, because they both come on the same iLife DVD from Apple.

You don't have to worry about iDVD's system requirements; if you can run iMovie, you can also run iDVD. But here again, faster computers work a lot better than slow ones.

iDVD also requires Mac OS X 10.4.9 or later.

What You're In For

In the following chapters, you can read about integrating movies, still pictures, and sound in very flexible ways; overriding Apple's design templates; and unlocking iDVD's darkest secrets. But especially at first, what most people do is much simpler: They create the movie in iMovie, and then hand it off to iDVD for burning. Or they burn a DVD directly from the camcorder, using the OneStep DVD feature.

This chapter guides you through both of those rituals. Most of what you're about to read, though, covers the iMovie-to-iDVD sequence, which entails six broad steps:

1. **Prepare your audio, video, and pictures.**

   In addition to movies, iDVD can incorporate audio and graphics files into your shows. iDVD doesn't, however, offer any way to *create or edit* these files. You must prepare them in other programs first.

2. **Export the finished iMovie video.**

   iMovie '08 can no longer hand off a finished movie directly to iDVD. It can, however, shunt your movie into the Media Browser (page 282)—and iDVD can fetch it from there.

3. **Insert chapter markers.**

   In a commercial Hollywood DVD, you can jump around the movie without rewinding or fast-forwarding, thanks to the movie's *scene menu* or *chapter menu*. It's basically a screenful of bookmarks for certain scenes in the movie. (You can no longer create these markers right in iMovie, but there are workarounds; read on.)

4. **Design the menu screen.**

   In iDVD terms, a *menu* doesn't mean the kind that drops down from the top of the screen. Instead, a DVD menu is a menu *screen,* usually containing buttons that you click with the remote control. One button, called Play, starts playing the movie. Another, called Scene Selection, might take you to a second menu screen full of individual "chapter" buttons, so your audience doesn't have to start watching from the beginning if they don't want to.

DVD menu design is at the heart of iDVD. The program lets you specify where and how each button appears on the screen, and also lets you customize the overall look with backgrounds and titles.

5. **Add the movies to the DVD.**

Remember those videos you exported in stage 2? Now that you've got a handsomely designed menu screen ready and waiting, you can drop them into place.

6. **Burn your DVD.**

To create a DVD, iDVD compresses your movie into the universal DVD file format, called *MPEG-2*, and then copies the results to a blank recordable DVD disc. This process, called *burning*, lets you produce a DVD that plays back either in a computer or in most set-top DVD players.

This chapter covers the details of these six steps.

Phase 1: Prepare Your Video

For the most professional results, prepare your video in iMovie (or another video editing program) before importing it into iDVD. Here are a couple of key issues to keep in mind.

Overscanning and You

Millions of TV viewers every day are blissfully unaware that they're missing the big picture.

In TV's early days, the little cathode-ray guns inside the TV worked by painting one line of the TV picture, then turning around and heading back the opposite direction. To make sure that the screen was painted edge to edge, these early TVs were programmed to overshoot the edges of the screen—to use the technical term, to *overscan* the screen.

TV technology is much better now, but even modern standard-definition tube TVs exhibit overscanning. The amount varies, but you may be missing as much as 10 percent of the picture beyond the left and right edges (and often the top and bottom, too).

TV producers are careful to keep the action and titles in the part of the frame that's least likely to be lost in the overscan. If you're being a film editor, the TV-safe area is suddenly your concern, too. The overscanning effect means that when you show your iMovie productions on a TV, you'll lose anything that's very close to the edges of the frame.

In particular, broadcasters refer to two danger margins of a video image: the *title-safe area* and the *action-safe area*. (See Figure 18-1.)

Tip: Flat-panel TV sets like plasmas and LCDs don't have picture tubes, and therefore don't overscan.

The title-safe area

When a TV chops off parts of your title, making it difficult or impossible to read, your audience can't help but notice. (See Figure 18-1.) In some old versions of iMovie, you had to be careful when preparing onscreen credits and titles; if you chose the largest font size, they could wind up getting lopped off at the outer limits of the screen.

In iMovie '08, however, you don't have to worry. iMovie doesn't allow a title to expand into the outer 10 percent on either side.

TItle-safe boundary   Action-safe boundary

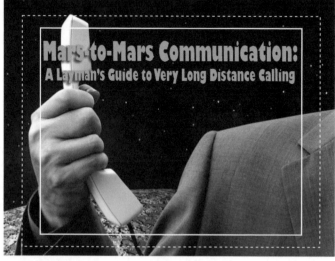

Figure 18-1:
Top: Avoid placing key visual action outside the action-safe zone of your video. Objects that appear outside the title-safe area may be cropped; objects outside the action-safe region almost certainly will be cropped by North American picture-tube TV sets.

Bottom: Although you should keep all key visual elements within the title-safe zone, you may allow non-vital portions of those elements (such as the knuckles and cord in this example) to stray into the action-safe zone.

The action-safe area

Professional broadcasters also refer to the *action-safe* area of the screen. It's not quite as broad a margin as the title-safe area, because your audience can usually figure out what's going on even if the action is slightly clipped at the outer edges of the screen. Still, it's vital that your action remains mostly within the central portion of the screen.

Imagine, for example, a science-fiction video. A mysterious enemy teleports your hero and his sidekick to a moon of Jupiter. The sidekick throws something to the hero—something that can save the day. In Figure 18-1 at top, for example, what's in the hero's hand may be obvious to you, but most TV viewers would have a hard time guessing what it is because it's outside of the action-safe zone.

In Figure 18-1 at bottom, the sidekick's hand and the phone he throws appear completely within the action-safe zone. Even if the TV winds up chopping off the outer edges of the picture, the visual story is preserved, and your hero can safely call home.

Note: Readers and their lawyers will please forgive the science of this example, in that (a) there is no such thing as teleportation; (b) there is no air to breathe on the moons of Jupiter, let alone to talk with; (c) the hero and his colleague would die almost instantly from catastrophic depressurization; and (d) even assuming the hero could make the call out, the speed of light ensures that it would take hours for his message to reach earth. When writing computer books, authors are limited by the royalty-free art collections they have on hand. The art used here appears courtesy of Ulead's Royalty-Free Media collection.

You can keep your action within the action-safe area in either of two ways:

- **Frame correctly to begin with.** Keeping important visual features and motion away from the edges of your video as you record it is by far the easiest solution.

- **Resize the footage.** You can resize your video and center it within the frame using iMovie's Crop tool (page 185). This approach, however, may degrade your video quality.

Phase 2: Export from iMovie

In its effort to play down the usefulness of the DVD as a movie-distribution channel, Apple has removed the "Send to iDVD" command from iMovie. There's no longer a one-step command for this.

Still, all is not lost. Once your project is finished, you have at least two ways to export it to a place where iDVD can find it later.

Export to the Media Browser

You can read about the Media Browser on page 282; it's a central repository of movies, photos, and music files on your Mac. It makes your multimedia goodies available to programs like Keynote, GarageBand, iWeb, iMovie—and iDVD.

To put your finished project there, choose Share→Media Browser. The dialog box shown in Figure 18-2 appears, asking which movie size you want to export.

Click Large, and then click Publish. Proceed to Phase 3 (if you want to add chapter markers) or Phase 4 (to go straight to designing the DVD).

Figure 18-2:
Here's the last thing you see before your movie goes to the Media Browser. Since your movie is destined for DVD greatness, choose Large. You need all the visual quality you can get. (If Large isn't available—because the resolution of the original isn't that high—use Medium.)

Export the Movie as a File

One funny thing about the Media Browser is that your exported movies aren't accessible *except* in the Media Browser. You won't see their icons sitting on the hard drive somewhere. (They're embedded in the package files of the projects themselves).

If you intend to use those movies in any program that doesn't have access to the Media Browser—iMovie 6, for example, or Final Cut—then you should export your iMovie projects to a *folder*, not to the Media Browser.

POWER USERS' CLINIC

Exporting from Final Cut

If you're reading this book, then you're probably using iMovie to edit your movies. But it's conceivable that you're using one of Apple's two more powerful programs, Final Cut Express or Final Cut Pro. And there's no reason you can't turn those movies into DVDs using iDVD, too.

Within Final Cut, click the sequence (movie) you want to export, and then choose File→Export→QuickTime Movie.

In the Save dialog box that appears, choose Chapter Markers from the Markers pop-up menu (if, of course, you've actually added these markers). Turn off "Make movie self-contained."

From the Setting pop-up menu, choose NTSC DV (the North American video standard) or PAL (Europe). Navigate to your Movies folder; click Save.

Final Cut creates a tiny QuickTime file on your hard drive—a reference movie, it's called—which is much smaller and faster to create than a full, self-contained QuickTime movie. As long as you don't delete the original movie files used in your Final Cut project, iDVD knows exactly what to do.

Finally, go to iDVD and add the movie to your menu screen as described in Chapter 19.

Follow the instructions on page 263, which guide you through creating a QuickTime movie file in the Apple Intermediate format.

Phase 2:
Export from iMovie

Tip: Save the file into your Movies folder. That way, iDVD will have easy access to it, as described later in this chapter.

Phase 3: Insert Chapter Markers

This phase is optional.

If you've ever rented or bought a movie on DVD, you're already familiar with *chapters,* better known as scenes (Figure 18-3).

Figure 18-3:
Most DVDs offer something called a scene menu, like this one (from the movie Ronin), which lets viewers jump directly to their favorite scenes in the movie. Your DVD scene menus probably won't be quite this elaborate, but you get the idea.

DVD chapters let viewers skip to predefined starting points within a movie, or pick up where they last left off watching, either by using the scene menu or by pressing the Next Chapter or Previous Chapter buttons on the remote control.

Unfortunately, as part of its effort to de-emphasize the DVD, Apple took the chapter-marker feature out of iMovie '08. You can still add chapter markers, but it's a lot more work.

Actually, there are three ways to go about it:

- **Export the movie to iMovie 6.** The older iMovie has a really great chapter-adding feature. When you're finished, iMovie 6 can then hand off the movie directly to iDVD with a single command. Use this method if you have other work to do in iMovie 6, like adding some of its visual effects or audio effects.

• **Export the movie to GarageBand.** GarageBand has convenient chapter-adding features, too—*and* a "Send to iDVD" command just like iMovie 6's. If you'll be using GarageBand to edit your audio tracks anyway (page 231), it might make sense to add your chapters at that point.

• **Use iDVD's automatic chapter-marker feature.** iDVD can add markers to a movie *for* you—but it places them at even intervals, like every 4 minutes. You don't have the freedom to place the markers where you want them—at logical scene breaks, for example.

The following pages cover all three methods.

Add Markers in iMovie 6

Begin by exporting your iMovie '08 project to iMovie 6; the instructions are on page 263.

Then, in iMovie 6, you have two different ways to add chapter markers. The easiest way is to press Shift-⌘-M at each spot where you want a chapter marker, even while the movie is playing. (That's the shortcut for the Markers→Add Chapter Marker command.) Although that's quick and easy, you still have to open up the Chapters palette to *name* the markers (Figure 18-4).

To create and manage chapter markers all in one tidy list, use the Chapters palette. Here's how that goes:

1. **In iMovie 6, click the Chapters button.**

   You'll find it among the other pane buttons, just to the right of the Editing button, as shown in Figure 18-4. When clicked, the Chapters pane opens.

2. **In the iMovie monitor, drag the Playhead along the scrubber bar to locate the position for your new chapter.**

   You may want to choose Edit→Select None (Shift-⌘-A) first, which ensures that no individual clip is selected. Now you can move the Playhead anywhere in your movie.

Tip: Use the arrow keys for precise Playhead positioning, or press Shift-arrow to jump 10 frames at a time.

---

3. **Click Add Marker.**

   You'll find this button near the bottom of the Chapters palette. iMovie adds the chapter to your list, as shown in Figure 18-4.

Tip: You can also use the keystroke Shift-⌘-M at this point, or even choose Markers→Add Chapter Marker.

---

4. Type a chapter title into the Chapter Title box.

Whatever you type here winds up as the chapter name in the finished DVD menu. Select a short but meaningful name.

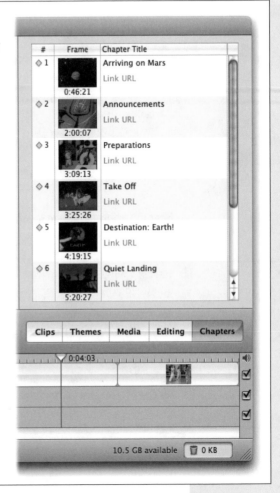

Figure 18-4:
If you've added any chapter markers using the Add Chapter Marker (Shift-⌘-M) method, you'll see them listed here, in the Chapters palette. They're named after the clip from which they originated, such as Clip 05/1 or Clip 02/7. The Chapters pane lets you add, remove, and name chapters. New iMovie chapters are numbered sequentially, as they appear in your movie from left to right. Chapter references appear in your timeline as small yellow diamonds, just above the video track. iMovie 6 can add up to 99 chapters per movie with the Chapters palette.

5. Repeat steps 2–4 until you've added all the chapters for your movie. Save your project.

Choose File→Save to save your iMovie project, including the chapter marks you just defined.

To change the name of a chapter, double-click it (in the Chapters pane) to open the editing box, and then edit away. To remove a marker, click its name in iMovie's Chapters palette, and then click the Remove Marker button.

Chapter-marker pointers

Here are a few key points to keep in mind about chapters:

- Chapter markers appear in the Timeline as small, yellow diamond shapes.

- **You can't move a chapter marker.** If you've used the wrong start frame when creating your chapter, you have no choice but to delete the chapter marker and create a new one with the correct starting point.

- **When you move, copy, or erase clips, chapter markers go along for the ride.** iMovie associates chapters with individual clips.

- **There's a "secret" unlisted chapter.** iMovie 6 and iDVD always create one more chapter than you see on the iDVD Chapters list. This extra chapter corresponds to the very beginning of your movie (00:00:00), and starts out with the label "Start". (You don't see it until you arrive in iDVD.)

- **Your finished iDVD screens can fit up to 12 buttons per screen.** That's "up to," because the actual number depends on the *theme* you pick.

Handing off from iMovie 6→iDVD

Once you've added your chapter markers in iMovie 6, you're ready to hand off the whole thing to iDVD, where you can do your menu design and DVD burning.

Start by saving your iMovie project. Then choose Share→iDVD and, in the confirmation dialog box, click Share.

Your hard drive whirs, thunder rolls somewhere, and after a few moments, you wind up in iDVD itself. Skip to page 338.

Adding Chapters in GarageBand

GarageBand has a handy chapter-adding feature, too. Using it to add chapter markers isn't as convenient as having a built-in iMovie '08 chapter feature would be. But if you plan to do some touch-up audio work in GarageBand anyway, you're not losing any time.

Start by exporting your nearly-finished iMovie '08 project to GarageBand. Follow steps 1 through 5 on page 232.

Then play the movie (Space bar), or position the Playhead using your mouse or the arrow keys on the keyboard. At each point where you want a chapter marker, press the letter P key (or, if you're being paid by the hour, choose Edit→Add Marker).

At this point, a handy chapter-marker editing console appears at the bottom of the window (Figure 18-5). Here, you can add, delete, or rename your markers.

When you're finished editing the markers, choose Share→Send Movie to iDVD.

At this point, iDVD opens automatically, with Play and Scene Selection buttons already in place. Proceed from page 338.

Adding Chapters in iDVD

As noted earlier, iDVD can add scene breaks for you, which saves you the detour to iMovie 6 or GarageBand. But iDVD adds them at regular intervals; you can't place them where you want them.

Figure 18-5:
Make sure that the "Marks a Chapter" checkbox is turned on; otherwise, you're creating navigation markers that won't transfer to iDVD. To rename a marker, double-click the existing name. To fine-tune the position of a marker, double-click its time code. And to delete a marker, click its row and then press Delete.

If you're still interested, then here's how it works. Place the movie onto your iDVD menu screen (page 357). Click the movie's button, once, to select it, and then choose Advanced→Create Chapter Markers for Movie. (This command isn't available if the movie *already* has chapter markers in it.)

Tip: Actually, you can Shift-click to select several movie buttons simultaneously. That way, iDVD creates chapter markers for all of them.

A tiny dialog box appears, offering to "Create chapter markers every __ minutes." Type in the number you want—2, for example—and click OK.

Now, when your viewers click that movie button, it doesn't begin playing immediately. Instead, it takes them to a secondary screen that offers a Play button *and* a Scene Selection button, which, in turn, opens a screen full of thumbnails called Chapter 1, Chapter 2, and so on. Those are the chapters that iDVD generated automatically.

Tip: If you change your mind about adding these scene-selection buttons, click the Scene Selection button, and then press the Delete key.

Phase 4: Design the Menu Screen

Once your movies are safely exported from iMovie, and you've added chapter markers if you want them, open up iDVD itself.

The opening screen offers four options (Figure 18-6, top):

- **Create a New Project.** In this program, "project" refers to a DVD that you're designing. It's not a "project" as iMovie refers to it.

- **Open an Existing Project.** Just burning a DVD doesn't mean the end of your project. You can open it up again later to burn another copy of that DVD, or make changes and *then* burn it.

- **OneStep DVD** is a one-click method of dumping a videotape onto a DVD, right from the camcorder, bypassing iMovie altogether. See page 353.

- **Magic iDVD.** This feature, too, avoids any iMovie involvement. But this time, Magic iDVD creates a DVD using a bunch of pictures, movies, and music files as its raw material. See page 354.

To create a new DVD for the first time, click Create a New Project. You now have three choices to make (Figure 18-6, bottom):

- **Name the project.** What you type here won't appear on the DVD; it's just a file name for organizational purposes on your Mac.

- **Choose where to save it.** iDVD suggests your Documents folder, but you can choose anywhere you like.

- **Choose an aspect ratio.** This is actually a pretty big decision; iDVD is asking what shape TV you'll be playing the DVD on.

    If you choose "Standard (4:3)", then the DVD will perfectly fit standard, traditional, squarish TV screens. But when played on widescreen sets, you'll get black vertical bars on either side of the picture.

    If you choose "Widescreen (16:9)", then the opposite will happen. The DVD will look fantastic on, and completely fill, high-def TV screens and other widescreen sets—but will have *horizontal* letterbox bars when played on an older, standard set.

Tip: You can always change your mind about the aspect ratio later by choosing Project→"Switch to Standard (4:3)" or "Switch to Widescreen (16:9)."

Once you've made your choices, click Create.

Note: If you've arrived here from iMovie 6 or GarageBand, you may not see the options shown in Figure 18-6. Instead, you might see a predesigned menu screen like the one shown in Figure 18-7.

If you added chapter markers, for example, you'll find two buttons: Play (meaning "Play the movie from the beginning") and Scene Selection. On the finished DVD, this button takes your audience to a second screen, which is filled with individual buttons for the chapters you created. In fact, this second screen may well have arrows that lead to *third and fourth* screens, since iDVD menus vary in the number of buttons that fit per screen.

Figure 18-6:
Top: You have four options. Or you can ignore this dialog box and choose commands from the File menu, like Open Recent.

Bottom: Choose a name, location, and aspect ratio for the movie.

All about Themes

The design of the DVD menu screen that's now before you is called a *theme:* a unified design scheme that governs how the menus look and behave, complete with attractive backgrounds, coordinated typography, and background music (Figure 18-7).

iDVD '08 offers over 150 of these themes, including 10 new ones. Each theme family contains a main menu screen, a chapter navigation screen, and an "extras" screen for bonus DVD features you can build with iDVD.

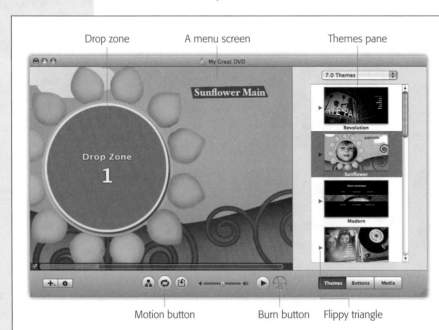

Figure 18-7:
In iDVD, you add, edit, and manipulate the buttons, pictures, movies, and titles that make up the menus for your DVD. The "drawer" at the right side is a permanent fixture, always open and always on the right. It's the portion identified here as the Themes pane.

It takes a lot of individual design decisions to make a theme. For example:

- **Background image or video.** Whatever art appears in the background, whether still images or video clips, is part of the theme. The movement of the desert in the Anime Pop theme is one example of video in action.

Tip: Many themes are animated with a repetitive looping; many have music, too. The Motion button (⟳) turns the looping motion and the music on and off while you're working on a DVD. (It does not affect the finished DVD, however.)

- **Button type.** The buttons in an iDVD project can be either little graphics or text phrases that your audience will click with the remote control.

- **Button look.** The look of your buttons can vary. Text buttons may have simple backgrounds; graphic buttons may have borders.

- **Button positions.** Each menu can accommodate up to 12 buttons, depending on the theme you've chosen. Themes are preset to place their buttons in certain favored positions.

- **Drop zones.** *Drop zones* are areas into which you can drag a favorite video clip (sometimes more than one) that plays continuously as a background for the main menu screen. If you've ever seen a commercial Hollywood DVD movie, you've seen this effect. One key scene from the movie plays over and over, looping until you choose one of the buttons on the menu screen—or go quietly insane.

Dynamic drop zones can even move across the screen, passing in front of each other, providing amazing visual effects.

Figure 18-8:
iDVD Themes can create strikingly different menu screens for similar projects.

Top: The Forever theme (shown in the traditional 4:3, squarish shape here) displays gracefully sliding photos (or videos) in the drop zones as they float from right to left; a string quartet plays.

Bottom: The Revolution Chapters Theme (shown in its widescreen, 16:9 shape) offers a stunning, high-tech look. Its features two counter-rotating cylinders, one bearing your project's name and the other displaying what you've put into the drop zones.

- **Text boxes.** Text boxes let you freely add text blocks to your menu screens. You could use one, for example, to provide instructions to your viewers, copyright notices, or details about what they're about to see.

- **Font selections.** Themes also specify the color, font size, and typeface for menu titles and buttons.

Figure 18-8 illustrates two very different looks for the same project. The difference lies only in the chosen theme.

Choosing a Theme

iDVD '08 starts up with a very cool-looking, high-tech, black-on-black theme called Revolution Chapters (Figure 18-8, bottom), but goodness knows, you're not stuck with that one. A wide range of canned themes awaits your inspection.

To see them, make sure that the Themes button is selected (lower-right corner of iDVD). Then choose a theme *set* from the pop-up menu at the top of the Themes palette. iDVD offers four built-in sets, each named for the version of iDVD that first included them: 7.0 Themes, 6.0 Themes, 5.0 Themes, and Old Themes (from iDVD 3 and 4). (Believe it or not, "7.0 Themes" refers to the new ones in iDVD '08.)

Within most themes, you can click the flippy triangle (Figure 18-7) to reveal *variations* of that theme—a complementary menu design for the scene-selection screen, for your DVD extras page, and so on.

If you've bought additional themes online, this pop-up menu may offer other choices. In any case, you can use this pop-up menu to switch between them, or just choose All to see all installed themes in a single scrolling list.

Scroll through the list of themes, clicking each one to see what it looks like in the main work area, or just rely on the little thumbnail icons to get a sense of the theme's overall flavor.

Note: All of the themes in the 6.0 and 7.0 collections appear, at first, to be suitable only for widescreen DVDs.

If you're making a standard 4:3 DVD, then every time you click one of these themes, the Change Project Aspect Ratio warning box appears, asking if you really intended to *change* the project to 16:9. It gets annoying fast. (Yes, you could turn on "Do not ask me again," but then it changes to widescreen every time *without* asking you.)

So for best results in looking over the themes, do so in widescreen mode, just to avoid being interrupted by that warning. You can always switch to the 4:3 version of a theme later by choosing Project→Switch to Standard (4:3).

If your DVD menu system consists of only a single screen—the main menu you've been looking at the whole time—it takes on your chosen theme instantly. A movie that has chapter markers in it, however, has at least one additional menu screen: your scene-selection screen.

In that case, when you click a theme thumbnail, iDVD asks if you want to apply the Theme Family to the entire project, so that the main menu and the Scene Selection menus match; almost always, this is what you want. Figure 18-9 shows how.

Note: You can also apply a theme to all the menus later by choosing Advanced→Apply Theme to Project. Or you can apply a theme only to the *submenus*—not the main screen—by choosing Advanced→Apply Theme to Submenus.

Figure 18-9:
As a rule, always use a single theme family for your entire project. When this message appears, turn on "Do not ask me again", and click OK. Doing this ensures that every screen in your project looks consistent with every other screen. Good idea, good design.

Apply Theme Family
Applying the master of a theme family to this project will change the theme for all menus in this project.

☐ Do not ask me again

Cancel   OK

When you're happy with the way the new theme looks, you're ready to proceed with your iDVD design work. Fortunately, you don't have to commit to a theme at this moment; you can swap in a different theme at any time until you actually burn the DVD.

Tip: You can buy additional themes, or download free samples, from other companies (such as *iDVDThemePAK.com)*. Install them by creating a folder called Favorites in your Library folder (the Library folder in the main hard drive window, not in your Home folder), and then putting them inside.

The Inevitable Paragraphs about Aspect Ratio

As you probably know, there are two popular *aspect ratios*—screen shapes—for television these days: standard 4:3 and widescreen. See page 109 for details.

iDVD '08, as it turns out, can create DVDs in either format; see Figure 18-10. You're asked to choose which format you want when you first create a project, and you can switch to the other format at any time, using the Project menu.

Now, it turns out that all of the iDVD 6.0 and 7.0 themes have been cleverly designed to look great on *both* standard and widescreen TV sets. Figure 18-10 explains all.

So if the menu screens will always look good, regardless of TV shape, why not just choose widescreen format for *every* DVD you make?

Because the *video* on your DVD isn't so accommodating! If it's been shot widescreen, and it's played back on a standard set, you'll probably wind up with letterbox bars above and below. And if it's been shot in standard 4:3 format, then playing it on a widescreen set will result in black bars on the sides.

The bottom line: Choose the aspect ratio for your DVD according to the aspect ratio of the video that's on it.

Figure 18-10:
*Each of the "widescreenable"
themes comes in two versions: a
standard 4:3 version (top) and a
widescreen version (bottom). The
question is, what happens if you
create a widescreen DVD—and then
play it on a 4:3 standard television?*

*If you'd like to find out, choose
View→Show Standard Crop Area.
iDVD responds by dimming the
outer right and left edges of the
picture, showing you which portions
won't appear on a 4:3 traditional
television. What you'll discover is
that Apple has cleverly designed
the widescreen themes so that all
the important stuff—drop zones,
buttons, titles, and so on—are close
enough to the center that they
won't be chopped off on a standard
TV. In fact, in most cases, there's
very little difference between the
4:3 version of a theme (top) and
the not-chopped-off portion of a
widescreen theme (bottom).*

*The bottom line: Choosing wide-
screen format for a DVD generally
means that the menus will play
beautifully on both standard and
widescreen TV sets. But the video
on the DVD is another matter.*

Drop Zones: The Basics

Drop zones let you use video, slideshows, or stills as the backgrounds of your menu screens. They're purely decorative, designed to entertain your audience as they study their choices on the menu. (You install these videos or pictures by *dropping* them into the designated *zones* in the menu design—hence the name.)

Not every theme offers drop zones, but most of the iDVD 5, 6, and 7 themes do. As if you couldn't guess, the words "Drop Zone" (Figure 18-11) indicate where the drop zones are.

Tip: If you don't see the telltale phrase "Drop Zone" followed by a number, choose iDVD→Preferences. Click the General icon, and then turn on "Show drop zone labels." (Turning off this checkbox just hides the words "Drop Zone," not the drop zones themselves.)

Note, by the way, that not all drop zones may be onscreen at once; the drop zones in several themes take their time in parading onto the screen, or rotating through it. To see all the drop zones in your chosen theme, click the Show Drop Zones button below the screen. As shown in Figure 18-11, you're now shown thumbnail placeholders for all of the drop zones in this theme's animation.

Filling drop zones

iDVD offers four different ways to fill these empty gray spaces with videos and pictures:

- **Drag directly into the full-size rectangle.** This technique is shown in the top example in Figure 18-11. Most of the time, you'll be dragging videos or pictures from the Media Browser. (Click the Media button at the lower-right corner of iDVD, and then click either Photos or Movies at the top.)

- **Drag into the Drop Zone editor.** To open the new Drop Zone editor, click the Editor button identified in Figure 18-11. Thumbnails appear beneath the menu screen with dotted lines, all present and accounted for, so that you don't have to wait for them to cycle into view in the main display window.

Note: The drop zone wells are also navigational bookmarks; if you click one, the monitor window displays that moment in the menu animation.

Figure 18-11:
Double-click any drop zone, or click the Drop Zone Editor button, to bring up the interactive Drop Zone editor shown here. Note that drop zones aren't always perfect rectangles or squares, so your video or photo may get clipped around the edges. You can fill drop zones with individual photos, bunches of photos (for a slideshow effect), or movies.

Drop Zone Editor   Open Drop Zone Editor   Media button

- **Let iDVD fill the zones.** Choose Project→Autofill Drop Zones. iDVD loads photos or movies—of its choosing—into the drop zones of the theme automatically.

- **Choose a picture or movie from the hard drive.** Control-click (or right-click) a drop zone; from the shortcut menu, choose Import. Find and open a movie, slideshow, picture, or folder full of pictures. iDVD uses that material to fill the drop zone.

Drop zones: the details

No matter which view of the drop zones you're using, here's how things work:

- **Hiding the drop zones.** Drop-zone animation can be stunning, but filling the zones can take time and tweaking. When you're in a hurry, or when you actually prefer the theme design *without* those zones, you can remove the drop-zone elements from the theme entirely. Choose View→Inspector (or press ⌘-I), and then turn off "Show drop zones and related graphics."

- **Adding to a drop zone.** Drag any video, photo album, image, or collection of images right into a drop zone outline to install it there. You can drag icons out of the Finder, or directly out of the Media pane.

Tip: Albums in drop zones can display 99 images at most. What you'll get is a mini-slideshow, right there within the drop zone. (More on dragging out of the Photos pane in Chapter 19.)

- **Replacing items in a drop zone.** Just drag something new into the drop zone.

- **Removing items from a drop zone.** To empty out the drop zone, drag away from the spot, just as you'd drag something off the Mac OS X Dock or the Sidebar. You get a cute little puff of smoke to indicate the movie or picture's disappearance.

- **Turning on motion.** If you've installed video into a drop zone and it doesn't seem to be playing, click the Motion button (⟳) at the bottom of the iDVD window, or press ⌘-J.

  Turning off Motion also turns off any background audio track and brings motion menus and motion buttons to a standstill.

Note: The status of the Motion button has no effect on the final DVD, which always shows the animations and plays the music.

- **Editing a drop-zone slideshow or movie.** If you've created a movie or slideshow drop zone, you have some additional editing powers available to you—like deciding what order the photos appear in the slideshow, or which part of the movie loops within the zone. Much more detail on Drop Zone editing appears in Chapter 20.

Redesigning the Theme

You can change every tiny aspect of your theme—if you have the time and patience. If you're so inclined, turn to Chapter 20 for a full discussion of theme creation.

Phase 5: Add Your Movies

See page 357 for details on the many ways to install movies and pictures into the guts
of your DVD.

Phase 6: Burning Your DVD

You're almost ready to burn the DVD. Before you go using up a blank disc, however, test
it to make sure that it works on the virtual DVD player known as the Macintosh.

Previewing Your Project

iDVD's Play button (▶) lets you test your DVD to avoid unpleasant surprises. It enters
Preview mode, which simulates how your DVD works on a standalone set-top DVD
player. You even get a simulated remote control to help you navigate through your
DVD's menus, movies, and so on, as shown in Figure 18-12.

To return to iDVD's edit mode, click Exit or Stop (■).

Tip: Instead of using the arrow buttons on the remote to highlight and click screen buttons, just use your
mouse. You'll find it's not only less clumsy, but also a decent indication of how your DVD will play back on
computers that can play DVDs.

Figure 18-12:
*To "click" your onscreen
buttons, use the arrows
on the remote to high-
light the one you want,
and then click the Enter
button in the middle of
the remote. Click the
◄ or ► buttons to skip
back or forward by one
chapter, or hold them
down to rewind or fast-
forward.*

Checking for Errors

A DVD is a complex beast. Behind the scenes, there's all kinds of programming and linking going on—and any number of things could result in a DVD that doesn't work right after it's burned.

Before you proceed, then, click the DVD Map icon identified on page 363. On the map, red stop-sign icons or yellow exclamation-point triangles appear on any screen of your DVD where problems await. For example:

• You created a slideshow, but forgot to add slides to it.

• You created a new menu screen, but didn't add anything to it.

• You haven't filled in all the drop zones.

Work through these alerts, resolving the problems one by one.

Maximum DVD Playback Time

When a DVD-burning program goes to work, it faces an important decision. Given that a blank single-layer DVD contains a limited amount of space (4.7 GB or so), how much picture-quality data can it afford to devote to each frame of video?

GEM IN THE ROUGH

Secrets of the Theme Scrubber

iDVD's scrubber bar (the thin white scroll bar beneath the menu screen) lets you preview the animation for a certain theme. You can let it play automatically (click the Motion ↻ button) or you can drag the scroll handle to zip through it, watching how the theme changes over time. Or press the arrow keys to step one frame at a time.

Many themes, including the one shown here, include a "play once" introduction—a preliminary animation that plays before your menu buttons even appear. It's represented in iDVD by a crosshatched area of the scrubber bar, to the left of the main section (which represents the looping portion of your menu animation). Some themes also have a crosshatched area at the end, a "play-out" portion that helps link back to the beginning of the loop.

At times, you might want to turn off that introductory animation—for example, when you're designing secondary

menu screens (like the Scene Selection screen). If you turn off the checkbox to the left of the scrubber, you hide the crosshatched section of the scrubber bar. You also eliminate the introductory portion, both as it plays in iDVD and on the final, burned DVD. Now only the main, looping portion of the menu-screen animation plays. (You can always restore the intro by turning the checkbox back on again.)

Similarly, the checkbox at the right end of the scrubber hides the play-out animation.

Speaking of scrubber-bar secrets: If you turn off the Motion (↻) button at the bottom of the iDVD screen, you bring the menu's animation to a halt. (This step doesn't affect the motion in the finished DVD.) Once Motion is turned off, you can drag the scrubber.

Oh, and you can choose View→Hide Motion Playhead to tuck the scrubber bar out of sight and View→Show Motion Playhead to bring it back.

---

iDVD offers three approaches. (You make your choice for the *current* project by choosing Project→Project Info, or for *future* projects by choosing iDVD→Preferences and clicking the Projects button.)

As Figure 18-13 shows, your options are:

- **Best Performance.** Your video will look fantastic, and your Mac can burn the disc relatively quickly.

  On the downside, the DVD you burn this way can contain a maximum of 60 minutes of video for standard DVDs. (You get about 120 minutes for dual-layer DVDs; see page 351.)

  The Best Performance option thinks like this: "Since I don't have to fit very much video on this disc, then hey—I can devote the maximum amount of data to each frame of video, for great quality. But it's a fixed amount. Not having to calculate how much data to allot to each frame will save me time and make the burning process go quickly."

Tip: Part of what makes this method burn your disc so fast is that it does a lot of advance work in the background *while* you're designing your DVD. That's good because it saves you time, but bad because, on slower Macs, it can make iDVD feel sluggish.

If your Mac bogs down, choose Advanced→Encode in Background to turn off that feature.

Figure 18-13:
This panel offers all the details of your DVD: how much material is on the disc, which aspect ratio, what kind of DVD (single- or dual-layer), and so on. Note: As the white arrow moves from green (excellent) into yellow, orange, and then red on the Quality graph, the video quality goes down. You'll see that if you change the encoding setting for a one-hour video from Best Performance to Professional; you'll see that the Pro option gives superior results.

Before you burn a disc, confirm that a check mark appears next to each *asset* (that is, each picture, movie, soundtrack, or what have you).

- **High Quality.** This option lets a standard DVD hold up to 120 minutes of video (or, on double-layer blanks, nearly four hours' worth). The tradeoff: It takes a lot longer to burn your DVD, since iDVD performs a deep analysis before burning.

This option makes iDVD think, "I'm going to use every micron of space on this blank DVD. I'm going to analyze the amount of video, and divide it into the amount of space available on the DVD. The amount of data used to describe an individual frame of video will vary from project to project, and it will take me a lot longer to burn the DVD because I'm going to have to do so much analysis. Also, I can't get started with that analysis until after the whole DVD is done; Background Encoding, described on the previous page, is not available with this setting. But at least my human will get two hours of great-looking video per disc."

The High Quality setting uses the same trick that movie studios use on their Hollywood DVDs: *variable bit-rate (VBR) encoding.* Professional DVD companies use advanced software to analyze each piece of the movie, using more or less data to describe each frame, depending on how much action is visible. The disc conserves data for when the video needs it the most.

The trouble is, the analysis required by VBR encoding takes a very long time. That's why High Quality takes longer to burn a disc than Best Performance.

- **Professional Quality.** This advanced encoding method, new in iDVD '08, is what you should use for the really important stuff. It takes twice as long as High Quality to burn a DVD, because it takes *two* passes through your material, one frame at a time. It's *double* variable bit-rate encoding. The result is better, richer color and, especially, sharper-looking photo slideshows.

The Professional method can fit two hours of video onto a single-layer blank DVD—and produces truly amazing-looking discs.

One Last Techie Look

Part of iDVD's job is to *encode* (convert) your movies, music, and pictures into the MPEG-2 format required by standard DVDs. It's actually a big, hairy job, one that Apple and iDVD try to hide from you, for fear of freaking you out.

Nonetheless, if you inspect what's going on with your encoding before burning the disc, you'll be a better person for it.

To do so, open the Project Info Window (choose Project→Project Info, or press Shift-⌘-I). The dialog box that appears shows how close you are to filling up the DVD with your movies, menus, and other elements. Figure 18-13 has the details.

Tip: If you click the tiny storage-space readout at the right end of the graph ("4 GB," for example), it cycles among different displays: how many minutes' worth of material your DVD will have, and how many separate tracks (individual playable bits) you've set up.

Shopping for Blank DVDs

iDVD can burn most kinds of blank DVDs. As you shop, pay close attention to what you're buying:

- **DVD-R.** These are single-sided blanks that you can record only once—permanently. Of all these formats, DVD-R is the least expensive and the one that will play on the most DVD players. (Capacity: 4.2 gigabytes, or 2 hours of video.)

- **DVD+R.** At one point, this competing format caused no end of grief to people whose Macs could burn only DVD-R—and weren't paying attention to the + sign when they bought blanks. Today, all Macs can burn DVD+R just as easily as DVD-R, and all but the most ancient DVD players can play both types.

- **DVD-RW or DVD+RW (Rewritable).** Same idea, except that you can erase these and use them again. (When you insert a DVD-RW that you've used before, iDVD automatically offers to erase it.) Some older DVD players can't play these, though.

- **DVD+R DL (Double Layer).** This kind of blank holds 7.7 gigabytes—close to four hours of video. All current Mac models can record onto these blanks, and all current DVD players can play them after they've been burned.

  Older Macs may not be able to record onto double-layer discs, however.

Tip: To find out if your Mac can burn double-layer discs, choose Project→Project Info. If the DVD Type pop-up menu offers a choice of Double-Layer (DL), then you're one of the lucky ones.

The Burn

When you've finished editing your disc and testing it thoroughly, it's time to proceed with your burn. This is the moment you've been waiting for.

1. **Choose File→Save Project (⌘-S).**

   This might be a good opportunity to confirm that your hard drive has some free space, too. It needs *twice* the amount of free space that your project itself takes up. Use the Project Info graph (Figure 18-13) as your guide.

2. **Click the Burn button twice.**

Figure 18-14:
The first click on the gray, closed Burn button "opens" it, revealing a throbbing yellow-and-black button. The second click begins the encoding and burning process, which can take hours.

See Figure 18-14.

3. Insert a blank DVD when the Mac asks for it.

Be sure you're using the correct kind of disc for your DVD burner. For example, don't attempt to burn 1x or 2x blanks at 4x speed.

4. Wait.

It can take iDVD a *very* long time to process all of your audio, video, and photos, encoding them into the proper format for a DVD. Your wait time depends on how complex your project is, how fast your Mac is, and which encoding setting you've chosen. The bottom line is that this period is usually measured in hours, not minutes.

For best results, make sure that no background programs are busy—downloading e-mail, playing iTunes music—while you're capturing directly to DVD. A busy computer may introduce video glitches (like dropped frames) into the video capture.

Eventually, though, a freshly burned DVD pops out of your drive.

Tip: After your new DVD pops out, a message says, "Your disc has been created. If you want to create another DVD, insert another disc now." Sure enough, if you want to spin out multiple copies of your project, you can insert another blank DVD right then, so that iDVD can record it without having to repeat all that time-consuming encoding.

Otherwise, click Done.

OneStep DVDs, Magic iDVDs

If you've read this far, you now know that even a simple iMovie-to-iDVD transfer can involve quite a bit of effort and learning.

That's why Apple came up with not one, but two, different ways to shorten the distance between your camcorder and a finished DVD:

- **OneStep DVD.** This is a one-click method of dumping a videotape onto a DVD. You just plug in a camera and record directly to a DVD, bypassing iMovie altogether. The result is exactly like the cassette, with the same footage in the same order as you shot it on your camcorder.

  In effect, OneStep DVD turns a *tape* camcorder into one of those *DVD* camcorders. It's a handy way to offload footage from a bunch of tapes, either because blank DVDs are cheaper than tapes, or because tapes have a more limited shelf life.

- **Magic iDVD.** Here again, the idea is to automate a lot of the gruntwork involved in designing a DVD. But this time, instead of using raw material straight from your camcorder, Magic iDVD knits together existing files on your hard drive. You choose a bunch of pictures, movies, and music files, and boom—iDVD produces the disc for you.

The result doesn't have to be a finished product. You wind up with an iDVD project that you *could* burn right away, but that you're also welcome to edit and fine-tune.

Here's a walk-through of both features.

OneStep DVD

As noted above, OneStep DVD is designed to convert the tape in your camcorder into an identical DVD in your Mac. It's very simple, and very limited. For example:

- iDVD can record only from a prerecorded MiniDV tape in a camcorder or a movie file on your hard drive. It can't record from the TV, a cable box, an analog-digital converter box, or your digital camcorder's video pass-through feature. It also can't record from a *high-def* tape camcorder or any tapeless camcorder.

- You can't edit the video or choose which parts to include.

- You can't customize your project in any way. The resulting DVD won't have a theme, a menu screen, or buttons. Instead, it will be an autoplay DVD—a disc that begins playing automatically when inserted into a DVD player.

Note: Like iMovie, OneStep DVD does not play well with 12-bit audio, which is the standard audio-recording setting for most new digital camcorders. Record your video using the 16-bit setting (which you change in the camcorder's menus); otherwise, your audio and video may drift apart on the DVD.

Here's how you use OneStep to copy a tape onto a DVD:

1. **Insert a recorded DV tape into your camcorder, and connect the camcorder to your Mac using a FireWire cable. Turn on the camcorder and set it to VCR or Play mode.**

   Chapter 4 offers details.

2. **In iDVD, choose File→OneStep DVD.**

   If your Mac's DVD drive has a slide-out tray, it now opens automatically.

Tip: If, instead, you choose File→"OneStep DVD from Movie," you can choose a finished QuickTime movie from your hard drive. iDVD turns it into a DVD that will play automatically and instantly, in "kiosk mode," when inserted into a DVD player.

---

3. **Insert a blank recordable DVD.**

   Close the DVD tray, if necessary.

4. **Wait.**

   iDVD takes over your camera, automatically directing it to rewind, play back, and stop (Figure 18-15).

Tip: You don't have to let iDVD rewind your tape to the beginning. You can specify where you want the transfer to begin, just by cueing up the tape in the camcorder before you begin the steps above. Then, the instant iDVD begins rewinding the tape, press Play on the camcorder right away. You've convinced OneStep that the tape has just been rewound completely. iDVD starts the capture at that point.

Figure 18-15:
The OneStep DVD process automates capturing, preparing, processing and burning a DVD from the contents of your camera's tape. OneStep doesn't actually begin recording the disc until after its video-encoding phase, which can take minutes or hours after the video-capturing process is complete. You can click the Cancel button at any time during this processing (encoding) stage to quit without burning. No harm done.

Ordinarily, iDVD imports video until the end of the tape, or until it sees 10 seconds of blank tape, whichever comes first. But you can override this setup, too. Whenever you feel that you've transferred enough of the tape, press the Stop button on your camcorder to end the capture process. OneStep moves right ahead to the compression and burning stages.

After the capture process is complete, iDVD takes the normal amount of time to compress your video and burn it to disc, so schedule the whole thing for a time (a *long* time) when you won't be needing your Mac. Go get coffee, found a new religion, or do something else that will occupy you as the tectonic plates move on inexorably and California continues its long, slow slide into Alaska.

Magic iDVDs

The magic of Magic iDVD all happens in a single dialog box, shown in Figure 18-16. It's a fun, easy way to put together a project for iDVD, or even to skip the whole editing thing and put together an instant DVD. You choose the movies and photos you want to include, choose the theme (menu design) you prefer, and then click Create Project to produce a new, ready-to-edit (or ready-to-burn) iDVD project.

Magic iDVD isn't *completely* on autopilot, however. You have to exhibit just a tiny bit of effort:

- **Name your DVD.** Edit the text box to the right of DVD Title.

- **Choose a theme.** All of the menu-screen templates (themes) are listed in a horizontal scrolling list; the pop-up menu above groups them by iDVD version (7.0, 6.0, and so on). (See page 339 for details on themes.)

Figure 18-16:
Using Magic iDVD is just like going shopping. "I'll take these movies, that slideshow, those audio clips, that theme…and wrap them up to go, please." Select the media you want to use, and then drop them in the wells on the lower left of the window. Click Create Project to start a new project using all your selections, or click Burn to create an instant DVD.

- **Add movies.** Click Movies (top right), and then drag the icons of the videos you've selected into the movie wells. (You can also switch to the Finder and drag them into the wells right from the desktop.) If you drop several movies at once, iDVD reassigns them to their own individual wells.

- **Add slideshows** Click Photos (top right), and then drag pictures into a Photos cell. What you're creating here is a slideshow, so don't drag *individual* photos. Either drag albums from your iPhoto list, or select *batches* of photos that you drag en masse into a well.

To add music to this new slideshow, click the Audio button to view your iTunes master list. Now you can drag either an individual song or a complete playlist onto any well where you've already installed some pictures. A ◄)) icon appears superimposed on that cell.

- **Remove stuff if necessary.** If you change your mind about something, you can remove a movie or slideshow by dragging its icon out of a well (or by selecting a well and then pressing the Delete key).

And what about audio? The only way to remove audio from a slideshow is to remove the slideshow itself. You can, however, change the audio by dropping a new music track on top of an occupied slideshow well.

- **Preview your DVD.** Click the ▶ button to see what iDVD has built for you using the raw ingredients you fed to it (Figure 18-17).

Figure 18-17:
A Magic iDVD has only two buttons on its main menu: Movies and Slideshows. It autofills all drop zones with selections it makes from the movies and pictures you've included.

- **Create a new iDVD Project—or burn, baby, burn.** If it all seems close enough to something you can use, click Create Project. iDVD builds a standard iDVD project containing all the elements and choices you've set up in the Magic iDVD window. You're free to edit, rearrange, delete, or otherwise tweak the elements; you've still saved a lot of time.

Or if the preview makes you think that what iDVD has done is just perfect—or good enough—click the Burn button twice. iDVD asks you for a blank DVD. The rest is just a matter of waiting.

DVD Menus, Slideshows, and the Map

C hapter 18 shows you how easy it is to convert a single iMovie project into a genuine DVD. But iDVD is capable of far more. You can use it, for example, to make a DVD that contains *six* of your greatest iMovie masterpieces all on one disc. Or you can create a *slideshow* DVD, which happens to be one of the world's greatest methods for displaying digital photos. (In iDVD '08, you can even incorporate movies *into* a slideshow.) And you'll never know joy like that of designing your own navigational menu system, complete with menus within menus.

This chapter shows you how, by doing a few more things manually, you can gain far more power and freedom.

Adding Movies

When you get right down to it, all iDVD really does is add window dressing—menus, buttons, and so on—to movies, music, and photos created in *other* programs.

Take movies, for example. As Chapter 18 makes clear, you can transfer an iMovie project into iDVD via the Media Browser. But that's just the beginning of the ways you can add movies to your iDVD projects. You can also:

- Use the File→Import command.
- Drag movies into the iDVD window from the desktop.
- Choose movies from the Media Browser.

The following pages take you through these additional methods.

The Import Command

iDVD's File→Import command lets you install video, audio, pictures, and background movies onto whatever menu screen you're editing; see Figure 19-1.

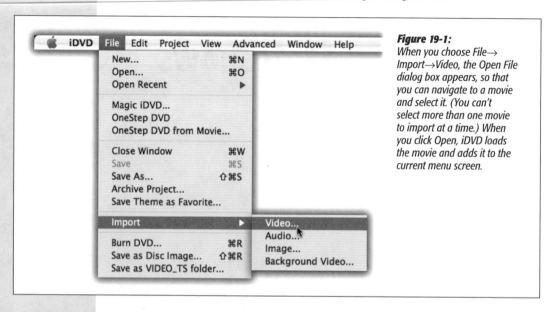

Figure 19-1:
When you choose File→ Import→Video, the Open File dialog box appears, so that you can navigate to a movie and select it. (You can't select more than one movie to import at a time.) When you click Open, iDVD loads the movie and adds it to the current menu screen.

Figure 19-2:
Here's a quick way to install a movie into one of your menu screens: In the Finder, position the window that contains the movie so that you can see it and the iDVD menu screen at the same time. Then just drag the movie onto the displayed menu and drop it there.

The Finder

Another great way to install a movie into an iDVD menu screen is to drag it there, either right off the desktop or from an open folder window. Figure 19-2 tells all.

The Media Browser

Dragging files in from the Finder is great, but it assumes that you know where your movies are. Fortunately, if you're a little fuzzy on where you've stored all your movie files, iDVD can help.

Click the Media button, and then click the Movies button at the top. (See Figure 19-3.)

Tip: The Media Browser shows the movies in your Movies folder. But you can also tell iDVD to list the movies it finds in *other* folders on your Mac. Choose iDVD→Preferences, click the Movies tab, click Add, and then navigate to, and select, the additional folder you want it to monitor for movies. Repeat for additional movie folders.

Figure 19-3:
At the top of the Media Browser, you see all of the movies in all of the logical places on your Mac: your iMovie projects, movie files in your Movies folder, camera movies from iPhoto, and non-commercial videos from iTunes. Expand the flippy triangle of one of these categories to see what's in it. Drag the movie you want into the menu screen to make it part of your DVD-in-waiting.

Submenus ("Folders")

Depending on the theme you've chosen, iDVD may impose a limit of six or 12 buttons on a menu screen. Fortunately, that doesn't mean you're limited to 12 movies

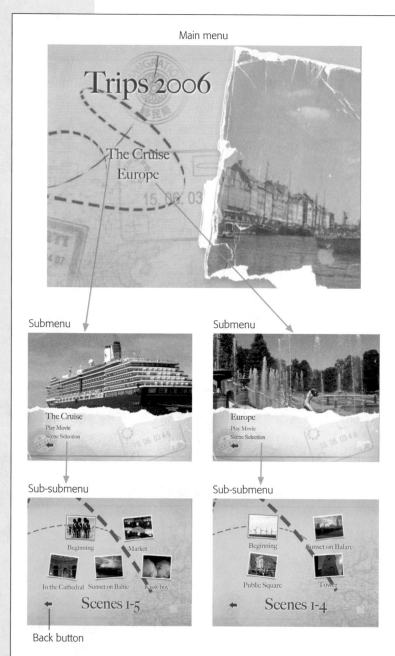

Main menu

Submenu

Submenu

Sub-submenu

Sub-submenu

Back button

Figure 19-4:
An iDVD menu screen can't hold more than six or 12 buttons. If you try to place any more, you'll have to branch off into submenu screens, or even sub-submenu screens.

This DVD has two movies, each of which has chapters within. When your audience clicks a movie's name (with the remote control), they go to a submenu screen with a Play button (to play the whole movie) and a Scene Selection button (to open yet another menu screen, this one showing your chapter markers so that the audience can choose a point to begin playback).

These submenus create extra room for navigation through your project. As your projects grow more complex, you must use folders (submenus) to add enough space to showcase all your pictures and movies.

per DVD. You can accommodate more movies by creating *submenus*—additional menu screens that branch off from the main menu. You can even make *sub*-submenus (Figure 19-4).

You may have seen this effect already, in fact, if you've tried to create an iMovie DVD containing more than a handful of chapter markers.

You can also create this effect manually. Whenever you choose Add Submenu from the + pop-up menu at the lower-left corner of the screen, iDVD adds a submenu button to the current menu screen. In some themes, especially those that began life in previous versions of iDVD, this button looks like an actual folder; in most, it's simply a new text button.

Behind the scenes, though, this button represents a second menu screen, a blank canvas with room for yet another six or twelve buttons.

Navigating Submenus

Navigating iDVD folders while building your project is pretty easy, once you master these tips:

- **Open by double-clicking.** Double-click any folder or submenu button to "open" it—that is, to bring up the menu screen it represents.

- **Return by clicking the arrow.** Each submenu screen contains a Back arrow. Click it to return to the parent menu.

WORKAROUND WORKSHOP

Temporary Buttons

When you try to add more buttons to a menu screen than iDVD can handle, the program gracefully announces that you've added too many buttons.

If you click OK, iDVD eliminates the new button you tried to add. If you click Temporarily Allow—often a more convenient choice—iDVD permits you to add those extra buttons to your menus for now, so that you have the convenience of (for example) cutting and pasting them to other menu screens.

Too Many Buttons
There are too many buttons in the current menu to add a new one.

☐ Do not ask me again

Cancel   Temporarily Allow   OK

The maximum number of buttons per menu is 12. You can temporarily add more than 12 buttons to a menu, but make sure there are only 12 buttons before you burn your project to a disc.

But with great power comes great responsibility. iDVD wants you to understand that you can't actually burn a DVD with too many buttons on a menu screen. If you forget to dispose of the extra buttons before clicking the Burn button, another warning message appears, and your burning efforts come to a grinding halt.

Avoid over-buttoned menus by creating generous and well-thought-out submenus.

• **Names may not match.** A folder/submenu button's label doesn't have to have any relationship to the title that appears on the corresponding screen. You can edit the text individually in both places.

• **Themes don't have to match.** Each menu screen can have its own theme. If you change a screen's theme and want to apply it to the entire project, choose Advanced→Apply Theme to Project. Want to apply a theme to just the submenus below the currently displayed menu? Choose Advanced→Apply Theme to Submenus instead.

• **Mind your minutes.** The more folders and more themes you add to your project, the closer you come to iDVD's video menu limit of 15 minutes.

Reaching that limit isn't such a remote possibility, either; 1-minute video loops on seven menu screens take up nearly all your available space, even if you use the same background video on every menu.

Note: When you try to add a new menu that takes up too much space, you'll see a message that says, "Total menu duration exceeds 15 minutes." Click Cancel to eliminate the new menu you tried to add. Click Ignore to add the menu despite the warning, with the understanding that you'll have to solve the space issue manually before you burn the DVD. Or click Fix to make iDVD shorten the menu's loop so that it fits within the remaining video menu space on your disc.

The DVD Map—and Autoplay

As you can see, menus and submenus can build up with alarming rapidity. At times your projects may grow out of control; pretty soon, you feel like Hansel and Gretel with not enough bread crumbs.

iDVD's Map pretty much eliminates these navigation problems. It's a living, interactive diagram whose icons represent your DVD's menus, videos, and slideshows and reveal how they're connected. As your menu and button layouts grow more complex, you can use the map screen to help you keep track of your menu structure.

To view the map, click the Map button at the bottom of the main iDVD window; it's identified in Figure 19-5. The element you were working on appears with colored highlighting (Figure 19-5).

When you're finished working with the Map, click the Map button again, or click Return.

Tip: Each menu tile includes a flippy triangle. Click it to expand or collapse that limb of the menu tree, for ease in managing complex projects.

Editing in the Map

The Map is interactive; you can actually design and edit your DVD on this single screen. For example:

- Delete a bunch of menu screens or other elements all at once. Select them by Shift-clicking them individually (Shift-click a second time if you select an icon by mistake), and then press the Delete key.

- Similarly, you can quickly apply new themes to the menu screens of your DVD without ever leaving the Map. Select the relevant menu icons, and then click the new theme on the Themes pane.

- You can even add new menu screens and slideshows on the Map screen.

  Start by highlighting a menu screen's icon in the Map. When you choose Project→ Add Submenu or Project→Add Slideshow, you'll see that it now links to a secondary screen.

Figure 19-5:
You can view the map either as a horizontal tree or a vertical one. Use the size slider to adjust the icons' size. Option-drag the background to scroll the whole window diagonally—a much faster method than adjusting the scroll bars individually. Open a menu or slideshow for editing by double-clicking its icon. Watch out for yellow exclamation points, which indicate problems you should fix before burning.

Main menu   Flippy triangle (collapses this tree limb)

Horizontal/Vertical layout   Map button   Size slider

At that point, you can specify *which* movies or *which* photos you want on those new screens by clicking Media, then either Photos or Movies, and then dragging your selections onto the newly created Map tile.

- iDVD lets you apply change characteristics of multiple menu screens simultaneously using the Map. Just Shift-click to choose the menu icons you want, choose View→Show Inspector (⌘-I) to open the Inspector palette, and then make any changes you like. You're affecting all of those menu screens at once.

- Watch out for the yellow triangle exclamation points. When you see one, point to it with your cursor (Figure 19-5). You'll see that iDVD has identified some problem with that menu screen—it contains no buttons at all, for example, or it's got drop zones that you haven't filled.

Autoplay

The Autoplay tile is the key to a *great* iDVD feature: It lets you create DVDs that start playing instantly when inserted into a DVD player. No menus, no remote control—just instant gratification.

Hollywood DVDs use this Autoplay behavior to display video *before* the menu screen appears. You know—a bright red FBI warning, previews of coming attractions, or maybe just a quick snippet of the movie on the DVD.

You can do that, or you can use the Autoplay feature to create a DVD that *never* gets to the menu screen—a DVD consisting *only* of Autoplay material. That is, you insert the DVD, and the whole thing plays automatically.

You could design a project this way for the benefit of, for example, technophobic DVD novices whose pupils dilate merely contemplating using a remote control. Or you could design your DVD that way for use in a kiosk, or just to avoid having to muck around with menu designs.

The key to this feature is the Autoplay tile, the very first one in Map view (at the top or the left, depending on the view you've chosen); see Figure 19-6. Whatever you drag onto it will play automatically when the DVD is inserted, before your viewers even touch their remote controls.

These are the kinds of things you can put on the Autoplay tile:

- **A video clip.** Click the Media button, and then click Movies at the top of the pane. Drag the movie you want directly onto the Autoplay tile to install it there.

- **A still image.** Click the Media button, but this time click Photos at the top. Now iDVD shows your complete iPhoto collection, including all of your albums. To use one of these images as a startup screen for your DVD project, just drag it onto the Autoplay tile. (You can add audio to it, too, just as you'd add audio to a slideshow—by dragging in an audio file from the Audio section of the Media pane.)

Tip: If you tinker with the graphics tools in a program like Photoshop or AppleWorks, you could come up with a decent replica of the standard FBI warning that appears as the Autoplay of a commercial DVD. You could precisely duplicate the wording and typographical look—or you could take the opportunity to do a hilarious spoof of the usual warning.

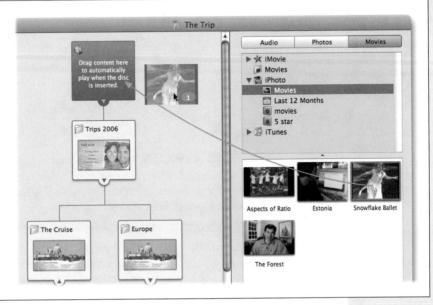

Figure 19-6:
If you decide to add or replace your Autoplay material, just drag new stuff right onto it. Or, to eliminate the Auto-play segment, drag it right off the tile. It disappears in a tiny puff of Mac OS X cartoon smoke.

- **A slideshow.** Once you've got the Photos list open as described above, you can also drag an entire iPhoto album onto the project icon. Alternatively, you can click and ⌘-click just the photos you want, and then drag them en masse onto the Autoplay icon. In fact, you can even drag photos—as a group or in a folder—right out of the Finder and onto this icon.

To control how long your still image remains on the screen, or how quickly your Autoplay slideshow plays, double-click the Autoplay tile. You arrive at the Autoplay slideshow editor, a screen just like the one shown on page 369, where you can adjust the timing, the transitions, and even the audio that plays behind the picture(s).

Note that unless you also turn on looping, described next, the DVD will eventually have to show *something* after playing the Autoplay material. For that reason, it's a good idea to designate a basic main-menu screen anyway—something to appear after the Autoplay cycle is complete.

Looping

If you highlight the button for a movie, slideshow, or Autoplay tile—either in Map view or on a menu screen—and then choose Advanced→Loop Movie (or Loop Slide-show), you unleash another raft of possibilities. You can make a DVD that repeats the highlighted material (a slideshow or movie) over and over again and, in fact, *never* gets back to the menu screen.

Tip: In the Map, a ↺ icon appears in the corner of any element you've set up for looping.

That would be a great way to create a DVD containing a self-running, self-repeating slideshow of digital photos to play on a TV at a party or wedding reception. You could also use it to create a self-looping kiosk display at a trade show.

In any case, the DVD will loop endlessly—or at least until it occurs to someone in your audience to press the Menu or Title button on the remote, which displays your main menu. At this point, the Menu button redisplays the previous menu screen; the Title button causes a return to the main menu.

DVD Slideshows

The DVD may be the world's best delivery mechanism for digital photos. Your friends sit there on the couch. They click the remote control to walk through your photos (or, if you choose, they let the slideshow advance automatically). Instead of passing around a tiny pile of fragile 4 x 6 prints, your audience gets to watch the photos at TV-screen size, looking sensational—accompanied by a musical soundtrack of your choice.

In iDVD '08, in fact, you can incorporate *movies* into your slideshows. Sure, this feature may seem to violate the very definition of a slideshow, but whatever—the ability to mix stills and videos adds a lot to the visual record of your life.

If you've installed movies into an iDVD menu screen, installing photos will seem like a piece of cake. Once again, you can do so using several different methods, each with its own advantages:

- **iPhoto albums.** Click Media, then click Photos. **iDVD** presents your entire iPhoto picture collection, complete with the albums you've used to organize them.

  The great thing about this system is that iPhoto albums contain well-defined image progressions. That is, you presumably dragged the photos into an emotionally satisfying sequence. That's exactly how iDVD presents the pictures—as they appear in the album, from the first image to the last.

- **Folder drag-and-drop.** If the pictures you want to add aren't in iPhoto, you can also drag a folder full of them right off the desktop (or from a Finder folder) and onto an iDVD menu screen. iDVD creates a slideshow from the images, all right, but puts them into an unpredictable sequence.

- **Slideshow Editor.** iDVD features a special window called the Slideshow Editor, in which you can add individual photos to the slideshow and drag them into any order you like. This approach takes a little work, but it gives you the freedom to import images from many different sources without having to organize them beforehand.

Tip: A DVD slideshow (*any* DVD, not just those produced by iDVD) can contain at most 99 slides, and one DVD can contain at most 99 slideshows. The designers of the DVD format obviously recognized that there's a limit to the patience of home slideshow audiences.

iPhoto Albums

You can use either of two approaches to create iDVD slideshows from your iPhoto album collection. One way begins in iPhoto; the other begins in iDVD.

Starting in iPhoto

As part of the much-heralded integration of iPhoto, iTunes, iMovie, and iDVD, iPhoto offers a menu choice that exports albums and slideshows to iDVD. In the iPhoto Source list, click the album or slideshow you want to export, choose Share→Send to iDVD, and then wait as iPhoto transfers the data.

Tip: If you do a lot of this, you can add a Send to iDVD button to your iPhoto toolbar (at the bottom of the window). Just choose View→Show in Toolbar→Send to iDVD.

Now, although the steps are the same for the iPhoto entities called *albums* and *slideshows*, the results in iDVD are different.

- If you export an iPhoto *slideshow* (a set of photos to which you've applied music, panning and zooming effects, specific crossfade styles, and even individual, per-slide timings), iDVD treats the result as a movie. Your audience will see a frozen slideshow when they press the Enter or Play buttons on their remote. They'll see the pictures in the sequence, and with the timings, *you* specified; they'll have no control over the show.

  You can work with this movie as you would any other movie you've imported.

- If you export an *album* (a "folder" full of photos, assembled and arranged by you), iDVD treats the result as a *slideshow*—a collection of pictures that your DVD audience can peruse, one at a time, using the arrow buttons on their remote controls.

  The rest of this discussion applies to these DVD slideshows.

In iDVD, an album slideshow is represented by a like-named submenu button. Double-click it to view the list of pictures inside, change their sequence, and make other adjustments, as described on page 369.

Tip: If, while in iPhoto, you make changes to your album—by adding photos or rearranging them, for example—click iPhoto's iDVD button again. Instead of adding a second copy to your DVD project, iDVD is smart enough to update the existing slideshow. This way, you can update your albums as often as you like without any adverse affects on your iDVD project.

Note, however, that you *don't* enjoy this luxury when you use the Photos pane within iDVD. Dragging an album out of the Photos pane onto a menu a second time gives you a second copy.

Starting in iDVD

If you haven't already been working in iPhoto, there's an even easier way to turn iPhoto albums into living slideshows. Just click the Media button, then the Photos button, and voilà: You're presented with the tiny thumbnails of every digital photo in your collection. You even get to see the list of albums, exactly as they appear in iPhoto (Figure 19-7). From here, you can drag either albums or arbitrary groups of selected thumbnails onto a menu screen to become a slideshow.

Figure 19-7:
To add a new slideshow, drag an album (from the Photos pane)—or even a batch of selected photos—onto your iDVD workspace. You can also select several and drag them en masse. (The usual multiple-selection tricks apply: ⌘-click several albums or photos in turn to select all of them, for example.)

Drag Folders from the Finder

Suppose you don't keep all your pictures in iPhoto. (Hey, it could happen.)

In that case, you may prefer to drag a folder of photos out of the Finder and onto an iDVD menu screen. (Make sure that the folder contains nothing but pictures and movies. If it contains any other kind of document, or even other folders, iDVD may complain that it can't handle the "Unsupported File Type: Unknown Format.")

The folder shows up on the menu screen as a new slideshow button. You're ready to edit your slideshow, as described below.

Add a Slideshow, Worry about the Pictures Later

If all of your photographic masterpieces aren't already together in iPhoto or even in a Finder folder, you can also bring them into iDVD individually.

To do that, start by creating a new slideshow folder: From the + pop-up menu (lower-left corner of iDVD), choose Add Slideshow (or choose Project→Slideshow, or press ⌘-L). iDVD creates a new, empty slideshow. Double-click it to enter the Slideshow Editor described next.

The Slideshow Editor

No matter how you got your slideshow folder button into iDVD, you still edit it the same way: by double-clicking it to open iDVD's Slideshow Editor. See Figure 19-8 for a quick tour.

Figure 19-8:
The iDVD Slideshow Editor lets you build and customize your slideshows. Each slide appears in order, with its number and a thumbnail; you can move them around by dragging, delete the ones you don't want, or add new ones by dragging graphics from the desktop or the Media pane of the Customize drawer. The buttons in the lower-left corner switch between a list view and an icon view (shown here). Click Return to go back to iDVD's menu-editing mode.

Adding or omitting slides and movies

If you want to add new pictures to the slideshow, use the following techniques:

- **Drag from the Finder.** Drag an image, a selection of several images, a folder of images, or some movies directly into the slide list.

- **Click Media, then Photos or Movies.** Drag a picture, a set of several shots, an iPhoto album, or a movie into the slide list.

- **Import an image.** Choose File→Import→Image. Navigate to any picture file, select it, and then click Open.

Tip: Before clicking Open, you can highlight several photos to bring them all in at once. If the ones you want appear consecutively in the list, click the first one, and then Shift-click the last one, to highlight all of them. If not, ⌘-click each photo file that you want to import. Either way, click Open to bring them all into iDVD simultaneously.

To remove a picture or a movie from the list, just click it and then press the Delete key. You can also remove a whole bunch of pictures or movies simultaneously by first Shift-clicking them or ⌘-clicking them, exactly as described in the previous Tip, before pressing Delete.

Reordering slides and movies

To change the sequence of slides and movies, just drag them around. Once again, you can select multiple thumbnails at once (see the preceding Tip) and then drag them en masse.

Renaming slides or movies

Click the name below each thumbnail to open a name-editing box.

Slideshow Settings

iDVD offers some useful options when you click the Settings button at the bottom of the Slideshow Editor window:

- **Loop slideshow.** If you turn on the "Loop slideshow" checkbox, the slideshow repeats endlessly, or until your viewer presses the Menu or Title button on the DVD remote control.

- **Display navigation.** When you check this option, you'll see navigation arrows on the screen as your slideshow plays. Your viewers can click these buttons with their remote controls to move back and forth within your slideshow.

  Navigation gives your viewers a feeling of flexibility and control. On the other hand, they can always use the < and > buttons on their remote controls even if no arrows appear on the screen. (Furthermore, you may consider the majesty of your photography marred by the superimposed triangle buttons.)

- **Add image files to DVD-ROM.** When iDVD creates a slideshow, it scales all of your photos to 640 x 480 pixels.

  That's ideal for a standard television screen, which, in fact, can't display any resolution higher than that.

  But if you intend to distribute your DVD to somebody who's computer savvy, you may want to give them the original, full-resolution photos. They won't see these photos when they insert the disc into a DVD player. But when they insert your DVD into their *computers,* they'll see a folder filled with the original, high-res photos, for purposes like printing, using as Desktop wallpaper, and so on. (In other words, you've created a dual-format disc that's both a DVD-video disc and a DVD-ROM.)

- **Show Titles and Comments.** You can add comments for each image in your slideshow—and then, at your discretion, have them appear onscreen during the slideshow.

When you click Settings, and then turn on "Show titles and comments," you're telling iDVD to display photo names and comments *both* in the Slideshow Editor *and* on the TV screen when the DVD plays.

Now you can click the gray "Add comments" text below each slide title to add your custom text.

Tip: This can be a great feature if you've named your pictures, say, "Martha gives Dad a kiss," but not so great a feature for pictures named "IMG_NK01219", "IMG_NK01222," and so on. If you want to use photo titles and comments, keep them succinct, meaningful, and easy-to-read.

- **Duck audio while playing movies.** In iDVD '08, you can now incorporate movies into your slideshow. You can nestle videos right in among your still photos; they begin playback automatically during the slideshow.

  But what happens if you've added some background music to your slideshow—and it drowns out the talking in the movies? Or, worse, what happens if the video has a music track of its own—and now you've got two clashing soundtracks?

  This option is supposed to make your slideshow music automatically lower its volume whenever a movie plays, to avoid these clashes.

Note: As of iDVD '08 version 7.0.1, this checkbox does nothing. Slideshow background music *always* lowers itself to about 50 percent when a movie plays, whether this option is on or off.

Slideshow Options

Other Slideshow Editor features include:

- **Slide Duration.** Using this pop-up list, you can specify how much time each slide spends on the screen: 1, 3, 5, 10 seconds, Fit to Audio, or Manual. Manual, of course, means that your audience will have to press the Next button on the remote control to change pictures.

  Fit to Audio appears in the pop-up menu only after you've added a song or playlist to your slideshow. In this case, iDVD determines the timing of your slides automatically—by dividing the length of the soundtrack by the number of slides in your show. In other words, if the song is 60 seconds long, and you've got 20 slides in the show, each slide will sit on the screen for 3 seconds.

Tip: Fit to Audio offers a nifty way to create a simple, no-fuss DVD "mix tape" that you can play on your home theater system. Drop a song into the Audio well (see the next page) but add only one photograph, which may be the album art for that song or a graphic showing the song's title. Make a series of "slideshows" this way.

Once you burn the whole thing to a DVD, you can choose a song to start playing in its entirety with the album cover on the screen. (If you add an album-in-a-playlist instead of just one song, you can choose an album to play in the same way.)

- **Transition.** You can specify any of several graceful transition effects—Dissolve, Cube, and so on—to govern how one slide morphs into the next. You can try each of these styles for yourself by selecting one and then watching your slideshow. (Click ▶ to start the show; click it again to return to the editor.) Viewing just a few slides shows you how the transitions work on real images.

The transition you specify here affects all slides in the show; you can't set transitions on a slide-by-slide basis. Note, too, that transitions *add* to the time your slides spend on the screen. If you've chosen 3 seconds for the slide duration, each slide will actually hang around for nearly 5 seconds, when you consider the time it spends morphing.

Slideshow audio

Music has a profound impact on the effect of a photo slideshow. You can't appreciate how dramatic the difference is until you watch the same slideshow with and without music playing.

The easiest way to add music to a slideshow is to click Media, and then click the Audio button at the top of the pane. Conveniently enough, iDVD shows your entire iTunes music collection, complete with any playlists you've assembled, as well as any GarageBand pieces you've made (Figure 19-9).

Figure 19-9:
The Music list includes your iTunes tunes, plus any music you've created using GarageBand. Such songs make great soundtracks, because you've tailored them to the mood and the length of the slideshow. (Your GarageBand pieces show up in iDVD only if you've opened GarageBand's Preferences, clicked the General tab, and turned on "Render an audio preview when saving." Oh, and one more thing: iDVD won't see your GarageBand pieces unless you keep them in your Home→Music→GarageBand folder.)

When you find suitable musical accompaniment, drag its name out of the GarageBand or iTunes list and onto the Audio well (also shown in Figure 19-9). You can even drag an entire playlist into the well; the DVD will play one song after another according to the playlist, so that the music won't die ignominiously in the middle of the slide show.

You can also drag a sound file from any Finder window or the desktop—and directly onto this Audio well.

Tip: When it's empty, the Audio well looks like a small speaker (◀⫶). When it's occupied, its icon identifies the kind of audio file you've installed; the little icon says, for example, AIFF, AU, or MP3. The icon used when you add a playlist rather than a single song varies, usually showing the first audio file type used in the playlist.

To try out a different piece of background music, drag a new song or audio file into the Audio well. And if you decide that you don't want music at all, drag the file icon directly out of the Audio well and onto any other part of the screen. An animated puff of smoke confirms your decision.

Leaving the Slideshow Editor

To return to iDVD's menu editor, click Return at the bottom.

Burning Your Slideshow

Once you've designed a slideshow DVD, previewing it and burning it onto a blank DVD works exactly as described beginning on page 347.

Since most people have never thrilled to the experience of viewing a digital-camera slideshow on their TV sets, a few notes are in order:

- Your viewers can use the remote control's Next and Previous buttons to move forward or backward through the presentation, no matter what timing you originally specified when you designed the show.

- They can also press the ❚❚ button to freeze a certain picture on the screen for greater study (or while they go to the bathroom). Both the slide advancing and music stop until they click the Pause or Play button, again.

- If the audio selection or playlist is shorter than the slideshow, the song starts over again.

- Your viewers can return to the main menu screen by clicking the Menu button on the remote.

- When the slideshow is over, the music stops and the main menu screen reappears.

IMOVIE '08 & IDVD: THE MISSING MANUAL

Designing iDVD Themes

S ome of Apple's iDVD themes offer great backgrounds but weak audio. Others provide terrific sounds but so-so text. Some create a nearly perfect package, while others seem broken beyond repair. Fortunately, in the end it doesn't matter, because iDVD lets you adapt themes to your taste and save them as new *Favorites*.

Favorites let you move beyond built-in themes and presets to create truly customized DVD menu systems. You can change fonts for titles, adjust the length of the looping background video, move buttons around and change their styles, switch the fonts and colors for button and menu titles, move text around the screen, substitute new background art or background patterns, replace or remove the audio loop that plays when the main menu is onscreen, and much more. Let this chapter be your guide.

Tip: One thing you'll notice in this chapter, and in iDVD in general: Learning the ⌘-I keystroke is incredibly useful. That's the shortcut for the View→Show Inspector command. It opens a floating black panel, illustrated often in this chapter, filled with formatting options that are specific to whatever was selected: a button, a text block, or the menu screen itself. (You hide this panel the same way: with another ⌘-I.)

---

iDVD's Built-in Themes

iDVD's built-in themes vary in complexity. Some offer completely realized presentations. Others provide little more than colors and fonts, leaving it up to you to mold them. Either way, the built-in themes, both old and new, provide an excellent jumping-off point for your DVDs.

All five collections—7.0 Themes, 6.0 Themes, 5.0 Themes, Old Themes and Favorites—appear in the Themes pane. As you study the scrolling list, you'll notice that:

• **Favorites appear together.** When you choose Favorites from the pop-up menu at the top of the pane, all Favorites (themes that you've created) appear together in the same list. (This list is empty when you start out using iDVD.) Themes you've bought from other companies (like *www.idvdthemepak.com*) are listed separately in the pop-up menu.

• **You can view several sets at once.** To view just one Theme set, select its name from the Theme Set pop-up menu. To view all themes, choose All instead.

• **The ribbon means Favorite.** A gray prize ribbon appears in the lower-left corner of certain themes. This icon lets you know that the theme is a Favorite—a theme that you created yourself. You'll find out how to create Favorites later in this chapter.

Editing Buttons

When iDVD was first introduced, its flamboyant button thumbnails generated a lot of excitement. Each button could show a small video or photo, offering visual previews of the linked material.

Times have changed. These days, text buttons have quietly replaced the old button designs. In the 6.0 and 7.0 theme collections, *no* main-menu buttons display videos or pictures; all the buttons are simple text labels.

If you choose one of the older themes for that reason, you don't have to be content with the proposed button style. You can move your buttons around, change the labels on them, and so on.

Changing Button Names and Fonts

To change what a certain button is called, click the name once, pause, and then click a second time to open the editing box. As shown in Figure 20-1, you can both retype the name and change the type size and font.

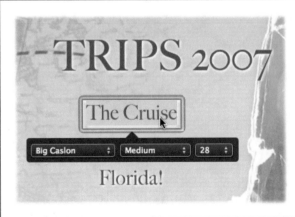

Figure 20-1:
In iDVD '08, little font, size, and style menus appear right beneath any text box or button that you're trying to edit. You can use only one text style per text box, however.

Keep these points in mind when working with iDVD text:

- **Be succinct.** DVD screens are small, so there's not much room for long and involved text.

- **Be contained.** Don't let one text box overlap another.

- **Spell check.** Nothing speaks worse of your attention to detail than a lovingly crafted masterpiece called "For Mouther's Day."

Tip: If your buttons' text labels are crashing into each other, try making the text wrap into a narrow column, so that it's several lines long. Just press Return to start a new line.

Button Styles

When you sit there and hit the arrow buttons on your DVD player's remote, how does a commercial Hollywood DVD indicate which onscreen option you've selected?

Well, that button sprouts some kind of highlighting. It lights up, or changes color, or gets underlined, or sprouts an indicator bullet. All of these options, and more, are now available in iDVD's new Buttons panel (Figure 20-2).

But wait, there's more. Just because a theme comes with text-only buttons doesn't mean you have to be content with that. The Buttons panel lets you turn them into picture or movie-preview buttons.

Here's how to use the Buttons panel:

1. **Select the buttons you want to change.**

   Most of the time, you'll want to choose Edit→Select All Buttons (⌘-A), so that all the buttons on a menu screen will match. But you could, in theory, make different buttons highlight in different ways.

2. **Click Buttons (lower-right corner of the screen).**

   The Buttons panel appears, filled with button design options (Figure 20-2).

3. **Choose a button style from the pop-up menu at the top.**

   The first three (Text, Bullets, Shapes) all create text-only buttons, but they're somewhat inconsistent.

   For example, the options in the **Text** and **Bullets** categories affect only what happens when a button is highlighted by the remote control. That is, the button has *no* special graphic treatment when it's *not* selected; it's just words on the screen. When it's selected with the remote, the affected buttons indicate that they're highlighted either by displaying a fancy underline (Text styles) or a bullet shape next to their names (Bullet styles, shown at lower left in Figure 20-2).

   The **Shapes** panel, on the other hand, adds a colorful background to the chosen buttons even when they're *not* selected (lower right in Figure 20-2). You have no control over the visual presentation of a button when it's *highlighted;* that effect is built into the style. (It's usually a starburst that appears next to the button's name.)

If you choose any of the bottom four commands from the pop-up menu, you turn the buttons into picture- or movie-preview buttons. Figure 20-2 shows you how.

Figure 20-2:
Choose the button or buttons you want to change (top). Click Buttons (lower-right). To turn text buttons into picture or movie buttons, choose Frames, Artistic, Rectangle, or Rounded from the pop-up menu. Click the shape you want; the selected buttons sprout picture or movie previews. (To turn them back into text-only buttons, choose Text, Shapes, or Bullets from the pop-up menu.)

4. **Click the button style you want.**

   You've now changed the text or picture/movie style for the selected buttons, including what graphic they use to indicate that they're selected. But you haven't yet decided what *color* highlighting those selected buttons will have.

5. **Click an empty spot on the menu screen. Choose View→Show Inspector (⌘-I).**

   The floating Menu Info window opens.

6. **Click the Highlight button.**

   Now the Color Picker dialog box opens.

7. **Choose the color you want for the highlighting.**

See page 204 for details on using the Color Picker. The point is that you're changing the color for the underline, bullet graphic, or starburst that appears when the selected button is highlighted.

8. **Click the ▶ button to try out your new buttons.**

iDVD's DVD-player simulation mode appears, complete with virtual remote control.

Justification, Drop Shadows, and Thumbnail Size

iDVD '08 sports a new floating palette that's dedicated exclusively to button editing. To open it, click a button and then choose Show→Inspector (or press ⌘-I.)

As shown in Figure 20-3, this panel looks different depending whether you're editing text-only buttons or picture buttons.

Figure 20-3:
Left: This version of the Button Info panel lets you control the button's name's font, size, color, style, shadow, and alignment within its box.

Right: For picture buttons, you get more controls. They cover the picture's size, looping point (or slideshow "poster frame"), and where its label appears relative to the picture: Right, Left, Above, Below, or Center.

Moving Buttons

Each theme comes with predetermined locations for your buttons. In fact, internally, each theme stores separate layout maps: one that specifies the button positions if you have *three* buttons, another for *four* buttons, and so on.

iDVD lets you move your buttons around just by dragging. In fact, a new iDVD '08 feature makes it easy to align them (Figure 20-4).

Tip: In general, buttons snap into alignment automatically. But if you really, truly want totally free rein to drop buttons anywhere (even though the result might be a little ugly), click the background of the menu, and then choose Show→Inspector (or press ⌘-I). In the Menu Info panel, click "Free positioning."

Removing Buttons

To remove a button from a menu screen, click it once, and then press the Delete key.

Tip: You can also click the first button, and then Shift-click another button, to highlight all of the buttons in between. Or ⌘-click individual buttons to highlight only those.

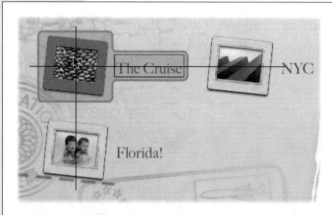

Figure 20-4:
As you drag buttons around, you'll know when you've got them lined up with each other. Horizontal or vertical guidelines appear, as shown here, and you feel a subtle snapping, at the instant when the thing you're dragging is lined up with something else on the screen.

Of course, if you're removing a button in order to move it to a different menu screen, you can use the Cut and Paste commands in the Edit menu.

Editing Picture and Movie Buttons

In some themes—including all of the iDVD 6.0 and 7.0 main-menu screens—the buttons on your menu screen are just bits of text.

But in some of the older themes, and in the chapter screens of some newer ones, buttons are actually tiny pictures or tiny movie clips that preview the movie or slideshow that's in store. And you can turn any text-only buttons *into* picture or movie buttons easily enough, as shown in Figure 20-2.

Here's how you control what appears on these preview buttons.

1. **Click the preview button once, pause, and then click a second time.**

   Don't just *double-click;* you'll actually open another menu screen or movie.

   Some controls appear above the button, as shown in Figure 20-5.

2. **Drag the slider to the spot you want.**

   The slider is a map of your entire movie or slideshow, from start to end. Pinpoint where you want the button's video playback to begin. Or, if it's a slideshow button, you're setting the *poster frame:* the one photo that appears on the button itself.

Then again, if your button links to a movie, it doesn't have to have an animated preview. You can turn on the Still Image checkbox to choose a still poster frame from the movie, something that doesn't actually play.

Tip: The picture on a button doesn't have to be a scene from the movie or slideshow. It can be any graphic you want. Click the button, choose View→Show Inspector, and then drag any graphics file right onto the "Custom thumbnail" image, either from the Finder or the Media panel. You'll see the button change instantly.

Figure 20-5:
Here's where you control where the video loop begins on a button preview. For buttons that link to movies, you get to pick the starting frame. For buttons that link to slideshows, you pick which photo appears on the button.

3. **Click anywhere on the background to deselect the button.**

Turn on the Motion button (⇄) to see the video play in the button.

Editing Text

Although most people focus primarily on iDVD's drop zones, video buttons, and so on, text also plays a critical role. It's a dependable, instantly recognizable part of a DVD menu system.

The text that you can fiddle with falls into two categories (in addition to button labels, of course):

- **Menu titles** help viewers figure out where they are in the DVD menu system by providing clues to the current context: "Our Vacation," "Pictures (Week 1)," and "Scene Selection," for example. Title text usually appears at the top of the screen, although you can put it anywhere you like.

- **Text boxes** can appear anywhere on your screen. You can fill them with whatever explanatory text you think is appropriate: instructions, introductions, a description of the project, and so on.

Tip: In iDVD, as in life, brevity is the soul of captions.

Here is a boatload of techniques to help customize your text. Each method changes the selected text on only the *currently displayed* DVD menu screen.

- **Create a text box.** To add a text block, choose Project→Add Text (⌘-K). Double-click the placeholder text and type away.

- **Select the text box.** Click it once. Colored highlighting appears. Now you can drag the box to move it, press Delete to remove it, Shift-click another text box to highlight both at once, use the Copy command so you can paste them onto another menu screen, and so on.

- **Change the text.** To highlight a piece of text, double-click anywhere inside it. You'll note that iDVD automatically highlights the entire phrase, meaning that you can just begin to type, replacing the entire text blob, without first dragging across it. (Of course, if you want to edit only part of the existing text, drag with the mouse first.) Press Return or Enter when you're finished.

Figure 20-6:
Two ways to format a text block. Top: When you click to edit, you get this miniature pop-up panel of font options.

Bottom: If you hit ⌘-I, you get a more complete formatting panel, which now includes shadow, color, and justification options.

- **Choose a font, size, weight, color, and alignment.** Whenever you're editing the text, you can use the mini-formatting palette to change the typeface (Figure 20-6). For more options, use the Text Info palette (also shown in Figure 20-6).

  You're not allowed to mix and match fonts *within* a text box, but each *text block* (each button label, title, and text box) can have a different look.

- **Add (or remove) a drop shadow.** Use the Shadow checkbox in the Text Info palette to add a faint shadow behind and below the text that creates an easier-to-read, almost 3-D effect.

- **Position the title or text box.** You can drag titles and text boxes anywhere on the screen you like. Be careful not to park one where the *overscanning* effect of older TVs (page 329) might chop off some of your letters. To avoid this problem, choose View→Show TV Safe Area before you drag, taking care to keep the text inside the superimposed guideline rectangle.

Editing Backgrounds

The menu-screen background provides a look and atmosphere that defines the entire screen. As a result, choosing a new background can add a unique twist to an existing theme.

Here's what you can use as a replacement for the Apple-supplied backgrounds.

A Still Photo

Yep, you can replace the one that came with the Apple theme. In some cases, this simple action makes the theme look *completely* different.

Note: iDVD never distorts a photo that you install as a background. If it's not the right shape for your TV screen, you'll wind up with black letterbox bars to fill the gap.

If you really care, you can prepare the photo in a program like Photoshop or Graphic Converter before installing it as a menu graphic. The dimensions for a *standard TV set* should be 720 x 540 pixels; for a *widescreen set*, use 854 x 480. (For the PAL system used in Europe, use 768 x 576 for standard, 1024 x 576 for widescreen.)

To bring this change about, drag the photo from the Media Browser (click Media, then Photos) or the Finder into any of these three spots:

- **Any empty spot on the menu.** Avoid the drop zones.

- **The Menu Info panel.** See Figure 20-7 for details on the Menu Info panel, also known as the Inspector panel.

- **The Drop Zone editor.** You met this handy row of drop-zone wells in Chapter 19, but they harbor a little secret: Another version of the Background well lurks at the left side. See Figure 20-8.

A Group of Photos

You can also drag an album full of photos, or just a handful of random ones, onto any of the Background areas described above. They become a slideshow that plays while the menu is on the screen.

Background well (drag a picture or movie here)

Figure 20-7:
Click a blank spot on the menu, and then press ⌘-I to open the Inspector window for the menu itself. You can now drag a new photo into the Background well shown here.

To make this work, drag the photos into the Drop Zone editor's Background well (Figure 20-8). You can't drag them into an empty spot on the menu, or into the Inspector panel.

A Movie

Now, instead of a photo background, you can also create moving, animated, *video backgrounds,* just like the ones on many commercial Hollywood DVDs.

Here again, Apple wanted to make sure you'd find a way to install a movie background, so it gave you several places to aim for:

- **Any empty spot on the menu.** Avoid the drop zones. Drag a movie's icon directly onto the background—but as your cursor arrives, press the ⌘ key. A shortcut menu sprouts from your cursor, offering two choices: "Add movie" or "Replace background." Can you guess which one to click? (Hint: "Replace background.")

- **The Inspector panel.** See Figure 20-7 again.

- **The Drop Zone editor.** See Figure 20-8 again.

Once you've installed the movie, you can control how *much* of it loops on the menu screen. Click the menu background, press ⌘-I to open the Menu Info panel (shown in Figure 20-7), and then adjust the Loop Duration slider.

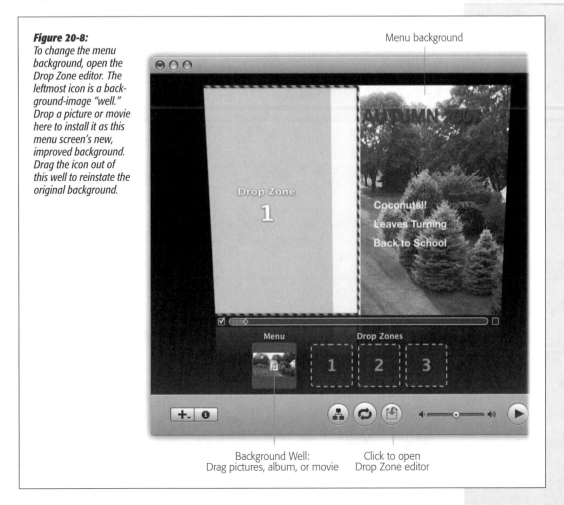

Figure 20-8:
To change the menu background, open the Drop Zone editor. The leftmost icon is a background-image "well." Drop a picture or movie here to install it as this menu screen's new, improved background. Drag the icon out of this well to reinstate the original background.

Menu background

Drop Zone

1

AUTUMN 2007

Coconuts!!
Leaves Turning
Back to School

Menu

Drop Zones

1   2   3

Background Well:
Drag pictures, album, or movie

Click to open
Drop Zone editor

Some Notes

Before you delve into the exciting new career of background replacement, keep these points in mind:

- **Your video will loop.** Your background video file will play, then restart and play again as long as your audience leaves the menu on the TV screen. There's no way to make a video background play just once. Unless you take special care when creating your video, menu looping will create sudden, sharp, sometimes distracting transitions between the end and start of your video.

- **Video tends to move.** If you're not careful, video can hide or overwhelm your titles, buttons, and drop zones. "Audition" your videos and make sure they work with your menus before you burn. In particular, watch for moving objects and scenes that are too bright or too dark.

- **One menu only.** These techniques change only the currently displayed menu screen. To apply the change to *all* menu screens, choose Advanced→Apply Theme To Project.

Note: The total durations for *all* videos on *all* your menus can't exceed 15 minutes. Weird, huh?

Menu Audio

Some of Apple's canned themes come with musical soundtracks, and some don't. If you'd like some music to play during, for example, the Shelves theme, you'll have to install it yourself.

You can also *replace* the music that comes with any of Apple's themes with a song you like better. In the case of musically challenged themes like Anime Pop, this ability is a true blessing, possibly saving lives and sanity.

Installing a menu-screen soundtrack is a heck of a lot like installing a menu-screen background movie.

Designing Video Loops in iMovie

Background videos don't have to jump between the end of one play-through and the beginning of the next. If you're willing to take a little time in iMovie, you can eliminate sudden visual changes that create unpleasant jumps. Consider these techniques:

Fade Out. Create a smooth fade-out at the end of the movie clip, and a smooth fade-in at the beginning, using the Fade Through Black transition style described in Chapter 8.

Use Cross Dissolve. If you prefer, you can design your movie so that the end cross-dissolves into the beginning each time it loops.

Use the Split Clip command in iMovie to break off the final 4:02 (four seconds, two frames) of your movie. Now drag this clip to the front of your movie, and add a 4-second cross

dissolve between this clip and the original start of your movie; finally, export your work.

You can choose a different length for the crossfade; just make sure that the moved ending clip lasts at least two frames longer than the desired transition time. This method works particularly well on stock footage, such as windswept grass, fish in an aquarium, and so forth.

You may discover a couple of drawbacks to this method. First, the start and end audio and video will overlap, and you may not like the results. Second, the background video will, unfortunately, start with the crossfade. There's no way yet to make it start playing from an un-crossfaded spot, unless you do some clever cutting and pasting in iMovie. iDVD 10, perhaps?

What to Drag

You can drag an audio file or QuickTime movie, either from the Finder or from the Music pane in iDVD (click Media in the lower-right, and then Audio at the top). For example, you can drag a song—or even a whole playlist—out of your iTunes list.

Tip: That's not a typo; you can drag QuickTime movies, too. iDVD harvests only the soundtrack and ignores the video.

Where to Drag

Once again, you can drag audio into any of three spots:

- **The existing background.** That is, drag an audio file or movie directly into an empty spot on the menu, as shown in Figure 20-9. (Avoid the drop zones.)

- **The Menu Info panel.** Click an empty spot on the menu screen, and then press ⌘-I to open the Menu Info panel. At center (see Figure 20-7) is an "audio well," where you can drag an audio or movie file in or out.

- **The Drop Zone editor.** See Figure 20-8. You can drag an audio file onto the same spot where you'd drop a background *movie*.

Figure 20-9:
If you've got a decent music collection already in iTunes, adding background music is easy. Keep in mind that some of the most satisfying and appropriate soundtracks of all are the ones that you create yourself, using GarageBand. Any finished compositions that you've exported from GarageBand show up in this iTunes list, too. (In fact, even the soundtracks included with iDVD were made in GarageBand! Apple's a company that eats its own dog food, as the saying goes.)

Incidentally, iDVD doesn't do much to help when your background video and background audio aren't the same length. If the music is too short, it repeats until the video is finished playing, cutting off the music if necessary to start in sync with the video track. If the music is too long, the video repeats until the music ends, cutting off the video mid-repeat. Use the Duration slider in the Menu Info panel (Figure 20-7) to set the loop time, which applies to both sound and video.

Or, if you're really a perfectionist, you could always use GarageBand to match the soundtrack length to the video. Create a nice fade-out at the end of the audio, and a fade-in at the beginning, so that the looping won't be quite so jarring.

Note: Remember, this technique affects the background music of only the currently displayed menu screen. To apply the change to *all* menu screens, wrap up by choosing Advanced→Apply Theme To Project. And make sure you don't exceed your total menu-length budget (15 minutes).

Replacing Menu Audio

To replace a custom audio file with another, repeat the steps you used to install the music to begin with. iDVD replaces the current track with the new one.

Removing Menu Audio

To remove audio, drag it out of the Audio well, either the one in the Menu Info panel or the one in the Drop Zone editor. Puff! When the audio well is empty, it shows a speaker icon (◀)).

If you want to remove *all* audio from your menu screen, you may have to drag twice: Your first drag removes custom sounds, and the second removes the theme sound, if one exists.

Adjusting Menu Audio Volume

You can control your menu screen's audio volume using the slider in the Menu Info panel (Figure 20-7). Don't forget to check your audio before burning; this slider affects the final DVD.

Saving Favorites

After applying all the techniques described so far in this chapter, you may end up creating masterpieces of adapted iDVD themes. Fortunately, iDVD allows you to save and reuse these modified themes after you adjust them to your liking. Here's how to go about it:

1. **Choose File→Save Theme as Favorite.**

   The Save sheet (dialog box) appears at the top of the window.

2. **Type the name for your new theme. Turn on "Shared for all users," if you like.**

   If you're the only person who uses your Mac, never mind. But if you share a Mac with other students, co-workers, or family members, each of whom has a Mac OS

X *account,* the "Shared for all users" option makes your new theme available to other people who use the machine. (Otherwise, your masterpiece appears in the list only when *you* use iDVD.)

When you save a Favorite, you no longer need to keep the original theme on which it was based, as far as iDVD is concerned. Feel free to discard, rename, or move the original theme files from their original locations on your hard drive.

(The box below offers the details.)

3. **Turn off "Replace existing" if you want to create a new entry in the theme list.**

   If you turn *on* "Replace existing," iDVD treats your adapted theme as a replacement for the one you based it on.

4. **Click OK.**

   iDVD saves your theme as a new Favorite. You'll be able to apply it to other DVDs in the future by choosing its name from the Themes pane. (Choose Favorites from the pop-up menu to see its listing.)

POWER USERS' CLINIC

Secrets of the Theme Files

Whenever you save a new Favorite theme, iDVD does a fair amount of administrative work. Behind the scenes, it creates a new theme file on your hard drive. If you decided to share your theme with other account holders, this file appears in the Library→iDVD→Favorites folder. If not, it winds up in your Home→Library→iDVD→Favorites folder. Unlike regular themes, whose names end with the suffix .theme, Favorites use a .favorite file name extension.

Why is this important to know? Because it tells you how to remove a saved Favorite: Just drag the .favorite file out of the secret folder and into the Trash. The next time you open iDVD, that favorite no longer appears in the Themes pane pop-up menu.

It's also worth noting that when you create a Favorite, iDVD copies all relevant materials, including background audio and video, to the newly created theme. (Don't believe it? To view these materials, navigate to the saved .favorite file. Control-click or right-click its icon; from the shortcut menu, choose Show Package Contents. Then open the Contents→Resources folder.)

IMOVIE '08 & IDVD: THE MISSING MANUAL

Advanced iDVD

Although iDVD appears simple, straightforward, and direct, there's more power lurking inside than you might expect. You can see, change, and control things you never knew you could—if you're willing to try new and unusual approaches. Some of these approaches require add-on software programs. Others demand nerves of steel and a willingness to dive into hidden iDVD files.

In this advanced chapter, you'll discover how some of these sideways (and backward and upside-down) methods can expand your iDVD repertoire.

iDVD: The DVD-ROM Maker

iDVD's ability to add data files to the DVD-ROM portion of your disc may be its least-known feature. When it creates a DVD-ROM, iDVD sets aside a portion of your DVD for normal computer files. This area of the disc won't show up on a DVD player—only on a computer.

With iDVD, you can store any variety of data on your DVD. Here are just a few ways you can use this feature to enhance your disc:

- **Store documents that relate to your DVD contents.** The DVD-ROM area provides a perfect place to store copies of documents that concern the material presented in the DVD. This might include the script used to film a movie, the different versions that eventually led to a final event invitation, extended family narratives, copies of email and other correspondence, and so on. Remember: TV sets aren't much good for displaying text, but a DVD-ROM and a computer can come to the rescue.

    Or store the full-resolution versions of the digital photos featured in your DVD slideshow (one of the most common uses for this feature).

• **Store Web pages.** Web pages are perfect additions to the DVD-ROM disc area. Create a Web site that relates to your DVD and add your source files to the disc. When it's distributed, your viewers can open these files with an ordinary Web browser. For example, a DVD with a training video can contain supplementary lessons in HTML (Web page) format.

• **Store email-quality versions of your video.** Use the DVD-ROM area of your disc to store small, compressed versions of your video, or "wallet-size" pictures from a slideshow, suitable for email. Now your audience can share your movie experience with other people.

Adding Files to DVD-ROM

iDVD's DVD-ROM file management couldn't be simpler. Just drag icons out of the Finder and into the DVD-ROM Contents list (Advanced→Edit DVD-ROM Contents), as shown in Figure 21-1.

Drag icons into this window from the Finder

Figure 21-1:
By using the Add Files button or by dragging, you can store documents, folders, programs, and other computer files on a DVD. Anyone who receives a copy of your disc can access these files on a computer. In other words, iDVD can burn DVDs that go beyond the realm of simple video.

Organizing DVD-ROM Contents

The DVD-ROM Contents pane lets you organize your files in several ways:

• **Add folders.** Click New Folder to add a folder to your list.

• **Remove things.** Either drag files or folders right out of the list, or select them and then press the Delete key. (Dragging out of the list gives you the cool puff-of-smoke animation.)

• **Move items into or out of folders.** You can drag icons into one of the little folder icons to file them there—or drag them out again to remove them.

• **Create subfolders.** Drag one folder into another to create subfolders.

• **Rename a folder.** Double-click the name of a folder to select and edit it. Press Return or Enter when you're finished typing.

- **List/hide folder contents.** You can click a folder's flippy triangle to expand it and see what's inside, exactly as in Finder list views.

Uncover Your DVD Project File

Behind the scenes, iDVD stores all the pieces of your project inside the .dvdproj "file" that you created when you first saved your work. However, the .dvdproj file isn't really a file, even though it looks like a single icon on your desktop. It's actually a *package*—a disguised Mac OS X folder—that contains many subfolders and files. To peek inside, follow these steps:

1. **Quit iDVD.**

   Never mess with your project files when iDVD is running.

2. **Control-click (or right-click) the project file. From the shortcut menu, choose Show Package Contents.**

   You've now opened that "file" into a folder window.

3. **Open the Contents→Resources folder.**

   You're in. Here are all the different files that make up your DVD. (See Figure 21-2 for an example.)

Figure 21-2:
Your .dvdproj file stores all the movies, sounds, graphics, and data associated with your iDVD project in a series of hidden subfolders and files. This column-view shot shows the progression of folders within folders.

So what is all this stuff?

- Your **ProjectData** file stores all the settings for your DVD project, in the form of a binary *property list.* It tells iDVD how to put together the menus, sound files, graphics, and other pieces that comprise your DVD.

Tip: If you're an inquiring soul, drag the ProjectData icon onto the icon of a binary XML editor, like Apple's (free) Property List Editor. Turns out ProjectData is just a humble XML file, and—as long as you're careful not to make or save any changes—you can pass an enlightening afternoon studying its contents to discover how it's structured.

- iDVD stores compressed video files—the ones that your audience will actually see on the DVD player—in the **MPEG** folder. If you really want to, you can play one of these files right on your Mac. To do so, copy it to the desktop, add an .m2v suffix to its file name, and watch it using a program that can play MPEG-2 files (like VLC, a free movie player from *www.videolan.org/vlc*).

- If you're using an older theme, one whose buttons are represented as little pictures or videos, then a **Thumbnails** folder stores the tiny QuickTime videos that play on the buttons. Double-click one of them to play it in QuickTime Player right on your Mac.

iDVD doesn't fill the remaining folders until it actually burns the DVD. At that point, iDVD uses these folders to store intermediate files as it works. For example:

- In the **Menu** folder, iDVD stores MPEG-2 (.m2v) files that represent the video loops used on your menu screens, complete with buttons, thumbnails, and so on.

- As you could probably guess, the **Slideshow** folder stores all the digital pictures and movies you've chosen for use in your slideshows, and the **Audio** folder contains all the sound files. (You could double-click one of the sound files to play it in QuickTime Player, if you really wanted to.)

- The **Overlay** folder holds *menu overlays* (videos that animate buttons when your viewers highlight them) and *motion overlays* (animations that play on top of drop zones—the Theater theme curtains or the Brush Strokes paint effect, for example).

AppleScripting iDVD

As any power user can tell you, AppleScript is one of the best features of the Mac operating system. It's a built-in, relatively easy programming language that lets you control your programs by writing little software recipes known as *scripts*—and lets your programs control each other by issuing invisible commands. (Not all programs respond to AppleScript commands, but, happily, iDVD does.)

As it turns out, you don't have to compose your own AppleScript programs to capitalize on iDVD's AppleScript-friendliness. Apple has created a series of useful scripts that you can download and install right now, for free, and use without having to type up a single line of code.

You'll find them on Apple's iDVD scripting page. Visit *www.apple.com/applescript/idvd* to read about them and download them.

Tip: Once you've downloaded these AppleScripts, you'll want to drag them into your Home→Library→Scripts folder, so you can trigger them by choosing their names from the Script menu. (If there isn't already a tiny black scroll icon on your menu bar—the Script menu—here's how to put it there. In Mac OS X 10.3, open your Applications→AppleScript folder and double-click Install Script Menu. In Mac OS X 10.4, use the AppleScript Utility program to add the menulet instead.)

In any case, choosing an AppleScript's name from this menu is a very convenient and quick way to run it.

In the following list, only the items identified as droplets or applications don't belong in your Script menu.

Here are some of the canned AppleScripts for iDVD:

- **iDVD Companion.** This is an actual application (not a script) that endows iDVD with the floating palette shown in Figure 21-3. This palette offers a number of useful controls that aren't available in iDVD alone, like one that snaps your menu buttons back into horizontal or vertical alignment (buttons that you've dragged freely, for example).

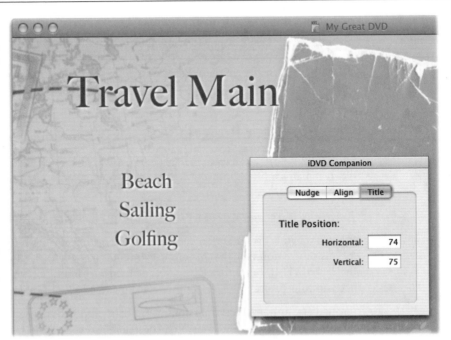

Figure 21-3:
iDVD Companion, a free program from Apple, isn't actually an AppleScript, but it uses AppleScript to add new features to iDVD—like the ability to align buttons that you've dragged by hand, or to specify the exact position of a text box on the screen.

iDVD Companion also offers a menu of all your menu screens, so that you can jump directly to any portion of your menu system; a list that lets you jump to any slideshow in a certain DVD project; a quick menu command that lets you turn the automatic button grid on or off; and more.

- **Create DVD From Folder.** This script is a *droplet*—a little application icon that does its work when you drag and drop something onto it. In this case, when you drag a folder of files onto this droplet, it opens iDVD and creates a new project automatically, based on the folder's contents and hierarchy. Complete instructions and examples come with the download.

- **Photoshop to iDVD.** This script automatically converts whatever document is currently open in Photoshop into a background image for the current menu screen in iDVD. It can be a real timesaver if you like to create your own DVD backgrounds.

- **iTunes to iDVD.** You know from Chapter 20 how to turn an iTunes song into the background music for a menu screen. But if you're already *in* iTunes, you can use this script to turn a selected track into the audio background for the current menu.

- **Sequential Movie.** This droplet creates a series of iDVD menu screens that guide your audience through a sequence of movies. It results in a well-structured and well-ordered movie sequence that's ideal for how-to projects (letting your viewers follow the steps in order), video treasure hunts (keeping your viewers from skipping ahead to clues before they're ready), educational videos (increasing the complexity of your instruction gradually as the lessons proceed), and so on.

Note: These scripts are getting pretty old. They still work, but they haven't been updated in ages. Some, like the iTunes to DVD script, aren't even useful anymore. (iDVD has its own window into your iTunes collection.)

Archiving Your Project

Ordinarily, iDVD doesn't store any videos, photos, or sounds in your iDVD project file. It remains a tiny, compact file that stores only *pointers* to those files elsewhere on your hard drive.

That's why, if you delete or move one of those media files, iDVD mildly freaks out.

In early versions of iDVD, you couldn't transfer a project from one Mac to another for this very reason. And that meant that you couldn't *design* a DVD on one Mac (one that lacked a DVD burner, for example), and then *burn* it on another. You also couldn't back up your project file, content that you'd included all of its pieces.

Fortunately, in more recent versions, Apple came up with a solution. The Archive Project command lets you completely "de-reference" your project, so the project file *contains* every file that you've incorporated into your project: movies, photos, sounds, theme components, and DVD-ROM files. Your project file is now completely self-contained, ready for backup or transfer to another computer.

It's also now really, really huge.

Follow these steps to produce your archive:

1. **Save your project.**

   If you forget this step, iDVD reminds you.

2. **Choose File→Archive Project.**

   The Save As panel shown in Figure 21-4 appears.

Figure 21-4:
The Archive Project's Save As panel lets you specify whether you want to include themes and encoded files in your archived project. You can save quite a bit of disk space by leaving these options unchecked. The Size indicator to the right of "Include themes" tells you how much space your project will occupy.

3. **Turn checkboxes on or off, if you like.**

   "Include themes" copies your theme files into the project—something that's unnecessary if you're using standard Apple themes. This checkbox is important only if the themes you've used come from other companies, were designed by you, or are modified versions of Apple's originals.

   "Include encoded files" is the more important option, because it's very unlikely that all of your sounds, photos, and movies are also on the destination Mac.

   Turn the boxes on and off to see how much space you'll recover.

4. **Name the archive file, choose a folder location for it, and then click Save.**

   Wait as iDVD builds the new archive. This can take a few minutes, so be patient. You may be working with *very* large files.

Archived projects look like any other projects, in that they use the same .dvdproj extension. But inside, they're very different. For proof, simply open it as a package (Control-click its icon; from the shortcut menu, choose View Package Contents). Inside its Contents→Resources folder, new folders called Assets and Themes store the extra archived elements (Figure 21-5).

Tip: In order to turn your photos and videos into DVD material, iDVD must *encode* (convert) them into a format called MPEG. Depending on your Preferences settings, iDVD may constantly be working on this time-consuming task, or it may do the job only when you burn the DVD.

Either way, an archived project also stores any MPEG files iDVD has created so far. They'll save you time when you burn the DVD, but they'll make the archive's file size balloon up like a blimp.

If you'd rather keep the file smaller, choose Advanced→Delete Encoded Assets before saving the archive. iDVD removes the encoded MPEG files—but you'll pay for this gesture in re-encoding time when you're ready to burn your discs.

Figure 21-5:
When archiving a project, iDVD creates additional folders within the new project bundle. The Assets folder stores original copies of your audio and video files (in the "av" subfolder), DVD-ROM content (in "data") and images (in "stills"). If you've chosen to save themes, they show up in the Themes folder.

Copying the Archive to a Different Mac

Suppose that you've designed a DVD using a Mac that lacks a DVD burner. Now, as Apple intended, you've used the Archive command to prepare it for transfer to a Mac that *does* have a burner.

Transfer the archive project using any convenient method: copy it across a network, transfer it using iChat, copy it onto an iPod, or whatever. (It's too big for email, of course, but you could instead post it on a Web site for downloading.)

The project opens normally on the other machine, with all of its pieces intact, ready to touch up and burn.

Disk Images

Thanks to a handy iDVD feature, you can save your project as a computer file called a *disk image*.

You may have run into the disk-image (.dmg or .img) format before; it's a popular storage format for software you download. It's so popular because you get a single, self-contained file that *contains* many other files, arrayed inside exactly as though they're on a disk. When you open a disk-image file, in fact, it turns into a little hard-disk icon on your desktop, with all of its contents tucked inside.

Note: Don't confuse a disk image with a project archive; they're two very different beasts. A disk image is a virtual disk, a bit-for-bit copy of the data that would appear on an actual, physical DVD—it just happens to be stored on a hard drive rather than a DVD.

Project archives, in contrast, contain all the source project material used by iDVD. The only thing that can read or "play back" a project archive is iDVD itself.

To turn an iDVD project into a disk image, save it. Then, choose File→Save as Disc Image (Shift-⌘-R). Choose a file name (for example, *Summer Fun.img*) and a location, and then click Save. Now wait as iDVD compresses your movie data and saves it to disk. All of this takes just as long as an actual DVD burning, so now's your chance to catch up on some magazine reading.

When it's all over, you'll find a new .img icon—a disk image—on your desktop.

Disk images are amazingly high-octane, cool stuff for two reasons:

- **You don't have to burn a disc to watch your movies.** Mac OS X's DVD Player program can play back a disk image just as though it's a real DVD. You see all the menus, slideshows, and other iDVD features you've grown to love.

  As shown in Figure 21-6, the trick is to open the Video_TS folder. Never heard of it? Well, it's an important folder on *every DVD ever made*—it's where all the video files reside—and there's one on your disk image, too.

Tip: This is a handy way to test a DVD before you use up a perfectly good blank. The tip doesn't work for dual-layer DVDs, though, because disk images don't indicate where the "break" is between dual layers.

- **You can burn a new copy whenever you want, without waiting.** You can use Roxio Toast (a beloved commercial burning program) or Mac OS X's own Disk Utility program to burn the disk image onto a real DVD—without having to wait for the excruciating multihour encoding process again. Figure 21-7 provides the amazingly simple instructions for this long-sought solution.

Professional Duplicating

Maybe you've organized a school play, and you want to sell copies of the performance to parents as a fundraiser. Maybe you want to send out "new baby" videos to your family circle. Or maybe you've used iDVD to create a video brochure of your small business's products and services.

In each of these cases, burning the DVDs one at a time on your own Mac looks like a time-consuming, expensive hassle. Furthermore, home-burned DVDs involve a laser recording a pattern on an organic dye, which deteriorates over time. On commercial DVDs, the signal is stamped directly into the plastic.

Accordingly, when you want to make more than a handful of copies of your DVD, you might want to consider enlisting the aid of *a DVD service bureau.* (DVD service bureaus are middlemen between you and the large replication plants, which don't deal directly with the public.)

Figure 21-6:
Apple's DVD Player utility (in your Applications folder) can play back disk images as well as physical DVDs. In the Finder, double-click the disk image to make the virtual DVD appear on your desktop. In DVD Player, choose File→Open DVD Media, as shown at top. In the dialog box that appears, choose the Video_TS folder you want to play. Navigate into the disk image, choose the Video_TS folder, and click Choose. Press the Space bar to start playback.

Technically, these companies offer two different services:

- **Duplication.** Duplicated discs are copies of your original DVD. Service bureaus use banks of DVD burners, five or 10 at a time, that churn out copy after copy on DVD-Rs (the same kinds of blanks as you used).

  You pay for materials and labor, usually by the hour. (Discs with less data burn more quickly, producing more discs per hour.) This is the way to go if you need fewer than 100 copies of your disc. (On the other hand, remember that some DVD players don't play DVD-R discs.)

- **Replication.** Replication is designed for huge numbers of copies, 200 and up. In this process, the company actually presses the DVDs just the way Hollywood movie studios do it—and the results play back in virtually every DVD player.

Replicated discs are produced in factories. When replicated, the data from your master DVD-R is placed on a pressed 4.7 GB "DVD-5" disc—a standard DVD, not a DVD-R.

You can also replicate to dual-layer discs. Just ask your salesman for details.

Expect to pay about a dollar per disc for a run of 1,000 discs. Smaller runs will cost more per disc, larger runs less, but $1,000 is about the least you'll pay for a replication job.

Note: DVD service bureaus often call themselves *replicators,* even though they offer both duplication and replication.

Figure 21-7:
Double-click your disk image in the Finder to make its virtual disk appear. Then open Disk Utility (in your Application→ Utilities folder), click the virtual disk, and choose Images→Burn. Disk Utility prompts you to insert a blank DVD. Do so, and then click Burn.

Prepare to Copy

All DVD service bureaus accept DVD-R masters, of the sort that iDVD burns. Nevertheless, keep these tips in mind:

- **Submit two.** Always submit two copies of your master. It costs you almost nothing in materials and time, and can save your project if one of the discs fails.

- **Use name brands.** Burn your masters on the best-quality discs available. Brand-name blanks, like Verbatim, Maxell or TDK, are less likely to lead to duplication problems. (One replicator complains that if you hold those cheapie 30-cent discs up to the light, you can see light pass right through them!)

- **Use DVD-Rs.** Despite the format wars in DVD standards (DVD-R vs. DVD+R), the -R standard is better for replication. Many factories, in fact, don't accept +R discs, which leads to manufacturing problems.

- **You don't need a DVD burner.** If your Mac doesn't have a DVD burner, most service bureaus can create the DVDs from a disk image (which you can create directly from iDVD). You'll pay a little extra for the conversion.

- **Collect your copyright documentation.** Every replicator will ask you to sign a copyright release stating that you have permission to use the material on your disc. (If you're not asked about this, run away screaming. It's a red flag that you're dealing with an unsavory replicator.)

As a rule, anything you've videotaped is yours. You own it. If you use music from a friend, then a simple signed and dated letter will do: "Casey is my friend and has the right to use my music." If you're using royalty-free material, make a note of it.

And if you're using music you bought from the iTunes music store (or ripped from a commercial music CD), well, you may be on thin ice.

Choosing a Replicator

When choosing a service bureau or reseller, start by getting references—preferably on *recent* projects. Do your legwork and make the calls. You can also check with the Better Business Bureau to see if a service bureau has a history of customer complaints.

Tip: Choose a licensed replicator. Replicators and manufacturers must pay a small royalty on every DVD they produce, because DVDs are copyrighted technology. Some factories, even in the U.S., operate with questionable practices—some pay all their fees, some pay part of their fees, some don't pay fees at all. Reputable service bureaus don't work with gray-market replicators.

Take cost into account when picking a service bureau, but keep in mind that you often get what you pay for. It may be worth paying extra to find a technically savvy reseller that will ask the right questions, hold your hand as needed, and make sure that your project turns out right.

Working with Replicators

When submitting a work order, be *very* specific. Unless you specify Amray cases (the Blockbuster-style cases, with a little plastic hub that holds the center of the DVD) and cigarette-stripped shrink wrap (standard clear plastic wrapping, so named because you pull a strip to open it, just as on a pack of cigarettes), you may end up with DVDs shoved into CD jewel cases. Sit down with your salesperson and go through all the options, from packaging to turnaround time.

Complex packaging takes more time and costs more. Consider ordering your discs in bulk paper sleeves or "slimline" cases (the most basic DVD delivery cases), without printing on them, to save on costs and time. To save even more money, you may be able to set up a deal where you pay to replicate 1,000 discs but package only 200 of them.

Fulfillment

If you're interested in *selling* your DVD masterpieces, you may want to hire yet another company to package, mail, and collect payment for them. *Fulfillment* companies, many run by DVD service bureaus, build a basic Web site, take orders, and mail out your discs. All you have to do is provide your iDVD masters, sign the contracts, pay the setup bills—and start working on your Oscar acceptance speech.

UP TO SPEED

Making DVDs Last

Your homemade DVDs (which are "burned" using dyes) probably won't last the 100 years expected of commercial DVDs (which are etched with lasers). But don't get too depressed by the occasional article about homemade DVDs "going bad" in a matter of months. Most cases of "DVD rot" come down to one of two things: problems created during manufacturing or poor handling by their owners.

There's not much you can do about manufacturing errors, apart from buying name-brand blank DVDs.

As for handling, these tips should ensure that your recordable DVDs will last for years:

Store your discs in a cool, dry place. DVD-Rs are sensitive to both temperature and humidity. In an ideal world, DVDs would love to live in a cupboard that's 68 degrees Fahrenheit with 30 to 50 percent humidity. In the real world, room temperature is fine as long as temperature swings aren't a fact of life. Recordable DVDs hate large changes in humidity, too.

Keep your discs out of the light. Prolonged exposure to ultraviolet light degrades the organic dyes in the recordable layer, possibly making the data on your discs unreadable. Regular light may also hurt your discs, primarily through heat.

Don't flex your discs. With their laminated polycarbonate layers, recordable DVDs are very sensitive to bending or flexing. In fact, the quickest way to destroy your disc is to bend it.

So don't. Store your discs in soft envelopes or in cases where you pinch a center hub to release the DVD. Don't store them in CD jewel boxes that have a snap-on hub.

Hold discs by the edges. Fingerprints, scratches, and dust on the disc surface interfere with a laser's ability to read data. DVDs are much more sensitive than CDs in this regard, because the data is crammed together so much more tightly.

Don't stick on labels. Adhesive labels throw off the disc's balance—and might even ruin your drive when the heat makes the glue melt. Instead, use a CD-safe marker to write on your DVD-Rs.

Part Five:
Appendixes

5

iMovie '08, Menu by Menu

As you've certainly noticed by now, iMovie doesn't look like a standard Mac program. Part of its radical charm is that almost all of its functions are represented visually onscreen. There simply aren't many menu commands. But don't get complacent: You'll miss some great features if you don't venture much to the top of the screen.

Now, documenting the iMovie menu commands is tricky, because they're constantly changing. The command that says **Select All Events** one minute might say **Select All** another, and **Select Entire Clip** a minute after that. The wording is always driving at the same gist—delete things, select things, and so on—but changes according to the situation.

Here's a rundown of the commands in iMovie's menus:

iMovie Menu

In Mac OS X, the first menu after the a menu is named for the program you're using—in this case, iMovie.

About iMovie

This command opens the "About" box containing the requisite Apple legal information. There's really only one good reason to open the About iMovie window: It's the easiest way to find out exactly which version of iMovie you have.

Preferences

Opens the Preferences window (Figure A-1). (*Keyboard shortcut:* ⌘-comma.) Here's a tour.

- **Display Timecodes.** Ordinarily, iMovie shows you the lengths of clips and selections using seconds—for example, "8.5s," meaning 8.5 seconds.

  Experienced video editors, however, are used to looking at timecode displays, which take the form of minutes:seconds:frames—for example, "02:08:15." If you turn this checkbox on, then iMovie adds the frames to all time readouts. Instead of "8.5s," you'll see "8:15." (There are 30 frames per second in North American video.)

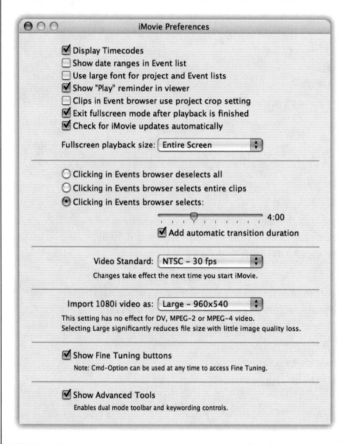

Figure A-1:
You can get to this box quickly by pressing ⌘-comma, which isn't so hard to learn considering it's also the keystroke that opens the Preferences box in iPhoto, iTunes, GarageBand, and most other Apple and Microsoft programs.

What isn't typical, though, is the way Apple has split apart two sets of preferences. In this box, you'll find options that govern the entire iMovie program. In the Project Preferences box, there are options that you set independently for each movie editing project.

- **Show date ranges in Event list.** If you turn this option on, then each Event in your Event list sprouts, in tiny lettering, a legend like "Oct 25, 2007 – Nov 1, 2007," to let you know the time period covered by the video inside.

- **Use large font for project and Event lists.** You guessed it: This option enlarges the type size in these two lists.

- **Show "Play" reminder in viewer.** From the day you first tried iMovie, you might have noticed the message that appears in the Viewer window whenever you're pointing to a filmstrip: "Press the space bar or double-click to Play." Apple wanted to make really, really sure that you knew how to play your video.

Once you've got that technique under your belt, though, you might feel that this message is unnecessary. You can turn it off with this checkbox.

- **Clips in Event browser use project crop setting.** You can read about the aspect-ratio problem on page 109. And you can read about how you want your project to *handle* the aspect-ratio problem on page 111.

  But the choice you make for handling mis-fitting footage in your *project* doesn't do anything in the *Event browser.* That is, setting up letterbox bars for the project itself doesn't create letterbox bars as you peruse your source clips in the Event browser—unless you turn on this option. Then the Event browser displays your clips with the same Crop or Fit setting you've selected for the project.

- **Exit fullscreen mode after playback is finished.** Pretty much what it says. If this option is turned on, then every time you finish playing back a movie in full-screen mode, you return to iMovie. If it's off, then you stay in full-screen mode for more playback experimentation.

- **Check for iMovie updates automatically.** If this option is turned on, then iMovie sends out an electronic feeler each time it's open and you're online, checking to see if a new update is available. If so, you're invited to download and install it.

- **Fullscreen playback size.** See page 136 for details on this option.

- **Clicking in Event browser...** These three options let you control what happens when you click a filmstrip in the Event browser. On a freshly installed copy of iMovie, you get a 4-second selection. But you can also opt to have one click select the entire clip, or to deselect everything (because you prefer to drag to make selections, not click).

- **Add automatic transition duration.** Suppose you prefer the factory setting, "Clicking in Event browser selects" 4 seconds—or whatever you've specified using the slider. The question here is: If you've told iMovie to add transition crossfades between clips automatically (page 166), do you want the durations of those transitions included in the slider's calculations? If so, turn this box on.

- **Import 1080i video as: Large/Full.** Page 89 offers a full description of this option, which pertains solely to video you import from high-definition camcorders.

- **Show Fine Tuning buttons.** The "buttons" referred to here are shown in Figure 6-12 (page 143). They appear when you point to a filmstrip without clicking. And when you click one of these little buttons, you get the orange vertical clip-cropping handles that let you lengthen or shorten a clip by up to 1 second.

  If the appearance of that little button confuses you or clutters your life, you can hide it by turning off this button. Even then, you can still make those orange clip-cropping handles appear when you want them—just by pressing the Option and ⌘ keys.

• **Show Advanced Tools.** This may not be Apple's finest interface-design moment, but whatever: When you turn on this option, a motley assortment of additional features shows up in random iMovie places. On the central toolbar, the Keyword button appears. "Paint to select" editing becomes available (page 134). So does "Paint to reject" or "Paint to mark as Favorite" editing (page 146). And in the Video Adjustments panel, individual sliders appear for Red, Green, and Blue color intensity (page 182).

Shop for iMovie Products

This isn't so much a command as it is a marketing ploy. It opens your Web browser to a page on Apple's Web site that offers to sell you camcorders, plug-ins, blank DVDs, and other accessories.

Provide iMovie Feedback

This command takes you to a Web form on Apple's site where you can register complaints, make suggestions, or gush enthusiastically about iMovie. (Don't expect a return call from Steve Jobs, however.)

Register iMovie

This is a link to yet another Apple Web page. Registering iMovie simply means giving Apple your contact information so you can access Apple's online support documents, receive upgrade notices, get special offers, and so on. There's no penalty for not registering, by the way. Apple just wants to know more about who you are, so that it can offer you exciting new waves of junk mail.

Check For Updates

If iMovie isn't set to check for Apple patches and bug-fix updates automatically, you can make it check manually on your command, using this option.

Services

This submenu lists the standard Mac OS X Services (see *Mac OS X: The Missing Manual*), like Summarize and Reveal in Finder. None of them work in iMovie.

Hide iMovie, Hide Others, Show All

These aren't iMovie's commands—they're Mac OS X's.

In any case, they determine which of the various programs running on your Mac are visible onscreen at any given moment. The Hide Others command is probably the most popular of these three. It zaps away the windows of all other programs—including the Finder—so that the iMovie window is the only one you see.

Tip: If you know this golden Mac OS X trick, you may never need to use the Hide Others command: To switch into iMovie from another program, hold down the Option and ⌘ keys when clicking the iMovie icon in the Dock. Doing so simultaneously brings iMovie to the front and hides all other programs you have running, producing an uncluttered, distraction-free view of iMovie.

Quit iMovie

This command (*keyboard shortcut:* ⌘-Q) closes iMovie after offering you the chance to save any changes you've made to your project file. The next time you open iMovie by double-clicking its icon, the program reopens whatever project document you were working on.

File Menu

As in any Mac program, the File menu serves as the program's interface to the rest of the Macintosh world. It lets you import movies and video, manage Events, create or duplicate projects, or quit the program.

New Project

Creates a new project in the Projects list, ready for filling with video snippets from the Event browser.

New Folder

Creates a simulated file folder in the Projects list, into which you can drag individual projects. It's a tool for managing long project lists as your editing skills grow.

Duplicate Project

Creates a duplicate of the project you're working on. This is a great trick for generating alternate versions—a shorter edit, a raunchier one, and so on.

The great thing about creating and duplicating projects, of course, is that you're not using up any more hard drive space. A project is, behind the scenes, just a tiny text file; it doesn't store any video. The instructions in that text file just refer to the video that's actually store in your Events.

Project Properties

This command opens the all-important Project Properties dialog box (Figure A-2), which is a lot like Preferences except that the settings you make here apply only to one project—the one you're working on.

Here you'll find these controls:

- **Aspect Ratio.** This pop-up menu specifies the movie-frame proportions of your project, as described on page 111.

- **Transitions.** Here, you control whether or not iMovie puts in transition effects automatically between all clips in your project—and if so, which transition, and how long you want it to last. Details are on page 166.

- **Title Fade Duration.** This slider controls how long the text of your titles takes to fade in and fade out during their appearances in your movie.

- **Photo Duration.** When you first drag a photo into your storyboard, it turns into a "still video" clip. This slider lets you specify how long those clips play when first placed into the storyboard. (You can always adjust their timing later, of course.)

- **Applies to all transitions.** If you opt for this choice, the duration slider affects all photos, those already placed and those you have yet to place. (It means that you'll lose all custom duration adjustments you've already made to photos in the project.)

- **Applies when added to project.** This one means "Leave the durations of the photos I've already adjusted alone. But make all incoming photos this long."

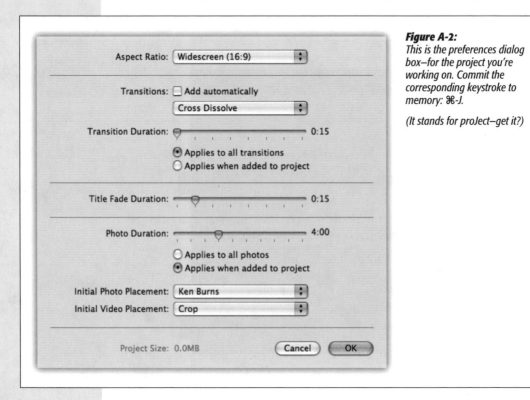

Figure A-2:
This is the preferences dialog box—for the project you're working on. Commit the corresponding keystroke to memory: ⌘-J.

(It stands for proJect—get it?)

- **Initial Photo Placement.** This pop-up menu tells iMovie how to handle photos that don't exactly fit the aspect ratio of your movie project. It can either Crop them (enlarge to fill the frame), Fit in Frame (add letterbox bars), or Ken Burns (perform a slow zoom and pan).

- **Initial Video Placement.** Similarly, this pop-up menu controls what happens when you add mis-fitting video to a project. iMovie can either enlarge it to fit the frame (Crop) or add letterbox bars (Fit in Frame).

Move to Trash

To delete most things in iMovie, like transitions, titles, or sound clips, you just click the item and then press the Delete key.

Things that represent more effort, however, like projects, Events, and imported video, require more effort to delete—and those steps always begin with this command, whose wording changes to reflect whatever is highlighted (for example, "Move Event to Trash" or "Move Rejected Clip to Trash").

They wind up in the Macintosh Trash, as described on page 109, so that you can recover them if you change your mind.

Merge Events

iMovie generally splits imported video into Events—shots that were filmed on the same day. You may sometimes find it useful, however, to combine several Events into a single Event, like the three days' worth of video from a single weekend getaway.

To use this command, first highlight the Events that you want to merge. (Click one, and then ⌘-click each additional one.) Then choose this command. You'll be asked what you want to name the new, combined Event.

Split Event Before Selected Clip

Conversely, you may sometimes want to split an Event in two. That's the purpose of this command. Highlight a filmstrip within the Event, and then choose this command; iMovie creates a second Event containing the selected filmstrip and everything that followed it. If the first event was called Vacation, the second one is called Vacation 1.

Move Rejected Clips to Trash

You can read about this command on page 153. It moves all footage that you've marked as rejects into the Trash, for permanent removal from your hard drive.

Space Saver

This command is another way to reclaim a lot of disk space. It rounds up all your unwanted or unused video and purges it from your hard drive; details are on page 155.

Import from Camera, Import iMovie HD Project, Import Movies

Every video-editing project begins with one of these three commands, which bring in the raw materials for your project from either a camcorder, an older iMovie version, or a movie file on the hard drive. Chapter 4 describes all three methods in great detail.

Page Setup, Print Project

It might seem peculiar to find a Print command in a video editing program. But there are times when the Print command might be helpful:

- You're working on a long project that doesn't fit into the iMovie window. By making a printout, you can see the big picture.

- You might want to share a visual representation of your project, identifying particular transitions, clips, or titles for someone who isn't sitting there in front of your screen with you.

- Your Event browser is overflowing with clips, and you're sorting through them, trying to decide which to trim or delete.

In all of these cases, you can print your events or projects for a handy reference.

Tip: Use the Print Preview button to get an accurate view of your output before you commit it to ink and paper.

Note, however, that:

- The Print command prints whatever project or Event(s) you have selected, so be sure to select the proper ones in the left-side list before you begin. (Remember, you can select more than one project or Event by ⌘-clicking them.)

- The Print command respects the magnification levels you're using to view your clips. That is, the half-second zoom means a lot of frames on your printed page; the 30-second zoom means very few.

- iMovie attempts to fit everything on a single page. If it can't, it reduces the thumbnail sizes of the entire printout as much as necessary, all in an effort to fit the number of "preferred" pages you've specified (Figure A-3).

Figure A-3:
If you choose iMovie from the third pop-up menu, you discover that two handy options have been lurking. "Preferred number of pages" determines iMovie's target maximum for the printout, although if your project is too long to fit this number of pages even with tiny thumbnails, additional pages will come out.

- When you print Events, you get a divider on the printout that identifies each Event.

Edit Menu

The Edit menu contains all of the editing commands described in Chapters 5 and 6. In fact, along with the various drag-and-drop editing techniques described in this book, the commands in the Edit menu are the only tools you need to build your movies.

Undo

In iMovie, you can take back not only the last editing maneuver, not only the last 10, but an infinite number of steps, all the way back to the last time you opened iMovie. The ability to change your mind, or to recover from a particularly bad editing decision, is a considerable blessing.

The wording of this command changes to show you which editing step it's about to reverse. It might say Undo Merge Events, Undo Split, and so on. *Keyboard shortcut:* ⌘-Z.

Redo

We're only human, so it's entirely possible that sometimes you might want to undo your Undo.

For example, suppose that you've just used the Undo command a few times, retracing your steps back to a time when your movie was in better shape, and then decide that you've gone one step too far. That's when the Redo command is useful; it tells iMovie to undo your last Undo, so that you can step forward in time, redoing the steps that you just undid. (If you haven't yet used the Undo command, then Redo is dimmed.) *Keyboard shortcut:* Shift-⌘-Z.

Cut, Copy, Paste

You can use the Cut, Copy, and Paste commands just as you would in any other program: to move stuff around. You can cut, copy, and paste whatever you've selected: entire filmstrips or just chunks of them.

For example, you can cut a selection out of a clip and paste it into another spot, or you can copy a selection and paste it into another project.

Cut, Copy, Paste, and Clear also work when you're editing text, such as the names of your clips or the text for your credits and other titles.

Tip: To get an interesting "instant replay" effect, try this trick. Copy a short bit of interesting video, such as your friend tripping over his shoelace and hitting the ground. Paste the snippet twice, so you wind up with three copies of the same short snippet all in a row. Now watch the playback and enjoy the fun!

Paste Adjustments

Once you've painstakingly edited the look of a clip (color correction, for example), a photo (a Ken Burns effect, for example), or some audio (boosting the volume, for example), you can rapidly enhance a bunch of other footage in the same way. Just copy the first clip, and then, after selecting the other clips, use the Paste Adjustments commands (either the Video, Audio, or Crop submenu).

Tip: The Crop command means "cropping, or anything else you did in the cropping window, including letterboxing or applying the Ken Burns effect."

Delete, Delete Entire Clip (Reject, Reject Entire Clip)

More ways to get rid of stuff. If you've selected only a portion of a filmstrip, you can use the Delete command (or press the Delete key) to snip out just that segment. Or add the ⌘ key to get rid of the entire clip, even though only a piece is highlighted.

The command might also say Delete Selection, depending on what's highlighted.

In the Event browser, these commands say Reject instead of Delete, but only because rejecting, in iMovie, is the first step toward deleting footage for good. Page 153 has the details.

Select All Events

This command is a chameleon. It always means "Select All," but the wording changes.

- If a portion of a clip is selected in the Event browser, it says Select Entire Clip.
- If an Event is selected in the Events list, it says Select All Events.
- If a clip is highlighted in the storyboard, the command says Select All (meaning all filmstrips).
- If some text is highlighted in a text box, the command says Select All (meaning all text in this box)

Keyboard shortcut: ⌘-A.

Select None

Memorizing this command (or better yet, its keyboard equivalent, Shift-⌘-A) is an excellent idea. It deselects everything, including clips and pieces of clips. That's useful when, for example, you want to use one of the "clip-painting" techniques described on page 134, which require that nothing is highlighted.

Trim to Selection

Use this command to trim excess ends off a storyboard clip after you've isolated a portion of it using the triangular handles under the Scrubber bar. *Keyboard shortcut:* ⌘-B.

Trim Clip End

You can fine-tune a clip's length with these commands—or, more practically, with the keyboard equivalents, Option-left arrow or Option-right arrow. Each press makes the clip one frame shorter or longer. (You're changing either the beginning or the end of the clip, whichever is closest to your cursor.)

Trim

Choose Trim to open up the Trim window, where you get a map view of the entire audio or video clip, the better to designate which portion you want to use. *Keyboard shortcut:* ⌘-R.

Split Clip

It's often convenient to chop a clip in half, or even into three pieces; this command does the trick. Make a selection in any storyboard filmstrip; iMovie splits the clip at the beginning of the yellow selection border. (If the border doesn't go all the way to the end of the clip, you'll wind up with *three* pieces.)

Join Clip

If, having split a clip as described above, you want to rejoin the pieces, place them consecutively in the storyboard, and then use this command.

Reveal in Event Browser

This handy option lets you click a clip in the storyboard, and then jump to the corresponding raw source clip in the Event browser. Seeing the original clip gives you a lot more information; for example, you can see how much of the clip you've used, whether or not you've used pieces of the clip elsewhere in the project (as indicated by the orange stripes), whether or not you applied any cropping or color correction to the master clip, and so on.

Arrange Music Tracks

This command refers to background music tracks, the sort of floating background audio that plays from the beginning of the project (page 215). If you've set up more than one of these tracks, this command opens a window (page 219) that lets you change their sequence.

Un-Pin Music Track

Again, page 217 has more details. But this command applies to background music tracks that you've dragged horizontally, thus pinning them to specific video frames. And it means "Un-pin this puppy, so that it floats freely against the left side of the project."

Spelling

You use Mac OS X's built-in spelling checker only when creating iMovie titles (Chapter 10).

Special Characters

You're creating a subtitle for an interview with the CEO of "I've Got a ¥en™" Productions. But how the heck do you type the ¥ symbol—or the ™ symbol? Easy one. You choose this command and double-click the symbol you want from the palette arrayed before you. *Keyboard shortcut:* Shift-⌘-S.

View Menu

This menu is mostly about changing the way iMovie displays your video clips while you work.

- **Favorites Only, Favorites and Unmarked, All Clips, Rejected Only.** These commands hide or show filmstrips in your Event browser, according to how you've branded them: as favorite clips, rejected clips, or neither (Chapter 7). If you're ever looking for a filmstrip that you're sure you once had, check this menu; they may just be hidden.

- **Events by Volume, Events By Month, Most Recent Events at Top, Separate Days in Events.** All of this options control the way your Events are listed at the left side of the window. Chapter 5 has details.

- **Play, Play Selection, Play from Beginning, Play Around Current Frame, Play Full Screen.** These are pretty much self-explanatory, no? For details, see page 136. And learn the keyboard shortcuts.

- **Snap to Ends.** Wow, talk about obscure. When you're dragging an audio stripe, photo stripe, or text stripe in the storyboard, would you like iMovie's assistance in lining it up with the exact beginning of the filmstrip? If so, turn on this option. You'll feel and see a little snap of your cursor as you drag the stripe close to the clip end.

- **Audio Skimming.** When you skim (page 123), iMovie generally plays the audio simultaneously, which may sound fragmented and disturbing. Turn off this command if you'd rather skim in silence.

- **Playhead Info.** When you turn this option on, a balloon pops out of the Playhead when you move it, identifying the date and time that video was shot, and pinpointing your cursor's location from its beginning point.

Text Menu

This menu is useful only when you're editing titles for your movie. All of its commands affect your typography, and all of them are described in Chapter 10.

Share Menu

In theory, anyway, the whole point of video editing is to produce a finished flick that you want to show somebody. This menu offers you six different ways to export the finished product:

- **iTunes** is the first step toward landing your movie on an iPod, iPhone, or Apple TV.

- **Media Browser** is the best bet if you want to burn the movie to a DVD (using iDVD), or if you want to use the movie in Keynote, GarageBand, or iWeb.

- **YouTube** is YouTube, the world's most popular free video-sharing Web site.

- **Export Movie.** Like Share→Media Browser, this command offers a dialog box that lists four canned screen sizes. But like Share→Export using QuickTime (described below), it offers you a chance to store the resulting file with a name and folder location of your choice.

- **Export using QuickTime** turns your movie into a video file on the hard drive. But unlike Export Movie, this command gives you full access to the dozens of QuickTime options that give you infinite control over frame size, frame rate, audio compression, video compression, and more.

- **Export Final Cut XML.** If you have one of Apple's more powerful video editing programs, like Final Cut Express or Final Cut Pro, you'll be grateful for this option. It turns your entire iMovie project into an XML file, an exported project file. Later, you can open up this exported file in Final Cut to complete the editing with a far more powerful suite of tools. See Figure A-4 for some caveats and limitations.

Note: The exported file doesn't actually contain any video. It's just a description of your project—your edits—and references to the original captured video files that sit in your iMovie '08 Events folders. Final Cut therefore works from the original, unmodified clips, preserving all of their quality.

Figure A-4:
The exported project file doesn't completely reproduce your iMovie work. As noted here, there's quite a bit of stuff that doesn't make it through the transfer alive (music, titles, and so on). But that's OK; if you plan ahead, you'll never miss them. The whole point is to dress up the rough cut in Final Cut anyway.

You'll also find Re-publish and Remove commands here, for use when your published masterpiece has been edited or has outlived its usefulness.

Chapters 14 through 17 cover all of these exports in detail.

Window Menu

This window is fairly standard in Mac OS X programs. The Minimize and Zoom commands are almost always present; they let you minimize iMovie (hide its window by collapsing into a Dock icon) or expand the window to fill your screen.

The other commands here are "Hide/Show" commands for the various panels of iMovie: **Project Library, Event Library, Keyword Filter, Viewer, Music and Sound Effects, Photos, Titles,** and **Transitions**. It's great to remember that these exist when you're trying to make room on your screen for editing.

The **Viewer** command is a bit different. There's no way to hide the Viewer window—it would be a little tough trying to edit a video without being able to see it—but these three sub-commands let you change its size.

Tip: You can also make the Viewer almost any in-between size by dragging iMovie's central toolbar up or down.

Figure A-5:
The Help Center's first screen offers big-ticket links like "What is iMovie?" and "Sharing Your Video Project." Most people, however, start by typing a phrase into the search blank and then clicking Search (top).

You get a list of Help pages that the Mac thinks might contain the information you want (middle). The Relevance graph indicates how confident the Help program is. (A longer bar means more occurrences of your search phrase relative to the text on that help page.)

Double-click a topic to read the corresponding help page (bottom). Click the Back button at the top of the screen to return to the list of topics.

Finally, the **Swap Events and Projects** command flips the top and bottom halves of the editing screen, so that the storyboard is now on the bottom. The advantage is that there's no Viewer on the bottom, so you get an even more expansive workspace.

Help Menu

iMovie doesn't come with a manual—if it did, you wouldn't need this book. Instead, you're expected to learn its functions from the online help.

iMovie Help

Choose this command to open the Macintosh Help window, where you'll see a list of iMovie help topics (Figure A-5).

You can use this Help program in either of two ways:

- Keep clicking colored links, burrowing closer and closer to the help topic you want. You can backtrack by clicking the left arrow button at the top of the window, exactly as in a Web browser.

- Type a search phrase into the top window, such as "importing pictures," and then click Search (or press Return), as shown in Figure A-5.

Either way, you'll probably find that the iMovie online help offers a helpful summary of the program's functions, but it's a little light on "what it's for" information, illustrations, tutorials, speed, and jokes.

Welcome to iMovie

Opens the Welcome screen that appeared the first time you ran iMovie (page 83).

Video Tutorials

Takes you to Apple's Web site, where a selection of handy video tutorials on iMovie basics awaits.

Getting Started PDF

Opens the 47-page electronic PDF help "booklet" that comes with iMovie.

Keyboard Shortcuts

This is really just another link into the iMovie Help system, but a particularly valuable one. It takes you to a table showing about 50 keyboard shortcuts in iMovie. (They're among the listings in Appendix C of this book.)

Service and Support

Opens your Web browser and takes you online to Apple's iMovie help Web site. Which, by the way, is a pretty great resource for asking questions and getting answers.

Troubleshooting

Apple was facing a big challenge when it wrote iMovie '08. It was creating a gigantic new program from scratch, with the capacity of handling several additional kinds of footage and camcorder, and designed to export the results to several new kinds of audiences. And you know what that means, right? Right: glitches.

Still, iMovie '08 strikes a lot of people as more stable than the old iMovie, whose deep-seated, intermittent bugs drove a lot of people batty.

Here's an impressive compendium of the problems that may occur—and the world's best attempts at solving them.

Two Golden Rules

If there's any common wisdom at all about iMovie, here it is: a pair of golden rules that will stave off a huge number of problems down the road:

- **Use the latest version.** Each ".01" or ".1" upgrade zaps a whole host of bugs and glitches. These updates are free, so when your Software Update program advises you that one is available, jump at the chance to install it.

- **Set your camcorder to 16-bit audio.** The typical tape camcorder can record its audio track using either 12-bit or 16-bit audio. The factory setting is 12-bit, which gives people who aren't computer owners a chance to overlay a second audio track without erasing the original camera sound. Trouble is, 12-bit audio may slowly drift out of sync with the video when you burn the finished project to a DVD.

  Use your camera's menu system to switch to 16-bit audio. You, an iMovie aficionado, can easily overlay additional audio using your computer, so you give up nothing—except a lot of frustration. (Make this change *now*, before you record anything important.)

General iMovie Troubleshooting

Let's start general, shall we?

Weird Inconsistent Problems

When a program's preferences file becomes scrambled, all kinds of peculiar behavior can result. Buttons and functions don't work. Visual anomalies appear. Things just don't work right.

If iMovie starts having a bad hair day, suspect its preferences file. Quit the program, open your Home→Library→Preferences folder, and throw away the files called *com. apple.iMovie7.plist* and *com.apple.iApps.plist.*

The next time you run iMovie, it automatically builds a new preferences file. This file will have the original factory settings (for the options in, for example, the Preferences dialog box), but at least it will be healthy and whole.

Note: The same advice applies to iDVD. If the program begins flaking out on you, unexpectedly quitting or otherwise acting odd, open your Home→Library→Preferences folder, and throw away the file called *com.apple.iDVD.plist.*

Keeping Your Hard Disk Happy

Remember the old expression "If Mama ain't happy, ain't nobody happy"? Well, if your hard disk isn't happy, iMovie won't be happy, either.

Here's a short list of maintenance suggestions. A little attention every week or so may help keep minor hard drive problems from becoming major problems:

- After installing or updating any software, use Disk Utility to repair permissions. (Disk Utility is in your Applications→Utilities folder. Click the First Aid tab, click your hard drive, and then click Repair Permissions.)

- Mac OS X runs three behind-the-scenes Unix maintenance programs at regular intervals between 3 a.m. and 5 a.m. If your Mac is asleep or turned off every night, the maintenance probably isn't being done, because the Mac doesn't wake itself up to do the maintenance.

  If you don't regularly leave your Mac running overnight, take a minute, every month or so, to run MacJanitor—a free program that runs those same maintenance programs, but at your command. (You can get it from the "Missing CD" page at *www.missingmanuals.com,* among other places.)

Starting Up and Importing

Trouble getting going? Here's some advice.

iMovie Doesn't See the Tape Camcorder

Try these checks, in this order:

Check the FireWire cable connections. Turn the camcorder off and then on again. Quit iMovie, turn the camcorder on, and then reopen iMovie. Restart the Mac. Try a different FireWire cable.

Do you have a high-def tape camcorder (that uses the so-called HDV format)? If so, delve into the menus and make sure that the camcorder's output matches what you recorded.

See, these camcorders can record either standard-definition or high-definition video on the same tape. But when you connect the camcorder to a TV or a Mac, it has to know which format to transmit.

Usually, you get a choice of DV (which means standard definition, 4:3), HDV (high definition, widescreen, 16:9), and Auto. But Auto doesn't always work. If you're having problems, choose DV or HDV manually.

iMovie Doesn't See the Tapeless Camcorder

First, note that some camcorders refuse to enter PC connection mode unless they're plugged into a power outlet. They won't even consider entering PC mode when running on battery. (The camcorder's fear is that it will run out of battery power in the middle of the transfer, possibly corrupting and ruining some of your video scenes.)

Second, keep in mind that your Mac can't import video from AVCHD-format camcorders (page 19) unless it has an Intel processor. Check your camcorder's box or manual—or just read the logos on its body—to find out if it's an AVCHD camcorder. Back on your computer, choose →About This Mac to see if you have an Intel Mac. (You'll actually see the word Intel on the resulting information screen. All Macs models developed since January 2006 have Intel processors.)

Finally, try plugging the USB cable into one of the USB jacks on the Mac itself, rather than into the USB jack on the Mac's keyboard. (The one on the keyboard is for low-powered gadgets only.)

If you've double-checked all three of these conditions, then quit iMovie and reopen it. Now, at long last, the Import screen should appear.

Video Looks Interlaced

You know the cool iMovie Preview window (page 93), where you get to see and even play the thumbnails for the video on tapeless camcorders before you actually import any video?

Sometimes, that preview playback looks awful. It might be jerky or have nasty interlace lines, for example.

Rest assured that this is all just a problem with the preview. Once you actually import this footage, it looks fine.

No Sound from Tape Camcorder

If you're used to the old iMovie, you might wonder why you can't hear anything as you import footage from your tape camcorder.

That's because iMovie no longer plays audio through the Mac when you're importing. If you want to hear the soundtrack as you import, leave the camcorder's screen open, so that you hear the audio from the camcorder itself.

iMovie Crashes on Startup

If you can't even make it past the startup phase, start by deleting the preference files as described earlier.

Also consider rebuilding the iPhoto library; iMovie checks in with iPhoto every time you open it, and if there's something wrong with your iPhoto library, iMovie chokes. To rebuild the iPhoto library, quit iPhoto, then reopen it while holding down the ⌘ and Option keys. In the resulting dialog box, you're offered several diagnostic options. Turn on all five, click Rebuild, and wait a very long time.

When it's all over, iMovie should be much happier about doing business with the clean, fresh iPhoto library.

Can't Import from DVD Camcorder

See the note on page 96.

Dropouts in the Video

A *dropout* is a glitch in the picture. DV dropouts are always square or rectangular. They may be a blotch of the wrong color, or may be multicolored. They may appear every time you play a particular scene, or may appear at random. In severe circumstances, you may get lots of them, such as when you try to capture video to an old FireWire hard drive that's too slow. Such a configuration may also cause tearing of the video picture.

Fortunately, dropouts are fairly rare in digital video. If you get one, it's probably in one of these three circumstances:

- **You're using a very old cassette.** Remember that even DV cassettes don't last forever. You may begin to see dropouts after rerecording the tape 50 times or so.

- **You're playing back a cassette that was recorded in LP (long-play) mode.** If the cassette was recorded on a different camcorder, dropouts are especially likely.

- **It's time to clean the heads on your camcorder.** The electrical components that actually make contact with the tape can become dirty over time. Your local electronics store sells head-cleaning kits for just this purpose.

If you spot the glitch at the same moment on the tape every time you play it, then the problem is on the tape itself. If it's there during one playback but gone during the next, the problem more likely lies with the heads in your camcorder.

Tip: Different DV tape manufacturers use different lubricants on their tapes. As a result, mixing tapes from different manufacturers on the same camcorder can increase the likelihood of head clogs. It's a good idea, therefore, to stick with tapes from one manufacturer (Sony, Panasonic, or Maxell, for example) when possible.

Editing

Once you've learned the program's ins and outs, there's not much that can go wrong during editing.

Can't Drag Certain Photos into the Movie

If you open the Media Browser and try to drag an iPhoto photo into your movie, but you get a "The file could not be imported" error message, it's probably a RAW file. (That's a high-end photo file format created by semiprofessional SLR cameras and intended for processing later on a computer.)

The solution: Return to iPhoto. Make a tiny change to the photo, like a small crop or brightness adjustment. When you exit editing mode, iMovie applies the change and, in the process, turns the RAW photo into a JPEG or TIFF-format photo, which iMovie can import.

Can't Use Audiobooks in Soundtrack

Yep, you can't use audiobooks as an iMovie soundtrack. They show up in the Media Browser, all right, but if you drag them into iMovie, nothing happens. Them's the breaks.

Filmstrips Don't Reflect Changes

It's true: If you crop a filmstrip, or apply color adjustments to it, you'll see the changes on playback—but not on the filmstrip itself. iMovie always displays its original filmstrip, no matter what changes you make to it.

That can be a little upsetting when, for example, you've rotated a photo 90 degrees and you don't see the change in the filmstrip. But there's nothing you can do about it.

Exporting

When it's all over, certain roadblocks may stand in between you and your adoring fans.

"Compatible Version of iDVD Required"

If you get that message when you try to export a movie, you've probably renamed or moved one of the iLife programs.

Don't do that.

They're supposed to have their original names (iMovie, iPhoto, iDVD, iWeb, iTunes), and they're supposed to be in your Applications folder.

YouTube Turns You Down

If you export a movie to YouTube that has exactly the same duration as one you've already posted, YouTube may see the second movie as a duplicate and refuse to accept it—even if the two movie have different names.

The solution is simply to change the duration of the second movie, even if it's by only one frame.

Text Chopped Off on DVD

You create a movie in iMovie, and create some good-looking titles and credits—and yet when you send the movie to iDVD for burning, you discover that the text is getting chopped off by the TV.

Unfortunately, iMovie '08 doesn't seem to know about the TV-safe area that iDVD knows about (page 329). It's left to you to figure out how to avoid these margin areas of the screen. For example, keep your titles short and centered. And don't use subtitles at all, so they won't get chopped off at the bottom. Or just make your own title designs, as described on page 207.

Where to Get Help

You can get personal iMovie help by calling Apple's help line at (800) 500-7078 for 90 days after you bought the iLife DVD or a new Mac. (Technically, you can call within the first 90 days of *ownership,* but the clock really doesn't start until your first call.) After that, you can either buy an AppleCare contract for another year of tech-support calls ($170 to $350, depending on your Mac model), or pay $50 per individual call!

Beyond 90 days, however, consider consulting the Internet, which is filled with superb sources of fast, free technical help. Here are some of the best places to get your questions answered:

- **Apple's own iMovie discussion forum.** Here, you can read user comments, ask questions of knowledgeable iMovie fanatics, or hang out and learn good stuff (*www.apple.com/support/imovie/*).

- **iMovie List.** There's a mailing list—several, actually—dedicated to iMovie and only iMovie. These lists are perfect places to ask questions without embarrassing yourself. Sign up by visiting *www.egroups.com* and searching for *imovie.*

- **Official iMovie help pages.** Apple doesn't freely admit to bugs and problems, but there's a surprising amount of good information in its official iMovie answer pages (*www.apple.com/support/imovie*).

- **Official iMovie tutorials.** Apple offers step-by-step instructions and movies at *www.apple.com/ilife/tutorials/#imovie.*

Master Keyboard Shortcut List

As you know, iMovie '08 was conceived with a single goal in mind: speed, baby, speed. And part of gaining speed is mastering keyboard shortcuts, so you don't waste time puttering around in the menus. So here it is, by popular, frustrated demand: The master list of every secret (or not so secret) keystroke in iMovie '08. Clip and post to your monitor (unless, of course, you got this book from the library).

Tip: There are also a million shortcut menus—the contextual menus that appear when you Control-click (or right-click) almost anything on the screen. Most of the time, the commands you find there just duplicate what's in the menus. Learning the keyboard shortcut is still faster.

Panes, Panels, and Windows

Minimize iMovie	⌘-M
Show/Hide Photos pane	⌘-2
Show/Hide Titles pane	⌘-3
Show/Hide Transitions pane	⌘-4
Show/Hide Video Adjustments window	V
Show/Hide Keywords window	K
Show/Hide Music and Sound Effects	⌘-1
Show/Hide Audio Adjustments window	A
Show/Hide Voiceover window	O
Viewer size small/medium/large	⌘-5, ⌘-6, ⌘-7

Event Browser and Storyboard

Scroll to top/bottom	Home/End
Scroll up/down	Page Up/Page Down
Show clip time/date	⌘-Y
Project Properties	⌘-J
iMovie Help	⌘-?
New Project	⌘-N
Delete project	⌘-Delete
Print Event browser or storyboard	⌘-P

Playback

Play from cursor	Space bar
Play the 2 seconds around cursor	[(left bracket key)
Play the 6 seconds around cursor	] (right bracket key)
Play selected footage	/
Play project (or Event) from start	\ (backslash)
Play selection full screen	⌘-G
Exit full-screen mode	Esc

Editing

Import from camera	⌘-I
Export as file	⌘-E
Select All (or whole filmstrip)	⌘-A
Deselect All	Shift-⌘-A
Cut, Copy, Paste	⌘-X, ⌘-C, ⌘-V
Paste copied adjustments	Shift-⌘-V
Paste video adjustments only	Option-⌘-I
Paste audio adjustments only	Option-⌘-U
Paste crop/Ken Burns adjustments	Option-⌘-R
Adjust duration (photo, transition)	⌘-R

Working with Clips

Add selection to storyboard	E
Mark selection as a Favorite	F
Mark selection as a Reject	R (or Delete, in Event browser only)
Unmark selection	U
Shift selection border	arrow keys (left, right)

Restore 1 hidden frame to clip	Option-right arrow (cursor near end of clip) or Option-left arrow (cursor near beginning)
Shorten clip by 1 frame	Option-left arrow (cursor near end of clip) or Option-right arrow (cursor near beginning)
Trim to Selection	⌘-B
Open Trimmer window	⌘-R
Apply numbered keyword	1, 2, 3, 4…
Remove all keywords from selection	0 (zero)
Undo	⌘-Z
Redo	Shift-⌘-Z

Music and Audio

Show/Hide Music and Sound Effects	⌘-1
Show/Hide Audio Adjustments window	A
Show/Hide Voiceover window	O
Audio during skimming on/off	⌘-K

Editing Titles

Show/Hide Titles panel	⌘-3
Show/Hide Fonts panel	⌘-T
Bold	Shift-⌘-B
Italic	Shift-⌘-I
Underline	Shift-⌘-U
Outline style	Shift-⌘-O
Increase/decrease type size	⌘-plus sign, ⌘-minus sign
Left, center, right-justified text	⌘-{, ⌘-|, ⌘-}
Tighter/looser spacing (kerning)	Option-⌘-left arrow, Option-⌘-right arrow
Cut, Copy, Paste	⌘-X, ⌘-C, ⌘-V
Copy text formatting	Option-⌘-C
Paste text formatting	Option-⌘-V

Visual Cheat Sheet

iMovie, as you've probably gathered, is completely different from any program you've seen before—including previous versions of iMovie. It's filled with handy visual cues as to what's going on. But especially at first, learning all of those cues can become a full-time job.

iMovie is teeming with thin stripes over and under your filmstrips (in green, blue, or purple); horizontal colored lines drawn right across them (in red, green, and orange); little white "badges" huddled in the corners of filmstrips; faint little corner badges that appear only when you *point* to a filmstrip; gigantic green or purple bubbles lying behind your entire project map; cryptic radiation symbols, building-block badges, and yellow exclamation points; and on and on.

You practically need a cheat sheet to remember what they're all for—and on the next two pages, you'll find it.

Broadcast waves:
Has been posted online

Solid sun badge:
Color adjustments
have been applied

Blue stripe:
Photograph

Faint badges:
Click to adjust color,
cropping, or volume

White squares:
Has been exported
in these sizes

Solid speaker badge
(straight sound waves):
Audio has been
"normalized"

Clock bad
Opens Trim
window

Yellow ! triangle:
Has been edited
since posting online

Green top stripe:
Flagged as Favorite

Solid speaker badge
(round sound waves):
Volume has been adjusted

Blue stripe:
Title or credits

Solid crop symbol:
Has been cropped
or rotated

Green bubble:
Background music

Corner arrows:
Click to lengthen
or shorten clip slightly

Purple stripe:
Recorded narration

Green stripe:
Sound effect

Purple bubble:
Background music
pinned to video

Inter-clip icons:
Transition effect

s – West Coast Sunrise

15s – Voiceover Recording

4s – Bell Buoy

que Blues Long

10s

5:00 total

5s

Orange bottom stripe:
Has been used in this project

Red top stripe:
Flagged as Rejected

Index

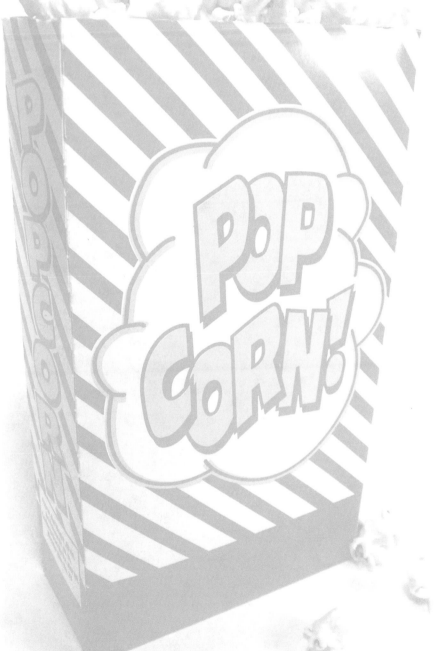

Index

Colophon

This book was written and edited in Microsoft Word X on various Macs.

The screenshots were captured with Ambrosia Software's Snapz Pro X *(www. ambrosiasw.com)* for the Mac. Adobe Photoshop CS *(www.adobe.com)* and Macromedia Freehand MX *(www.macromedia.com)* were called in as required for touching them up.

The full-page photos that introduce each part of this book and many of the scenes that appear in this book's "home movie" ilustrations were graciously provided by iStockPhoto.com.

The book was designed and laid out in Adobe InDesign CS2 on a PowerBook G4, PowerMac G5. The fonts used include Formata (as the sans-serif family) and Minion (as the serif body face). To provide the and ⌘ symbols, custom fonts were created using Macromedia Fontographer.

The book was then generated as an Adobe Acrobat PDF file for proofreading, indexing, and final transmission to the printing plant.